Global Homophobia

Global Homophobia

States, Movements, and the Politics of Oppression

Edited by Meredith L. Weiss
and Michael J. Bosia

UNIVERSITY OF ILLINOIS PRESS

Urbana, Chicago, and Springfield

© 2013 by the Board of Trustees
of the University of Illinois
All rights reserved
Manufactured in the United States of America
1 2 3 4 5 C P 5 4 3 2 1

∞ This book is printed on acid-free paper.

Library of Congress Control Number: 2013946225

Contents

Acknowledgments

Our path to this volume has been more fortuitous than purposive, driven more by events on the ground than by a conscious research agenda. While we each study the nexus between social movements and the state—with sexuality just one aspect of wider movement politics—neither of us had quite conceptualized homophobia as something other than a constraint or background. It was the almost eerie parallels we started to see among developments in the far-removed contexts on which we each focused that pushed us to look deeper, not just to wonder how homophobia *really* functions as a part of a political order, but also to question what those dynamics mean for how we understand social mobilization.

The turning point in our interest in political homophobia is evident in our own contributions to this volume. For Bosia, it was the remarkable similarity between the acts of sexualized torture at Abu Ghraib and those he had read about in Bosnia a decade earlier, both counterpoised against what he knew of, for instance, how LGBT activists from the north and south strategized in response to negligent or hostile state actors. He began by excavating testimonies from Bosnia and the wider Yugoslav wars, and later sought to consider strategies of persecution outside these contexts through the work he was doing with HIV/AIDS activists in Paris, including immigrants and exiles from countries experiencing a rapid rise in homophobic politics. Bosia thanks Michael Loriaux, Audie Klotz, Isabella Alcañiz, and Rahul Rao for their thoughtful reading of and commentary on earlier iterations of his chapter, as the work developed.

For Weiss, questions of how the "we" of social mobilization developed propelled her to explore the context against which collective identities form. It was a prior project on student activism that really sparked this inquiry; in particular, the difficulty of parsing what makes a student recognize that identity as both collective and political. While she worked through those quandaries, claims around gender identity and sexuality—both for and against tolerant accommodation—started to cluster disproportionately in the Southeast Asian states on which her research focuses. Primed by that earlier work on student identities, Weiss started to investigate where these new identity claims and assignations came from, and why so small and substantially mute a minority should suddenly be painted as such a threat.

Bringing these overlapping interrogations together just as the news from Uganda revealed an unsettling twist in the politics of state homophobia (as Kaoma details herein), we organized a panel for the 2010 American Political Science Association annual meeting in Washington, D.C. By that point, we had identified a number of other scholars engaged in work on sexual minorities, gender identity, LGBT rights, social movements, and postcolonial politics who were likewise eager to think through how to theorize political homophobia as a distinct phenomenon, equally as deserving of study as the LGBT rights it contests. We appreciate the support of Paisley Currah, Cecelia Lynch, and Cricket Keating in that effort, and of a large and enthusiastic audience, whose comments, critiques, and questions helped spur us to move toward a book. We thank Saint Michael's College student Nicholas Hogan, too, for then organizing a similarly fruitful event on homophobia in which Bosia, Weiss, and Kaoma participated. Along the way, we have received tremendously helpful feedback, as well, from presenting portions of the research at conferences from Madrid, Spain, to Portland, Oregon. Thanks especially to Dennis Altman and Susanne Beechey, as well as to our anonymous manuscript reviewers, for their thoughtful and thought-provoking suggestions and encouragement. But our deepest gratitude goes out to our editor, Larin McLaughlin, who could not have been more enthusiastic, helpful, and responsive throughout the entire process, from germ-of-an-idea to manuscript.

For better or for worse, this project has revealed to Bosia and Weiss both that we are well-matched in compulsive pursuit of an intriguing project, commitment to "relevant" scholarship, and obsessive attention to semantic detail. Our process of co-authoring and co-editing has been appropriately challenging—sometimes across oceans and sometimes side by side at cafés—

but also mutually reinforcing, supportive, and generative. It has been a fun ride. The best part, of course, was the opportunity to work with so fantastic, insightful, and diligent a community of contributors. Their hard work and zeal made completing this volume not just a comparatively speedy matter, but tremendously intellectually rewarding.

Most importantly, Bosia thanks his husband, Steven Obranovich, who has provided the space and support needed to reflect and write, or to travel for conferences and research, the critical enthusiasm necessary for the hard work of self-improvement, and a world of diverse adventures and pleasures far beyond the political. Weiss, as usual, thanks Ruth Burdick for her near-endless patience.

Global Homophobia

1

Political Homophobia
in Comparative Perspective

MICHAEL J. BOSIA
AND MEREDITH L. WEISS

The way I see it, homophobia—not
homosexuality—is the toxic import. Thanks to the
absurd ideas peddled by American fundamentalists, we
are constantly forced to respond to the myth—debunked
long ago by scientists—that homosexuality leads to
pedophilia. For years, the Christian right in America
has exported its doctrine to Africa, and, along with it,
homophobia. . . . Not all Ugandans are homophobic.
Some say there are more pressing issues to worry about
than gay people and believe we should have the same
rights as anyone else. But they are not in power and
cannot control the majority who want to hurt us.

—Frank Mugisha, "Gay and Vilified in Uganda"

The wave of anti-authoritarian revolts that began to roll across the
Middle East and North Africa in 2011 coincided with another contemporary trend: a widespread, caustic focus on sexuality, in the form of overtly
political homophobia. Egypt figures in both. Among the most striking
incidents in contemporary homophobia was Cairo's 2001 "Queen Boat"
case, which saw fifty-two men prosecuted in a special national-security
court on charges related to same-sex intimacy. A decade later, as Hosni
Mubarak toppled from power, the Muslim Brotherhood and the military
filled the vacuum; after decades of authoritarianism, few other social forces
could hope to do so. Given the extent to which Mubarak had suppressed
Egyptian civil society, one would hardly expect to see active mobilization

either for or against sexuality rights at that point. Yet homophobia hit the ground running. When the Brotherhood joined forces with old enemies in the junta to support a set of constitutional amendments in Egypt's first post-Mubarak vote in 2011, mysterious forces issued warnings that a defeat would bring a triumphant secularism that would unveil women, ban the call to prayer, and—echoing apocryphal global discourse—permit men to marry men (Slackman 2011).

Of all the fears contending forces could summon to reinforce their political stature in Egypt, why leap to sexuality? Or if sexuality be the target, why skip past far more globally prevalent calls from Western leaders and international institutions for the decriminalization of same-sex sexuality, directly to imagined demands for same-sex marriage, as if sexual minorities everywhere claim the same rights that define LGBT organizing in only a handful of countries? Egyptian sexual minorities have no durable networks; the small LGBT organization Bedayaa was founded only in 2010, primarily for social and educational purposes.[1] A joint statement they issued with other Arab sexual minority groups in May 2011, still in the heady first months after Mubarak's ouster, called merely for "peaceful coexistence" and denied any intent "to persuade you to accept our gender identity."[2] Marriage equality has hardly been a priority.

The invocation of such incongruous marriage fears demonstrates the particular power of homophobia, not as some deep-rooted, perhaps religiously inflected sentiment, nor as everywhere a response to overt provocation, but as a conscious political strategy often unrelated to substantial local demands for political rights. This volume seeks to understand and explain *political* homophobia as a state strategy, social movement, and transnational phenomenon, powerful enough to structure the experiences of sexual minorities and expressions of sexuality. We consider political homophobia[3] as purposeful, especially as practiced by state actors; as embedded in the scapegoating of an "other" that drives processes of state building and retrenchment; as the product of transnational influence peddling and alliances; and as integrated into questions of collective identity and the complicated legacies of colonialism. Specifically, we target the open deployment of homophobia in political rhetoric and policy, as a remarkably similar and increasingly modular phenomenon across a wide range of countries. While the more brutal examples of hatred and violence grab headlines, we see this dynamic just as clearly in less overtly repressive contexts—for instance, the Philippines, where an emerging LGBT-rights movement has begun to contest the clout of the Catholic church in the (constitutionally secular) state (see Weiss, this volume). This broad application of more and less oppressive homophobic strategies suggests that homophobia may be better globalized than homosexuality (Murray 2009).

In our analysis, "unexpected" forms of political homophobia must be examined as typical tools for building an authoritative notion of national collective identity, for impeding oppositional or alternative collective identities that might or might not relate to sexuality, for mobilizing around a variety of contentious issues and empowered actors, and as a metric of transnational institutional and ideological flows. Moreover, policy and organizational reactions to repression both locally and globally often take up LGBT rights rhetoric in ways that constitute new sexual identities where LGBT rights had not been invoked before. Today's homophobic political strategies range from straightforward or seemingly "rational" processes of marginalization— of branding gay rights, like so often women's or ethnic minorities' rights, as either "special interests" and thus not a priority, or as a threat to the nation—to often violent vilification and abuse. The most familiar example of the latter is the dehumanizing humiliation of Muslim men at Abu Ghraib, in Bosnia, and elsewhere, through forced (homo)sexual postures and brutal sodomy. Such sexualized violence parallels wider racialized, misogynist, and militarized forms of Islamophobia (Hersh 2004; Puar 2005), even while Western "saviors" bewail Muslim states' paucity of human rights, especially for women, but also for sexual minorities.

Such processes of identification and ostracism have long been recognized as part of state formation when couched in terms of race, including the crystallization of racial categories and ever-stronger ethnic claims in the course of nation building and as part of the legitimization of political and economic power (Marx 1998; Olzak 1983). That same effort to control populations and to mold citizens toward a certain norm, both as an end in itself and a means to consolidating authority, applies equally well to sexuality, even where LGBT rights are more secure. The politically charged homophobia that can enforce heteronormativity or prod citizens to suspect and fear a new category of social evil seems, in this light, a "natural" part of state making and interstate intervention, however underexamined previously.

We seek in this volume to explore the how and why of the transnational diffusion and domestic enactment of political homophobia, including (with varying degrees of specificity) transphobia.[4] We trace evidence of parallel processes in cases ranging from contemporary Uganda, where Kapya Kaoma reveals how U.S. evangelical Christian activists have joined forces with local political, social, and religious leaders to promote newly repressive policies; to Iran, as examined by Katarzyna Korycki and Abouzar Nasirzadeh, where sodomy may now be punished with death by hanging; to Indonesia, where Meredith Weiss finds that pressures for Islamization are increasingly refracted through lenses of gender and sexuality; to postcommunist Europe, where as Conor O'Dwyer details, Polish and Russian authorities have targeted small gay-rights movements for sometimes violent and public suppression. As these and the other chapters herein demonstrate, contemporary homophobia subsumes—and indeed, frequently elides—complex dimensions of gender and sexuality.

In many ways, these patterns outline the development of a modular notion of homophobia as part of U.S. national security strategies during the Cold War, as David Johnson describes, and stepped up anew particularly against the backdrop of the "war on terror" and crises of sovereignty, as Michael Bosia details, as well as the Bush administration's transnational evangelical activism (as Kaoma explores). Presaging contemporary modularity, too, is the spread of homophobia under Western colonial flags in the nineteenth century (Binnie 2004: 77–78; Sanders 2009) and as a tool of health professionals particularly in the twentieth (Terry 1999). Embedded in Western imaginaries, but exported and adopted alongside economic and technological practices, homophobia brings to mind a range of "globalized localisms" (Santos 2006) that arise in the West but grow roots in the rhetoric and policies of powerful actors much farther afield.

"Homophobia" likewise has become political both as part of a larger push to delegitimize in advance rights that have not been claimed and as a diversion from larger crises and threats to existing authorities, including those arising from the pressures of globalization. David Murray evocatively captures this sleight of hand, with reference to Barbados, "These discourses [against homosexuality], combined with the absence of local gay and lesbian voices in the media, result in what I call a 'spectral' sexuality that haunts the Barbadian mediascapes, where a threatening, perverted and/or sick sexualized body or group of bodies are continually incarnated in discourse but never fully instantiated in the flesh. These deviant ghostly bodies haunt the dominant media discourse of a national body imagined to be heterosexual and masculine, which is perceived to be under attack from outside and inside forces" (2009a: 148). Such diversions reflect a complex but little-heeded dimension of neoliberal globalization in which the sexual politics of national identity and bodily discipline can either distract from (as in Uganda) or undercut (as in Malaysia) economic deregulation, depending on the position of those who exploit homophobic politics. By promoting the "fear of small numbers" (Appadurai 2006)—of minorities—state and social opinion leaders incriminate a tiny, sometimes barely or not (yet) self-identified minority, often drawing more on imported than domestically sourced language, agendas, and strategies.

A set of core similarities thus undergirds this modularity within individually distinctive cases and dynamics. To tease out that common thread, which runs through all the chapters to come, we first explore better ways to conceptualize homophobia as a specifically *political* and *modular* force, then examine how homophobia has been studied thus far and why researchers and policy makers have so clearly and chronically bypassed or misconstrued it. Finally, we consider the practical and theoretical implications of a careful, critical focus on politicized homophobia. Analytically, we differentiate overt claims to political legitimacy through homophobia from private, religious, and interpersonal sentiments that have not been taken up as political tools, with the understanding that there is no necessary and fixed relationship between political homophobia and extant private homophobia or even local sexual discourse.

While we recognize that private, religious, and interpersonal sentiments are *political* in that they are produced and reproduced in contexts of power, the discourses and policies of modular political homophobia in fact have had the power to reshape local structures of sexuality.[5] This is not to say that Presidents Mugabe of Zimbabwe and Kaczyński of Poland, or Prime Ministers Mahathir and Najib of Malaysia, for instance, have not been motivated by personal religious belief in pressing homophobic agendas, or that they lacked social allies who shared these sentiments. Whether in Louisiana, Russia, Singapore, or Malawi, we can and must distinguish between private beliefs and political homophobia, even while acknowledging the potential for private or religious sentiments to pervade political contests or processes of state and nation building. We suggest that the salience of these attitudes as strategic tools has more to do with local and global politics than with private meditations, as evidenced by similar models of political homophobia across traditions and in both secular and religious states.

Conceptualizing Homophobia as Political and Modular

More often than not, social scientists and queer theorists have largely ignored or mischaracterized the emergence of political homophobia, despite its often stunningly violent and repressive aspects as well as its frequent absurdity. As this wave of repression increases in virulence, coming to encompass imprisonment and harassment as well as torture and execution, the study of sexuality has missed the fact that political homophobia requires no substantive self-defined LGBT community or local, above-ground organizing among sexual minorities before splashing onto shore and seeping into elites' political strategies. Similarly overlooked is the role of Western leaders in offering sustenance and support to the birth of more specifically tailored, localized homophobia, as embodied, for instance, in the passage of a constitutional amendment in 2005 in Uganda banning "gay marriage" in line with U.S. (but not Ugandan) iconography. It seems the all-too-rosy glow of Western leadership in exporting LGBT rights has rendered the West's equally prominent role in the diffusion of homophobia nearly invisible.

In fact, this homophobic wave is despite, and profoundly contradicts, the significant progress that LGBT rights have made in a handful of Western states and even fewer localities outside the West. While political homophobia is invoked where fundamental rights to sexual and gender self-determination remain unclaimed and sexual minorities have not thought in terms of a shared political identity or full legal equality, it lingers, too, as an easily accessible form of social differentiation and privilege, even where legal equality is achieved or in sight. Homophobia has, in short, gone modular, being imposed in a consistent way across diverse contexts. Sexuality itself lacks similar wings: as much research demonstrates, it is not similarly modular (Blasius, this volume; Broqua 2013; Epprecht 2005; Hoad 2000).

Meanwhile, the fact that so much research focuses narrowly on the transformation of sexual identities leaves us without concepts needed to theorize either the mutual influence of such changes on homophobia and sexuality or the global diffusion of similar forms of homophobia. As the study of sexuality has moved beyond the West, scholars have trained their gaze on the influence (or not) of Western models of sexuality spread by global LGBT activists or tourists, not on the politics of the homophobia local sexual minorities increasingly face on their own streets. Even while historians have examined homophobic state policies in the past, and anthropologists, its sociocultural manifestations (e.g., Rubin 93; Murray 2009b), researchers concerned with the contemporary nexus of social movements and the state limit their analysis of homophobia to its manifestation as a target of LGBT rights activism, decoupled from the state. In fact, there is no focus on *specifically* state-sponsored or politically charged homophobia to match the emphasis on specifically LGBT human-rights activism, nor do we have a theoretical framework for understanding homophobia as a named and explicit feature of political contestation over state authority, tracing its influences, origins, and multiple global manifestations. Even queer theory, given its disciplinary proclivities, focuses on homophobia often as a facet of heterosexism that forms and transforms the sexual subject who is organizing to claim certain rights.

This emphasis on LGBT human rights activism rather than on a repressive apparatus might itself be a reflection of lingering homophobia within academic circles. Political science, for example, continues to treat gay politics as marginal to and outside the parameters of state and society proper—a tendency that is part and parcel of the enduring dismissal of research on marginal identities across the social sciences, including work done by gays and lesbians, who are simultaneously derided as "frivolous" and feared as "uniquely powerful" (Duggan 1994: 2). In the reductionist views of mainstream academics, LGBT politics represents only one application (and a rarely considered one at that[6]) of new social movement theory, so that homophobia-as-politics is reduced to nothing more than a variable reflecting static religious values and traditional attitudes about sexuality, whether organized by public opinion or by political leadership.

Alternately, misguided tolerance might produce a similar misconception: as liberal theorists and social scientists consider the homophobe, they mistakenly render him or her exogenous both to the state and to analysis. These approaches come to mirror popular theories of sexuality that "predict" or "privilege" the progressive normalization of lesbian and gay identities and disappearance of outdated dogmas of the past, a view long favored among activists and increasingly prominent in the media. Recently, for example, pundits have seized on survey data to foretell not only the ultimate success of marriage equality in the United States, but the death of homophobia. Yet suggestions of homophobia's much-touted end, like those of history and Mark Twain, have been greatly exaggerated. Homophobia remains not just alive, but aggressively kicking.

Homophobia and Research: Beyond "Sexual Modernization Theory"

To understand how academics and policy makers have largely failed to address politicized homophobia, even when they understand sexuality as an overt and contentious aspect or product of political action, we distinguish five key approaches that dominate the relevant work. One common approach considers the diffusion of LGBT politics, primarily within a human rights framework, and theorizes homophobia (if at all) as constraint; a second views the politics of sexuality as a contest between LGBT advocates and their antagonists, framing state homophobia as a reaction to the diffusion of an "American" model of LGBT activism; a third mirrors popular understandings to associate homophobia with tradition, ignorance, paranoia, or other forms of social ill; and a fourth, a kind of sexual modernization theory, sees homophobia as unnecessary to theorize, as it belongs to a social past we will eventually overcome. The fifth strand comprises scholars who view same-gender desires and gender identity within structures of heternormativity or masculinity. Each of these strands has informed and/or been informed by public advocates in the field of LGBT human rights. It is important to keep in mind that though much of the activism and research on sexual identity does not seek explicitly to complicate or even to comprehend the politics of homophobia, it still adds significantly to our knowledge of sexuality as such.

The first approach, which fits within a broader literature on social movements, often uses concepts like diffusion and brokerage (Chabot and Duyvendak 2002) or the availability of transnational networks through which policy or political frameworks are adopted or adapted (Della Porta and Tarrow 2005) to consider how deeply a Western model of sexuality has seeped into communities across the globe. Those who view global LGBT politics through this lens explore links across national contexts, the interplay of global and local forces that impel social practice, and the kinds of resources available in the contexts in which LGBT sexuality has implanted, starting with the export of models for sexual identities across the Atlantic and later outside the United States and Europe (e.g., Adam, Duyvendak, and Krouwel 1999; Gevisser and Cameron 2004; Wright 2000). Homophobia through this lens is a local backdrop, not what is diffused.

Dennis Altman has been a leader in this school through his work examining the mix of global and local forces that shape sexual identities in contexts around the world (for example, Altman 1996, 2004, 2008). Altman considers the transformations brought about by capitalism and economic globalization, for example, as each propels urbanization, impinges on extended families, provides resources for greater autonomy from existing social forms, undermines authority, and provides access to novel ideas. Other scholars join Altman in exploring the effect of the HIV/AIDS pandemic as a global force necessitating a response in communities around the world, particularly as international institutions and transnational activism have framed AIDS through rights rhetoric and access-based policies across new contexts (Peacock, et al. 2009; Roberts 1995; Weiss 2006; also Altman himself, 1998, 2000, 2008). A growing literature on sexual citizenship, too, interrogates sexuality and sexual rights as forms of international governance and mobility that provide an "escape from locality, family, and history," empowering citizens as they weaken sovereignty (Stychin 1998; 2000: 603). Related work explores how rapid, recent changes in the laws applicable to lesbians and gay men in particular have reshaped not just their legal rights and options, in ways simultaneously empowering and constraining, but also their legal consciousness and relative "equality" (Harding 2011; Vaid 1995).

Much of this research has yet to offer a compelling theory of political ostracism and oppression, or of how sexual identities and stigmatization align. For instance, while homosexuality and AIDS are in many ways associated by scholars and policy makers, that association is not linked through specific histories or contexts even to a set of identifiable social institutions or actors. As well, these approaches examine how social or political life "constrains" or "inhibits" LGBT organizing, particularly in the European context, where, for example, scholars argue that official hostility in France to independent social organizing challenged the elaboration of U.S.-style LGBT activism and inhibited some policies of integration such as marriage equality (Duyvendak and Fillieuile 1996; Fassin 2001). Similarly, when Bosia unlocked a genealogy of orientalizing and Americanizing homophobia in the French context, he was more concerned with the effect of homophobia on activism or AIDS politics than with the reason state actors deploy homophobia, other than its rhetorical sense (Bosia 2005, 2009).

The second pattern of research builds from the first, homing in on the implications of transnational diffusion. This approach proposes that the global Westernization of same-gender sexual intimacy has coupled LGBT activism and homophobia within the framework of a sexual "clash of civilizations" waged domestically as well as globally. While Thomas Linneman argues that spiraling perceptions of anti-Christian sentiment in a broader domestic culture embracing LGBT people spurs the U.S. Christian right's homophobia (Linneman 2004), Joseph Massad provocatively indicts a "Gay International" composed of activists at organizations like the International Lesbian, Gay, Bisexual, Trans and Intersex Association (ILGA)[7] and the U.S.-based International Gay and Lesbian Human Rights Commission (IGLHRC) as well as primarily U.S.-based gay scholars (Massad 2007). Responding to growing Western polemic and activism challenging Muslim states that imprison or execute men who engage in male-to-male sexual and social activity, Massad blames this Gay International for an "incitement to discourse" that imposes homosexuality and a concomitant Western sexual binary upon local cultures that have more fluid understandings of sexuality. This discourse, claims Massad, has led Muslim countries to punish self-identified "gay" Muslims in their midst and threaten the well-being of men who merely practice same-gender sexual intimacy. Massad's analysis, which spans colonial and neo-colonial experience across various sites in the Muslim world, endows his Gay International with the discursive legacies of Western orientalism and the institutional power of government ministries and universities.

While broadly sensitive to local practice, Massad's conceptualization of state homophobia as a reaction to Western LGBT strategies is radically limited.

In geographic terms, he fails to account for the similar strategies of state homophobia across the United States and Europe, like the political homophobia, sponsored or encouraged by political and religious officials, that has thrived amidst a surge of xenophobic nationalism and angry boundary drawing in postcommunist Russia or Poland (Kon 2010; Graff 2010). Massad is silent about the variety of challenges "at home" for his LGBT imperialists during the decades he outlines, including the religious right, the spate of antigay initiatives in the United States (see Duggan 2004), and the decimation of the AIDS pandemic, and so ignores the serious damage to their domestic agendas, let alone their global reach, in the 1980s and '90s. In brief, Massad's Gay International seems a weak challenger to state and social actors in positions of authority. Even when supranational pressures, particularly from the EU, and domestic political alignments have turned many activists from "commercial" or popular identity-building mobilization to more exclusive, formal policy remedies (e.g., Bernstein 1997), these efforts target specific acts and regimes, like condemning the 2005 execution of sexual minority youth in Iran. Most importantly, even if Massad is right that contemporary repression arises directly in reaction to global LGBT incitements, he does not address the variety of local and global factors that move state actors from indifference to repression, so foregrounding LGBT organizing unsatisfactorily casts the external incitement itself as sufficient to provoke a state's internal homophobic repression.

A similarly critical and engaged scholarship emerging in the aftermath of "9/11" interrogates the often mutually reinforcing association of LGBT rights, nationalism, and Islamophobia. These scholars have identified "homonationalism" as a new variant of LGBT activism. Central to this project is a kind of "pinkwashing," through which state actors not only encourage LGBT activists to condemn homophobia in Muslim communities, but also themselves embrace LGBT rights to cloak their own racist and oppressive policies against Muslims (Ahmed 2011; Duggan 2003; Haritaworn 2010–11; Kunstman 2008; Puar 2006, 2011; also Keating, this volume). While homonationalism is a powerful new force in politics, much of this work has yet to analyze the persistently oppressive homophobia that pushes either a vapid LGBT rights agenda devoid of social justice or a militant and racist nationalism. Cohen's work on the persistence of homophobia in the African American community and its effect on the response to HIV/AIDS clarifies the limits that scholarship on homonationalism has yet to broach (Cohen 1997). In order to understand the cleavages and divisions that structured AIDS politics as a series of secondary marginalizations, Cohen outlines both the politics of race that define African American sexuality and the structures of power within the community. Homophobia enfeebles community organizing against AIDS, then, due to the strategies that empowered actors pursue to seek legitimacy by defying racial categories and challenging racial mythologies. As Cohen's approach suggests, a full interrogation of homonationalism would consider homophobia as one aspect of a system of inequality (inclusive of racism and misogyny) that compels LGBT activists to pursue strategies of normalization and legitimization.

The third pattern of research has sought conceptually to undermine (and depoliticize) homophobia as akin to a social disease: dangerous, certainly, but on the cusp of a cure. This approach includes considerations of homophobia as backward or prejudiced, as well as pychosexually primitive. Theorist Martha Nussbaum's musings on disgust and marriage equality are very much in this vein (2004, 2009, 2010). She characterizes the "problem" of LGBT rights, such as opposition to military service or marriage, as a manifestation of disgust. The disgust impulse, Nussbaum explains, though a nearly universal human response, is also a "visceral" one (2010: 13), arising from a disorienting psychological process that separates the self from the body's more animalistic and mortal nature. Through a series of sub-rational cognitive extensions, individuals project their disgust on other individuals or social groups; by implication, disgust becomes the public policy variant of a deeply primordial reaction, leading to "panic" and fear of contamination. Other scholars reach similar conclusions, by simply equating the religious motivations of opponents of marriage equality with hatred and disdain (Denike 2007), or by detailing the similar, long-standing pathologization of both racial and sexual difference (Somerville 2000).

Such feelings of disgust or disdain are significantly under-theorized. Disgust, in fact, might be deliberately cultivated as an aspect of good taste (Korsmeyer 2002). Indeed, we see such a process in the details Nussbaum draws from homophobes themselves, who revel in discussing the gory details of same-gender intimacy. Homophobes may incite the vicarious enactment of that which gives them disgust—witness Abu Ghraib, which Bosia considers as an aspect of securitized national sexuality in his chapter. They can also willfully cross the contamination line, soaking themselves in the very bodily fluids they find disgusting, as their fists draw blood or as they rape to "correct" and humiliate.

The fourth category of research is a variant of the third, but in this strand, homophobia is often dismissed as religious or traditional, with some explanatory variable offered as a (poorly specified) antidote to homophobia. The classic work along these lines is Boswell's *Christianity, Social Tolerance, and Homosexuality*. Boswell argues that urbanization increases tolerance for same-gender sexual intimacy and de-urbanization, the rejection of such sexualities (Boswell 1980). Scholars on contemporary politics likewise offer urbanization as a predictor of tolerance, along with factors more traditional to social movement analysis, while homophobia appears only among the religious, moral or traditional forces that array against LGBT rights (Wald, Button, and Rienzo 1996). That the widely celebrated work of urban planner Richard Florida (2002) finds the most economically promising cities to be those that score well on a Gay Index, a proxy for tolerance of "creative class" nonconformity, has sparked similar strategies and analysis, in contexts from Cincinnati to Singapore. Opening up to gays is taken as both harbinger of and facilitator to economic vitality, and thus as an all but inevitable stage in development—notwithstanding evidence to the contrary, of domestic agendas nested in conservative mores that ultimately trump steps to lure global capital (Weiss 2005). Similarly, quantitative analyses of recent votes on marriage equality have suggested that homophobia, measured as rejection of marriage equality, correlates with such factors as age, religiosity, ideology, and born-again Christianity (Egan and Sherrill 2006, 2009).

Considerations of disgust or tradition too frequently treat homophobia only as the public manifestation of a private attitude. Homophobia might serve as an appeal to or justification for individual choice, a collective statement of aspiration or reprobation, or a constraint on politics. This reading is emblematic of both U.S. politics itself and of methods commonly used to study politics in the United States, which tend to see in voting behavior or public opinion the root "causes" of political practice. Homophobia in these approaches is never theorized as related to the state in a deep and profound way, and these approaches are of little use in attempting to understand the politics of homophobia outside settings in which opinion polls, interest group lobbying, and referenda are standard features of political life. While certainly, leaders can channel popular sentiment, we must also move farther from contexts in which state practice even appears tied to public opinion or beliefs, where we are left only with powerful state and social actors. These forces choose homophobic repression absent a public call to do so, often providing details about *foreign* LGBT organizing (or sexual practices) in order to arouse—not respond to—popular disgust. In the democratic West, as Johnson explores in this volume, homophobia is less private belief than public compulsion that defines and describes the very "love that dare not speak its name" in order to stimulate condemnation and anxiety.

Even when forms of urbanization that foster diversity and tolerance are considered, homophobia itself remains something to be overcome in good time, suggesting an approach with all the anticipations and shortfalls of the sexual equivalent of that "modernization theory" which predicted a similar liberal democratic end from processes of industrial development. Undergird-ing Egan and Sherrill's statistical analysis, for instance, is the growing percep-tion that younger voters will inevitably bring about a generational change that will all but eliminate the homophobic impulse in society, notwithstanding the diversity of possible incentives for such an impulse. They conclude that the transformation in attitudes across recent ballot measures relating to marriage indicates a "swift pace" unprecedented in U.S. politics (2009: 15). Likewise, political analyst Nate Silver of the popular blog FiveThirtyEight has modeled the future of same-gender marriage ballot initiatives in the United States, predicting that within four years, nearly half the states will vote to oppose a marriage ban, concluding with the fiftieth, Mississippi, in 2024 (Silver 2009).

The International Lesbian and Gay Association is among those policy groups subscribing to this variation of modernization theory. Reporting on state homophobia, ILGA notes that such policies of repression are both arti-facts of "a certain time and context in history," linked to the colonial past or religious beliefs, and a product of "conservative interpretations of religious texts" (Ottosson 2007: 4). ILGA's analysis effectively privatizes such laws as the result of ignorance, fear, and intolerance. Finally, ILGA inverts historical chronologies to conclude that the emancipation of sexual minorities is a pre-cursor to democracy, thus nicely closing the loop between the urbanization assumptions that support both political and sexual modernization theories.

These recent efforts parallel earlier studies that place sexual identity on an historical continuum that culminates with a Western-style sexual binary, in which heterosexuality and homosexuality stand opposed. The emerging con-sensus is that sexual identity does not evolve along a shared trajectory, even after exposure to Western influence. The roster of available forms and practices of same-gender social or sexual intimacy does change in response to both global and local influences, but not per any uniform pattern of modernization—raising two issues of concern. First, changes in sociability related to sexuality might not address state homophobia absent the prior evolution of domestic LGBT identity and politics, and, in fact, evolving practices do not necessarily indicate even a shared pattern of politicization. Second, evidence suggests that while politicized homophobia is imbedded in both local and global dynam-ics, state actors and their allies tend to adopt a shared and apparently modular characterization of Western LGBT organizing as a foil. Even where homopho-bia serves some local political purpose, then, that purpose has no necessary relationship with patterns of sociability and mobilization among local sexual minorities (for instance, Msibi 2011). Former Kenyan president Daniel arap Moi offered a classic (and revealing) example when he noted, "Now we are seeing men wear earrings to make it easier for them to be identified by other men." Moi seems to have forgotten that many Kenyan men, including Maasai warriors, wear earrings.[8]

Finally, a set of scholars, including those in queer theory, do focus explicitly on oppression, but without conceptualizing political homophobia as we have described it (Sedgwick 1990; Warner 1993). Following Foucault, such approaches consider sexuality as an encompassing discursive structure that propagates normal and abnormal possibilities, elaborating, too, on the ways feminist and race theorists have unlocked the social power and meaning of gender and race. This perspective also extrapolates a critique of LGBT activists as bounded sexual subjects, pulled by, even as they contest, the forms of their marginalization, though often without naming homophobia's practitioners, as feminists sometimes did with misogynists. Included in this strain is constructivist or postmodern work on "queer" identities that meshes poorly with positivist policy making (c.f., Duggan 1994: 4, 9–10).

For instance, Gayle Rubin (1993) embraces the turn to the social reproduction of sexuality, and condemns the essentialist politics that have been reborn today in defense of sexual minorities. She compels scholars to address the persistence of certain ideological formations that not only determine "normal" sexuality, but create categories of forbidden or persecuted sexuality. Rubin examines both state prosecution and social policing of homosexuality to trace a genealogy of an oppression that is just as creative as it defines same-gender sexuality as it is destructive in its suppression of it. Nevertheless, she references "homophobia" only in passing, using it as shorthand for specific claims made against LGBT activists. As such, Rubin's analysis of repression does little to help us understand why persecution becomes an institutionalized political strategy, rather than just part of a broad system of sexual subjectivity. Even as Sedgwick (1990) invokes homophobia much more directly, it remains similarly ambient, if powerfully so. Left out is a comparative understanding of why and how political and social leaders transform homophobia from a normalizing discursive structure into a hotly contested political object. While the state is heteronormative and masculine, heteronormativity and masculinity are not themselves "homophobic"; they might remain dogmatic yet uncontested (Boellstorff 2004), or they might as easily normalize some sexual minorities through the grant of marriage as they might block such equality (e.g., Bonthuys 2008).

Homophobia: Mapping a New World Order

While these disparate traditions each make meaningful contributions to our understanding of both sexuality and patterns of mobilization around same-sex intimacy, none directly addresses the process and implications of the global spread of politicized homophobia. Instead, we can start with Altman (1998:16), who defines homophobia as "all forms of discrimination/ persecution/denial which are related to hostility to homosexuality." The most ambitious attempt thus far to apply this framework to political processes is Murray's *Homophobias* (2009b), although some contributors to that volume either bypass the active engagement of the state or problematize the very concept of homophobia as a raced and gendered construct. The result is an avowedly more anthropological collection that troubles conventional wisdom on relations and structures of inequality without targeting the particularity and modularity of the new wave of political homophobia.

We attempt here to remedy that gap—to trace the roots of homophobia as a state strategy, political movement, and transnational phenomenon with potentially critical impacts on sexual minorities' experiences and expressions of sexuality. Our approach proceeds through four core dimensions: exhuming the purposeful, conscious dimensions of political homophobia, especially as practiced by state actors, and of the "fear of small numbers" that drives politicized homophobia more broadly; examining the role of transnational influence peddling and alliances; probing questions of collective identity; and weighing the legacies of colonialism for subsequent trajectories.

We start with the same assumptions as Murray and his collaborators—that homophobia is socially produced, variously manifested, and entangled in enduring patterns of gender, class, and racial inequalities (Murray 2009c: 3–4)—but then train our gaze on its implications as a fundamentally *political* phenomenon. First, we stress that homophobia is a purposive strategy, adopted by state and social actors. This cohort includes the obviously empowered elites in a given society, as well as close allies and associates of those elites. But we might also consider actors in the context of competition over state institutions and authority, including those seeking either to dislodge current leaders or curry favor with them. By focusing on the purposeful nature of political homophobia, we join with studies of nationalism that home in on the public and political manifestation of hate as it affects or is a product of policy and politics (Snyder 2000).

This dimension sits apart from existing structures of normative sexuality that might independently constrain same-sex intimacy. As performed both publicly and in private, normative sexuality often provides alternative avenues for sexual expression; at the same time, it rarely rises to the level of popular invective associated with political homophobia, given the fundamentally (inter-)personal rather than public stakes at issue. In fact, structures of normative sexuality can contradict the claims made by political homophobia and must change to conform to the new demands of the state. So, for instance, tacit permission of or willful lack of attention to private same-sex intimacy, or uncritical acceptance of a "third sex" as cultural status quo, falls victim to the codification and politically charged standardization of new gender and sexual roles across a range of temporal and regional contexts.

Second, comparative analysis reveals clear transnational patterns, not only in the diffusion of LGBT rights across borders, as so much of the extant literature suggests, but at least as importantly in the diffusion of homophobia. This process has profound predicates. Just in terms of brute demographics, in no context in the world are LGBT citizens the threat they are made out to be; the ubiquitous specter of married, child-rearing gay men or lesbians inflates a tiny, often meek and nearly or fully invisible minority to nation-destroying stature, much as anti-Semitism has done, and frequently at the same time. Similar to the protection racket described by Tilly (1985), in which the state extracts taxes or other resources to secure its constituencies against dangers the state itself has conveniently defined, homophobic state and social actors create a gay peril against which they seek to organize state efforts. In the process, those elites secure their own privileges. Indeed, political homophobia often takes root before a critical mass of sexual minorities even begins to think of itself as "lesbian," "gay," or "transgender," let alone to endow these identities with any collective, political significance or policy claims, threatening or otherwise—since that "identization" process is far from automatic or assured (Mansbridge, 2001; Melucci, 1995).

This dynamic suggests our third point—one we cannot overemphasize. The diffusion of a certain set of human rights claims in LGBT organizing now is at best coincident with and in fact often *follows* the diffusion of a political homophobia. In many cases, it is the homophobes who import a model of same-sex intimacy in terms of Western concepts of LGBT community. Theorizing the spread and political nature of homophobia allows us to explore the implications of such preemptive homophobia—based as it is on borrowed images and rhetoric rather than local ones—on the subsequent development locally of the collective identities of emergent sexual minorities.

In this way, while recognizing prejudice to be just as constructed and contingent in the global North as South (contra Murray 2009b: 7–8), we recast the trajectory of the social development of sexuality to take homophobia, especially in this modular form, as the initial point of departure. In other words (generalizing for the sake of argument), political homophobia incites a Western sexual binary, which in turn structures reactive organizing among sexual minorities through identities that draw from the Western binary. This framework differs from theorizing about race that sees locally prevalent notions of difference as deeply rooted in *local* histories and political struggles (Marx 1998). Nevertheless, our approach precludes any tidy linear progression from normative homophobia to LGBT liberation. Locally and globally, sexual minorities as well as veteran and emergent LGBT movements fight shifting, simultaneous wars against both existing structures of sexuality and newly mobilized forms of modular homophobia, their foils and foes at the same time domestic and transnational. That tension goes far to explain the constitutionalization of similar marriage laws in California and Uganda, as the same manifestation of a kind of politico-sexual eternal return.

Lastly, given the postcolonial contexts into which imported homophobia increasingly intrudes, we see value in considering colonial legacies specifically. Such legacies are hardly deterministic, but cannot be ignored: colonial laws and prejudices, as well as particular processes of anticolonialism and postcolonial nation building, feed or quell politicized homophobia. Homophobia as state practice has been a legacy of (primarily) British colonialism, which compelled the adoption of sodomy laws across the empire (Sanders 2009; also Kaoma, this volume). Furthermore, changing local sexual practices outside the West often responded to an emerging metropolitan conceptualization of sexuality in the nineteenth century, with significant changes in both sexual and gender practices (Najmabadi 2005). Later, national liberation leaders used political homophobia to stigmatize the West, without irony reinforcing or imposing Western laws against same-sex intimacy (Epprecht 2005; Hoad 1999; Lee 2011: 140). And throughout, local activists and sexual minorities in much of the world have been obliged to negotiate not only inherited hegemonic legacies with regard to sexual identity and behavior, but also a precarious balance between Western disdain for homophobic policies presumed drawn from Islam, and an equally repressive homophobia drawn from U.S. standards applied outside the United States—as Zeidan illustrates with reference to Lebanon in his chapter.

With these dimensions in mind, we return to our original empirical puzzle. Put simply, given that a majority of countries have decriminalized same-gender sexual relationships, many of them in the last decade, we might forgive those who see LGBT rights as on the march globally. Same-gender sexual intimacy (particularly between women) is legal somewhere on every continent and nearly everywhere on some continents, and stereotypes notwithstanding, there are no clear patterns among the holdouts. Muslim-majority Turkey lifted restrictions in 1857, as did Jordan in 1951. Communist Vietnam and Cuba ended legal prohibitions decades ago. Fourteen countries in Africa have never had a criminal prohibition on the books, and fifty-four countries worldwide now also prohibit discrimination in employment on the basis of sexual orientation, of which nineteen also prohibit discrimination on the basis of gender identity. Seven countries include antidiscrimination clauses in their constitutions (Bruce-Jones and Itaborahy 2011: 8–14).

On the other hand, we find simultaneously the paradoxical persistence and resurgence of politicized homophobia. Sexual minorities in fourteen countries face a higher age of consent—including in the U.S. states of Virginia and, in some circumstances, Nevada, as well as in Canada, notwithstanding other steps toward full equality. Seventy-six countries currently restrict same-gender sexual intimacy by law. Of those, all or part of seven states deem these forms of sexual expression capital crimes. In this last category is Iran, which adopted explicit prohibitions on homosexuality (beyond criminalizing fornication) only in the 1990s, as well as Uganda, which just recently considered extending capital punishment to cases of "aggravated homosexuality." Indeed, the last decade has seen criminalization strengthened, positive rights repealed, new restrictions adopted, and statutes manipulated to imprison sexual minorities and LGBT and HIV/AIDS activists, across the globe. Governments and their allies have used the power of both media and religion to launch broad campaigns against same-gender sexual expression.

Nor does transnational governance burnish the picture. In February 2011, the UN declined to reinstate ILGA's full consultative status (granted in 1993, then suspended the following year after a campaign by Christian-right activists), nor has the UN adopted a policy against the criminalization of homosexuality advanced by a diverse consortium of members.[9] Yet activists applauded when four months later, the UN narrowly passed a resolution introduced by South Africa merely to commission a study of discriminatory laws and violence against individuals on grounds of sexual orientation and gender identity, to be followed by a panel discussion and determination of a plan of action for redress.[10] The resultant report, issued in November 2011, urged member states to take immediate legal or other steps to monitor and safeguard rights related to sexual orientation and gender identity and expression, and for the Human Rights Council to "investigate and report" violations (Human Rights Council 2011: 25). Even U.S. Secretary of State Hillary Clinton's strident declaration at the UN Human Rights Council that December that "gay rights and human rights . . . are one and the same"[11] is undercut by the fact of LGBT citizens' dubious *de jure* and *de facto* equality in the United States itself.

Egypt occupies a pivot point in the story of contemporary political homophobia, not only as it surfaced after Mubarak's fall, but for the Mubarak regime's explicit prior use of homophobia to secure its legitimacy against the rising Muslim Brotherhood. To return to the notorious case mentioned earlier: the men arrested in 2001 at the Queen Boat dance club faced charges of "debauchery" and "public obscenity" because Egypt has no specific sodomy law. These arrests occurred in a period of challenge to the regime, following the Muslim Brotherhood's significant showings both in the 2000 parliamentary elections and in subsequent elections for the national Bar Association.[12] Tortured with anal exams akin to "virginity tests" the military later conducted on female democracy activists in 2011, these men were tried at a special national-security court under emergency laws dating to the time of Sadat's assassination in 1981, while media published their names and addresses, as U.S. newspapers did of those arrested at bars and clubs in the 1950s. Accused of undermining the state, two dozen were convicted. The Queen Boat incident demonstrates not deep cultural or religious tendencies—the crackdown was of unprecedented severity, and the Muslim Brotherhood remained a beleaguered if strengthening opposition force—but the state's use of homophobia to claim social legitimacy. The broadcast over state media of a TV miniseries based on the notoriously anti-Semitic *Protocols of the Elders of Zion* a year later followed the same pattern, using demonization to distract critics and drum up a "rally round the flag" effect.

As pivotal as the Queen Boat trials were, seen in a wider context, they followed, rather than set, a trend. Zimbabwe's Robert Mugabe, for one, has used homophobia as political strategy at key moments throughout his career in government. In 1997, facing rising discontent that culminated in a massive general strike, as well as a growing HIV epidemic, his government prosecuted the country's first post-liberation president, by then long retired, on sodomy charges stemming from accusations based on his tenure in office. Again in the 2011 run-up to parliamentary and presidential elections, confronting international pressure even from neighboring states, Mugabe's allies in an insurgent branch of the Anglican church battled regime critics in the church leadership in Zimbabwe over the ordination of openly gay men in the United States. Similarly, Malaysian authorities twice (though not successfully) prosecuted former deputy prime minister and later opposition figure Anwar Ibrahim on sodomy charges in the context of direct internal and external challenges to the regime. Meanwhile in Poland, the nationalist Kaczyński twins exploited a small and embattled LGBT movement to build a right-wing party that challenged the European Union's impingement on Polish sovereignty, earning then-president Lech Kaczyński the sanction of the European Court of Human Rights in 2007 for banning LGBT pride events in 2004–5 as mayor of Warsaw. Poland even extracted a protocol allowing an opt out of the EU Charter of Fundamental Rights in the drafting of an EU constitution, justified specifically to free Poland from embracing those same-sex unions that European institutions have not, in fact, required of any state (O'Dwyer, this volume).[13]

Global neocolonial networks have also embraced state homophobia (Kaoma 2009 and this volume). While Uganda has received much international attention for repressive policies fueled by a network of evangelical Christian missionaries, other states fit the same pattern, among them the Democratic Republic of the Congo, Zambia, and Zimbabwe. International outcry secured a pardon for a gay couple sentenced in 2010 to an extended jail term in Malawi,[14] where same-sex relations between women were also newly criminalized the following year. Moreover, the notion of homosexuality as imported, which extends from myths of "moral imperialism" to those about foreign sponsorship of homosexual recruitment, is widespread. Conflation of homosexuality with neocolonialism entwines conservative Christian agendas with nationalist tropes, enhancing church leaders' sociopolitical power—notwithstanding the genuinely imperialist interventions of U.S.-based activists in Uganda, Liberia, and elsewhere.

The Theoretical Implications of Homophobia as a Target of Research

The study of political homophobia extends well beyond the experience of (homo)sexuality and its stigmatization or repression. Importantly, situating homophobia as part of the process of state and national self-definition and legitimation helps to explain how authorities create a "we" among the majority of citizens, at the cost of framing a minority as outsiders; such an approach highlights the politics and *process* of collective identity and the invention or imagining of political traditions and practices that forge and enforce those identities (Anderson 1991; Hobsbawm and Ranger 1983). Understanding how political homophobia becomes modular, and with what effects, adds to our knowledge, too, of collective action and social (counter)mobilization, and particularly of how similar discourses and policy proposals travel as tools and practices in political contention, including among states themselves. And such study enables us to refine our toolkit for combatting repression *and* expanding rights.

Moreover, our focus on the interplay of formal and informal, and local and translocal, politics not only recognizes sexuality in context as a core part of political identities and agendas, but allows us to broach subtle dimensions of a neoliberal model's ever-increasing sway as sometimes a constraint and sometimes a compulsion on states and regimes. Amy Lind's chapter on Ecuador particularly targets these dimensions, in examining the confluence of discourses of citizenship, political economy, sexuality, and "the family." Although legal strictures on sexuality have been dramatically relaxed since the late 1990s, negotiation of neoliberal political and economic reforms has kept LGBT activists' and adversaries' focus on policy making, extending to legislating, for example, what sort of family is entitled to full consideration by the state.

Such connections between neoliberalism and sexuality can seem like a perversion of Polanyi's "double movement" (Polanyi 2001: 136), in which states that embrace globalization economically and otherwise as their ticket to "development" at the same time protect themselves from the domestic upheaval structural adjustment and integration invite, but in these cases by vociferously restricting bodies and cultural change instead of markets. Central to this project is maintenance of a particular order entangled with sexuality and gender, sometimes affirming locally couched heteronormativity, other times transforming gender and sexual norms, yet always readied for battle against mythical foreign dangers known as "LGBT activists," who stand as surrogates for the financial capital and international institutions that have compelled social transformation and limited the regulatory capacity of the state. LGBT forces both hypothetical and real are glossed as narrow special interests ranged against the common good, that represent useful "signifiers of the 'crisis' of liberal politics itself" (Duggan 1994: 2). As the chapters by Bosia and by Korycki and Nasirzadeh clarify, however, targeting non-normative sexualities and identities as part of a state project of conformity and control may proceed through, against, or absent economic liberalization; these processes, rather, are part of the machinery of state power, thrown into relief at times of sociopolitical strain on or of challenges to that power.

Decades of research have asserted and reaffirmed the centrality of gender and sexuality to our experience of political life. Yet that research has largely sidestepped the equally political challenges to those very identities, even as national leaders define the body politic as heterosexual, as political activists condemn as antinational those who flout authority, and as transnational powers press the adoption of ever more repressively discriminatory policies. Sexuality—its manifestations as well as its suppression—must be acknowledged as not just a worthy target for social scientific study as well as activism, but as a truly central one, particularly amidst the steady onward march of present-day politics of violent intolerance and exclusion. Indeed, our focus on political homophobia activates oppression as a category of analysis that is produced and productive, remarkably transmutable as it is available to political and social leaders as a means of legitimation and control, but at the same time defining of sexuality in ways that constrain and construct a specific, Western-oriented response. In other words, a Western trope of political homophobia has seized the terrain. It is on that field that sexual minorities in locales around the world and globally are forced to do battle in their own defense.

Finally, the limits to current research present clear policy implications. Political homophobia is subject to intervention in a way sexuality and gender identity have not been: the spread and calculated deployment of homophobia may be stemmed through domestic and international condemnation (including of the actions of a given state's own agents) and isolation—part of what Weiss (this volume) terms "homopositivity." The EU has been a particularly important force toward that end. EU pressure compelled Romania, for instance, finally to repeal the last vestiges of sodomy laws, whittled down over the course of decades, in 2000. On the other hand, the EU is hardly omnipotent in this regard, as Polish repression demonstrates (See O'Dwyer's chapter for further discussion of the implications of EU conditionality, particularly for postcommunist Europe.)

Or we can compare international responses to state homophobia specifically. While the United States equivocated on a response to Uganda's 2009 sweeping antigay legislation (dubbed the "Kill the Gays" bill), despite the importance of U.S. funding to Uganda generally and specifically in the fight against HIV/AIDS, the UK and Canada issued staunch statements of reprobation and Sweden determined to cut all development assistance to Uganda.[15] One reading might see such condemnation as quasi-imperialist, and hence itself reprehensible. However, that reading ignores both the fact that political homophobia is so often substantially imported—borrowed by segments within those countries with power to condemn rather than an organic local impulse—and the reality that without basic rights to dignity, livelihood, and self-realization, local activists may be powerless to contest political homophobia independently, absent "boomerang" activism from abroad (Keck and Sikkink 1998). Using available tools of diplomacy and transnational activism to combat political homophobia—as a complement to defending the political rights of sexual minorities—clears a path for domestic activists to claim and enjoy rights in accordance with local priorities and mores, to develop their collective identities absent preemptive suppression, and to block the further diffusion and exploitation of politicized homophobia.

Organization of the Volume

The chapters to come move through conceptualizations of the character and genesis of political homophobia to the complications of struggles for rights in its wake. We seek to present not a comprehensive vision of the world, but exhumations of particular (overlapping and intersecting) patterns and dynamics toward the refinement of theory: a conceptualization of state homophobia specifically as a strategy of security, authority, and governance when the state is contested or state actors are under threat from above or below (Bosia); the ways in which homophobia is codified and exported from the West as policy and practice (Johnson and Kaoma); modularity in how homophobia thus comes to be deployed by state actors in struggles over authority (O'Dwyer); the extent to which a new model of homophobia stands in for or supplements larger/different anxieties over gender roles and family structures, in ways that shape the space available for mobilization around identity (Lind and Weiss); and the need thus to think critically about not just identity categories, but the provenance and progress of activism *for* rights as well as *against* oppression, within a framework in which political homophobia is but one aspect of the governance of sexuality (Korycki and Nasirzadeh; Zeidan). We conclude with two chapters that interrogate both our analysis and the political implications that flow from it: the first considers state homophobia within a broader context of sexual governance and intercultural dialogue, addressing the implications of global LGBT rights discourse and sexual personhood for a politics of social justice (Blasius); the second, by Keating, considers how best to negotiate the poles of homophobia and what she terms "homoprotectionism," toward the goal of sexual justice.

Through this approach, we hope to bring political homophobia to the forefront, with the explicit recognition that this prejudice is neither "natural" nor inevitable, nor will it simply fade into impotence with the passage of time. Rather, homophobia is a core instrument of governance in the contemporary world, all the more nefarious for being misunderstood.

Notes

1. Bedayaa uses "LGBTQI" to include queer and intersex alongside LGBT. Launched in July 2010, Bedayaa's website, http://bedayaa.webs.com, had 172 members a year later; its companion page on Facebook, http://www.facebook.com/bedayaa, had 188 fans. See also http://www.calem.eu/bedaaya-egypt-sudan-LGBTQI.html (accessed 17 June 2011).

2. Joint Statement of Arab LGBT Groups, The International Day against Homophobia & Transphobia (trans. Hossein Alizadeh), 17 May 2011, available online, http://www.iglhrc.org/cgi-bin/iowa/article/takeaction/partners/1400.html (accessed 17 June 2011). This framing is also noteworthy in its placement of their identity within concepts of gender and not sexuality.

3. While the term had been used previously, Boellstorff (2004) seems the first to have developed this concept theoretically.

4. *Homophobia* as a term offers us two benefits. First, it is an easily understood, familiar shorthand, used both within academia and outside; and second, it describes a set of discourses and policies linked to the West and now increasingly modular.

5. Jin Haritaworn (2010–11) traces how activism related to hate crimes travels, too (with its own racialized, carceral aspects).

6. But consider, for example, Adam, et al. 1999 as an exception to the rule.

7. ILGA's board is composed of at least two representatives from each region of the world, selected by local delegates at regional conferences.

8. Stephen Brown provided this anecdote. Reported by Reuters in 1999 and available at www.glapn.org/sodomylaws/world/kenya/kenews001.htm (accessed 20 June 2011).

9. "Committee on Non-Governmental Organizations Recommends Special Consultative Status for 12 Groups; Roster Status for Another; Postpones 16 Applications," UN Economic and Social Council press release, February 4, 2011, http://www.un.org/News/Press/docs//2011/ecosoc6460.doc.htm (accessed 17 June 2011); Gamson 1997: 183–86.

10. United Nations Office of the High Commissioner for Human Rights, press release, "Council establishes mandate on Côte d'Ivoire, adopts protocol to child rights treaty, requests study on discrimination and sexual orientation," 17 June 2011, http://www.ohchr.org/EN/NewsEvents/Pages/DisplayNews.aspx?NewsID=11167&LangID=E (accessed 17 June 2011).

11. Steven Lee Myers and Helene Cooper, "U.S. to Aid Gay Rights Abroad, Obama and Clinton Say," *New York Times*, 6 Dec. 2011.

12. "Muslim Brotherhood List Dominates Elections for Egypt's Long Delayed Bar Election," Al Bawaba News, February 25, 2001, http://www1.albawaba.com/news/muslim-brotherhood-list-dominates-egypts-long-delayed-bar-election (accessed 17 June 2011).

13. The protocol, applicable to Poland and the United Kingdom, but for very different purposes, prohibits European courts from overturning domestic laws on the basis of the charter.

14. See Jon Henley, Xan Rice, and David Smith, "Love in the Dock," *The Guardian*, 22 May 2010.

15. Steve Williams, "Uganda Gay Death Penalty Bill: Sweden Threatens to Withdraw Aid, Should the USA?" available at http://www.care2.com/causes/human-rights/blog/ugandan-gay-death-penalty-bill-one-week-closer-to-passing-another-week-of-protest/ (accessed 16 June 2011).

Bibliography

Adam, Barry D., Jan Willem Duyvendak, and André Krouwel, eds. 1999. *The Global Emergence of Gay and Lesbian Politics: National Imprints of a Worldwide Movement.* Philadelphia: Temple University Press.

Altman, Dennis. 1996. "On Global Queering," *Australian Humanities Review* 2 (July). Available at http://www.australianhumanitiesreview.org/archive/Issue-July-1996/altman.html.

——. 1998. "Commentary: HIV, Homophobia, and Human Rights." *Health and Human Rights* 2, no. 4: 15–22.

———. 2000. "Confronting AIDS: Human Rights, Law, and Social Transformation." *Health and Human Rights* 5, no. 1: 149–79.

———. 2004. "Sexuality and Globalization." *Sexuality Research and Social Policy* 1, no. 1: 63–68.

———. 2008. "AIDS and the Globalization of Sexualities." *Social Identities* 14, no. 2: 145–60.

Anderson, Benedict. 1991. *Imagined Communities: Reflections on the Origins and Spread of Nationalism.* New York: Verso.

Appadurai, Arjun. 2006. *Fear of Small Numbers: An Essay on the Geography of Anger.* Durham, NC: Duke University Press.

Bernstein, Mary. 1997. "Celebration and Suppression: The Strategic Uses of Identity by the Lesbian and Gay Movement." *American Journal of Sociology* 103, no. 3: 531–65.

Binnie, Jon. 2004. *The Globalization of Sexuality.* Thousand Oaks, CA: Sage.

Boellstorff, Tom. 2004. "The Emergence of Political Homophobia in Indonesia: Masculinity and National Belonging," *Ethnos* 69, no. , no. 4: 465–86.

Boonthuys, Elsje. 2008. "Possibilities Foreclosed: The Civil Union Act and Lesbian and Gay Identity in Southern Africa." *Sexualities* 11, no. 6: 726–39.

Bosia, Michael J. 2009. "AIDS and Postcolonial Politics: Acting Up on Science and Immigration in France," *French Politics, Culture & Society* 27, no. 1, : 69–90.

———. 2005. "*Assassin!*: AIDS and Neoliberal Reform in France," *New Political Science* 27, no. 3: 291–308.

Boswell, John. 1980. *Christianity, Social Tolerance, and Homosexuality.* Chicago: University of Chicago Press.

Broqua, Christophe. 2013. "Male Homosexuality in Bamako: A Cross Cultural and Cross Historical Comparative Perspective," in S. M. Nyeck and M. Epprecht, eds., *Sexual Diversity in Africa: Politics, Theory, and Citizenship.* Translated by Michael J. Bosia. Montreal: McGill-Queen's University Press.

———. 2010. "La socialization du desire homosexual masculine à Bamako," *Civilisations* 59, no. 1: 37–58.

Bruce-Jones, Eddie, and Lucas Paoli Itaborahy. 2011. "State Sponsored Homophobia: A World Survey of Laws Criminalizing Same-Sex Sexual Acts between Consenting Adults," International Lesbian, Gay, Bisexual, Trans and Intersex Association (ILGA), available at http://old.ilga.org/Statehomophobia/ILGA_State_Sponsored_Homophobia_2011.pdf.

Chabot, Sean, and Jan Willem Duyvendak. 2002. "Globalization and Transnational Diffusion Between Social Movements: Reconceptualizing the Gandhian Repertoire and the Coming Out Routine," *Theory & Society* 31 : 697–740.

Della Porta, Donatella, and Sidney Tarrow, eds. 2005. *Transnational Protest and Global Activism.* Lanham, MD: Rowman and Littlefield.

Denike, Margaret. 2007. "Religion, Rights, and Relationships: The Dream of Relational Equality," *Hypatia* 22, no. 1: 71–91.

Duggan, Lisa. 1994. "Queering the State," *Social Text* 39: 1–14.

Egan, Patrick J, and Kennith Sherrill. 2006. "Same Sex Marriage Initiatives and Lesbian, Gay, and Bisexual Voters in the 2006 Election," National Gay and Lesbian Task Force Policy Institute, available at http://www.thetaskforce.org/downloads/reports/reports/MarriageAndLGBVoters2006.pdf.

———. 2009. "California's Proposition 8: What Happened and What does the Future Hold?" National Gay and Lesbian Task Force Policy Institute, available at http://www.thetaskforce.org/downloads/reports/reports/pi_prop8_1_6_09.pdf .

Epprecht, Marc. 2005. "Black Skin, 'Cowboy' Masculinity: A Genealogy of Homophobia in the African National Movement in Zimbabwe to 1983," *Culture, Health, & Sexuality* 7, no. 3: 253–66.

Fassin, Eric. 2001. "Same Sex, Different Politics: Gay Marriage Debates in France and the U.S.," *Public Culture* 13, no. 2: 215–32.

Fillieuile, Olivier, and Jan Willem Duyvendak. 1999. "Gay and Lesbian Activism in France: Between Integration and Community-Oriented Movements," in Barry D. Adam et al., eds., *The Global Emergence of Gay and Lesbian Politics: National Imprints of a Worldwide Movement*, Philadelphia: Temple University Press, : 184–213.

Florida, Richard. *The Rise of the Creative Class: And How It's Transforming Work, Leisure, Community and Everyday Life*. New York: Basic Books.

Gamson, Joshua. 1997. "Messages of Exclusion: Gender, Movements, and Symbolic Boundaries," *Gender and Society* 11, no. 2: 178–99.

Graff, Agnieszka. 2010. "Looking at Pictures of Gay Men: Political Uses of Homophobia in Contemporary Poland." *Public Culture* 22, no. 3: 583–603.

Gevisser, M., and E. Cameron,eds. 1995. *Defiant Desire: Gay and Lesbian Lives in South Africa*. London: Routledge.

Harding, Rosie. 2011. *Regulating Sexuality: Legal Consciousness in Lesbian and Gay Lives*. New York: Routledge.

Haritaworn, Jin. 2010–11. "Queer Injuries: The Racial Politics of 'Homophobic Hate Crime' in Germany," *Social Justice* 37, no. 1: 69–87.

Hersh, Seymour. 2004. "Torture at Abu Ghraib," *The New Yorker*, May 10.

Hoad, Neville. 1999. "Between the White Man's Burden and the White Man's Disease," *GLQ: A Journal of Lesbian & Gay Studies* 5, no. 4: 559–80.

———. 2000. "Arrested Development or the Queerness of Savages: Resisting Evolutionary Narratives of Difference," *Postcolonial Studies* 3, no. 2: 133–58.

Hobsbawm, Eric, and Terence Ranger (ed.). 1983. *The Invention of Tradition*. New York: Cambridge University Press.

Kaoma, Kapya. 2009. *Globalizing the Culture Wars: U.S. Conservatives, African Churches, and Homophobia*. Somerville, MA: Political Research Associates.

Keck, Margaret E., and Kathryn Sikkink. 1998. *Activists beyond Borders: Advocacy Networks in International Politics*. Ithaca, NY: Cornell University Press.

Kon, Igor´. 2010. "Homophobia as a Litmus Test for Russian Democracy." *Russian Social Science Review* 51, no. 3: 16–37.

Korsmeyer, Carolyn. 2002. "Delightful, Delicious, Disgusting," *The Journal of Aesthetics and Art Criticism* 60, no. 3: 217–25.

Lee, Julian C. H. 2011. *Policing Sexuality: Sex, Society, and the State.* New York: Zed Books.

Linneman, Thomas. 2004. "Homophobia and Hostility: Christian Conservative Reactions to the Political and Cultural Progress of Lesbians and Gay Men," *Sexuality Research and Social Policy* 1, no. 2: 56–76.

Marx, Anthony W. 1998. *Making Race and Nation: A Comparison of South Africa, the United States, and Brazil.* New York: Cambridge University Press.

Massad, Joseph. 2007. *Desiring Arabs.* Chicago: University of Chicago Press.

Mansbridge, Jane. 2001. "The Making of Oppositional Consciousness," in Jane Mansbridge and Aldon Morris, eds., *Oppositional Consciousness: The Subjective Roots of Moral Protest,* Chicago: University of Chicago Press, 1–19.

Melucci, Alberto. 1995. "The Process of Collective Identity," in Hank Johnston and Bert Klandermans, eds., *Social Movements and Culture.* Minneapolis: University of Minnesota Press, 41–63.

Msibi, Thabo. 2011. "The Lies We Have Been Told: On (Homo)Sexuality in Africa." *Africa Today* 58, no. 1: 54–77.

Mugisha, Frank. 2011. "Gay and Vilified in Uganda," *New York Times,* December 22.

Murray, David A. B. 2009a. "Homo Hauntings: Spectral Sexuality and the Good Citizen in Barbadian Media," in David A. B. Murray, ed., *Homophobias: Lust and Loathing Across Time and Space.* Durham, NC: Duke University Press, 146–61.

———. 2009b. *Homophobias: Lust and Loathing Across Time and Space.* Durham, NC: Duke University Press.

———. 2009c. "Introduction," in David A. B. Murray, ed., *Homophobias: Lust and Loathing Across Time and Space.* Durham, NC: Duke University Press, 1–15.

Najmabadi, Afsaneh. 2005. "Mapping Transformations of Sex, Gender, and Sexuality in Modern Iran," *Social Analysis* 49, no. 2: 54–77.

Nussbaum, Martha. 2004. *Hiding from Humanity: Disgust, Shame and the Law.* Princeton, NJ: Princeton University Press.

———. 2009. "A Right to Marry: Same Sex Marriage and Constitutional Law," *Dissent* (Summer): 43–55.

———. 2010. *From Disgust to Humanity: Sexual Orientation and Constitutional Law.* New York: Oxford University Press.

Olzak, Susan. 1983. "Contemporary Ethnic Mobilization," *Annual Review of Sociology* 9: 355–74.

Ottosson, Daniel. 2007. "State-Sponsored Homophobia: A Worldwide Survey of Laws Prohibiting Same Sex Activity Between Consenting Adults," International Lesbian and Gay Association, available at http://ilga.org/historic/Statehomophobia/ State_sponsored_homophobia_ILGA_07.pdf.

Peacock, Dean, Lara Stemple, Sharif Sawires, and Thomas J. Coates. 2009. "Men, HIV/AIDS, and Human Rights," *Journal of Acquired Immune Deficiency Syndromes* 51: Supp. 3, pp. S119–S125.

Polanyi, Karl. 2001 [1944]. *The Great Transformation: The Political and Economic Origins of Our Time.* Boston: Beacon Press.

Puar, Jasbir K. 2005. "On Torture: Abu Ghraib," *Radical History Review* 93: 13–38.

———. 2007. *Terrorist Assemblages: Homonationalism in Queer Times.* Durham, NC: Duke University Press.

———. 2011. "Citation and Censorship: The Politics of Talking About the Sexual Politics of Israel." *Feminist Legal Studies* 19, no. 2: 133–42.

Roberts, Matthew. 1995. "Emergence of Gay Social Movements and Gay Identity in Developing Countries," *Alternatives* 20: 243–64.

Sedgwick, Eve Kosofsky. 1990. *Epistemology of the Closet.* Berkeley: University of California Press.

Sanders, Douglas. 2009. "377 and the Unnatural Afterlife of British Colonialism in Asia," *Asian Journal of Comparative Law* 4, no. 1, available at http://www.bepress.com/asjcl/vol4/iss1/art7.

Silver, Nate. 2009. "Will Iowans Uphold Gay Marriage," FiveThirtyEight blog, April 3, available at www.fivethirtyeight.com/2009/04/will-iowans-uphold-gay-marriage.html.

Slackman, Michael. 2011. "Islamist Group is Rising Force in a New Egypt," *New York Times*, March 24.

Somerville, Siobhan. 2000. *Queering the Color Line: Race and the Invention of Homosexuality in American Culture.* Durham, NC: Duke University Press.

Santos, Boaventura de Sousa. 2006. *The Rise of the Global Left: The World Social Forum and Beyond.* New York: Zed Books.

Snyder, Jack L. 2000. *From Voting to Violence: Democratization and National Conflict.* New York: Norton.

Stychin, Carl. 1998. *A Nation by Rights: National Cultures, Sexual Identity Politics, and The Discourse of Rights.* Philadelphia: Temple University Press.

———. 2000. "A Stranger to its Laws: Sovereign Bodies, Global Sexualities, and Transnational Citizens," *Journal of Law and Society* 27, no. 4: 601–25.

Terry, Jennifer. 1999. *An American Obsession: Science, Medicine, and Homosexuality in Modern Society.* Chicago: University of Chicago Press.

Tilly, Charles. 1985. "War Making and State Making as Organized Crime," in Peter Evans, Dietrich Reuschemeyer, and Theda Skocpol, eds., *Bringing the State Back In.* New York: Cambridge University Press, 169–91.

Human Rights Council. 2011. "Discriminatory laws and practices and acts of violence against individuals based on their sexual orientation and gender identity." Report of the United Nations High Commissioner for Human Rights, A/HRC/19/41 (17 November).

Vaid, Urvashi. 1995. *Virtual Equality: The Mainstreaming of Gay and Lesbian Liberation.* New York: Anchor Books.

Wald, Kenneth D., James W. Button, and Barbara A. Rienzo. 1996. "The Politics of Gay Rights in American Communities: Explaining Anti-Discrimination Policies and Ordinances," *American Journal of Political Science* 40, no. 4: 1152–78.

Michael Warner. 1993. *Fear of a Queer Planet: Queer Politics and Social Theory*. Minneapolis: University of Minnesota Press.

Weiss, Meredith L. 2005. "Who Sets Social Policy in Metropolis? Economic Positioning and Social Reform in Singapore," *New Political Science* 27, no. 3: 267–89.

———. 2006. "Rejection as Freedom? HIV/AIDS Organizations and Identity," *Perspectives on Politics* 4, no. 4: 671–78.

Wright, Timothy. 2000. "Gay Organizations, NGOs, and the Globalization of Sexual Identity: The Case of Bolivia," *Journal of Latin American Anthropology*, 5, no. 2: 89–111.

2

Why States Act

Homophobia and Crisis

MICHAEL J. BOSIA

As the U.S. war on terror shifted to Iraq during the winter of 2002, French police arrested more than twenty members of Act Up Paris when they splattered fake blood on the walls of the Saudi embassy. There to denounce the beheading of three men punished for same-sex intimacy, they demanded that their government extend the right to exile to sexual minorities and challenged French support for regimes that engage in persecution. Such actions indicate a shift in the LGBT struggle. Though global organizing began with the International Lesbian and Gay Association (ILGA) in 1978, and the International Gay and Lesbian Human Rights Commission (IGLHRC) followed in 1990, much political action remained local and national for another decade, even as scholars considered the global diffusion of a rights-based model for mobilizing among sexual minorities. But in this century, and following the work of AIDS activists, LGBT politics focused on global issues linking locations of relative success with experiences of rights deprivation. In Britain and France, then across Europe, and finally in North America with the swift reaction to the suppression of the rights of sexual minorities in Uganda, LGBT activists have turned the struggle against homophobia into a universal campaign for human rights.

But, as this volume argues, events have sometimes led research astray, as if the scholarly gaze is transfixed by that trompe l'oeil drawing of a beautiful young woman who might really be an aged and hunched figure. Optimistically, we are seduced by the transformative possibilities of generative youth in the expansion of human rights; we recognize the broken figure as a fading world of intolerance and superstition. Such constructs mislead theoretically and misread empirically. Instead, tossing aside elusive dichotomies favors a radically obvious question: Why do state actors embrace homophobic policies and rhetoric? In order to understand the global reach of twenty-first-century homophobia, this question privileges agency, even if constrained or impelled by crises and challenges brought by local and international change. By centering analysis on the state, we consider how the state when challenged is served by homophobia, what challenges homophobia addresses, and what problems it seeks to resolve; from Warsaw to Paris, Uganda to Tuzla, Kuala Lumpur to Harare, homophobia has its strategic effect. These phenomena are what I call "state homophobia," borrowing from Act Up Paris and ILGA. While "state" to some suggests law and policy, I consider state homophobia as the totality of strategies and tools, both in policy and in mobilizations, through which holders of and contenders over state authority invoke sexual minorities as objects of opprobrium and targets of persecution.

While my emphasis on agency envisions state actors, their proxies, allies, and competitors strategizing about policy and politics related to same-gender sexual intimacy, I do not deny that constraints shape political choice, including local history, culture, and domestic and international pressures. Like MacIntyre, I believe that the deeply contextual political reality undermining cross-cultural analysis is balanced by a focus in comparative studies on "cases where the will to achieve the same end was pursued with greater or lesser success" (1971, 271). For my purposes, it is neither profitable nor demonstrable to claim that state actors are constrained or compelled to adopt some form of state homophobia as "the same end" because of personal belief, the traditions of the past, or the emergence of LGBT demands. Instead, the power and "will" of the state is such that these policies and rhetorics can create, refashion, and impose tradition or identity rather than merely reflect them. More intriguing is the question of why states do so when constrained by domestic challenge, foreign pressure, or economic dislocation—or all three.

I start with the motif of governance in terms of sexuality presented by Blasius in this volume, where he considers political homophobia as embedded in forms of sexual governance and personhood. I propose a framework for research on one striking and prevalent aspect of the motif of governance—state homophobia—that I find to be flexible and adaptable as it shapes sexual governance in new ways. My framework follows three dimensions, focusing on purpose and will to target agency even when constrained, and on the work done by homophobia in periods of instability or uncertainty. The first dimension is homophobia in situations of violent confrontation resulting from profound changes in the international system, where processes of sovereignty and belonging are in question and an emergent national security apparatus seeks to reestablish authority. Here, state actors, their proxies, and their allies use homophobic repression as a tool for the reconstitution of belonging, not only as ethnic cleansing through expulsion and sexual assault, but in the ways brutal sexualized and gendered violence affirms authority within. Next, I consider ongoing pressures and crises, where competitors or allies threaten state actors, and state homophobia becomes a convenient tool for the affirmation of rule. Here, we see prosecution and condemnation as improvisational strategies introducing very public discussions of sexual differentiation. Finally, I look to the organization of strategic alliances to build state capacity when other resources run short, examining neocolonial networks that reinforce the imposition of sexual repression and the full articulation of an LGBT scapegoat within a Western sexual binary. Both Johnson and Kaoma in this volume consider similar processes, during the Cold War for the former and, like my discussion, in Uganda for the latter.

These are not empirically discrete categories, and by way of conclusion I examine their intersections in France. But they do provide a framework introducing how state homophobia can work. Neither is this a grand theory of state homophobia, as modularity is still paralleled by local imbeddedness. Moreover, much of my analysis centers on state homophobia constituted through male sexuality and gendered notions of masculinity. As the evidence in this volume demonstrates (the chapters by Kaoma, Weiss, and Lind, for instance), political homophobia targets women and transgender people as well as men. My focus does not suggest otherwise; it just offers an intensive analysis of three key examples of the relationship of state homophobia to crisis. Such limitations, however, should not prevent us from advocating for a full conceptualization of the "whys" and "whens" of homophobia in relation to the will of state actors to deploy gender and sexuality in contestations over or re-affirmations of state power.

"Why," for example, calls attention to the choice to embrace the rights of LGBT people made by South Africa's emerging elite in the aftermath of apartheid. In 1993, the African National Congress endorsed marriage equality, and the country's majority-rule constitution was the first in the world to explicitly prohibit discrimination on the basis of sexual orientation. The Constitutional Court overturned sodomy laws, and in 2005 it expedited the enactment of marriage equality. But a strong LGBT movement did not transform society against the forces of tradition, as apartheid policies, like forced conversion of gay men in the military and segregation and coercion, undermined fledgling LGBT organizing, leaving it weak and divided racially; and homophobia retains dangerous social power. Instead, majority rule and LGBT rights stem from the embrace of human rights and the choices of a variety of individuals in the complicated wake of repression (Palmberg 1999). Consider the response to prominent gay men like Simon Nkoli, who was first arrested in the 1976 student uprising, was prosecuted for treason, and convinced his co-defendants to recognize homophobia as a form of oppression: ANC national chair "Terror" Lekota asked at the time of Nkoli's death, "How could we say that men and women like Simon, who had put their shoulders to the wheel to end apartheid, how could we say that they should now be discriminated against?" (Gevisser 1998).

Yet this might be what U.S. civil rights leaders said to Bayard Rustin. Certainly the global zeitgeist was different in 1963, though probably more akin to 1994 than either period is to today. U.S. lesbians and gay men organized concurrently with the civil rights movement, and in 1958, the U.S. Supreme Court recognized the promotion of homosexuality as protected speech, something newly criminalized in parts of Russia in the twenty-first century. Three years after the court ruling, Illinois was the first state to repeal its sodomy law. Rustin's sexuality wasn't even a secret, having been entered into the congressional record and acknowledged in private. But his leadership of the 1963 march was not public, and Dr. Martin Luther King Jr. withdrew from an event at the 1960 Democratic convention after being threatened with Rustin's "outing" (D'Emilio 2004). This is not to suggest that King should or could have done more. Instead, it emphasizes the deliberate choice made later by ANC leaders, whom we should not have expected to act any differently with regard to Nkoli than King did with Rustin.

The contrast between positive embrace and silence confirms that the presumed binary—a new generation of human rights, or homophobic repression—is misleading. Indeed, we are unable to understand state homophobia until theory reflects that, in many contexts today, state actors, their allies and proxies, as well as those in direct contestation over state power have no need to embrace repressive policies because no local LGBT movements can make substantive and credible demands that force a response from the state. At the same time, choosing between repression and silence demonstrates that—while localized patterns and relationships, meanings, and understandings inform repression—state homophobia has shared attributes across contexts that require a comparative theory focusing on a modular set of strategies and rhetorics, despite differences of region, religion, culture, historical experience, state capacity, and regime.

When actors choose, instead of silence, increasing vitriol and repression, they do so because state homophobia serves state- and nation-building processes against the challenges facing the sovereign state, fends off specific challenges, or affirms governing alliances. This pattern is especially true as the state is under threat or compulsion locally or globally, with elite maneuvering on core issues significantly curtailed. State homophobia as such is not a mere artifact of tradition or belief, nor related in any specific way to local sexual minority organizing, but conceptualizes and produces tradition through an increasingly modular LGBT boogeyman as key claims in building state and nation. So the pull between international pressure and domestic politics is clearly one axis for fruitful research on state homophobia, highlighting "the struggles of an incumbent political elite to retain its hold on power as change in the international political economy gives rise to domestic political contestation and opposition" (Loriaux 89, 356). However, neither the external nor the internal pressures need relate to sexuality. Our examination, instead, seeks contexts where state sovereignty or maneuverability is in question, and homophobic repression is a tool to contest or reestablish authority. These intersections of international and domestic might be brought about by neoliberal globalization, where the state's existing opportunities for reward and redistribution are restricted by global players, and so state actors face conflicting demands from above and below. Intersections also occur when national security is challenged by the localized collapse of sovereignty, where state actors, their proxies, and their allies reconfigure the boundaries between national and foreign, friend and foe, combatant and civilian.

The role of state actors in processes of racial exclusion indicates an approach to research on state homophobia. While the imposition of a system of racial exclusion might produce economic and social benefits, reinforced through histories and cultures of racial differentiation and state action, Anthony Marx insists that "the key is to explain why states so act" (Marx, 1998; 2). He links the dynamics of exclusion to the building of state capacity through the state's ability to organize citizenship, extract resources, and allocate benefits—kind of a nationalist bargain. While racism retains its historic and cultural attributes, Marx looks to moments of crisis and/or opportunity, when state actors and emerging state actors affirm or refine patterns of racial exclusion in order to solidify a coalition that can maintain (or in some instances, seize) control over the state. Similarly, in the response to the pressures of colonialism and neocolonialism, state modernization as nation building is carried through the purposeful recalibration of sexuality and gender by state elites and their cultural allies (Najmabadi 2005).

National Security, Gender, and Sexuality

June 10, 1992. A cultural center in a Bosnian village. Seven Muslim fathers and their sons are marched onto the stage and forced to strip by their Serb captors. Possibly more than one hundred fellow Muslims held by the Serbs at the cultural center are compelled to watch as the men and boys onstage are forced to engage in oral sex. The Serbs begin to fire randomly at the "performers" onstage and into the "audience," and the Serb paramilitary who organized this tragedy places his rifle in the mouth of a sixteen-year-old boy and pulls the trigger (U.S. Department of State 1993). Estimates are that four thousand Bosnian male prisoners were subjected to sexual torture by their Serb paramilitary captors, which included castration and genital injury as well as rape and forced fellatio (Littlewood 1997; Olujic 1998).

Fall, 2003. The "midnight shift" at Abu Ghraib prison. Iraqi detainees are removed from their cells and forced to pose for a variety of photographs and videos by soldiers from the U.S. 372nd Military Police Company. Iraqi detainees are hooded and stripped of their clothing. They are forced to pile on top of each other, or ordered to sit naked on another's head. One photograph shows two men forced to simulate oral sex with each other, one man kneeling while the standing man's hands are placed on his head. In nearly every image, American soldiers are present, often smiling. Other humiliations at Abu Ghraib include that of a father forced into a sexual situation with his son (Hersh 2007). Elsewhere in Iraq, according to Amnesty International, soldiers from the American 82nd Airborne "felt welcome to come to the PUC tent on their off-hours to 'F**k a PUC,'" which was a euphemism for beating detainees (officially called "persons under control" or "PUC"). After the photographs from Abu Ghraib were published, soldiers from the 82nd destroyed digital evidence of abuse (Amnesty International 2005).

These parallel instances of torture as theatricalized same-gender sexual assault occur in contexts of similar state collapse. Under pressure to reform at the Cold War's conclusion, Yugoslavia was among the first victims of the New World dis-Order, when once-Communist regional autocrats turned to strategies of national security to legitimize rule. A decade later, Iraq fell in a preemptive war that served as the strategic innovation of the national security state post 9/11. In such cases, as aspects of the nation-state were usurped and then the state implodes, sexual violence becomes one method by which the military and paramilitary affirm sovereignty amidst disorder and inscribe new security upon and through bodies, where previous certainties of ethnic or communitarian belonging evaporate amidst international and localized pressures (Card

1996). Research on the Bosnian War demonstrates that sexual violence, as an act of ethnic or social cleansing, can be a process of disengagement, where the perpetrator engages the victim at a very intimate level, to expel them in the process of securing territory. A cultural act as much as a geographic one, sexual violence atomizes in order to "destroy a group's identity by decimating cultural and social bonds" (ibid., 8). The gendered nature of sexual violence in wartime is important, as it affirms group destruction and the domination of those feminized through acts of violation. Through sexual violence, masculinity can further genocide (MacKinnon 2006) by emasculating and thus disempowering men (MacKinnon 1991) and by inhibiting the possibility of procreation through dismemberment and injury (Sivakumaran 2005). Elsewhere, the refinement of sexualized violence as counter-insurgency strategies and tactics of occupation at Abu Ghraib calls attention to processes of gender disordering and reordering that work "within and through racial, imperial, and economic matrices of power" (Puar 2005, 28).

I differ from these approaches by looking to homophobic acts of torture as they reinforce belonging among the men and women who constitute the emerging security apparatus of the state, and not the separation of the victim from a territorial or social bond. Atrocities like those in Bosnia and Iraq cannot be understood outside an analysis of how violence in war acts on the body and "twists and subverts familiar meanings in ways planned and unplanned" (Culbertson, 2006; 63). In response, we must focus our attention on how homosexualized torture navigates violence and insecurity to control the tortured body as a national security project, and on the effect of sexuality and humiliation on the torturers as well as torture's victims. My intention is to explore the use of sexual violence against men to examine how such acts define and extract loyalty from the *perpetrator*, devising new meanings in contexts of destabilized authority, but always through a struggle against those who might subvert the national security apparatus. If national security reinforces a "gendered logic of the masculine role of protector" (Young 2003, 2), I follow Enloe in reading the practices I call homophobic through the "homegrown American sense of masculinity's fragility" (Enloe 2004), complicated by the uncertainties and mythologies of both internal and external differentiations. Importantly, Iraq and Bosnia point to the breakdown of boundaries that the national security state must reconstitute—between former neighbors and friends for the latter, potential allies in liberation for the former—requiring new variations of sexual and racial differentiation to reconstitute the securitized terrain.

With the collapse of authority in Bosnia and Iraq, what we might call "innovative war" takes hold as previously accepted rules of engagement are arrogated by a series of profoundly new directives and expectations, many of which are violations of both standards of conduct and international law. Facing an inability to contextualize, compartmentalize, and judge this new context of war, the soldier proves a weak link in the military chain of command, and loyalties need to be affirmed through practices that give meaning and sense to what would have been before unthinkable. Imagine, for the moment, the Serb paramilitary, raised in a multicultural Yugoslavia, where borders between ethnic or sectarian communities were not demarcated as politically meaningful and intermarriage was common and valued. In Bosnia, in particular, communities were multicultural, with historic mosques and churches that residents seemed to treat with equal indifference. For the military and paramilitary command, getting untrained paramilitary recruits to claim territory from their friends and neighbors compelled the imposition of a new system of meaning, enacted in violence on the bodies of Bosnian men to ensure the loyalty of the Serb soldier. In essence, the masculinity and patriotism of the Serb soldier was constructed through and against the emasculation of the Bosnian neighbor, inspiring and inspired by the feelings of loathing and disgust associated with same-gender sexual expression.

Iraq under occupation exhibited characteristics that are similar in effect to those evident in Yugoslavia. The new U.S. authorities failed to secure the borders, the institutions of government, and the weapons of war. An emerging insurgency challenged the assumption that Iraqi allies would be thrilled by an act of foreign liberation and reinforced a growing Islamophobia in the United States after 9/11. Facing instability and geographic dismemberment, the new "state" retreated within walled fortresses exemplified by the Green Zone. As well, this privatized war blurred structures of command. For the first time, armed contractors, professional soldiers, and National Guard troops operated more or less in the same theaters, and the role of women expanded to include direct combat when fired upon in a war with no front lines, with profound effects on notions of militarized femininity (Sjoberg 2007). Mingled responsibility and interlocking webs of command were nowhere more evident than at Abu Ghraib, with the CIA and their contractors, the National Guard, as well as regular soldiers working in separate but overlapping jurisdictions. In brief, this confusion of authority and allegiance was the real threat to unit cohesion, masked by the claim that open service for LGBT soldiers would be such a threat.

While sexual violence against women in the context of war also reinforces trust and cohesion as masculine habits, same-gender sexual torture does so by first undermining and then reinforcing both gender and sexual hierarchies that structure same-gender intimacy, feminizing specific sexual acts either arrayed across a gendered hierarchy or associated with a given sexual orientation (Herdt 1997; Murray 2000). This is how the staging of sexual violence in Bosnia and Abu Ghraib recasts raced and gendered boundaries where geographic and social borders no longer exist. With a repertoire of sexual torture moving in a modular pattern across zones of securitization, such violence is state-directed homophobia in that it "produces not only sexed bodies, but also a form of sexual differentiation" situated in the tension between "national normative sexuality and anti-national sexuality" (Axel 2002, 420).

By reconstituting gender through hierarchically arrayed sexual acts, order and control are imposed on the feminized and racialized threat. But, as importantly, cohesion and trust are shared among the now dominant masculinized aggressor—in the case of Abu Ghraib, regardless of their biological sex. So the system of sexual differentiation as elaborated along a complicated gender matrix (Puar 2005) on one level seeks to inoculate the perpetrator from the homosexualized bodies of subordinate peoples. Such tactics are only weakly associated with the lives of gay men in Europe or the United States, as they affirm this securitized system of gendered emasculation through sexual acts and brutal dismemberment. Still, we must ask if the gendered nature of this torture, coupled with its staged effect, truly distances the perpetrator from homosexuality. I suggest that the same-sex intimacy of the violence—as witnessed in groups and digitized among European and U.S. soldiers familiar with a contemporary sexual binary—implicates the perpetrator through his or her direction of it even as it attempts some degree of gender insulation and disengagement. If the purpose of the security state is internal and external, defending the borders and revealing "conspiracies of disaster and disruption" (Young 2003, 80), meanings must be uncertain, as the state sows the seeds of doubt—even self-perceptions of shame and implications of guilt—that are the paranoid justification of its necessity. In this context, same-gender sexual torture is used to shift between gender and sexual understandings in service to a national security "that postulates sex as not only a 'cause' of sexual experience but also of subversive behavior and extraterritorial desire" (Axel 2002, 420).

We can see such a use of homosexuality during the Cold War construction of the U.S. national security state against former Soviet allies through a witch hunt targeting hidden communists and homosexuals in the federal bureaucracy and the expanded public policing of same-gender sexual and social relationships (Johnson 2004; Carter 2004). Media documented the homosexual threat—arising in but outlasting the Red Scare—in newspapers and later on television and in "educational films" explaining "the homosexual," and published the names and addresses of those arrested on public morals charges. These engagements with the menace defined and refined a new danger, and indicated the ubiquity of the homosexual, fostering pervasive suspicion and doubt. Similar to the export of a kind of paranoid homophobia Johnson explores in this volume, state homophobia typically exhibits a constant engagement with same-gender sexuality as pervasive threat at the same time society promotes disengagement and shame (Najmabadi 2005). By layering mutual and self-suspicion within these acts of choreographed disengagement in Bosnia and Abu Ghraib, the national-security apparatus now requires a constant reenactment of masculinized loyalty through homosexualized violence and repression, a staging of the gender and sexual disgust that defines threats to security; this process implicates as well those who stage violence and repression, and so forces an ongoing but never complete reaffirmation of meaning and belonging through violence against a fragile masculinity and within a disordered world.

We can see similar strategies in Iran, where Korycki and Nasirzadeh (this volume) situate capital punishment for same-gender sexual expression within an affirmation of "sexual sovereignty," and security personal purportedly have raped men and women detained for protesting against the regime. Hostility to the established order, with the security command demanding a violent reaction from its troops on the streets, creates a crisis in comprehension and understanding, threatening authorities who fear that security personnel will not act. Policies of sexual violence inflicted on men and women seek to affirm state sovereignty and the logic of national security through loyalty: agents of the state enact the very crime whose existence is denied by the state but whose enactment both symbolically emasculates and vanquishes the state's enemies. But at the same time, this violence implants doubt within those bodies acting on behalf of the state.

Sexuality amidst Crisis

In a spectacular 2001 show trial before a national security court in Cairo, prosecutors won the conviction on charges of debauchery of twenty-one men arrested at a popular disco. The club served as a venue where Egyptians could meet European gay tourists, but nothing of a sexual nature occurred inside. The trial occurred in the shadow of a regime increasingly challenged by an Islamist movement at the same time that it implemented new engagements with the West—including neoliberal structural adjustment policies and currency devaluations—favoring exports and the financial sector but reducing food subsidies amidst stagnant job and income growth (Pfeifer 1999, Pratt 2007). The accused were brought before a specialized national security court originally constituted to pursue crimes against the regime during the transition crisis at the time of Anwar Sadat's assassination. Extensive press coverage sensationalized the judicial process and called attention to the men's association with Western homosexuality as part of the refiguration of social and sexual expression as a foreign menace to national sovereignty.

In explaining these events, Joseph Massad focuses our attention on the influential work of Sayyid Qutb, an intellectual leader of the Muslim Brotherhood in Nasser's Egypt, who wrote extensively about sexuality—including homosexuality—in the United States (Massad 2007). While we should carefully consider the histories that inform state homophobia, including the role of Qutb, my analysis considers the cases in this section as representative of a form of state homophobia that begins in Zimbabwe and Malaysia, where state actors turn to show trials in times of crisis or challenge, in particular where neoliberal reforms reduce economic maneuverability and embolden opponents: sometimes, state homophobia comes out as a shield for the liberalizing state; alternatively, it is a defense against the forces of liberalization. Moreover, these cases illustrate the improvisational interplay of sexuality and gender in the courtroom, where the trope of Western homosexuality is deployed alongside localized forms of sexuality and criminality.

But it was in the United States in the 1980s that homophobia was first coupled with neoliberal reforms and, after 9/11, with cowboy and crony capitalism. In the initial iterations in the Reagan years, the criminalization of HIV transmission and the isolation of people with AIDS were used to ostracize the LGBT movement as the real menace to society in the midst of economic dislocation and change, and the 2000s brought the affirmation of "traditional" marriage in parts of the United States where it had not been questioned. So the challenges facing the Mubarak regime in Cairo, and its response, are instructive but not unusual. In India, as well, where the British had imposed sodomy laws under colonial rule, the governing Hindu nationalist party in the 1990s made the first turn toward globalization to undermine both mercantilist and social policies at the same time it encouraged its adherents to rampage through movie theaters to protest a film depicting a love affair between two women (Kapur 2000). I argue that in these cases where states face such challenges and restrictions, a politics of hostility to the extension of human rights to sexual minorities, if not an outright repudiation of those who engage in same-sex expression, has become a modular response. In Egypt, this strategy supports the implementation of neoliberal reforms of the 1980s and 1990s that reduced the state's maneuverability at the same time they create economic conditions within which political challenges thrive. In Zimbabwe and Malaysia, which are my primary focus because they act first, state homophobia generates support for the government against those internal opponents and external forces pressuring the state in crisis.

Show trials are a defining tactic of this form of state homophobia, amidst public arrests and prosecutions similar to those pursued in the United States in the 1950s, and either separate from an enhancement of legal penalties or in conjunction with them. First, homosexuality on trial provides a public forum to define a surrogate foreign menace embodied by the accused, and behind whom lurk the international pressures on state sovereignty. The accused can then stand in for the foreign danger the state is attempting to resist, or for the disorder threatened by domestic opposition to the structural adjustments the government has embraced. Second, and as Arendt outlined, these processes are contradictory: they require a defendant who is individually the focus for the crime he or she committed; at the same time, the trial illustrates a social or historical force embodied in the defendant (1963). So it is not the accused that is paramount in the proceeding, but the way homosexuality is constructed, from scratch and with significant improvisation, as a danger to national integrity. Since the accused is a real human being who probably will not cooperate, this improvisation of the homosexual menace requires a compliant and supportive media in service to the state.

Zimbabwe is a leading innovator in this regard, adapting the homophobia of the liberation movement to link emerging homosexual activism with forces of Western imperialism (Epprecht 2005). Adopting structural reforms in the first half of the 1990s, Mugabe faced a rising tide of strikes and opposition to his regime as the economy failed to produce substantive gains. In 1995, after he was *shocked, shocked* to find gay men and lesbians at the international book fair in Harare, he targeted the homosexual as a white import, worse than dogs and pigs, wringing cooperation from state and allied media in his campaign. By 1997, neoliberal reforms had receded and land redistribution and economic indigenization were back on his party's agenda, while a year later Mugabe's intervention in the Congo brought economic sanctions from the West. Ahead of the next elections, homosexuality came to represent the threat of British and white domination (Drew 2005). After nearly losing the parliamentary contest, and with a collapsing economy, Mugabe's lawmakers focused on banning public "displays" of homosexuality, and later, forced into a power-sharing agreement and despite his Catholicism, Mugabe openly favored dissident Anglicans who moved to oust Harare's leading prelate over the ordination of lesbian and gay bishops in the United States.

Zimbabwe's chief contribution to state homophobia is the prosecution on sodomy charges of the country's first president, Canaan Banana. A Methodist minister, a leader of the internal opposition to the white minority regime who presided over the country during Mugabe's war against former allies, Banana stepped down from the presidency to make room for Mugabe as part of a peace accord. In 1997, a former aide on trial for murder charged that the crime stemmed from a sexual assault at the hands of Banana more than a decade before, and within months the attorney general charged Banana with sodomy and rape. A few days after the complaint went public, Michael Mawema, a liberation leader long associated with Mugabe's party, launched a "crusade against gays and rapists" that blamed the West for the crimes of sodomy and sexual assault of which Banana stood accused (Raath 1997). Whether an intentional manipulation to sideline a leader who might capitalize on Mugabe's weakness or the impromptu response to pressures brought as a result of those weaknesses, Banana's trial became a model for state prosecutions and enabled Mugabe to affirm his position in a new campaign of homophobia. In the aftermath of a conviction and Banana's flight to South Africa, Mugabe personally intervened, meeting with President Nelson Mandela to negotiate Banana's return. Since 1999, accusations of criminal homosexuality have become commonplace in Zimbabwe politics, lodged by and against Mugabe's government.

It might be mere coincidence that the most notorious prosecution of a public official on sodomy charges began immediately after in Malaysia, though Mugabe associated with long-serving prime minister Mahathir Mohamad, from Malaysia's assistance in easing the entry of Zimbabwe into the Commonwealth in 1980, to a 1999 delegation from Zimbabwe to learn how Malaysia resisted International Monetary Fund pressures. However inspired, the sodomy charges in Malaysia against then–deputy prime minister and Mahathir's once beloved protégé Anwar Ibrahim responded to both outside pressures for neoliberal reform and domestic opposition. Round one, in the wake of the 1997 Asian financial crisis and pressures from international financial institutions, targeted Anwar after his increasingly vocal support for neoliberal reforms pushed by global investors and his apparent intent to succeed Mahathir sooner rather than later. Opposed to both reforms and his own displacement, Mahathir lashed out against Anwar at the same time he identified a Western threat to Malaysia embodied by financier George Soros and "the Jews" the prime minister said were responsible for the financial crisis. More spectacularly, Anwar was accused of sexual degeneracy and homosexuality in a pamphlet entitled "50 Reasons Why Anwar Cannot Become Prime Minister," distributed at the governing party's 1998 conference and that Mahathir cited in his public dismissal of Anwar. In September, Anwar was charged with "unnatural sex," accused of forcibly sodomizing his wife's driver (Human Rights Watch 1999). Convicted, he served in solitary confinement until being acquitted of the sodomy charge and released in 2004. When Anwar assumed the leadership of the opposition after his release, he was again tried on similar charges.

For Mahathir and Mugabe, accusations of sodomy are situated within a contest over the authority and direction of the state. Homosexuality in these stories does not stand alone, an isolated accusation of immorality; the charges against Anwar and Banana took place against the backdrop of economic crisis and of pressures from international actors—structural reforms in the 1990s and pressure to withdraw from the Congo in the case of Zimbabwe, and on Malaysia to institute reforms in the aftermath of financial crisis. Similarly, Anwar's second trial takes place against rising demands for political reform, just as the growing domestic discontent threatening Mugabe's grip on power is also the backdrop to Banana's prosecution ahead of the 2000 parliamentary elections.

Importantly, these trials are improvisational, featuring loosely structured stories about same-gender intimacy and sexual minorities in order to bridge and to confuse categories of sexual and gender identity. Distinct from the strategic conflation of gender and sexuality in the national security state we saw earlier and from the wholesale adoption of Western homophobia we will see in the next section, these trials recast local notions by refiguring modern sexuality in newly localized terms, in the process displacing notions of "same-sex loving" described by Blasius in this volume. Initially, Western homosexuality is portrayed as violent and not consensual, penetrating national sovereignty as international financial institutions have threatened to do, and encapsulating associations of the active sexual role with masculinity. The victims become one possible national future under Western dominance, feminized, like Banana's accuser who committed murder when someone called him "Banana's wife." At the same time, "gay rights" stand in for Western democracy and human rights, which are juxtaposed against African and Asian values that reinforce authority and proper masculinity by condemning Western homosexuality. Finally, homophobic rhetorics and practices might even recognize the social and expressive aspects of homosexuality in order to spotlight once private intimacies, as in Zimbabwe's 2004 law expanding sodomy to include any physical contact offensive to public decency, like handholding and kissing between people of the same gender. In Egypt, the different figuration of the accused homosexuals as feminine mirrors Mubarak's different response to neoliberal demands: the accused as visible victims of Western intervention and foreign penetration mask the state's embrace of—not resistance to—Western financial institutions.

Charged with acts described as foreign, Banana and Anwar were prosecuted under revived colonial-era laws, even in Malaysia, where sharia offered a local alternative. Terms like gay and *homosexual*, or *homoseksual* in Malay, were used alongside *sodomy* or *liwat* and *unnatural*, demonstrating the unsettled nature of the emerging homophobic rhetoric, blurring any distinction between criminal acts and a new category of criminal attachments. "50 Reasons" portrays Anwar as corrupt, power hungry, "ravenous" in his sexual and political appetite, and the leading edge of a homosexual menace that might number twenty thousand men—all common tropes in Western homophobia. As well, he is a U.S. puppet (and the United States is often accused of being Israel's puppet), driving down the value of Malaysia's currency at the hands of his IMF and U.S. masters.[1] Banana's sexual violence becomes a useful tool to portray Mugabe's opponents as the allies of white predators. Whether or not average Malays or Zimbabweans understood same-gender sexual relationships to be of Western origins prior to the accusations, the association of alleged misconduct with apparent support from British, "Jewish," or U.S. interests begins the substitution of a new social category for once private acts of loving.

The courtroom has become modular in the decade since, with states facing domestic or international challenge hauling sexual minorities before prosecutors. AIDS activists in Senegal have been put on trial for crimes against nature, while Russian authorities have arrested LGBT activists at unauthorized rallies. In O'Dwyer's chapter in this volume, we see how Poland's late president fanned anti-European nationalism when he twice banned LGBT rights events as mayor of Warsaw, then later, as head of state, secured treaty concessions that limited the application of European Union rights to his country. Amidst rising opposition and a foreign currency crisis caused by the purchase of a presidential jet, a Malawi court sentenced a same-sex couple often caricatured by the media as "engaged" to the maximum penalty of fourteen years' hard labor for violating that country's colonial-era sodomy law, and at the same time the government prosecuted Peter Sawali for putting up signs that read "Gay Rights are Human Rights."

Capacity Building and the LGBT Menace

In many ways, Uganda seized the attention of global LGBT activists and some in the media as the most shocking example of state homophobia. While Ugandan state actors and their allies have not yet earned that title, the reputation stems from a series of repressive policies that have culminated in a proposal to strengthen the criminalization of same-gender sexual intimacy. Under debate after 2010, this proposal includes the extension of capital punishment to crimes described as "aggravated," including defendants who have HIV or so-called "serial offenders." Iran, Saudi Arabia, Yemen, Afghanistan, and northern Nigeria have existing capital punishment statutes that include hanging in Iran and stoning in Saudi Arabia. The Ugandan law would also ban advocacy or support for, and the failure to turn in, homosexuals.

As well, there is something to be said about the national-security aspirations of the Ugandan state, following decades of strife since the dictatorship of Idi Amin, including a period of instability and a series of insurgencies and armed-resistance movements after President Museveni assumed power in 1986. The most durable has been that of the Lord's Resistance Army, with its call for the imposition of the Ten Commandments as the guiding principles of state, indicating at least a rhetorical religiosity despite its brutality and plunder (Bevan, 2007). This might suggest that Museveni's homophobia is political contestation and domestic nation building through proof of faith. I grant these possibilities but suggest it is more fruitful to focus our attention on the strategic alliances built between Ugandan and American state actors and their proxies and allies as part of the neocolonial networks of financial support that sustain the Museveni regime and hence the contemporary Ugandan state. Local displays of faith carry great weight in these networks and so produce substantial and necessary resources to fight the insurgency and build state capacity. My argument in this section is that these neocolonial faith and financial networks provide the autocratic regime with resources that are not only necessary to marshal allegiance, but hard to come by given the free trade and structural adjustment demands of the neoliberal economic order.

In this volume, Kaoma explores the history and nature of these networks, and his work on Uganda's wholesale importation of the Western homophobes' "gay menace" is mirrored by the conceptualization of homophobic "anticipatory countermovements" in Southeast Asia developed by Weiss in Chapter Seven. But it is more than the violent rhetoric and draconian legal proposals that are strikingly evident and interesting in the Ugandan case. The "gay menace" is a paradoxical contrast with a Museveni regime once hailed for decisive, early, and innovative efforts to stop an out-of-control

AIDS epidemic—"everyone's favorite success story" in the words of Amitai Etzioni (2003). Now Museveni is condemned by many global AIDS activists and service providers for policies related to same-gender sexual intimacy that could in fact further the spread of the disease, even as the country has received the praises and prayers of American evangelicals like the Rev. Rick Warren.

One Ugandan AIDS prevention counselor and activist whom I have known since 2000, now an expatriate, explained this transformation. When my friend became HIV positive in the 1990s, there was little discussion of men who have sex with men in the African context, and despite this absence of social or political organizing, Museveni launched the first volleys of homophobia at that time. Even prevention programs provided nothing more than lessons about abstinence and condoms, as well as monogamy, and personal stories were about AIDS-related stigma. But in his outreach work with the AIDS Support Organization (TASO), my friend was asked with increasing frequency about male sexuality, and he decided to speak openly if impersonally, documenting these exchanges in his reports. Ultimately, he worked within the Positive Men's Union, a private space where men could talk about their sexuality, and it is here that he first found a kind of camaraderie around same-gender sexual intimacy among men who would not identify as gay and many of whom were married.

He described his own increasing awareness and activism against a backdrop of "fermenting stigma" and growing clashes with the prevailing politics, but he was not afraid of significant sanction and in fact received only warnings from his superiors at this time. He was even able to confront Museveni directly at the Great Lakes AIDS Conference in 2001, criticizing not just the silence, but the president's condemnation of homosexuality as a "foreign import." Even in such a context, he had little need to be concerned for his safety and told the delegates and the president about his work with men who had sex with men. But after growing intimidation led to his dismissal two years later for "advocating homosexuality," he left the country.

What changed in this period, and continued to change after my friend left in 2003, is the growing personal relationship between President Museveni, his wife Janet Kataha Museveni, who also has been a member of Parliament, and American evangelicals, as well as the strategies of AIDS prevention and treatment pursued from Washington under the Bush administration. Kaoma's chapter in this volume explores how these relationships extend deeply into Ugandan society through state allies and proxies, including local religious leaders, community-service organizations, and medical institutions benefiting from the financial implications of these personal ties. What could be a highly diversified and contested civil society awash in foreign funding, however, is brought together by the binding glue of state homophobia, which reinforces state authority through its ties to like-minded interests in the United States. As more American church delegations come to Uganda, they bring ideas about homosexuality, including fears of a "gay agenda" that incorporates animalistic promiscuity, pedophilia and recruitment, the danger of marriage equality to society, and faith-based cures for homosexuality as a package of policies, rhetoric, and practices perfected in the American context. Many of these introductions are facilitated through the secretive network of powerful American evangelicals, called "the Family," that spans government, business, and faith both in the United States and Uganda.

A report authored earlier by Kaoma for Political Research Associates indicates that the results are tangible. Since the 1990s, American evangelical churches have augmented or at times supplanted funding from mainline Protestant denominations, even that of the Anglican diocese in this former British colony. A Michigan Christian Reformed Church, for example, gave $115,000 directly to the Anglican Church in Uganda. Funding has been used for clerical salaries provided through the archbishop's office, SUVs purchased by the president for supportive clerics, as well as specific programming and services, and much of the funding is controlled and accounted for in the United States. But a full picture of these private bankrolls is nearly impossible.

With the faith-based initiatives of the Bush administration, we can see the strength of this relationship in a growing confluence of private funding and U.S. government programs, the latter including support for the Ugandan Christian University from USAID, and, most importantly, generous spending in Uganda by the President's Emergency Program for AIDS Relief (PEPFAR), ranking behind only South Africa, Nigeria, and Kenya.[2] In the 2009 budget, the Ministry of Health estimated that more than 80 percent of the country's AIDS-related funding was from foreign sources, which included the $30 million for treatment access. PEPFAR, which represents only part of U.S. funding overall, is one of the two largest contributors. PEPFAR also funds programs through a variety of American and local partnerships, which brought total American contributions to AIDS treatment, care, and prevention in Uganda from $90 million in 2004 to more than $230 million four years later.[3] The bulk of PEPFAR funding globally is for treatment and medical interventions that prevent mother–child transmission. More than a half million Ugandans receive some form of care through PEPFAR, and more than 100,000 have access to treatment. The majority of PEPFAR's prevention education funding internationally goes to abstinence/be-faithful program-ming, linked locally to faith-based programs and the Ugandan government, according to PEPFAR's own reports (PEPFAR, 2009: 3), but overall, U.S. funding to Uganda goes through a variety of primary sponsors, including universities and non-affiliated medical and service organizations.

The most visible American presence on the ground, tightly woven into the fabric of governance, is evangelical, and as a result, Uganda itself is kind of an American "faith-based initiative": a country-wide experiment where funding is driven by sympathetic global networks and where state actors, their local proxies who benefit from the new resources available, and their international allies who fund this array of community and service organizing all agree on a programmatic increase in hostility to homosexuality. Global financial resources build state capacity within this alliance, and a set of ex-panding services bring Ugandans closer to the alliance that is the bedrock of the state, even as the state pursues neoliberal reforms including evictions and land expropriations (Grainger and Geary 2011) partly associated with oil development. Though official hostility to homosexuality produced a backlash from sexual minorities, including a case in which the country's Supreme Court sided with two activists whose home had been illegally searched, the repressive policies continue to be directed through this evangelical alliance. While South Africa became the first in Africa to endorse marriage equal-ity in 2005, for example, Uganda became the first country in the world to institute a constitutional ban on gay marriage the same year, modeled on those state-level bans on gay marriage pushed by the Bush coalition across American states in the 2002 and 2004 general elections. As Kaoma points out, even the proposal to impose the death penalty for "aggravated homosexual-ity" and prohibit advocacy results from American initiatives, paralleled by an American conservative's admission on cable news that he would prefer a return to criminalization in the American context.[4]

Conclusion: France and the Persistence of State Homophobia

In a courtroom in northern France, it was the homophobe on trial in January 2006. Christian Vanneste, a center-right member of the National Assembly for the governing party, was convicted of making hateful remarks about ho-mosexuality, asserting inferiority, menace, and a "sectarian" nature.[5] While the verdict might suggest a wide embrace of LGBT rights, I call attention to this case to demonstrate the persistence of state homophobia even where

LGBT activism has been the most successful. France decriminalized sodomy under Napoleon, and President François Mitterrand abrogated one of the remaining inequalities soon after taking office in 1981. As well, the French Republic is predicated on an emphatic secularism that excoriates any intrusion of faith in political debate and a universalism that promises the same rights to all. But we find a supple and persistent state homophobia evident in Vanneste's commentary and among those who lined up to defend him.

Certainly, tradition and prejudice lurk as well. During the long debate over a civil-union law, Socialists failed to show up to vote on an earlier version authored by legislators from their own governing coalition, reportedly referring to it as "that fag law," and one right-wing member spoke in the National Assembly against the proposal while waving a Bible. The foot-dragging from the governing left and the unprecedented participation of the racist National Front at center-right opposition rallies might indicate the intrusion of private inspirations into considerations of the law. Nevertheless, it is more illuminating that the dominant parties ultimately structured debate around common forms of state homophobia that mimic anti-immigrant and racist impulses that had become a hallmark for some on the left and right at the same time the state embraced economic reform.

After 1984, structural adjustment policies and financial reforms restricted social solidarity and curtailed broad protections against the excesses of capitalism. While rapid modernization brought postcolonial patterns of migration, economic crisis coupled with demographic change proved opportune for the extreme right-wing National Front, and it gained adherents through a platform that foregrounded national identity and demographic anxieties (Gaspard 1995). Parties of the left and right pushed national identity onto the political agenda, but center-right leader Nicolas Sarkozy most unabashedly championed the nation in the new century (Noiriel 2007). If we substitute the values of the French Republic for the politics of "Asian values" in Malaysia, coupled with foreign pressures to reform felt in both contexts, we can understand how the pattern of accusations against Anwar in Malaysia serve the same ends as Vanneste's defense, when notions of French belonging get presented as under attack by forces of globalization described through long-held anxieties about U.S. civilization to the West and an Islamic one to the East (Lebovics 2004; Mangeot 2004; Roger 2002).

These deployments of exclusion and inclusion, targeting either Americanized homosexuals or orientalized Franco-Maghrebi, replace economic and social anxieties with fears of cultural loss and the disintegration or "Lebanonization" of social life brought about by demographic forces and not market ones. State actors, allies, and proxies position the evaporation of the French people through the loss of French values against certain identities, be they "gay" or "Muslim" (Bosia 2009). Once a social scourge akin to alcoholism, gay men are likely portrayed in this period as U.S.-inspired, as in the 1980s when officials reasoned that this association brought HIV to France. Or, like in the case of Anwar in Malaysia, some accuse activists of partaking in a conspiracy of foreign and Jewish menace, pursuing "sectarian" interests in ways that threaten collective interests; this is what is meant when even the left invokes a "gay lobby" and "gay community" as the right does a "Jewish lobby" (Bosia 2007, Mangeot 2004). Though Sarkozy himself might be more subtle than the Socialist politicians who fled the floor of the National Assembly, he embraced Vanneste and others more stridently homophobic, like he consistently prevaricated on the integration of Franco-Maghrebi. Indeed, Sarkozy's defense of homophobic political rhetoric despite its legal prohibition while also encouraging LGBT members of his party, and his support for a ban on both adoption and medically assisted procreation outside of state sanctioned heterosexual marriage, reinforce his proxies to his right, and so also mirror his attack on the children of immigrants as "thugs" as he appoints Franco-Maghrebi to new positions in the state.

Even after Sarkozy was replaced in 2012 by a government of the left promising marriage equality, politicians from each end of the spectrum deployed the old rubric associating demands for the integration of Franco-Maghrebi with those for LGBT family equality. One newly elected Marxist spoke out against marriage equality after his election, while on the right, a former minister restated the conviction that marriage equality would threaten "the balance in French society."[6] Both had in the past invoked images of isolated Muslim women wearing the Burqa to portray the values of at least some immigrants as hostile to those shared by the French.

While state homophobia is a subtle feint to trump claims that economic reform causes social disintegration, the opposition to lesbian and gay parenthood is also a response to demographic anxieties and national-security concerns that reach back to the Republic's refounding after the German invasion of 1870. Preoccupied with the next war, French governance came to rest in part on natalist security imperatives. Today, the rhetoric of immigration is always about the demise of the French Republic, and consistently the right and left speak about homosexuality and immigration as overlapping threats to the reproduction of the nation (Bosia 2007). For the right, this is basic demography, as in Vanneste's claim that homosexuality unfettered would lead to the end of humanity. For the left, it is situated in a supposedly natural difference between men and women as parents, from which flow all systems of differentiation that children must learn, and so all understanding of society (Fassin 2000). In both, homosexuality is removed from the system of normalized gender and becomes threatening to national survival, either because it is naturally so or because its contemporary claims are not refuted. While both are the foundation for arguments against the right of same-gender couples to access medically assisted procreation or adoption, they also implicate heterosexual couples who refuse to procreate.

While France presents the complication of categories, in each of the examples I have sketched, we see how state homophobia is about capacity and security, the contestation over and consolidation of power, along sexual and gender lines. We should not target our research on deeply held social values or preconceptions, but on the politics of repression that produces and reproduces historical patterns and tradition, through processes of diffusion or adaptation and in response to the rise of new challenges and crises. State homophobia is the choice to *do* something, taken by people in authoritative positions, to serve specific purposes that only rarely have to do with the control of often not-yet-emergent sexual minorities. I suggest three dimensions where a choice has been taken by state leaders, but these dimensions are neither necessarily discrete nor complete. As analytical tools, they indicate possible directions research should take, and they demonstrate a set of parameters that might extend to new theories and approaches. Certainly, the cases I highlight indicate a systematic intersection of state homophobia with race and gender, particularly striking in the post-9/11 era.

Finally, I return to my primary claim: we can neither set homophobia aside nor remove it from its central position as an aspect of state governance and nation building. If, as Veena Das warns, in the post-9/11 world—and echoed by Blasius in his chapter—our theories might "provide scaffolding to this picture of untranslatability despite our understanding of diversity" (Das 2001, 1), the interrogation of state homophobia requires us first to be wary about the analysis of identity politics outside of our own cultural comfort zone, and then to acknowledge the collusion of a variety of Western and global forces where the state remains central to repression.

Notes

1. http://todaymalaysia.wordpress.com/2008/05/21/50-reasons-why-anwar-cannot-become-prime-minister-yesterday-journalism-for-today-to-ponder/.

2. http://www.pepfar.gov/countries.

3. PEPFAR Country Operation Plan for Uganda, 2007 www.pepfar.gov/about/82442.htm, and the PEPFAR country profile for Uganda www.pepfar.gov/press/countries/profiles/116321.htm.

4. In a February 2, 2010, broadcast of *Hardball* on MSNBC, Peter Sprigg of the Family Research Council said, "I think there should be a place for criminal sanctions against homosexual behavior."

5. Act Up Paris, July 5, 2005. http://www.actupparis.org/spip.php?article2013.

6. The former was Deputy Patrice Carvahlo (http://francaisdefrance.wordpress.com/2012/07/15/un-depute-com/) and the latter, Valérie Pécresse (http://yagg.com/2012/07/09/pour-valerie-pecresse-louverture-du-mariage-aux-couples-homos-bouleverserait-les-equilibres-de-la-societe-francaise/).

Bibliography

Amnesty International. 2005. Summary, "Leadership Failure: Firsthand Accounts of Torture of Iraqi Detainees by the U.S. Army's 82nd Airborne Division." http://hrw.org/reports/2005/us0905/1.htm#_Toc115161399.

Arendt, Hannah. 1992. *Eichmann in Jerusalem: A Report on the Banality of Evil.* New York: Penguin.

Axel, Brian Keith. 2002. "The Diasporic Imaginary." *Public Culture* 14, no. 2: 411–28.

Bevan, James. 2007. "The Myth of Madness: Cold Rationality and Resource Plunder by the Lord's Resistance Army," *Civil Wars* 9, no. 4: 343–58.

Bosia, Michael J. 2009. "AIDS and Postcolonial Politics: Acting Up on Science and Immigration in France," *French Politics, Culture & Society* 27, no. 1: 69–90.

———. 2007. "Guilty as Charged: Accountability and the Politics of AIDS in France," in *The Global Politics of AIDS*, P. Siplon and P. Harris, eds. Boulder, CO: Lynne Reinner Publishers.

Card, Claudia. 1996. "Rape as a Weapon of War," *Hypatia* 11, no. 4: 5–18.

Carter, David. 2004. *Stonewall: The Riots that Sparked the Gay Revolution.* New York: St. Martin's Press.

Culbertson, Roberta. 2006. "War and the Nature of Ultimate Things: An Essay on the Study of Post-War Cultures." In Asale-Angel Ajani and Victoria Sanford, eds., *Engaged Observer: Anthropology, Advocacy, Activism.* pp. 60–75. New Brunswick, NJ: Rutgers University Press.

Das, Veena. 2001. "Violence and Translation," *Anthropological Quarterly* 75, no. 1: 105–12.

D'Emilio, John. 2004. *Lost Prophet: The Life and Times of Bayard Rustin.* Chicago: University of Chicago Press.

Enloe, Cynthia. 2004. "Wielding Masculinity Inside Abu Ghraib: Making Feminist Sense of an American Military Scandal," *Asian Journal of Women's Studies* 10, no. 3: 89–102.

Epprecht, Marc. 2005. "Black Skin, 'Cowboy' Masculinity: A Genealogy of Homophobia in the African National Movement in Zimbabwe to 1983," *Culture, Health, & Sexuality* 7, no. 3: 253–66.

Etzioni, Amitai. 2003. "Fight HIV with Straight Talk," *Christian Science Monitor*, March 4.

Fassin, Eric. 2000. "The Politics of PaCS in a Transatlantic Mirror: Same Sex Unions and Sexual Difference in France Today," Sites 4, no. 1: 55–64.

Gaspard, Françoise. 1995. A Small City in France. Cambridge, MA: Harvard University Press.

Gevisser, Mark, and Edwin Cameron. 1995. Defiant Desire: Gay and Lesbian Lives in South Africa. New York: Routledge.

Gevisser, Mark. 1998. "A Leading Light of Gay and AIDS Activism in South Africa," Sunday Times, December 6. www.aegis.org/news/suntimes/1998/ST981202.html.

Grainger, Matt, and Kate Geary. 2011. "The New Forest Company and its Uganda Plantations." Oxfam Case Study. http://www.oxfam.org/sites/www.oxfam.org/files/cs-new-forest-company-uganda-plantations-220911-en.pdf.

Hersh, Seymour M. 2007. "Annals of National Security. The General's Report: How Antonio Taguba, Who Investigated the Abu Ghraib Scandal, Became One of Its Casualties," The New Yorker, June 25, pp. 58–69.

Human Rights Watch. 1999. World Report. http://www.hrw.org/worldreport99/asia/malaysia.html.

International Criminal Tribunal for the Former Yugoslavia, Richard Goldstone, prosecutor. Indictment of Dusan Tadic, case number IT 94-1-I, February 13, 1995.

Johnson, David K. 2004. The Lavender Scare: The Cold War Persecution of Gays and Lesbians in the Federal Government. Chicago: University of Chicago Press.

Kapur, Ratna. 2000. "Too Hot to Handle: The Cultural Politics of Fire," Feminist Review 64: 53–64.

Lebovics, Herman. 2004 Bringing the Empire Back Home: France in the Global Age. Durham, NC: Duke University Press.

Lesselier, Claude. 2002. "Préférence familiale, préférence nationale, ordre moral." Journal du Ras l'front 86, www.raslfront.org.

Littlewood, Roland. 1997. "Military Rape," Anthropology Today, 13, no. 2: 7–16.

Loriaux, Michael. 1989. "Comparative Political Economy as Comparative History," Comparative Politics 21, no. 3: 355–77.

Mangeot, Philippe. 2004. "'Communautés' et 'communautarisme' Premier Partie: La rhétorique 'anti-communautariste' a l'épreuve des 'communautés homosexuelles." LMSI: Communautarisme, http://lmsi.net/-Communautarisme.

Marx, Anthony. 1998. Making Race and Nation. New York: Cambridge University Press.

Massad, Joseph. 2007. Desiring Arabs. Chicago: University of Chicago Press.

MacKinnon, Catherine, 2006. Are Women Human and Other International Dialogues. Cambridge: The Belknap Press of Harvard University Press.

——, 1991. "Sex Equality under Law," The Yale Law Journal 100, no. 5: 1281–1328.

MacIntyre, Alasdair. 1971. Against the Self Image of the Ages. South Bend, IN: University of Notre Dame Press.

Najmabadi, Afsaneh. 2005. "Mapping Transformations of Sex, Gender, and Sexuality in Modern Iran," Social Analysis 49, no. 2: 54–77.

Noiriel, Gérard. 2007. *À Quoi Sert L'Identité "Nationale."* Marseille: Éditions Agone.

Olujic, Maria B. 1998. "Embodiments of Terror: Gendered Violence in Peacetime and Wartime in Croatia and Bosnia-Herzegovina," *Medical Anthropology Quarterly* 12, no. 1: 31–50.

PEPFAR. Celebrating Life: 2009 Annual Report to Congress (Highlights).

Pfeifer, Karen. 1999. "Parameters of Economic Reform in North Africa," *Review of African Political Economy* 26, no. 82, 441–54.

Palmberg, Mai. 1999. "Emerging Visibility of Gays and Lesbians in Southern Africa: Contrasting Contexts," in Barry D. Adam, Jan Willem Duyvendak, and André Krouwel, eds., *The Global Emergence of Gay and Lesbian Politics: National Imprints of a Worldwide Movement*, pp. 266–92. Philadelphia: Temple University Press.

Pratt, Nicola. 2007. "The Queen Boat Case in Egypt: Sexuality, National Security and State Sovereignty," *Review of International Studies* 33: 129–44.

Puar, Jasbir K. 2005. "On Torture: Abu Ghraib," *Radical History Review* 93: 13–38.

Raath, Jan. 1997. "Crusade to Whip, Castrate Gays and Rapists Falls Flat," *Deutsche Presse Agentur*, March 5.

Roger, Philippe. 2002. *L'ennemi américain: Généalogie d'antiaméricanisme français.* Paris: Seuil.

Shaw, Drew. 2005. "Queer Inclinations and Representations: Dambudzo Marechera and Zimbabwean Literature." In Flora Veit-Wild and Dirk Naguschewski, eds., *Body, Sexuality, and Gender: Versions and Subversions in African Literature.* Amsterdam: Editions Rodopi B.V.

Sivakumaran, Sandesh, 2005. "Male/Male Rape and the 'Taint' of Homosexuality," *Human Rights Quarterly* 27, no. 4: 1274–1306.

Sjoberg, Laura. 2007. "Agency, Militarized Femininity, and Enemy Others," *International Feminist Journal of Politics* 9, no. 1: 82–101.

U.S. Department of State Dispatch. 1993. "Eighth Report on War Crimes in the Former Yugoslavia" 4, no. 30: July 26 (Washington, D.C.: Bureau of Public Affairs), http://dosfan.lib.uic.edu/ERC/index.html.

Young, Iris Marion. 2003. "The Logic of Masculinist Protection: Reflections on the Current Security State," *Signs: Journal of Women in Culture and Society* 29, no. 1: 1–25.

3

America's Cold War Empire

Exporting the Lavender Scare

DAVID K. JOHNSON

In 1952, in the midst of the Cold War struggle that dominated international relations and effectively divided the world into two armed camps,
Canadian officials discovered a security breach within the Communications
Branch of the National Research Council (CBNRC), the highly secret agency
that monitored radio signals from the Soviet Union. They discovered that
a middle-management employee in the CBNRC was gay. Although uncon-
cerned about his loyalty or integrity, they immediately sought his resignation.
As a Canadian intelligence expert explained, "The authorities feared more
than anything that the Americans would find out." Canada's closest neighbor and ally, the United States, was in the midst of a moral panic over the
threat posed by both communists and homosexuals to its national-security
apparatus. Whether they agreed or not, during the Cold War, Canada, the
United Kingdom, and other American allies conformed to American policies concerning national security or risked being cut off from America's vast
military-industrial network (Sawatsky 1980, 124).

Although the United States is now associated with exporting an agenda of
human rights that includes equality for gay men and lesbians, its Cold War–
era views were radically different. Indeed, a fear of homosexuals characterized
American Cold War security concerns, leading to the establishment of policies,
procedures, and personnel throughout the executive branch of the U.S. government to uncover and remove all suspected gay men and lesbians from public
service.[1] This fear of the corrosive influence of homosexuals on state policy
was so pervasive that the U.S. government made an explicit effort to export it
overseas. The story of the CBNRC's dismissal of a gay employee illustrates the
power of the U.S. federal government during the Cold War to export its fear of

deviant sexuality. This essay examines how this state-sponsored homophobic panic was exported to America's Western allies and international organizations such as the United Nations, the International Monetary Fund, and the World Bank. It shows how U.S. officials pressured foreign officials and the heads of international organizations to adopt American-style security procedures and purge their agencies of anyone guilty of homosexual conduct. Fearing the loss of either American financial aid or contact with the U.S. intelligence-gathering apparatus, most sought to comply. It explores the ways in which state homophobia functioned in the United States during the Cold War both on the national and state levels—with an intricate enforcement network involving the FBI and local police—and then how it was exported overseas both as explicit government policy and as a cultural model.

An American Lavender Scare

In February 1950, in what should have been an unremarkable Lincoln-day address to a Republican women's club in Wheeling, West Virginia, U.S. Senator Joseph McCarthy (R-Wisconsin) made the audacious claim that 205 card-carrying Communists had infiltrated the State Department. "I have here in my hand a list of 205—a list of names that were made known to the Secretary of State as being members of the Communist Party and who nevertheless are still working and shaping policy in the State Department," McCarthy reportedly told the women's club, although recordings of the speech went missing. Charges about subversion in the diplomatic corps were old news, but because McCarthy claimed to possess a specific list, the accusation captured tremendous national attention. Under intense media pressure, McCarthy began to modify his charges—205 communists became 57 "loyalty risks" and then 81 "bad risks." When McCarthy finally detailed his alleged cases of subversion, several centered on homosexual employees. On the floor of the Senate, McCarthy explained the connection between political and sexual deviance. He had recently had a conversation about why some people were so "fanatically Communist" with a Washington intelligence expert. "If you had been in this work as long as we have been," the expert told McCarthy, "you would realize that there is something wrong with each one of these individuals. You will find," he asserted, "that practically every active Communist is twisted mentally or physically in some way." To McCarthy and many others in Cold War Washington, homosexuality was a type of psychological maladjustment that led some people toward communism.[2]

Under attack from McCarthy, U.S. State Department officials denied that the department employed or had employed any Communists. But under intense congressional questioning about its new security system, Deputy Under Secretary John Peurifoy revealed that the department had dismissed a number of employees, and that among these were ninety-one homosexuals. Many interpreted this as a sign that the State Department—perhaps the entire government—was infiltrated with perverts. Seeming to confirm McCarthy's charges, Peurifoy's revelation prompted concern and outrage throughout the nation, heated debates on the floors of Congress, several congressional committee investigations, countless newspaper articles, and numerous White House meetings. In a joint memorandum to the president, three of Truman's advisors told him that "the country is more concerned about the charges of homosexuals in the Government than about Communists." Newspapers reported that a sampling of McCarthy's mail revealed that only one-quarter of letter writers expressed concern about "red infiltration," while three-quarters expressed "shocked indignation at the evidence of sex depravity." As one woman from Long Island wrote to the *New York Daily News*, "the homosexual situation in our State Department is no more shocking than your statement that 'they are uncertain what to do about it.' Let every American who loves this country get behind McCarthy or any committee which will thoroughly investigate and expose every one of these people . . . This is no time for compromise. Democrats or Republicans—we must rid our Government of these creatures."[3]

The Peurifoy revelation was part of an orchestrated attempt by senior Republican officials to push McCarthy's campaign away from the issue of Communists in government toward the more politically promising issue of homosexuals in government. Many fellow Republicans doubted McCarthy could prove there were fifty-seven card-carrying Communists in the State Department—labeling his charges "too wild." They suggested McCarthy might have more success if he focused on "bad security risks." As early as 1947, they had quietly pressured the State Department to institute the first postwar governmental security program as a means to target the threat of both communists and homosexuals. They had passed the "McCarran rider," legislation permitting the secretary of state to dismiss any employee at his "absolute discretion" if deemed advisable in the interest of national security with the understanding that it would cover both communists and homosexuals. In the wake of the McCarthy charges, the focus on homosexuals intensified. Senator Kenneth Wherry (R-Nebraska) subpoenaed the head of the D.C. vice squad and coaxed him into estimating that the District of Columbia was home to five thousand homosexuals— three-quarters of them on the federal payroll. By comparing this to an estimated one thousand political subversives in the city, they suggested the real menace facing the nation's capital was not political but sexual deviance. As one Republican told an audience in McCarthy's home state of Wisconsin, "When they admit discharging ninety-one homosexuals it doesn't look good . . . A man doesn't have to be a spy or a Communist to be a bad security risk. He can be a drunkard or a criminal or a homosexual." Such security risks, these Republicans intimated, were more numerous, easier to catch, and just as dangerous.[4]

Although "security risk" covered a variety of offenses, it often functioned as a euphemism for homosexual. A security risk was someone who might divulge secret information, either because they were careless or coerced. Those with relatives behind the iron curtain fell into this category, as did the loquacious, the alcoholic, and the homosexual. But of these three sins, homosexuality was the only one to be illegal, thereby enlisting every police force in the nation in its enforcement. It was the only one that warranted a full-scale congressional investigation, the only one requiring specialized security officers, the only category about which government departments kept specific records. As a result, in most statistics about security risks, homosexuals constituted the largest contingent. The Eisenhower security program, which expanded the Truman loyalty program and shifted the focus from political deviance to issues of character and suitability, was the ultimate triumph of this effort to shift from communists to homosexuals. In 1953, when Republicans took control of the White House, Eisenhower quietly signed an executive order that included "sexual perversion" as grounds for dismissal. By combining issues of loyalty and security and granting final authority to agency heads, it effectively expanded the security authority originally given to the State Department and a few military agencies at the start of the Cold War to the entire federal government. Under the Eisenhower administration, national security would require not only political loyalty, but also proper morality.[5]

Even before the new Eisenhower security program, the federal government stepped up its efforts at weeding out homosexuals. To respond to the public and political clamor created by McCarthy's charges, the Senate in 1950 authorized a full-scale investigation into "the employment of homosexuals and other sex perverts in government." Chaired by Senator Clyde Hoey (D-North Carolina) the committee investigated the claim that homosexuals posed a threat to national security and considered changes to existing government policies and procedures to ensure their removal from sensitive government agencies. After months of investigation and interviews with scores of security officers, the committee discovered little evidence to back up the claim. It never found a single example of a homosexual American citizen who had been blackmailed into revealing state secrets. Claiming these officials all agreed that homosexuals posed a security risk, they produced only one example—Colonel Alfred Raedl, a World War I–era Austrian intelligence officer. Even here, it appears the government manipulated the story. Raedl was a homosexual double agent, but all accounts suggest he betrayed Austria for financial gain, not as the result of blackmail. The committee did uncover considerable difference of opinion, even within the U.S. government, over whether foreign governments attempted to blackmail homosexuals.

Despite this lack of evidence, the Hoey Committee's final report stated emphatically that all of the intelligence agencies of the government that testified "are in complete agreement that sex perverts in Government constitute security risks." It asserted that Russian intelligence agents had been given orders to find weaknesses in the private lives of American government workers. And while acknowledging that other weaknesses might pose as much of a threat, it asserted that such comparisons were beyond the committee's mandate. Through the Hoey Committee's final report, the notion that homosexuals threatened national security received the imprimatur of the U.S. Congress and became accepted as official fact. The report was sent to American embassies and foreign intelligence agencies around the world, became part of the U.S. government security manuals, and would be quoted for years by the government of the United States and its allies as justification for excluding homosexuals.[6]

Francis Flanagan, the committee's chief counsel, had grandiose plans to mimic the tactics of the House Committee on Un-American Activities, which for years had maintained its own extensive files of suspected Communists and fascists. Flanagan planned to establish "a central card index" of homosexuals, a tool that government agencies could consult in screening potential or current employees. To maximize its effectiveness, the list was to include names of anyone a government agency had reason to suspect of homosexuality, whether a government employee or private citizen. At the very least, Flanagan hoped to consolidate a number of existing lists of sex deviants already compiled by various government agencies, including the navy, army, State Department, Washington, D.C. Police, and U.S. Park Police. He estimated such a combined list would give him the names of some 16,500 suspected homosexuals. These agencies, however, refused to turn over their files to Flanagan, and his plans for a master file of American homosexuals remained unfulfilled.[7]

As a result of McCarthy's charges and the subsequent Hoey Committee investigation, members of Congress pressured all government agencies to shore up their security procedures. But the pressure was particularly high on the State Department. With the growing public perception that it was a haven for sexual deviants, the State Department set up a veritable dragnet for homosexuals. Every applicant was checked against the State Department's master list of three thousand alleged homosexuals compiled from previous

interrogations and investigations. All male applicants were personally interviewed to help detect sex deviants. Investigators were to note "any unusual
traits of speech, appearance and mannerisms." The investigators checked
credit and police records and interviewed character references. Invoking the
"guilt by association" technique, the investigators checked whether any of the
employee's friends or associates were homosexual. If suspicions were high
but evidence lacking, those suspected might be placed under surveillance to
determine whether they frequented "known homosexual places" or associated with "known homosexuals." By 1953, under the Eisenhower administration, the State Department established a special investigative branch known
as the "Miscellaneous M Unit" to handle homosexual and other "morals"
cases. The Miscellaneous M Unit's preferred techniques to detect homosexuals were personal interviews and the polygraph examination. If information
suggested an applicant or an employee was homosexual, the unit would confront the individual and attempt to procure a confession. The "opportunity"
of a lie-detector examination was offered as the only alternative. As a result
of such intensive investigative work, according to the head of Security and
Consular Affairs, more than 80 percent of those confronted with evidence
against them confessed.[8]

The vehemence of the State Department's antigay campaign can hardly
be overstated. At the height of the Cold War, the State Department security
office became a de facto sex squad. The chief of every mission received a
memorandum underscoring the need to eliminate the homosexual problem.
Inspectors sent to every embassy, consulate, and mission were given special
training sessions on "methods used in uncovering homosexuals," instructed
to be "continually on the alert" to discover homosexuals, and asked to brief
others on the topic during their tours of inspection. Recruiters in the Office
of Personnel were given similar briefings and cautioned to "do everything
possible to ferret out individuals with homosexual tendencies before final
selection."[9] Testifying before Congress at the very beginning of the Eisenhower administration, Carlisle Humelsine, the State Department security
officer, defended his department's antigay campaign. "It is quite clear to me,"
Humelsine testified, "that these homosexuals are sick people, and they just
don't know what they are doing, they do some of the most foolish things,
which lead to the compromising of our particular type of work." Although
publicly the department had a loyalty/security system, in fact it had two systems—one for political deviants and one for sexual deviants. Homosexuals
were not simply one of many types of security risks officials tracked—they
were given unprecedented attention. In an unguarded internal memorandum,

one official made the point quite explicit by referring to the department's "loyalty system" and its "homosexual system."[10]

McCarthy's time in the spotlight was brief. He did not follow the advice of his more senior colleagues to pursue the more promising issue of homosexuals in government. Instead, he initiated wild smear campaigns about alleged Communist conspirators, including powerful generals such as George Marshall. His antigay campaign soon dropped out of the headlines. By 1954, his Senate colleagues voted to censure him, and he subsequently slowly drank himself to death. But the lavender scare he unleashed did not go away. It became institutionalized in the bureaucracy of the national security state and remained standard civil-service policy until the 1970s. The Department of State's aggressive program of uncovering and removing suspected homosexuals became the model that Congress pressured other departments to follow. The State Department's security system focusing on Communists and homosexuals became the standard for the entire federal government and eventually its Cold War allies.

The total number of persons affected by the anti-homosexual purges is impossible to determine with any precision, especially since so many of its victims resigned quietly under pressure rather than face a public scandal. Nevertheless, some published figures give a sense of their scale. According to the Hoey congressional committee, between 1947 and 1950, over four hundred federal employees resigned or were dismissed for sexual perversion—about one hundred per year. This represents only the first few years of the purges, before McCarthy's charges and congressional pressure gave them momentum. In the two years between May 1953 and June 1955, as the purges accelerated, there were over eight hundred such victims—about four hundred per year. By the 1960s, the State Department, the most aggressive federal agency in ferreting out homosexuals and in keeping records, had fired approximately one thousand alleged homosexuals. Since State Department firings represented about 20 percent of the total, according to government-wide statistics, it is likely that upward of five thousand suspected gay men and lesbians lost their jobs during the Cold War.[11] This does not include the large number of applicants or persons working in the private sector but who needed a government security clearance.

The impact of the purges spread to the private sector. Millions of private-sector employees who worked for government contractors were required to have security clearances. Although those denied a security clearance could theoretically do nonclassified work for such companies, in practice they were often fired. Because the government did not reveal to private companies the reason for a security-clearance denial, it cast a shroud of mystery over the employee. As Bernard F. Fitzsimmons, a security officer for Douglas Aircraft, told a congressional committee in 1955, "we feel that if a man is a security risk when he has access to classified materials, he is a security risk wherever he is in our plant." Other private industries, with no direct federal contracts, adopted the policies of the federal government—the nation's largest single employer. The perceived need to rigorously examine the background of employees became so pervasive that it spawned a new industry, as investigative agencies formed to act as "miniature FBIs." Fidelifax, Inc., offered "fact-finding and personnel reporting services for business organizations" in thirty cities. Staffed largely by former FBI officers, these consulting businesses used high-pressure promotional techniques that stressed the importance of following the government's lead in probing the lives of veteran and potential employees alike. One such agency listed "homosexuals" in bold print on its letterhead among the types of "undesirables" it specialized in uncovering.[12]

Although most intense at the national level, the antigay purges also spread to local and state governments. The Florida Senate in 1956 established the Legislative Investigation Committee to look into organizations that threatened the safety of citizens by violating the law—a clear reference to civil rights groups. But when the committee, named for its chairman Charlie Johns, failed to find any Communist ties among civil rights activists, its mandate shifted to include the investigation of "subversives" in public employment, with a particular focus on homosexuals in public universities and high schools. Like McCarthy and his Republican allies in the U.S. Senate, the Johns Committee saw that uncovering homosexuals was easier and garnered good publicity. Police forces in Miami and Tampa were already involved in a crackdown on gay bars and other public meeting places. One committee informant indicated that many of the civil rights activists at Florida State University and other campuses were homosexual. The committee began to interrogate hundreds of faculty and students, sometimes pulling them from class for interrogations with no opportunity for the advice of counsel. The state government sponsored training sessions in homosexual detection for law enforcement officials and recommended a statewide database of homosexuals open to private employers. Dozens of students and faculty at the University of Florida and the University of South Florida, as well as numerous secondary schools, were forced to resign (Bertwell 2005; Braukman 2012; Graves 2009; Schnur 1997).[13]

The Cold War American hysteria over the alleged threat caused by homosexuals was unprecedented. At a time when Americans felt threatened by an external enemy that seemed to be gaining strength and stealing its military secrets, the search for internal enemies ran rampant, and homosexuals proved an easy target. Over the previous decades, particularly during the disruptions of World War II, a homosexual subculture had flourished in American cities, particularly Washington, D.C., as it experienced unprecedented growth of the civilian and military bureaucracies. Many saw this as another sign of America's moral decline, a fear reinforced with the 1947 publication of the Kinsey Report, which indicated that American men engaged in high rates of premarital, extramarital, and homosexual sex. In this climate, the threat posed by homosexuals and that posed by Communists were easily conflated. Security officials claimed that Communists blackmailed homosexuals, but that was only one way to make the connection. In the popular culture of the 1950s, both groups seemed to comprise hidden subcultures, with their own meeting places, literature, cultural codes, and bonds of loyalty. Members of such subcultures were feared to have a loyalty to one another transcending that toward their class, race, or nation. Both groups were thought to be hostile to family formation and exhibit psychological or moral abnormalities that weakened America's defenses. And attacks against both groups proved useful in winning partisan political elections and expanding the apparatus of the national security state.

Purging the United Nations

Within the United States, the lavender scare spread on its own momentum throughout the private sector and down to local and state governments. But its spread to international organizations and foreign allies required government action. State Department officials, extremely zealous in rooting out homosexuals in their own agency, pressured agencies that it saw as part of the greater American foreign-policy apparatus to adopt its homophobic policies and procedures. Senator McCarran's Internal Security Subcommittee and a federal grand jury had already conducted investigations into the employment of Communists among the United Nation's American delegation. Shortly before leaving office, President Truman had signed an executive order requiring loyalty checks on American citizens working for international organizations and the United Nations had agreed to remove employees determined to be "disloyal" to member nations. However, the new International Employees Loyalty Board (IOELB) set up to administer this system had no authority to look into broader issues of character and morality. But the Eisenhower State Department, which relayed the results of these investigations to the UN and forty-six other international organizations, took on the extralegal function of forwarding information regarding the morality of employees, exerting considerable pressure to have its recommendations followed. During the first year of the Eisenhower administration, the State Department furnished the United Nations with derogatory "suitability" information on over two hundred employees. Finding such information to be often questionable or irrelevant, UN authorities terminated fewer than one-quarter of these employees. This failure to follow the State Department's security advice raised the hackles of officials, prompting them to increase the pressure.[14]

Aware that their moral views were not always shared by other cultures, American officials knew that they faced an uphill battle. As State Department security chief Scott McLeod acknowledged, "in large and important parts of the world, homosexuality apparently does not excite the same degree of opprobrium as in the United States." But they were concerned about a McCarthy-style controversy erupting over the harboring of homosexuals in the United Nations. As one official speculated, "in time Congress or an aroused public will charge officials of this department with sweeping homosexuals out of the back door of the State Department into the front door of the U.N." Desperate to avoid such a public-relations scandal, officials argued that fired homosexuals—unlike others fired as unsuitable—showed no remorse, resented their dismissals, and therefore should be considered untrustworthy.[15]

The State Department undertook an extensive lobbying campaign to ensure the ouster of homosexuals from all international organizations in which the United States held membership. In their routine briefings to twenty-six specialized international agencies, such as UNESCO, department officials included appeals for the need to purge homosexuals. They called upon their security colleagues at the Treasury Department to deliver the same message to the World Bank and the International Monetary Fund. McLeod made it clear to UN officials that a homosexual scandal in their organization could threaten U.S. financial support. "Notoriety accompanying some revelation of homosexual conduct among U.N. personnel," threatened Scott McLeod, "scandalous to the American public, might very easily have echoes in Congress unfavorable to the U.N."

Although it accused other governments of attempting to blackmail homosexuals, the U.S. government was engaged in some blackmail of its own. Henry Cabot Lodge, U.S. ambassador to the United Nations, made a clear threat directly to UN Secretary General Trygve Lie that failure to follow American policy with regard to homosexual employees would lead to a cut in funding. In a written message, Lodge told Lie that U.S. support would be "seriously undermined" if the United Nations retained homosexual American employees. How he argued this point in private can only be imagined. The secretary general had already dismissed nineteen of twenty-seven employees about whom the State Department had forwarded derogatory homosexual information. Unrelenting in its pursuit, the State Department wanted the remaining eight employees—all in clerical positions—removed as well, even though the charges against them were mostly "allegations and rumor." Under pressure, the secretary general agreed to the American request, but only if the State Department provided definitive proof documenting homosexual activities, such as a criminal conviction record. The department promised to reopen investigations to find more definitive proof. Although the U.S. government had no authority to provide such suitability information to international organizations, it continued to do so for nineteen years. Although no one ever challenged this practice, by 1972 the U.S. government quietly abandoned it, as U.S. federal courts had begun to limit the government's ability to fire civil servants on the basis of information not clearly germane to job performance.[16]

Pressuring Allies

The U.S. government also exerted pressure on its many Cold War allies to exclude homosexuals from government positions. The British, Canadian, and Australian security agencies all studied and copied, to varying degrees, the antigay policies and investigative procedures developed by the U.S. government. Whether or not they subscribed to the same beliefs about homosexuals, each feared that the disclosure that one of their secret agencies employed a homosexual would jeopardize their close relationship with American intelligence officials. Once the model for the rest of the federal government, the State Department's antigay policies and procedures became the model for much of the NATO alliance. Mimicking how the purges spread in the United States, in allied countries they often happened quietly, within the bureaucracy of the national security state and with little public scrutiny.

As the lavender scare unfolded in the United States, much of the British public thought that such witch-hunting tactics and fear mongering would never happen in Great Britain. The sense of moral condemnation that characterized the American lavender scare seemed less prevalent in the United Kingdom. As Reg Whitaker argued, in the United Kingdom, "successive British governments and opinion leaders made it clear that McCarthyism was not exportable to the U.K." But when British diplomats Guy Burgess and Donald MacLean went missing in June 1951, speculation immediately turned to their private lives. Burgess had recently been recalled from his position in Britain's Washington Embassy after having been caught repeatedly for speeding in Virginia with a hitchhiker. Insiders knew him to be quite open about his homosexuality ever since his college days at Oxford—the 1984 homoerotic film *Another Country* was based on his life. The *Sunday Dispatch* immediately suggested that the disappearance meant Great Britain should follow the American model and begin "weeding out both sexual and political perverts." The British government tried to downplay the issue, and the official white paper on the defections did not even mention homosexuality. By contrast, an FBI report referred to Burgess and MacLean as "a pair of pansies." American journalists like Westbrook Pegler used the defection as evidence that McCarthy had been right, after all—Communist sympathies and sexual perversion went hand in hand. That Maclean was a heterosexual married man and that the pair chose to spy for the Soviet Union for ideological reasons was ignored (Hodges 1983, 501; Whitaker 2000, 190).

In 1951, in the context of the Burgess and Maclean scandal, officials in the British Foreign Office had informal contacts with State Department officials about their policies and procedures regarding "the homosexual problem." Britain's unique relationship with the United States led the United States to exert extreme pressure on the British to follow its lead in matters of security and pay closer attention to the issue of homosexuality in its personnel security program. In 1952, following the American model, the British government introduced "positive vetting" for government employees—a thorough investigation of a person's background and character. In 1953, a top-ranking member of Scotland Yard spent three months in Washington consulting with FBI officials on a plan to weed out homosexuals from the government. An American interdepartmental committee looking into the control of military information continued to find deficiencies in the British personnel security system, specifically its lack of attention to "personal associations and to defects in character and personal traits." A series of transatlantic security conferences was held throughout the decade to discuss common threats, where the United States officially continued to pressure British security (Hodges 1983, 507; Whitaker 2000, 200).

Much of this pressure to adopt an American-style security system with a focus on homosexuality happened beyond the public gaze. But an Australian newspaper, less reticent than British papers about reporting on security matters, ran the headline "SCOTLAND YARD PLAN TO SMASH HOMOSEXUALITY IN LONDON." The plan, according to the London reporter for the *Sydney Sunday Telegram*, "originated under strong United States advice to Britain to weed out homosexuals." He also reported that Special Branch had begun compiling a "Black Book" of "known perverts" in high-level government jobs in the wake of the Burgess and Maclean disappearance. This new American-inspired initiative raised the hackles of some members of Parliament. In 1954, in a debate concerning the Atomic Energy Bill, a Labor MP demanded to know if "a homosexual is automatically now considered to be a security risk?" and questioned the efficacy of branding all such persons a threat. A government representative responded, "It certainly is in America. It is a result of the law as it is now" (Hodges 1983, 506; Whitaker 2000, 199; Wildeblood 1959, 45–46).

Canada seems to have been particularly vulnerable to pressure from the United States. Without an independent means of gathering foreign-based intelligence, it was dependent on the friendly intelligence services of the FBI and CIA. Canadian officials acknowledged as early as 1948 that American officials would share information with them only if assured of a tight security system meeting American standards. As one top-level Canadian government report put it, "Allied countries will not entrust Canadian officials and political leaders with secret information unless Canada has in place effective structures and procedures for detecting and preventing foreign espionage" (Robinson and Kimmel 1994, 324).

The influence of the American lavender scare emerged first in Canada's immigration policy. In December 1950, just as the Hoey Committee report came out asserting unequivocally that homosexuals posed a threat to national security, the Canadian Parliament was debating immigration-law reform. The Canadian governmental committee working on immigration reform added the category "homosexuals" to the list of persons excluded from visiting or immigrating to Canada. It remained in the Immigration Bill passed in 1952, marking the first time a Canadian act of Parliament referred to homosexuals as a class of person. This provision received almost no public comment at the time and seems not to have been the result of any public or partisan moral panic, as existed in the United States. Instead, it was the result of pressure from U.S. security officials on the Canadian government, particularly the Royal Canadian Mounted Police, to follow its lead in security procedures. Given the "world's longest undefended border" between the two counties, American officials feared that Canada represented a potential "weak link" in its security apparatus. Law professor Philip Girard labeled this change in the immigration bill "an act of appeasement" toward American security concerns. Although enforcement was minimal, this exclusion remained Canadian law until 1977, when the law was again reformed. The U.S. Congress passed in 1952 a similar immigration reform bill, which included a provision to exclude anyone exhibiting a "psychopathic personality," a term the Immigration and Naturalization Service and the courts continually interpreted as targeting homosexual persons. Relying on a determination of identity or inclination rather than proof of a particular act, the provision enhanced the federal government's ability to exclude or deport suspected homosexuals (Canaday 2011, 214–50; Girard 1987; Stein 2010).

The Canadian government also undertook an American-style purge of federal employees, one that had serious consequences for hundreds of Canadian citizens. The Royal Canadian Mounted Police (RCMP) was the principal agency behind these purges. Beginning in the late 1940s, as they began screening Canadian government employees, the RCMP began reporting not just on political deviance, but also "moral lapses" and "character defects" that made employees vulnerable to blackmail. This was largely the result of the Mounties' close relationship with the FBI and what political scientist Reg Whitaker calls their sharing an "American security paradigm." Although at first the civilian-oversight Security Panel objected to this focus, by 1952 their own cabinet directive included "character defects" as a formal risk category. Now with official authorization, the RCMP established a separate "A-3" unit to investigate homosexuals and two separate filing systems: pink forms for those with political problems, and yellow forms for those with moral problems. By the late 1960s, an average of one hundred adverse reports were being filed per year, most of them on suspected homosexuals. As Whitaker concluded, "there is no question that far more public servants suffered severe sanctions as a result of homosexual screening, which peaked in the 1960s, than as a result of political screening." The Mounties had collected information on over eight thousand suspected homosexuals, more than half of whom were not employed by the Canadian government. Prime Minister John Diefenbaker in 1958 questioned whether all homosexuals needed to be purged from government employment, but no change in government policy resulted. A 1959 security report prepared by Don Wall, the Security Panel secretary, quoted liberally from the U.S. Senate's Hoey Committee report. Although in the ensuing debate, some officials noted that no government civil servant had been successfully blackmailed into revealing state secrets, the policy remained unchanged (Robinson and Kimmel 1994, 332; Whitaker 2000, 202).

Similarities between the Canadian and American national security states' regulation of homosexuality are striking. Like the American security system, the Canadian system expanded from concerns with loyalty and "political subversion" to larger questions of "character weakness and moral flaws." Like the American purges that began in the State Department, the Canadian purge initially focused on the Department of External Affairs but spread to the entire federal workforce. Both bureaucracies established separate investigative offices and filing systems to concentrate on homosexuals. Both depended on local policing of gay men as a key investigative and enforcement mechanism, especially in their national capitals. As the head of the Washington, D.C., vice squad estimated that five thousand homosexuals lived in the U.S. capital area, the RCMP estimated that three thousand homosexuals called Ottawa home.

In some ways, Canadians officials not only shared the American obsession with ferreting out and removing gay and lesbian civil servants, they may have been more zealous.

Not content with merely creating a list of all the gay residents of Ottawa, the RCMP's A-3 unit tried to plot them on a map of the city. Like their American counterparts, they assumed that gay people, ostracized from mainstream society, lived and socialized in packs. They used red dots to indicate the presence of known homosexuals, hoping to locate others nearby. The map they purchased from the National Capital Commission was soon so saturated with red ink as to be useless. Undeterred, they purchased a larger map from the city of Ottawa, but it, too, was soon covered in red. They even made an unsuccessful attempt to get the Department of National Defense to create a larger map using aerial surveillance cameras (Sawatsky 1980, 127–28).

The Canadian government's most ambitious—and embarrassing—attempt to uncover homosexual public servants was known as the "Fruit Machine." In 1960, Security Panel secretary Don Wall was sent to Washington to report on the latest security screening procedures. He discovered that one of the principal means that American officials used to determine a subject's homosexuality was the polygraph machine. State Department officials boasted of a near perfect success rate. But Wall found the lie-detector method of measuring anxiety in reaction to aggressive questioning to be "an intrusive and essentially unfair process." So the Security Panel authorized the undertaking of a research program to study homosexual detection technologies and put a psychology professor from Carleton College in charge of the effort. Funded by the Canadian Department of National Health and Welfare, professor Frank Wake spent a year in the United States, where he found that pupillometric exercises at the University of Chicago offered the best hope. Research indicated that dilation of a subject's pupil corresponded with interest in what the subject was viewing. A marketing professor had used this technology to indicate consumer responses to product packaging. Canadian security officials determined that if used to measure a subject's reaction to pictures of naked men and women, it could indicate the subject's sexuality.

In some ways the motivations for developing what came to be dubbed "the Fruit Machine" were liberal—officials did not want to dismiss civil servants on mere hearsay or rumor. They sought a way to scientifically determine if the civil servant had something to hide and was therefore subject to blackmail. It also represented a movement away from the notion of homosexuals as gender inverts who would exhibit obvious physical characteristics or mannerisms. But after four years of attempts to record and measure pupillary responses to photos of landscapes, physique magazine images, and pin-up girls, the experiment failed. In addition to the technical difficulties of measuring tiny physical variations with any degree of accuracy, getting known homosexuals and a control group of "normal" adults to agree to be tested proved a major hurdle. The experiment also assumed only two categories of sexual identity (Kinsman and Gentile 2010, 168–88; Sawatsky 1980, 133–37).

As America's two closest allies during the Cold War, Great Britain and Canada were the countries most clearly subject to influence by America's homophobic national-security policies. But direct and indirect influences undoubtedly impacted America's other strategic partners. France was a more problematic ally of the United States and even withdrew from NATO's integrated military command. France also had much less of a history of homosexual persecution, having decriminalized homosexual sex in 1791. But France also experienced "a wind of Puritanism" in the postwar world and what one French historian calls "a progressive criminalization of homosexuality." The display of homosexual magazines was banned nationally, and the prefect of Paris banned same-sex dancing. Prosecutions for homosexual sex (under a Vichy-era law that criminalized same-sex activity with persons under twenty-one years old) rose each year from 1945 to 1958, totaling some three thousand. By 1960, the National Assembly added homosexuality to a list of social blights—along with alcoholism, tuberculosis, and prostitution—and extended to the government "all necessary measures to fight homosexuality" (Corrivieau 2011, 102–10; Jackson 2009, 37–50; Sidéris 2000, 121–24).

The campaign against homosexual expression, part of a larger campaign to crack down on immorality and threats to the family, was initiated by French naval officials, who had been concerned about the effect of homosexual prostitution on young, badly paid sailors. They noted certain bars that attracted sailors that were "centers of communist action and occasionally at the same time meeting places for homosexuals." They were also concerned about sailors' contact with "an idle and unsettled foreign colony that is sometimes suspect from the point of view of espionage." Historian Julian Jackson has uncovered evidence of a purge of a cadre of gay sailors from the French navy serving in Indochina in the mid-1950s. When one of the accused gay sailors asked his interrogators why they cared about his private life, they cited the cases of Burgess and Maclean. While there is no evidence of a wholesale American-style purge of homosexual public servants in France, and homosexual acts between consenting adults remained legal in France (unlike in the United States, the United Kingdom, or Canada), the recriminalizing of some homosexual activity in France was a result of the commingling of notions of homosexuality, Communism, and espionage as threats to national security—the same set of ideas that created a postwar lavender scare in the United States (Jackson 2009, 47; Sibalis 2002, 301–18).

Conclusion

The Cold War brought American military power and influence to much of the globe. Among the many unforeseen and largely undocumented consequences of that expansive "sphere of influence" was the exportation of homophobic government-security policies. The rise of the national security state provided an unprecedented means to regulate morality, both at home and abroad. In addition to the broader cultural influence it may have had, the United States during the Cold War, because of its military and intelligence dominance, imposed its unprecedented homophobic policies upon its strategic allies and the international organizations it supported.

Canada, Australia, the United Kingdom, and other countries may not have completely shared the American obsession with homosexuality, but they shared a desire to participate in a crucial Cold War national-security network of information and financial support. They succumbed to what Bosia calls "the influence of transnational networks," which encouraged them to adopt homophobic policies, as also happened in Uganda in the twenty-first century. And as in the case of Uganda, they may have occasionally exceeded the demands of that network. Canada's explicit prohibition on "homosexual" immigrants and its attempt to construct a "fruit machine" exceeded even the harsh antigay apparatus constructed by the American national security state.

Two ironic twists, however, frame this story. While America imagined that homosexuals and communists were somehow working together to steal state secrets, the Soviet Union was far from a homosexual paradise. Indeed, America's Cold War obsession with homosexuality was something it shared with its ideological opponent as both countries imposed "compulsory heterosexuality" as prerequisites to achieving full citizenship (Healey 2002). This suggests that the state-sponsored homophobia of the Cold War was facilitated on both sides by the rise of a national security state, the obsession with possible internal and external enemies, and the need to safeguard state secrets. But in another ironic twist, at least in the United States, the virulent level of homophobia unleashed by the Cold War conflict was instrumental in creating the first organized LGBT civil rights organizations. After resigning from the Communist Party USA because of his homosexuality, Harry Hay founded the Mattachine Society in Southern California in 1950 largely in response to the homophobic policies he saw spreading from Washington and the State Department. He feared that if homosexuals did not organize, homosexuals would become entirely unemployable in the United States. In the next decade, as the small American homophile movement became more militant and began to organize its first public demonstrations, it was led by Frank Kameny, a victim of the federal lavender scare. Overturning the federal government's antigay policies was one of the U.S. movement's first goals, something it largely achieved through a series of court suits culminating in 1969, just before the Stonewall riots in New York, often portrayed as the beginning of the modern gay-rights movement. An unprecedented era of homophobia, the 1950s also produced an unprecedented level of gay and lesbian activism.

Notes

1. This essay draws from and extends the argument I made in Johnson 2004.

2. *Congressional Record*, February 20, 1950, 1961–70; Senate, Subcommittee of the Committee on Foreign Relations, *State Department Employee Loyalty Investigation*, 81st Cong., 2nd sess., March 8–June 28, 1950, 1777.

3. Charles S. Murphy, George M. Elsey, and Stephen J. Spingarn to the President, July 11, 1950, "Internal Security—McCarthy—Charges #4," Box 70, George Elsey Papers, Harry S Truman Library; *Washington Star*, April 2, 1950, C-5; *New York Daily News*, March 27 and 29, 1950.

4. *Washington Times-Herald*, April 1 and April 16, 1950.

5. Executive Order 10450, "Security Requirements for Government Employment," *Federal Register*, April 27, 1953, 2489.

6. U.S. Congress, Senate, Committee on Expenditures in the Executive Departments, *Employment of Homosexuals and Other Sex Perverts in Government*, Senate. Doc. 241, 81st Cong., 2nd sess., 1950.

7. "Files Desired by Investigations Subcommittee, 40-1-9," Hoey Committee Case Files, RG 46, National Archives and Records Administration (NARA); Goodman 1968.

8. Draft of proposed manual for Special Agents, February 1952, Folder SY—General, 1952, Entry 1508, Office of Security and Consular Affairs, Lot File 53-D-233, Subject files of the Security Division, 1946–1953, RG59, NARA; "Security Clearance Procedures," Box 16, Decimal Files, 1953–1960, Bureau of Security and Consular Affairs, RG59, NARA. On the use of the polygraph machine, see Alder 2007, 235–41.

9. Boykin to Martin, "Homosexual Problem," December 21, 1950, "SY General 1947–51," Box 1, Security Division Subject Files, Lot 53-D-233, Bureau of Security and Consular Affairs, RG 59, NARA; U.S. Congress, House, Subcommittee of the Committee on Appropriations, *Department of State Appropriations for 1952*, 82nd Cong., 1st sess., March 2, 1951, 399–400.

10. Carlisle Humelsine, *Executive Sessions of the Senate Foreign Relations Committee, Historical Series, Volume V*, 83rd Cong., 1st sess., February 5, 1953, 70–71; Scott to Boykin, November 28, 1950, "Loyalty 1947–1950," Reading Files of Samuel Boykin, Bureau of Security and Consular Affairs, RG 59, NARA.

11. U.S. Congress, Senate, *Administration of the Federal Employees Security Program*, Hearings before a Subcommittee of the Committee on Post Office and Civil Service, 84th Cong., 1st sess., May–September 1954, 732; *Washington Post*, April 21, 1953.

12. U.S. Congress, Senate, Committee on Government Operations, Subcommittee on Reorganization, *Commission on Government Security*, 84th Cong., 1st sess., March 14, 1955; "Are You Now or Have You Ever Been A Homosexual," *One*, April 1953: 6–13.

13. Other southern states established "sovereignty committees" in this period to impede racial integration, but to what extent they also targeted homosexuals has yet to be determined.

14. *New York Times*, January 27, 1953, 1; *Washington Star*, June 3, 1953, A-2, and December 20, 1954; Caute 1978, pp. 325–38; USUN–New York to DOS-Washington, Mary 27, 1954, and U.S. Consulate General, Geneva, to DOS-Washington, both in "Suitability" folder, Box 12, Lot 88D3, Records Relating to E.O. 10422, 1946–1975, RG59, NARA.

15. Fletcher to Flinn, "Employment of homosexuals in international agencies," September 22, 1954, and McLeod to Phillips, December 30, 1954, both in "Suitability" folder, Box 12, Lot 88D3, Records Relating to E.O. 10422, 1946–1975, RG 59, NARA; *Congressional Record*, July 24, 1950, 10843.

16. Key to Lodge, January 4, 1955, Babcock to Key, January 18, 1955, and Phillipe to McLeod, January 26, 1955, and Carroll to Buffum, June 21, 1974, all in folder "Suitability," Box 12, Lot88D3, Records Relating to E.O. 10422, 1946–1975, RG 59, NARA.

Bibliography

Alder, Ken. 2007. *Lie Detectors: The History of an American Obsession*. New York: Free Press.

Bertwell, Dan. 2005. "'A Veritable Refuge for Practicing Homosexuals': The Johns Committee and the University of South Florida," *The Florida Historical Quarterly* 83: pp. 410–31.

Braukman, Stacy. 2012. *Communists and Perverts under the Palms: The Johns Committee in Florida, 1956–1965*. Gainesville: University Press of Florida.

Canaday, Margot. 2011. *The Straight State: Sexuality and Citizenship in Twentieth Century America*. Princeton, NJ: Princeton University Press.

Caute, David. 1978. *The Great Fear*. New York: Simon and Schuster.

Corrivieau, Patrice. 2011. *Judging Homosexuals: A History of Gay Persecution in Quebec and France*. Translated by Kathe Roth. Vancouver: UBC Press.

Girard, Philip. 1987. "From Subversives to Liberation: Homosexuals and the Immigration Act 1952–1977," *Canadian Journal of Law & Society* 2: pp. 1–27.

Goodman, Walter. 1968. *The Committee: The Extraordinary Career of the House Committee on Un-American Activities*. Baltimore: Penguin Books.

Graves, Karen. 2009. *And They Were Wonderful Teachers: Florida's Purge of Gay and Lesbian Teachers*. Urbana: University of Illinois Press.

Healey, Daniel. 2002. *Homosexual Desire in Revolutionary Russia: The Regulation of Sexual and Gender Dissent*. Chicago: University of Chicago Press.

Hodges, Andrew. 1983. *Alan Turing: The Enigma*. New York: Simon and Schuster.

Jackson, Julian. 2009. *Living in Arcadia: Homosexuality, Politics, and Morality in France from Liberation to AIDS*. Chicago: University of Chicago Press.

Johnson, David K. 2004. *The Lavender Scare: The Persecution of Gays and Lesbians in the Federal Government*. Chicago: University of Chicago Press.

Kinsman, Gary, and Patrizia Gentile. 2010. *The Canadian War on Queers: National Security as Sexual Regulation*. Vancouver: UBC Press.

Robinson, Daniel J., and David Kimmel. 1994. "The Queer Career of Homosexual Security Vetting in Cold War Canada," *Canadian Historical Review* 75 (September): 319–45.

Sawatsky, John. 1980. *Men in the Shadows: The RCMP Security Service*. Toronto: Doubleday Canada.

Schnur, James A. 1997. "Closet Crusaders: The Johns Committee and Homophobia," in John Howard, ed., *Carryin' On in the Lesbian and Gay South*. New York: New York University Press, pp. 132–63.

Sibalis, Michael D. 2002. "Homophobia, Vichy France, and the 'Crime of Homosexuality': The Origins of the Ordinance of 6 August 1942," *GLQ* 8, no. 3: 301–18.

Sidéris, George. 2000. "Des folles de Saint-Germain-des-Prés au 'Fléau social': Le discours homophile contre l'efféminement dans les années 1950," in Esther Benbassa and Jean-Christophe Attias, eds., *La Haine de soi: Difficiles identités*. Brussels: Complexe, pp. 121–42.

Stein, Marc. 2010. *Sexual Injustice: Supreme Court Decisions from Griswold to Roe*. Chapel Hill: University of North Carolina Press.

Whitaker, Reg. 2000. "Cold War Alchemy: How America, Britain and Canada Transformed Espionage into Subversion," in David Stafford and Rhodri Jeffreys-Jones, eds., *American-British Canadian Intelligence Relations, 1939–2000*. Portland, OR: Frank Cass Publishers, pp. 177–210.

Wildeblood, Peter. 1959. *Against the Law*. Harmondsworth, England: Penguin Books.

4

The Marriage of Convenience

The U.S. Christian Right, African Christianity,
and Postcolonial Politics of Sexual Identity

KAPYA J. KAOMA

In what seemed like a "win" for the progressive movement in Uganda and across the globe, the infamous Anti-Homosexuality Bill 2009 (hereafter referred to AHB 2009), authored and introduced in Uganda's eighth parliament in October 2009 by David Bahati, had not been acted upon when parliament closed on May 13, 2011. In February 2012, this private member's bill, also known as the "Kill the Gays" bill, was reintroduced in the ninth parliament of Uganda. In October 2012, the bill received new life after Canadian Foreign Minister John Baird challenged Ugandan Parliament Speaker Rebecca Kadaga at the Inter-Parliamentary Union in Quebec about her country's record on gays. Upon her return to Uganda, Kadaga promised to pass the bill as a "Christmas" present to Ugandans. While the bill remained on the agenda of the house throughout December 2012, it was not acted on when parliament adjourned on December 23, 2012. It is hard to tell what will become of this bill in 2013, but once passed, it would mandate that all those convicted of homosexuality serve prison terms and, in some cases, face execution (AHB 2009).

The reintroduction of the antigay bill, the murder of an openly gay man, David Kato, in 2011, and the cancellation of LGBT conferences in February 2012 and June 2012 continue to put Uganda's increasing persecution of LGBT persons in the international spotlight. Such persecution is not limited to Uganda. A gay couple was arrested and sentenced to fourteen years in prison in Malawi. While international outcry forced the late president Bingu Wa Mutharika—who in 2011 described gays to be "worse than dogs" (Frampton 2011)—to pardon the couple, it also mobilized what Weiss (this volume) called homophobic countermobilization in the country. In December 2010, the Parliament amended the Penal Code, and in January 2011, the Malawian president signed into law a bill criminalizing same-sex relations between women. Section 137A, captioned "Indecent Practices between Females," states that any female person who, whether in public or private, commits "any act of gross indecency with another female shall be guilty of an offence and liable to a prison term of five years."

Politically sanctioned homophobia is what the new Malawian president Joyce Banda inherited from the government of the late Mutharika in 2012. However, upon taking office, President Banda refused to sanction the persecution of sexual minorities. In contrast, Liberian president and Nobel Peace Prize winner Ellen Johnson Sirleaf defended her country's antigay laws. "We like ourselves just the way we are," Sirleaf told the *Guardian*, when asked about the law as well as proposals for even stricter antigay legislation in her country. "We've got certain traditional values in our society that we would like to preserve." When pressed as to whether she would work to decriminalize the current laws, she responded, "I have just said to you, we gonna maintain our traditional values" (*Guardian* 2012).

The future political ramifications of President Banda's position will be tested in 2014, when Malawi goes to the polls. Nonetheless, Banda's position suggests that homophobia grows or dies with political will. Since new antigay laws are also expected in the Democratic Republic of Congo, Zambia, Zimbabwe, and perhaps other nations, it remains to be seen how African political leaders will move to defend the rights of sexual minorities on the continent.

Michael Bosia and Sami Zeidan (both in this volume) analyze the intersection between international LGBT human-rights campaigns, colonial history, and today's African political discourse on human sexuality. While this intersection remains vital to understanding postcolonial politics of sexual identity on the continent, in *Globalizing the Culture Wars: US Conservatives, African Churches and Homophobia* (2009) and *Colonizing African Values: How the U.S. Christian Right is Transforming Sexual Politics in Africa* (2012), I make the case that U.S. religious conservatives' ideologies and activism are behind the growing violent homophobia in Christian Africa. While appealing to what Nyeck (2010) terms "colonial blackmail"—thereby accusing Western countries and progressives of imposing sexual deviance on African countries—U.S. Christian conservatives are influencing African political discourse on issues pertaining to human sexuality.

In spite of the established fact that homosexuality was practiced in traditional societies, the myth that sexual rights are Western impositions has taken solid root in African theological and political discourse. Right-leaning American and African religious and political leaders unabashedly claim that homosexual behaviors were introduced by Western progressives—giving them a neocolonial nexus. Sadly, scapegoating the West for what is essentially African diversity in sexual behaviors increases the culture of silence that surrounds sexuality across the continent.

However, there is undoubtedly a very public outcry or countermobilization against homosexuality in today's Africa. Postcolonial Africa is highly critical of colonial laws and values, but one colonial legacy is the English law that reads the same across Anglophone Africa. "Carnal knowledge against the order of nature" is illegal in many African countries today, just as it was in colonial times. Compounded by the religious teachings of Christianity and Islam, this law has been assimilated into all aspects of African society and is defended with pride.

Despite the number of constitutional reforms in most African countries, this "carnal knowledge" law has been retained and in recent constitutions, expanded on to include same-sex relations among women, the prohibition of same-sex marriages and adoption of children by gay couples, and, in some cases, the banning of gay clubs and organizations, as was the case in Nigeria in 2011. Worse still, political leaders defend these laws by alluding to traditional African beliefs and religions. Homosexuality is un-African, uncultural, un-Christian, and un-Islamic—thus illegal. In sum, these leaders claim that homosexuality violates God's law and attest to the judgment God brought upon Sodom and Gomorrah (Genesis 18–19; Quran 26). Tereza Samson, senior chief kachindamoto of Malawi, shared this perspective: "Sodom and Gomorrah were punished because of homosexual acts" (Samson 2011). Paramount chief Lundu Chapter of Malawi concurred, "If we go to scriptures Gen. 19:1–22 it states how Sodom and Gomorrah were destroyed due to homosexual acts. As chiefs we will not allow such acts to continue in our country, it is an abomination. We will not accept this, It is better to remain poor than to accept same sex marriage" (Lundu 2011). But Harold Williams, a white Malawian, asserted that this argument is also made to block meaningful discussion of human sexuality across Africa (Williams 2011).

The oft-repeated meme that LGBT persons are funded by American and European gays to practice homosexuality has been translated into a truism used by most African politicians and religious leaders who accuse Western countries of imposing homosexuality on the continent. When British Prime Minister David Cameron threatened to cut funding to African countries that persecute LGBT persons during the Commonwealth Heads of Government Meeting in Perth, Australia, in October 2011, African religious and political leaders did not just condemn the move as immoral, but also used it as evidence that homosexuality is another imperialistic instrument that Western nations employ on Africa. Across the continent, both independent and government news-media houses reacted with indignation, as the following headlines show: "Ghana tells off UK over threat on gays" (*Daily Nation, Ghana*), "Is the West still colonizing [the] Continent" (*Tanzania Daily News*), and "UK's Cameron Touched Wrong Button on Gays" (*The Observer, Uganda*). "[A]moral and horrendous culturally imperialistic" is what Mobhane Matinyi of the *Citizen in Tanzania* called Cameron's move (Matinyi, Nov. 3, 2011). While some responses, such as the one from *The Observer*, seem to accept homosexuality as part of the African heritage, most responses saw the prime minister's position as imposing homosexuality on the continent.

Similar responses were experienced when U.S. president Barack Obama and Secretary of State Hillary Clinton linked foreign aid to gay rights across the world and defined "human rights as gay rights and gay rights as human rights" on December 6, 2011. Many African political and religious leaders interpreted these statements as imperialistic and immoral, thereby confirming that the Western world is promoting homosexuality (Bosia, this volume). To some extent, these statements help both religious and political leaders to mobilize public resentment against what is perceived as an international gay agenda (Nyeck 2010). In Liberia, for example, explained Tamasin Ford on (American) National Public Radio, the backlash against LGBT rights began after Secretary Clinton defended gay rights as human rights. Those words sparked public outrage and led to the introduction of the antigay law that would imprison homosexuals for ten years (Ford and Martin 2012).

Such responses are representative of Africa's religio-political discourse on human sexuality. Long before both the British and American governments made those statements, Bishop Joseph Bvumbwe of the Malawi Christian Council (a group of twenty-seven Protestant churches) had accused Western nations and international donor agencies of using "their financial muscle to advance gay rights in Malawi" (*Maravi Post* 2010). But as Seodi White, the national coordinator for Women and Law in Southern Africa, argues, the plot to blame homosexuality on the donor community is just a way that governments that have become unpopular and have been questioned by the West can badmouth the West. These governments, she argues, contend that homosexuality is the reason why Western governments criticize their bad governance. In her words, "They [Western leaders] say we are bad because of homosexuality. They want to impose it on us but we are fighting for you . . . we know you don't want it" (White 2011).

It is important to note an insidiously inverse relationship between LGBT rights in the United States and in Africa; any advancement toward full equality in the United States is depicted as evidence of a growing homosexual threat to the world. U.S. conservatives—Scott Lively, Sharon Slater, Lou Angle, and

many others—have constantly employed this assumption in their mobilization of antigay movements on the continent. As a consequence, fears of equal
rights in Western countries and the slight possibility of having such rights
in Africa have invited stiffer penalties against LGBT individuals and their
allies across Christian Africa.

Despite such oppositions, the belief that LGBT rights are human rights
to be defended and protected has taken root among gay-rights activists. Just
as African religious and political leaders aggressively fight what they call a
"moral imperialism" from the Western world, African LGBT persons are
challenging their own governments to respect their God-given rights and
dignity—sometimes at the cost of their own lives. Even though the battle
is being fought on African soil, both groups have international allies, including, in the context of this chapter, the very groups involved in fighting
American culture wars. While progressive American human-rights groups
side with LGBT persons and insist that sexual rights are fundamental human rights, U.S. social-conservative groups side with African religious and
political groups in advocating the permanent criminalization of sexual minorities as both a religious and political duty. Although conservative groups
seem to be losing political battles in the United States, as evidenced by the
number of states legalizing same-sex marriages, their African counterparts
are on the winning side. Thus the real casualties in American culture wars
are LGBT persons in Africa, who lack political and religious power to defend themselves from political and religious forces. In other words, LGBT
persons suffer what I have called a "form of collateral damage" from the U.S.
culture wars, as every victory in the U.S. serves to mobilize social-religious
and political bigotry and violence against them in Africa (Kaoma 2009).

This observation, however, has been challenged by some critics who minimize the influence of American right-wing Christian groups in promoting
homophobia in Africa. For instance, Philip Jenkins, a professor of Humanities
at Pennsylvania State University, places Uganda's homophobia outside the
African culture by blaming it on the "Arabic pederasty culture" (Cromartie
text 2010; Kaoma 2010b:6). Jenkins cites the killing of some early converts
to Christianity in the 1880s (also known as the Uganda Martyrs), who refused to engage in same-sex relations with their king, Kabaka Mwanga, after
they converted to Christianity, as evidence that homosexuality is foreign to
Ugandans. To Jenkins, Uganda's homophobia is linked to issues of Islam and
tyranny; hence antigay activism is "not something that was dropped on the
Ugandan Christians from America" (Cromartie 2010). Elsewhere, I have responded to Jenkins's argument and will not repeat it here (Kaoma 2010a:6–7).
Suffice it to say that the association of King Mwanga's reign with same-sex

relations suggests that homosexuality was in Africa long before Christianity took hold of the continent.

This chapter will strengthen the argument that U.S. Christian conservatives of various backgrounds (Evangelicals, Catholics, and Mormons) mobilize around LGBT issues for various reasons. To make this case, I use extra data and new developments from various African countries. This chapter insists that when Americans and Africans oppose homosexuality, they do so with different worldviews. Thus the unqualified "homophobia" that unites these two groups can be termed a "marriage of convenience." I begin with the Ugandan case, since it is the best-known situation.

The Ugandan Case

Reminiscent of the 2005 publication of a "Top 50" list of alleged gays by the local newspaper *Anecdote* addressed by Nyeck (2010), the *Rolling Stone* newspaper (no relationship to the American *Rolling Stone* Magazine) published the names of people it called "top Ugandan homos" in 2010. The newspaper revealed their addresses and workplaces with the brazen words *"Hang Them,"* prominently displayed on the front page. In order to attract public hysteria, the paper followed U.S. antigay arguments that Western-funded homosexuals were out "recruiting 1 million children by raiding schools" (*Rolling Stone*, 2010; compare with Lively 2009; Slater 2009). On January 26, 2011, David Kato, an openly gay human-rights activist whose picture appeared on the front page, was viciously attacked at his home in Mukono and died on his way to the hospital. While the killer was sentenced to thirty years in prison, most activists linked this death to homophobia (BBC 2011).

The call to hang homosexuals might be alarmingly extreme. Yet the newspaper was only resuscitating public and international religious and political discourse on the Anti-Homosexuality Bill 2009 addressed above, which many people at the time thought dead (Kasozi 2010). The *Rolling Stone* newspaper's publication was followed by another seminal event: the second (Anglican) All-Africa Bishops' Conference held in August 2010. Hosted by the antigay archbishop Henry Luke Orombi of the Church of Uganda, over 400 African Anglican bishops gathered in Entebbe, Uganda. The conference attracted global media attention, not only because Rowan Williams, the then archbishop of Canterbury and head of the worldwide Anglican Communion (to which the gay-friendly Episcopal Church belongs), was in attendance, but also because the question of homosexuality was set to arise.

Many African Anglican bishops have been known for their opposition to the acceptance of LGBT persons in the Anglican Communion since the 1998

Lambeth Conference in Kent. Like their Asian counterparts, Africans have been outspoken in their grave disapproval of the consecration of an openly gay Episcopal bishop, Gene Robinson, in the United States in 2004 (Weiss in this volume). Bishops from Rwanda, Nigeria, Uganda, and Kenya have even gone so far as ordaining American conservative clergy opposed to gay rights in the Episcopal Church as bishops. These bishops operate under the guidance of the African bishops, a situation that has created a crisis for the Anglican Communion (Hassett 2007).

The presence of Rowan Williams, whom many Africans consider to be sympathetic to gay rights, provided fodder for antigay sentiments at the time when Uganda was considering the anti-homosexual bill. Bishops from Rwanda, Nigeria, Uganda, and Kenya used the African bishops' conference as an opportunity to speak out against the perceived moral imperialism of Episcopal Church and Anglican Communion leadership. Apart from bishops from Southern Africa (Ashworth 2010), the bishops unequivocally advocated the criminalization of homosexuality on the continent. Archbishop Orombi, as host, summarized their opposition as follows: "Homosexuality is evil, abnormal, and unnatural as per the Bible. It is a culturally unacceptable practice. Although there is a lot of pressure [from the West], we cannot turn our hands to support it" (Kasozi 2010). Ironically, Orombi did not condemn the involvement of U.S. conservatives in the infamous "Seminar on Exposing the Homosexual Agenda" in Uganda, which led to the drafting of the 2009 antigay bill.

SEMINAR ON EXPOSING THE HOMOSEXUAL AGENDA

There is a direct correlation between views of U.S. conservatives and conservative African clergy. Aside from the fact that African religious and political leaders with U.S. conservatives links helped draft the bill, the seminar was conducted by American antigay activists (Kaoma, 2009). While the conference was hosted by Stephen Langa's Uganda-based Family Life Network—with the goal of "restoring" traditional family values and morals in Uganda—the main speakers were from three U.S. antigay organizations: holocaust revisionist Scott Lively of Defend the Family and Abiding Truth Ministries (who in 2012 was sued in U.S. courts by Sexual Minorities Uganda for inciting persecution of gays there), Don Schmierer of the ex-gay group Exodus International, and Caleb Lee Brundidge of the International Healing Foundation.

No doubt, the seminar increased homophobia and ignited the flames that led to the drafting of the antigay bill. Generally, Ugandan religious leaders, parliamentarians, law enforcement agencies, educators, and concerned parents were aware of the existence of homosexuality in Uganda, but the U.S. antigay activists' seminar provided the ammunition for an aggressive fight against it. Evidently, the seminar alerted Ugandans to a supposed "international gay agenda" to control the world. It insisted that LGBT activists were part of a *powerful international gay movement* set to take over the world.

Scott Lively emerged as a star in Uganda, where he flaunted his extreme ideas on state radio and television, in churches, and in Parliament (where he spoke for more than four hours). In his presentations, Lively promoted his book *The Pink Swastika* (which claims that the Nazi leaders were gay) and Richard A. Cohen and Laura Schlessinger's *Coming Out Straight* (2000)—the book that equates homosexuality to child molestation, among other horrific claims, as scientific evidence against homosexuality—to an unsuspecting African audience.

As is common in American antigay politics, Lively blamed higher rates of divorce, abortion, child abuse, and HIV/AIDS on gays. He said legalizing homosexuality is on par with accepting molestation of children or having sex with animals (seminar recording hereafter referred to as AGR 2009).[1] He insisted that gay rights were not human-rights issues: "The people coming to Africa now and advancing the idea that human rights serve the homosexual interests are absolutely wrong." He added, "Many of them are outright liars and they are manipulating history; they are manipulating facts in order to push their political agenda." Lively even tarred abortion rights as "a product of the gay philosophy" meant to promote sexual promiscuity in order to "destroy the family" (AGR 2009).

Using American antigay talking points, Lively warned Ugandans about the radical homosexual agenda to indoctrinate an entire generation of children with homosexual values. He insisted that homosexuals' grand goal was to eliminate traditional family values and replace them with a new world based on sexual promiscuity, which will lead to unacceptable social chaos and destruction.[2] Frightening his audience, he contended that "the real danger of the gay movement is its necessary goal of the elimination of this moral system in order to achieve this [sexual freedom]" (AGR 2009; Slater 2011).

Citing antigay writer Richard Cohen, Lively argued that there is no definitive scientific study that has ever proved that homosexuality is innate or caused by genetic factors. Instead he said it is acquired. Those who are gays were recruited as children, and Ugandans should *protect* their children against the vice instead of "affirming a scientific hypothesis that has no actual truthful foundation." He enthusiastically explained to his audience that there's a whole network of gays "ready to simply inculcate you and enfold you into their world and they want more and more people in their world because they are in a campaign to change everything" (AGR 2009).

As if this were not enough, Lively emphatically equated homosexuality with pedophilia. He contended that although the majority of homosexuals are not oriented toward young people, there is a significant number that are. "Male homosexuality," he said, "has historically been not adult to adult [but] adult to teenager" (see also Slater 2009). He cautioned Ugandans to be wary of gay activists by pointing to homosexual successes in America: "We've seen the transformation of America, when at the pinnacle of its Christianity was probably in the 1950s. Ever since then it has been declining—why? Because of the sexual revolution! Where did the sexual revolution come from? The sexual revolution came from the activists of the American gay movement. For this very reason, they have taken over the United Nations, the United States government, and the European Union. Nobody has been able to stop them so far. I'm hoping Uganda can" (AGR 2009).

Just after leaving Uganda, Lively explained the purpose of his trip to Uganda on his Defendthefamily blog as follows: "The campaign was to teach about the 'gay' agenda in churches, schools, colleges, community groups, and in Parliament . . . The international 'gay' movement has devoted a lot of resources to transforming the moral culture from a marriage-based one to one that embraces sexual anarchy. Just as in the U.S. many years ago, they are leading with pornography to weaken the moral fiber of the people and propagandizing the children behind the parents' backs" (Lively 2009).

Like Sharon Slater, the president of Family Watch International (Slater 2009), Lively noted that the United Nations has been taken over by gay activists: "We exposed a book distributed to schools by UNICEF that normalizes homosexuality to teenagers." For this very reason, he expected "a massive protest by parents, who are mostly not aware that such materials even exist in their country, let alone in their children's [classrooms]." He predicted that the "campaign" would aggressively increase antigay activism in the country. In his own words, the "campaign was like a nuclear bomb against the 'gay' agenda in Uganda" (Lively 2009).

FAMILY LIFE NETWORK STRATEGIC MEETING

When I called Stephen Langa, the executive director of Family Life Network, the official sponsor of the antigay seminar, seeking an interview, he invited me to attend a strategic meeting on "Combating Homosexuality in Uganda" at Hotel Triangle in Kampala on March 15, 2009. Various organs of Ugandan society, among them the police, religious and political leaders, and parliamentary officers, attended the meeting. Although the meeting lasted over four hours, I captured it on video. Throughout the deliberations, Ugandans demanded stiffer laws against homosexuality. Echoing Lively's teachings, Langa called on parents to fight the international gay agenda or risk their children being recruited into homosexuality.

Harry Mwebesa of Family Life Network warned the agitated crowd that allowing gays to exist in Uganda will be to the detriment of their own lives and those of their children: "Dr. Scott told us about Brazil, where ten years ago, homosexuality was unheard of . . . Today it is the capital . . . There are people that have been against homosexuality that are having to leave because of the pressure and the threats that they are putting on them. That is how serious it is" (Strategic Meeting Recording on Video, hereafter referred to SMV 2009). Another participant, who identified himself as Elijah, praised Lively for alerting them to the international gay agenda:

> The man of God [Scott Lively] told us about . . . a movement behind the promotion of homosexuality and it is called gay movement. Me, I had never heard of that. But I got to know that there is a force behind homosexuality which we need to tackle with force. He also told us that these people who are behind this . . . evil, they have all resources that they need . . . to spread this evil. [In] Africa, Uganda in particular . . . it is more easy [sic] for the young generation to get attracted into the evil. Since that day . . . we need to stand firm to fight homosexuality. (SMV 2009)

Jeff Sharlet (2010:147) asserted that the anti-homosexuality bill was not a product of Lively's meetings but was "a catalyst for a process that had already been set in motion" in 2003. While antigay sentiment has clearly been present in Uganda as far back as 1998 (Hassett 2007; Kaoma 2009), participants at the strategic meeting blamed parliamentarians for their unwillingness to pass stiffer laws against homosexuality. In the presence of some parliamentary representatives, a female police officer complained that Uganda's anti-homosexuality laws were outdated. "We need stiffer laws, and when time comes to make new laws, every parent should stand up and demand new laws," she said. At the same meeting, a representative from Parliament told the audience that after Lively's presentation to lawmakers, "[The Parliament] feels it is necessary to draft a new law that deals comprehensively with the issue of homosexuality and . . . takes into account the international gay agenda . . . Right now there is a proposal that a new law be drafted" (SMV 2009).

The assurance that a new bill was in the pipeline did little to convince participants that the government was finally serious about cracking down on homosexuality. The participants resolved to publicly demonstrate against homosexuality and push the parliament to enact stiffer penalties against gays and lesbians. Should the parliament fail to enact new laws, they threatened to take the law into their own hands and "go door to door" looking for gays and lesbians until Uganda was cleansed from this vice (SMV 2009).

On Thursday, March 19, 2009, the Uganda Joint Christian Coalition—comprised of Anglicans, Catholics, and Orthodox—in conjunction with Family Life Network and Pentecostal Christians, demonstrated in the streets of Kampala and handed a petition to Parliament demanding stiffer laws against homosexuality. Religious leaders associated with the Lively Kampala meeting and American Christian Right, including Julius Oyet, Stephen Langa, and Martin Ssempa, were among the group of pastors who worked with Hon. David Bahati to draft the bill in April 2009.[3]

Despite the American Psychiatric Association's decision to remove homosexuality from the *Diagnostic and Statistical Manual of Mental Disorders* in 1973, the bill followed Lively in arguing that same-sex attraction "is not an innate and immutable characteristic" but a "mental disorder" that can be cured through therapy. The bill insisted that young people are "most vulnerable to recruitment into the homosexual lifestyle" (Kaoma 2009). It also argued that "research indicates that homosexuality has a variety of negative consequences including higher incidence of violence, sexually transmitted diseases, and use of drugs. The higher incidence of separation and break-up in homosexual relationships also creates a highly unstable environment for children raised by homosexuals through adoption or otherwise, and can have profound psychological consequences on those children. In addition, the promotion of homosexual behavior undermines our traditional family values" (AHB 2009). Following Lively's and other Americans' antigay rhetoric that the terms *sexual orientation* and *sexual rights* are basically code words "for homosexuality," the initial bill asserted that "sexual rights activists have created new euphemisms to promote [the gay] agenda such as 'sexual orientation,' 'gender identity,' 'sexual minorities,' and 'sexual rights'" (Lively 2009; Slater 2009:232–34).

The wording of this bill confirms Weiss's (in this volume) observations about anticipatory legislation. In many African countries, marriage and adoption of children are, of course, not issues that gays there are concerned about, yet bills or laws are passed in anticipation. In 2011, for example, the Senate in Nigeria passed the Same Sex Marriage (Prohibition) Bill 2011, which sought to outlaw same-sex marriage. The new Kenyan and Zimbabwean constitutions and the draft constitution in Zambia prohibit same-gender marriages. But why do such bills find support among Africans?

Homosexuality and the African Ethic of Procreation

The June 22, 2011, Pew Forum on Religion and Public Life's *Global Survey of Evangelical Protestant Leaders* showed that the majority of global evangelical leaders are social conservatives. "Nearly all (96%) say that abortion is always or usually morally wrong, with a slim majority of those polled (51%) saying it is always wrong." On homosexuality, 96 percent of African, 87 percent of Americans, and 45 percent of Central and South American respondents disapprove of same-gender relations (Pew Forum 2010). The above survey is in line with a 2006 Pew Forum survey, entitled *Spirit and Power*, that showed large majorities of Africans hold conservative views on same-sex relations. For example, 98 percent of Nigerians and 99 percent of Kenyans disapprove of homosexuality (Pew Forum 2006:8).

The above figures can be interpreted to mean that Africans have never had gays in their culture, which is evidently false. As already discussed, scholarly and historical findings by Marc Epprecht (1998; 1999), Neville Hoad (2007), Deborah P. Amory (1997), Judy Gay (1986), and James H. Chaplin (1963), as well as my field research in East, West, and Southern Africa, all suggest that homosexuality has been in Africa from precolonial days. For instance, Mellissa Mudiwa (name changed), a lesbian from Zimbabwe, suffered discrimination from the age of fifteen when her family realized she was queer. She was placed in juvenile probation school and later prayed for by various religious leaders, including African Christian prophets. Her exorcisms, however, ended after her grandmother said her body was inhabited by the ancestral spirit of her rich late uncle, who wanted to marry a woman. Given the imprimatur of traditional ancestor worship, she is now valued. "I am even allowed to drink by my family. (In Shona culture, only males are expected to drink.) We are Christians but they say that I have a male spirit" (Mellissa 2012). That Mellissa's family found support from traditional religions as opposed to Christianity suggests that the American rightists' claim that homosexuality is a Western vice being exported across the globe is false (Kaoma 2010a; Nyeck 2010). Sadly, many African religious and political leaders crusade against homosexuality on the assumption that it is an imposition from the West and has no African cultural roots.

Needless to say, U.S. conservatives are involved in African antigay politics with the premise that they are defending Africa's cultural and traditional *family values*. Aside from the fact that cultural values are not static, but change over time—which is true in Africa as elsewhere—most of these pastors know very little about African family values. Generally, African family values emphasize humanity as embedded in community of extended relationships beyond the nuclear family, a concept called *ubuntu*. Perhaps the difference in perception of human sexuality in the Western world vis-à-vis Africa is observable by how extramarital affairs are treated. Whereas in the

West, fathering a child outside marriage can possibly force one to resign one's public office, in Africa, such an act is considered a lesser evil or even amoral in African political discourse. Generally, Africans can accept a leader like President Jacob Zuma of South Africa despite his sexual misconducts. Unless celibacy is sanctioned by traditional religions, as is the case with Mellissa above, Africans can sympathize with a celibate priest's fathering of children in the community but oppose committed homosexual relationships. This is because homosexuality presented as a personal choice does not "promote" life as communally sanctioned, while the former behavior does.

Furthermore, the emphasis placed on extending the lineage somehow influences how many Africans react to homosexuality, family planning, and barrenness (Margolis 1997). Most African cultures place greater importance on intergenerational links than on conjugal ones, which gives great respect and power to the old. Since ancestors retain their identity through their living descendants, an ethical person is expected to meet the demands of the ancestors through lineage prolongation. Because same-sex marriages do not encourage procreation, they are viewed as an affront to the ancestors, who desire that their descendants multiply.

John C. Caldwell, Pat Caldwell, and Pat Quiggin argue that many Africans consider a virtuous person to be one who has many children. Marriage is centered on procreation and lineage prolongation, which is the greatest good (*summum bonum*). How one gets these children is of little importance to African morality. This morality, they argue, poses a stress on arresting the spread of AIDS, since "virtue is more related to success in reproduction rather than limiting profligacy" (Caldwell, Caldwell, and Quiggin 1989:187; Ukaegbu 1976). In this regard, homosexuality, like celibacy or family planning, once presented as "limiting profligacy," can be said to be an enemy of life. It is therefore understandable that same-sex relations can be perceived to upset the *ubuntu* fabric, once it is presented as destroying the family, the argument used in the United States. Thus the conservative misrepresentation of the LGBT community as a threat to the African family in part accounts for the unpopularity of the gay community and LGBT activists on the continent.

Despite conversion to Christianity, African Christian worldviews are still conditioned by traditional religious ideas and practices. For example, Osborne Joda-Mbewe, the general secretary of the Malawi Council of Churches, backed the traditional worldview: "our culture says a man should marry a woman, even the Bible says and I quote 'God created a man and a woman in his own image'; Genesis 1:27. You can also read Ephesians chapter 5:22–35. God created marriage and it is God who established marriage between a man and a woman to live together. In so doing the two may be able to procreate, Genesis.1:28; [and] multiply like sand of the beach. God did not refer to man and his fellow man. If that was not the case, God would not create a man and a woman. Even if we recall in the Garden of Eden, he created Adam a man and Eve a woman. If we say John should marry his fellow man, that is a total confusion, in fact we are copying from another culture" (Jordan-Mbewe 2011). Elsewhere I cite scholar Dominique Zahan's observation that

> African thought assigns man different modes of time depending on his marital status. The bachelor is placed in a false human perspective; he registers his life in linear time and follows a straight path with no possibility of returning. . . . The married man, by contrast, follows a curved line because he inscribes his life in cyclical time, and thereby finds himself in the true human perspective. Indeed, through marriage, and especially through fatherhood, man enters into a cycle of generations. He abandons the straight route in order to follow the gyrating movement of creativity and great undertaking; he becomes fully a man. (Kaoma 2010a:304)

This understanding does not just explain African "homophobia," but also affects how many LGBT persons choose to live their lives. Unless such persons find justification for their sexual orientation in traditional culture, like Mellissa above, the fear of childlessness will continue to force most of them to father and mother children of their own. This religious foundation is critical to understanding the intersection between African religious traditions, Christianity and Western influence on antigay politics in general.

But as Africa's population and the number of abandoned children explode, a good argument can be made for having some members of society be the reproducers, while others take different paths in life. While American conservatives associated with Evangelical, Catholic, and Mormon churches misrepresent the population crisis on the continent (Clowes 2010; Slater 2010), elsewhere I have argued that Africa has a serious population problem—a problem that has exacerbated conflicts and genocides (Kaoma 2010a). From Darfur to Cape Town, wars and interethnic conflicts have erupted because too many people laid claim to too few resources. It is perhaps possible that some can be excused from the need to reproduce. This, too, has been a traditional concept. There have always been people like Mellissa in African societies who played a different family role and did not need to bear children. In other words, voluntary limits on reproduction would both help Africa manage its environment and population and also give space for some to have a different sexual perspective.

Hiding by Religion:
The Effects of Western Influence

One important difference between Western and African Christians is how they relate to religion. As John Mbiti asserts, "Africans are notoriously religious" and "Religion permeates into all the departments of life so that it is not easy or possible to isolate it." In this regard, an attempt to study religion in Africa is also a "study of the people themselves in the complexities of both traditional and modern life" (Mbiti 1969:1). Mbiti's observation has implications for postcolonial homophobia in Africa. In a community where procreation is sanctioned by traditional religions, colonially influenced conservative Christian norms, and Islam, for example, the U.S. conservative positioning of gays as a threat to the African family and Christianity as a whole provides a new rationale for religiously sanctioned homophobia.

Similarly, this critical point resonates with the view that homosexuality is a postcolonial plot (Nyeck 2010). To some extent, their homophobia is, therefore, as much an expression of resistance to perceived Western imperialistic values as it is a statement about human sexuality. In other words, homophobia is used as a tool to mobilize resentment against perceived Western values of imperialism, manifested in globalization and ever-growing poverty on the continent.

In addition, homophobia works to the advantage of African leaders, who use it to divert attention from Western criticisms on issues of good governance. For example, Presidents Robert Mugabe and (the late) Bingu wa Mutharika, as well as Ellen Johnson Sirleaf, among many other African leaders, have employed homophobia to mobilize their citizens against the perceived exploitation of the Western world (Bosia, this volume).

The globalization of American culture wars does not just promote the dictum that "homosexuality is not African," but also presents LGBT persons as cronies of the West. While it is sometimes tagged as unbiblical and unnatural, the un-Africanness of homosexuality is recited widely across sub-Saharan Africa. During the strategic meeting addressed above, one police officer told the audience that "lesbianism was brought by girls whose parents were diplomats in Europe" (SMV 2009). As Zeidan (this volume) notes about India—where Hindus blamed homosexuality on Muslims, as in the argument made by Jenkins above—Paul Ssembiro of the Church of Uganda blamed same-sex relations on outsiders: "The issues of homosexuality seem to have penetrated [African culture] with the coming of Arabs, particularly in Uganda in the 1800s . . . The first history we dig up into homosexuality is based back then. Looking at my own culture, the Baganda culture, the formation of the family, the values and the proverbs, the values by which we were brought up, homosexuality is largely foreign" (Ssembiro 2009). Canon Joshua Foluso Taiwo of the Anglican Church of Nigeria pointed to the army and soldiers who were on peacekeeping missions in Europe as the source of homosexuality in Nigeria (Taiwo 2009). Archbishop Orombi concurs with this perception when he maintains that very rich homosexuals "are taking advantage of the abject poverty in Africa to lure people into their club" (Aruho 2008). In Nigeria, Anglican archbishop Akinola accused the Western world of employing large sums of money to lure young people into homosexuality (Akinola 2009).

The accusation of funding is not limited to gay activities, since African human-rights defenders are accused of being bought by U.S. progressives. Ironically, conservatives deny being bought. Aaron Mwasiye from the Church of Uganda put it as follows: "While liberals are out to buy Africans, the conservatives are saying, no, we have to maintain our own people . . . The conservatives are not by any means competing with Americans to buy Africa . . . The conservatives are in partnership with those who profess Christ crucified . . . who are in disagreement with homosexuality. Conservatives are in fellowship" (Mwasiye 2009).

However, not all conservative religious leaders situate homosexuality in the West. Martin Ssempa, one of the strongest anti-homosexual advocates and a key supporter of the anti-homosexual bill in Uganda, argued: "Kabaka Mwanga's [a Buganda King in the 1880s] homosexuality is an issue we tip-toed about for fear of offending the Buganda monarchy, which abhors homosexuality. But all historical accounts agree that Mwanga was a deviant homosexual who used his demigod status to appease his voracious appetite for sodomy by engaging in these unmentionable acts with his pages at the court" (Ssempa 2005:8). Wilson Mutebi, a retired Anglican bishop of Mityana in Uganda, more bluntly noted, "People who are saying that homosexuality is foreign are telling lies. They have not done enough research . . . To say no is to deny something we know very well and you are displaying ignorance . . . Such a statement is naïve" (Mutebi 2009). In Nigeria, Archdeacon Obioma Onwuzurumba of St. Matthews Parish in the Church of Nigeria also observed, "Even before Christianity got to my own locality, we had not ordinarily viewed homosexuality as very normal . . . Usually if anybody was found in that act, there were sanctions. One of them involved making sacrifices to gods. That was the thinking of my people, Igbo. It was considered as defiling the land" (Onwuzurumba 2009). Similarly, Nigerian Evangelical scholar Samuel W. Kunhiyop argues that it is historically false to blame homosexuality on the West since African cultures had homosexual male prostitutes (*yan daudu*), who, as early as the 1970s, danced annually in the open square (Kunhiyop 2008: 304). What does this mean for African politics?

The Marriage of Convenience: History of U.S. Conservatives in Africa

The history of the U.S. Christian conservatives in Africa should be seen on two fronts: political and religious. The political front is well documented by Sharlet in his book *The Family: The Secret Fundamentalism at the Heart of American Power*. Sharlet argues that U.S. political conservatives associated with the Family, also known as the Fellowship, have developed alliances with African politicians and dictators. In Uganda, President Yoweri Museveni and David Bahati, sponsor of the anti-homosexuality bill, are members of the Family.

Museveni's association with the Family first surfaced in 1990, when he asked Kenneth Kaunda of Zambia to host the first African Prayer Breakfast for African presidents in Lusaka, Zambia that November. This was after Museveni attended an American Prayer Breakfast, an annual U.S. event sponsored by the Family with U.S. conservative members of Congress. The Associated Press reported that Museveni wanted to organize something similar, but since "he was not a good Christian," he asked Kaunda to play host (quoted in Finnegan 1992:250).

While the Family was building relationships with African presidents, the American religious Right was partnering with African religious leaders. Aside from the number of U.S.-founded churches on African soil in the 1970s and 1980s, American conservative evangelists of all persuasions had exported their culture-war teachings to Africa in their attempt to "fight" the perceived communism of Pan-Africanist leaders such as Kaunda and Julius Nyerere of Tanzania. While originally opposed to African political leadership, today American religious conservatives have found political and religious support from both politicians and religious leaders in various countries.

This relationship is, however, recent. Generally, U.S. conservatives have sided with white regimes or dictators across Africa. For example, I have argued elsewhere that the neoconservative Institute on Religion and Democracy's executive director and former CIA operative in Africa, Mark Tooley, sought an apology from the National Churches in Christ (NCC) and the World Council of Churches (WCC) for supporting "Marxist" revolutionaries in Africa like Nobel Peace Prize Laureates Desmond Tutu and Nelson Mandela (Kaoma 2010a). Tooley's demand seeks to criticize the role that churches affiliated with the NCC and WCC played in the liberation of Africa. Aside from exposing crimes committed in the name of fighting communism, these churches provided financial and social support to displaced families in Africa, Asia, and South America (Kaoma 2009; Stoll 1991).

In addition to ignoring their embarrassing historical associations with colonial and post-independent African oppressors, U.S. conservatives broadcast their Christian Broadcasting Network and Trinity Broadcasting Network in sub-Saharan Africa. Although generally disinterested in helping poor blacks at home, in Africa these white American conservatives, in their drive to make Africa "a U.S. conservative colony," dominate social services; run orphanages, schools, and universities; and provide loans to poor Africans (Hearn 2002:54–55). Using such infrastructure, they have also redefined themselves as the true representatives of Western Christianity, effectively marginalizing mainline U.S. churches that once had strong relationships on the continent. In the Anglican Church, for example, right-wing groups have enticed African religious leaders to reject funding from mainline denominations—which require documentation of how the money is spent—and instead to accept funds from conservatives, further empowering the U.S. conservative viewpoint while giving local bishops the opportunity to enforce their authority on global Christianity (Hassett 2007; Kaoma 2009).

Africa has become a critical locale due to the demographic shift of the center of Christianity to the global South, where Christianity is growing rapidly (Jenkins 2002; Sanneh 2003). This growth has shifted the balance of power between African and Western churches. U.S. conservatives have exploited this change and have mobilized African religious leaders to work on their behalf as a mouthpiece for generating homophobia in Africa on the one hand and destabilizing American churches on the other hand (Kaoma 2009).

It is important to note that protestant churches in Africa are doctrinally evangelical; this is an element that makes them key partners to U.S. conservatives. However, they are also progressive on many economic and social issues, making them natural partners of politically liberal western Christians (Ranger 2008). But their religious orthodoxy provides the U.S. conservatives with an organizing opportunity. Because of the financial incentives African religious leaders currently get from their conservative alliances, they have been persuaded to switch their allegiance to U.S. conservatives over shared opposition to homosexuality.

On the conservative evangelical front, Lively and Angle are just two among a parade of right-leaning American Christians who have brought the U.S. culture wars to Africa. U.S. evangelicals like California's Rick Warren, pastor of Saddleback Baptist Church and bestselling author, have turned their attention to Africa as its role in global Christianity has grown. Within Africa, Warren seems to be progressive when it comes to fighting poverty, illiteracy, and HIV/AIDS. These efforts have painted him as a real partner in development. However, his antipoverty and education strategies also have been used to promote conservative institutional power and ideologies in Africa, including homophobia. As Warren's "purpose-driven" projects in Rwanda, Kenya, Nigeria, and Uganda have grown, so too have levels of active homophobia and the proposed laws against LGBT people. And Warren's allies are in the forefront of advocating for stiffer laws against LGBT persons in their countries (HRW and IGLHRC 2001; IGLHRC 2006; Johnson 2007; Thoreson and Cook 2011). In short, just as Warren has used his supposed religious moral superiority to campaign against gay rights in the United States, his African colleagues have constantly employed their religious authority to promote antigay dogmas on the continent.

Until 2009, Warren enjoyed ties to African religious and political leaders such as Uganda's first lady and Minister Janet Museveni and Orombi, Akinola, and Ssempa. During this time, Warren's opposition to gay rights in the United States was employed to justify discrimination against LGBT people in Africa. Warren's most quoted position on LGBT issues came during a March–April 2008 visit with African religious and political leaders in Rwanda, Uganda, and Kenya. He told reporters, "Homosexuality is not a natural way of life and thus not a human right" (Lirri 2008; Ssempa 2009).

Aside from making global news for showing gay pornography in his church and publishing the names of LGBT persons in the local press, Ssempa was a regular visitor to Saddleback until Warren distanced himself from him in 2009—after immense pressure from human-rights activists. But such distancing came at a cost to Warren's reputation. For example, when Warren condemned the antigay bill as "unjust, extreme and unchristian" (Warren 2009), Ssempa and other antigay activists in Africa and Uganda in particular viewed such a move as spiritual betrayal. In Uganda, Ssempa went as far as demanding an apology from Warren, whom he accused of bullying Uganda. In his rebuttal of Warren's statement on the antigay bill, Ssempa duplicated the same arguments that characterize American antigay arguments before reminding Warren that he denounced homosexuality both in the United States and when he visited Uganda in 2008 (Ssempa 2009).

CHANGING FACES: A NEW PARADIGM IN CONSERVATIVE ACTIVISM

Although Rick Warren's involvement in Africa is most fêted, and Lively's perhaps the most loathsome, they are not the first U.S. conservative evangelicals to influence African policies. Pat Robertson's television show *The 700*

Club is watched across sub-Saharan Africa. Aside from supporting ferocious dictator Mobutu Sese Seko of the Congo, Robertson also sided with war criminals Liberian Charles Taylor and Angolan rebel leader Jonas Savimbi. These men were linked to hundreds of thousands of civil-war deaths in their own countries.

In postcolonial Africa, conservative activism has taken another paradigm shift. Conservatives' opposition to Africa's liberation is already noted. Today, however, conservatives are working to stop the emancipation of LGBT persons and women through legal reforms. The American Center for Law and Justice (ACLJ) was, for instance, involved in the drafting of new constitutions in various African countries including Kenya and Zimbabwe. In American politics, ACLJ is notoriously homophobic. In Africa, however, ACLJ hides its neocolonial attitudes behind an African face, operating as the East African Center for Law and Justice in Kenya and the Africa Center for Law and Justice in Zimbabwe.

But this postcolonial relationship is fostered by religion. In Zimbabwe, for example, ACLJ used pastor Goodwill Shana, the president of the Evangelical Fellowship of Zimbabwe (a grouping of theologically conservative Churches in Zimbabwe), to gain access to political leaders in Zimbabwe. According to Jordan Sekulow, ACLJ director of international operations, Shana was familiar with the American group through its weekly broadcast "on the Christian satellite network Daystar" (Sekulow 2009). Of course, Robertson opposed the liberation of Zimbabwe, but through a "marriage of convenience," his group has found in Zimbabwe's Robert Mugabe's dictatorial government a perfect partner and is committed to represent the Zimbabwean government to the United States' government and the Church. By doing so at a time when progressive forces were pushing for good governance in Zimbabwe, ACLJ rebranded itself as a caring partner with the postcolonial oppressive government of Mugabe (Sekulow 2010).

In Kenya, Sekulow's association with that country began when an American pastor from Iowa introduced a Kenyan Bishop to ACLJ-USA. Sekulow claimed the bishop "wanted to make sure that he and the thousands of pastors that are part of his denomination knew how to properly comment on the draft constitution when speaking to their parishioners and the media. The Bishop and his fellow pastors have decided to speak out against the constitutionalization of the Sharia Courts and have called on the ACLJ to travel to Kenya to setup a full-time legal and government affairs operation in Nairobi where we'll work with church leaders on this crucial issue" (Sekulow 2009).

Sekulow assumes that Africans are too ignorant to engage in political activism without his organization's help, which is not true. His involvement in Kenya, for example, had little to do with Africa but with issues central to American culture wars—Islamphobia, homophobia, and abortion. Kenyans' proposed constitution stated that although "the life of a person begins at conception," it permitted abortion "if a trained health professional deems it necessary, or if the life or health of the mother is in danger." Using American culture-war rhetoric, Sekulow interpreted this section as permitting abortion on demand. He predicted that abortion would lead "the proposed constitution to its demise" (Sekulow 2010). The new constitution passed with 64 percent of the vote, in spite of ACLJ's "dire" prediction.

Furthermore, antigay and anti-abortion activist Brian Clowes of the Catholic organization Human Life International—which is dedicated to fighting American culture wars both in the United States and abroad—concluded in his Mission Report to Namibia in 2010 that Africans are pro-life but not in an American conservative way. In his words:

> ... many *Namibians have fallen victim to anti-life thinking, simply because they haven't heard the other side of the story* [emphasis his]. They did not comprehend why explicit sex education and contraception are intrinsically evil, and they found it very difficult to understand the scientific evidence and Church teachings on these issues. Some even thought that abortion could be acceptable under certain "hard case" conditions. Namibia is a prime example of how abortion is one hundred times harder to get rid of once it is established than it is to stop it from infecting the culture in the first place. (Clowes 2011:6)

Clowes warned that U.S. conservatives should continuously attempt to break up and soften this moral ground, which accepts abortion, if "the pro-life message is wholeheartedly accepted by the people." Clowes is wrong to attribute abortion to Westerners. Long before colonialism, Africans have made decisions to end certain pregnancies using various traditional methods. As Jackson Kaliponda, church elder in Masaiti, Zambia, noted, unlike homosexuality, "abortion is somehow tolerated in public discourse [and] most people look at it as normal and the most affected are youths from 15 to 28 years old" (Kaliponda 2011). Conservatives have packaged homosexuality as a "Western" vice; abortion, on the other hand is "African." Thus, those advocating safer abortions have found it easy to sell their arguments.

However, there seems to be another reason why abortion is hard to sell as an issue. First, abortion is very common in Africa. For example, all people interviewed in Zambia, Malawi, and Zimbabwe claimed to know someone who had aborted. This fact gives abortion a human face. In addition, the lack of international pressure to decriminalize abortion, on the one hand, and on the other, the silence of international voices and activists when women are arrested for alleged "illegal" abortions—although many Africans would turn a blind eye to abortions in general—has made it difficult for abortion to become a mobilizing issue in postcolonial Africa. One would argue that if arrests of women on alleged abortion charges raised similar outcries to those on homosexuality, African political and religious leaders would have used the issue to countermobilize against reproductive justice for political ends.

But American Evangelicals and Catholics are not alone in exporting homophobia. Mormon culture-wars activist Sharon Slater, the president of Family Watch International (FWI)—which enjoys consultative status at the United Nations—has frequented African countries promoting her antigay agenda. Aside from working with Uganda's antigay activist Martin Ssempa, Slater actively lobbies African governments to oppose any UN resolution that seeks to decriminalize homosexuality and abortion. "We ask African governments to spell it [marriage] out as male and female. We are opposed to the word sexual rights, comprehensive sexuality education and reproductive rights. The words are used by homosexual activists to destroy the family." When asked to how she has fared on these issues with African leaders, she responded, "I can say I have been very successful" (Slater 2012).

Slater's activities are not limited to the UN. In July 2011, Slater was a keynote speaker at the *International Law Conference on Challenges in Upholding the Rights of Women and Children in Nigeria*, attended by government leaders, social workers, lawyers, educators, and American antigay activists. While the conference sounds as though aimed at the progressive rights of children and women, Slater used it to call on Nigerians to resist U.S. president Obama and "the United Nations' calls to decriminalize homosexuality." Like Lively above, Slater, who boasted of consulting "to a number of African nations during UN negotiations on family issues," threatened that legalizing homosexuality meant losing religious and parental rights. As she put it, legalizing same-sex relations will curtail parents' rights to guide "the education of their children and remove the rights of churches and individuals to publicly practice their own religious beliefs in these areas" (Slater 2011:11).

After the conference, her husband and FWI's legal adviser, Greg Slater, informed supporters in an email: "As the most populous and one of the wealthiest African counties, Nigeria can serve as a strong role model for other governments in the region to follow on how to hold on to their family values despite intense international pressure. In fact, several days after the conference, the head of the Anglican Church called upon the Nigerian government to withdraw from the United Nations because of its push to further the cause of homosexuality" (Slater 2011).

In November 2011, the Nigerian Senate followed Uganda in passing "the Same Sex Marriage (Prohibition) Bill 2011," which criminalizes not just same-sex marriages, but also registration and operation of any gay organization or clubs in the country. Like the Ugandan antigay bill, anyone who witnesses same-sex marriage or "supports the registration, operation and sustenance of gay clubs, societies, organizations, processions or meetings in Nigeria commits an offense and shall be liable on conviction to a term of 10 years imprisonment." Is this just another coincidence in American conservative drama in Africa?

Conclusion

Despite historical evidence of homosexuality in Africa from long before the Europeans arrived, most African religious and political leaders now view homosexuality as a Western export and a form of imperialism and neocolonialism. Africans are sensitive to neocolonialism. The conservative claim that homosexuality is a donor-driven agenda gives African church leaders ammunition to fight it. On the political level, denouncing homosexuality—the very issue that the international community is dedicated to addressing across the globe—may be Africa's way of claiming certain power over the Western world. In this regard, when African leaders assert that homosexuality is un-African, they are pointing to a politics of postcolonial identity on the one hand, and fighting perceived western imperialism on the other.

Although American conservatives repeatedly accuse progressives of being imperialist, their dealings with Africa represent imperialism at its worst. Aside from their unethical business dealings with African dictators and rebel leaders, the conservative flow of funds creates a form of clientelism, with the expectation that the recipients toe the donors' ideological line. Elsewhere, I showed how sometimes conservatives put words into the mouths of their African allies, even writing or rewriting their anticolonial statements to reflect U.S. conservative concerns (Kaoma 2010a). In one of many examples, IRD reworked remarks Rev. Jerry Kulah of Liberia wrote in preparation for a 2008 Methodist conference to use as a general African statement, imposing its anti-Islamic politics on the African position (Kaoma 2009b). Slater's lobbying activities at the UN are another example of how conservatives use non-Western battlefields to fight American culture wars.

In contrast, U.S. mainline churches repeatedly demonstrate their opposition to neocolonialism of all sorts, not least by supporting the UN's Millennium Development Goals to fight poverty in postcolonial Africa. That said, the Western insistence that foreign aid should be linked to the defense of human rights for LGBT persons is just another side of fighting culture wars on African soil. While the principle is good, in reality, U.S. conservatives and their African allies will dismiss such efforts as imperialistic and neocolonial plots to force Africans into accepting homosexuality. Because homosexuality is said to destroy the family, antigay proponents are considered heroes in the public eye. But as already observed, when the U.S. Christian Right accuses LGBT activists of threatening family values, they speak of two very different social norms. Mbiti explains that Descartes' concept "I think therefore I am" is meaningless in Africa. Instead, Africans say: "I am because we are; and since we are, therefore I am." Nobel Peace Prize Laureate Archbishop Desmond Tutu says the African theological outlook of *ubuntu* affirms this interconnectedness and the sacred worth of all human beings regardless of their sexual orientation. Thus nobody can claim to defend human rights while ignoring the dehumanizing effects of homophobia in Africa today. Africans will definitely accept LGBT rights as human rights, but such acceptance will be gradual. For this very reason, Africa does not need "American culture wars" to achieve equality for all people.

Notes

1. The following quotes from Lively are based on audio and video recordings I took during the seminars in Uganda in March 2009.

2. Lively's talking point shared much with the *Public Advocate* email, 9 June 2011 08:20, Subject: Congress to mandate homosexual indoctrination?; townhallmessage@ townhallmail.com.

3. The principle of the April 2009 Anti-Homosexuality Bill was to "establish a comprehensive legislation to protect the traditional family by prohibiting (i) any form of sexual relations between people of the same sex; and (ii) the promotion or recognition of such sexual relations in public institutions as healthy, normal or an acceptable lifestyle, including in the public schools, through or with the support of any government entity in Uganda or any non-governmental organization inside or outside the country." The September 2009 version which was tabled in Parliament was edited down and does not have most of these statements. See Kaoma 2009, Appendix.

Bibliography

Adams, Marilyn McCord. 2008. "Shaking the Foundations: LGBT Bishops and Blessings in the Fullness of Time," *Anglican Theological Review* (Fall): 713–32.

Akinola, Peter. 2006. "Pastoral Letter to the Church." Available at http://www.anglicannig .org/pastrollttr_ibadan2006.htm, accessed May 13, 2009.

Aruho, Paul. 2008. "Archbishop Orombi Re-affirms Anti-gay Stand," *The Daily Monitor*, Kampala, July 11.

Ashworth, Pat. 2010. "African Bishops Split Over 'Ambushed' Agenda, but Together on Development." *Church Times*, September 3.

BBC. 2006. "Nigeria to Outlaw Same-sex Unions." 19 January. Available at http://news.bbc.co.uk/2/hi/africa/4626994.stm, accessed October 14, 2008.

Bujo, Bénézet. 1992. *African Theology in Its Social Context*. Maryknoll, NY: Obis Books.

Cromartie, Michael. 2010. "Have the Culture Wars Gone Global? Religion and Sexuality in the Global South." March 9, *The Faith Angle Conference on Religion, Politics, & Public Life*. Available at http://www.eppc.org/programs/faithangleforum/publications/pubID.4121,programID.37/pub_detail.asp.

Caldwell, John C., Pat Caldwell, and Pat Quiggin. 1989. "The Social Context of AIDS in Sub-Saharan Africa." *Population and Development Review* 15, no. 2: 185–234.

Clowes, Brian. 2010. "Mission Report: Namibia: October 2010," prepared for Human Life International. Available at http://www.hli.org/index.php/mission-field/1000-mission-report-namibia-october-2010, accessed April 20, 2012.

Epprecht, Marc. 1998. "The 'Unsaying' of Indigenous Homosexualities in Zimbabwe: Mapping a Blind Spot in an African Masculinity," *Journal of Southern African Studies* 24, no. 4: 631–51.

Finnegan, William. 1992. *A Complicated War: The Harrowing of Mozambique*. Berkeley: University of California Press.

Ford, Tamasin, and Bonnie Allen. 2012. "Nobel Peace Prize Winner Defends Law Criminalising Homosexuality in Liberia," *The Guardian*, UK. March 19. Available at http://www.guardian.co.uk/world/2012/mar/19/nobel-peace-prize-law-homosexuality, accessed March 19, 2012.

Ford, Tamasin, and Michel Martin. 2012. "Liberian LGBT Rights Under Spotlight," April 9. Available at http://www.npr.org/2012/04/09/150286293/liberian-lgbt-rights-under-spotlight, accessed May 18, 2012.

Frampton, Pam. 2011. "The Shocking Truth: Some People Are Gays," *The Telegraph*, UK. May 21.

Gettleman, Jeffrey. 2011. "Remembering David Kato, a Gay Ugandan and a Marked Man," *New York Times*, January 29. Available at http://www.nytimes.com/2011/01/30/weekinreview/30gettleman.html?, accessed February 4, 2011.

Hassett, Melinda. 2007. *Anglican Communion in Crisis: How the Episcopal Dissidents and Their African Allies Are Reshaping Anglicanism*. Princeton, NJ: Princeton University Press.

Hearn, Julie. 2002. "The Invisible NGO: U.S. Evangelical Mission in Kenya," *Journal of Religion in Africa* 32: 32–60.

Hoad, Neville. 2007. *African Intimacies: Race, Homosexuality and Globalization*. Minneapolis, University of Minnesota Press.

HRW and IGLHRC. 2001. *More than a Name: State Sponsored Homophobia and Its Consequences in Southern Africa*. New York: Human Rights Watch and the International Gay and Lesbian Human Rights Commission.

IGLHRC. 2006. *Voices from Nigeria: Gays, Lesbians, Bisexuals, and Transgender Speak Out about the Same-Sex Bill*. New York: International Gay and Lesbian Human Rights Commission.

Johnson, Cary Alan. 2007. *Off the Map: How HIV/AIDS Programming Is Failing Same-Sex Practicing People in Africa*. New York: International Gay and Lesbian Human Rights Commission.

Jacobson, Jodi. 2009. "Martin Ssempa Responds to Rick Warren on Uganda's Homosexuality Bill." Available at http://www.rhrealitycheck.org/blog/2009/12/19/updated-martin-ssempa-responds-rick-warren-ugandas-homosexuality-bill, accessed June 2, 2010.

Jenkins, Philip. 2002. *The Next Christendom: The Coming of Global Christianity*. New York: Oxford University Press.

Kaoma, Kapya. 2009. *Globalizing the Culture Wars: US Conservatives, African Churches, and Homophobia*. Somerville, MA: Political Research Associates.

———. 2009–10. "The U.S. Christian Right and the Attack on Gays in Africa," *Publiceye Magazine*, (Winter/Spring).

———. 2010a. *Ubuntu, Jesus, and Earth: Integrating African Religion and Christianity in Ecological Ethics*. ThD Dissertation, Boston University.

———. 2010b. "Who's Colonialist: African Antigay Politics in the Global Discourse," *Publiceye Magazine* 25, no. 3.

———. 2012. *Colonizing African Values: How the U.S. Christian Right Is Transforming Sexual Politics in Africa*. Somerville, MA: Political Research Associates.

Kasozi, Ephraim. 2010. "African Bishops Unite to Denounce Homosexuality," *Daily Monitor* (Uganda), August 29.

Kunhiyop, Waje Samuel. 2008. *African Christian Ethics*. Grand Rapids, MI: Zondervan.

Lirri, Evelyn. 2008. "Gay Row—US Pastor Supports Country on Boycott." Available at http://allafrica.com/stories/200803281265.html, accessed June 2009.

Lively, Scott. 2009. "Report from Kampala," March 10. Available at http://www.defendthefamily.com/pfrc/archives.php?id=2345952, accessed March 19, 2009.

Maravi Post. 2010. "Malawi Churches Tell Donors: Out with Your Gay Stuff." Available at http://www.maravipost.com/malawi-politics/district/4746-churches-tell-donors-take-gay-stuff-outside-malawi.html#ixzz1NyaEAXO8, accessed June 2, 2010.

Margolis, Pacqué Sara. 1997. "Population Policy, Research and the Cairo Plan of Action: New Directions for the Sahel," *International Family Planning Perspective* 23, no. 2: 86–89.

Nyeck, Sybille Ngo. 2010. "Accounting for Paradoxical Emptiness in Contentious Intersections: 'Colonial Blackmail,' Token Causation and Sexuality in Africa." Paper read at American Political Science Annual Meeting, at Washington, D.C., September 4.

Olukya, Godfrey, and Jason Straziuso. 2010. "'Hang Them': Uganda Paper Publishes Photos of Gays," *Washington Post*, October 19.

Pew Forum on Religion and Public Life. 2006. *Spirit and Power: A 10-Country Survey of Pentecostals*. Washington, D.C.: Pew Research Center.

———. 2009. "A Conversation with Pastor Rick Warren, Saddleback Church's Signature Issues," Pew Forum on Religion and Public Life, November 23. Transcript available at http://www.pewforum.org/Christian/Evangelical-Protestant-Churches/The-Future-of-Evangelicals-A-Conversation-with-Pastor-Rick-Warren.aspx, accessed August 2, 2012.

———. 2011. *Global Survey of Evangelical Protestant Leaders*, June 22. Washington, D.C.: Pew Research Center.

Ranger, Terence O. 2008. *Evangelical Christianity and Democracy in Africa*. New York: Oxford University Press.

Sanneh, Lamin. 2003. *Whose Religion Is Christianity? The Gospel beyond the West*. Grand Rapids, MI: Wm. B. Eerdmans.

Sekulow, Jordan. 2009. "The New ACLJ: All About the African Center for Law & Justice—Washington D.C. Foreign Policy, December 26.

———.2010. ACLJ Special Operations Unit: Zimbabwe, June 23, 2010, available at http://aclj.org/aclj/african-centre-for-law-justice---zimbabwe-update-, accessed August 2, 2012.

———. 2011. "Divisive Issues May Sink Kenya's Constitution," *Global Post*, May 18.

Slater, Greg. 2011. "Great Hope and Strength For the Family in Nigeria," July 25. http://www.familywatchinternational.org/fwi/newsletter/0530.cfm, accessed June 2, 2012.

Slater, Sharon. 2009. *Stand for the Family: Alarming Evidence and Firsthand Accounts from the Front Lines of Battle: A Call to Responsible Citizens Everywhere*. Gilbert, AZ: Inglestone Publishing.

———. 2011. "Human Rights Gone Awry: Myths and Facts Regarding International Human Rights Affecting Women and Children." Presented at the 2011 Nigerian Bar Association Conference in Lagos, Nigeria.

Sharlet, Jeff. 2009. *The Family: The Secret Fundamentalism at the Heart of American Power*. New York: Harper Perennial, 2009.

———. 2010. *C Street: The Fundamentalist Threat to American Democracy*. New York: Little, Brown.

Ssempa, Martin. 2005. *The New Vision*, June 3.

———. 2009. Uganda National Pastors Task Force Against Homosexuality Letter to Pastor Warren. available at http://wthrockmorton.com/2009/12/19/uganda-national-pastors-task-force-against-homosexuality-demand-apology-from-rick-warren/, accessed August 2, 2012.

Tamale, Sylvia, ed. 2007. *Homosexuality: Perspectives from Uganda*. Kampala: SMUG.

———. "Out of the Closet: Unveiling Sexuality Discourses in Uganda. *Feminist Africa*, http://www.feministafrica.org/index.php/out-of-the-closet, accessed June 8, 2011.

Thoreson, Ryan, and Sam Cook, eds. 2011. *Nowhere to Turn: Blackmail and Extortion of LGBT People in Sub-Saharan Africa*. New York: International Gay and Lesbian Human Rights Commission.

Throckmorton, Warren. 2011. "American Anti-Gay Campaign in Africa Opposes Fictitious Sexual Rights: How One Religious Fight Organization Lobbies Against Gays in the Developing World." *Religion Dispatches*, August 21. Available at http://www .religiondispatches.org/archive/sexandgender/4996/american_anti-gay_campaign _in_africa_opposes, accessed August 3, 2012.

Ukaegbu, Alfred O. 1976. "The Role of Traditional Marriage Habits in Population Growth: The Case of Rural Eastern Nigeria," *Journal of African International Institute* 46, no. 4: 390–98.

———. 2009. *Letter to Pastors of Uganda*. Available at http://www.thedailybeast.com/ newsweek/videos/2009/12/14/rick-warren-s-letter-to-the-pastors-of-uganda.html, accessed August 2, 2012.

LIST OF INTERVIEWEES

All interviews, Seminar on Exposing the Homosexual Agenda, and the strategic meeting were recorded on video or audio. Copies are available at Political Research Associates' Library.

Joda-Mbewe, Osborne, general secretary, Malawi Council of Churches, 04/09/2011.
Kaliponda, Jackson, church elder in Masaiti, Zambia, 2011.
Langa, Stephen, Family Life Network, Uganda, 03/15/2009.
Lundu, Chapter, Paramount Chief Lundu, 05/19/2011.
Mudiwa, Mellissa, Gays and Lesbians of Zimbabwe member, Harare, Zimbabwe, October 2011.
Mwebesa, Frank, Family Life Network, Uganda, 03/15/2009.
Mwesigye, The Rev Canon Aaron, Provincial Secretary Church of Uganda, 03/17/2009.
Onwuzurumba, Obioma Wuse II, chaplain to the vice president and vicar of St. Matthews Anglican Church, Abuja Church of Nigeria, 03/24/2009.
Samson, Tereza, Senior Chief Kachindamoto of Malawi, 05/06/2011.
Slater, Sharon, Family Watch International, 08/13/2012.
Ssembiro, Paul Wasswa, provincial coordinator of mission and evangelism, Church of Uganda, 03/14/2009.
Taiwo, Reverend Joshua Foluso, Provincial Communication Office, Church of Nigeria, 03/24/2009.
White, Seodi, Women in Law in Southern Africa, Lilongwe, Malawi, 05/18/2011.
Williams, Harold, secular humanist, Malawi, 05/23/2011.

5

Gay Rights and Political Homophobia in Postcommunist Europe

Is there an "EU Effect"?

CONOR O'DWYER

If the recent past has witnessed an international trend toward increasing recognition and contestation of the rights of lesbian, gay, bisexual, and transgender (LGBT) people, then postcommunist Europe is also, perhaps surprisingly, a part of the trend. Why should its inclusion be surprising? As I will describe below, communism left a profoundly destructive legacy in this sphere, bequeathing a history of state repression of gays, lesbians, and bisexuals,[1] broad-based homophobic attitudes in society (at least in comparison to Western Europe), and a more general phenomenon of weak civil society. These legacies made homosexuality a taboo topic after 1989, and the weakness of civil society organizations hampered efforts to demand new rights in the political arena. Though the timing of gay rights'[2] new prominence in the postcommunist region suggests the workings of broader global trends, it also suggests, more specifically, the influence of the European Union (EU). On closer inspection, however, the overall effect of the EU remains an open question. It can and has focused pressure on countries to improve their gay-rights records as the price of membership, but it can also be argued that, in the face of deeper homophobic attitudes, such pressure may later provoke a political backlash that undoes rights (Kochenov 2007; O'Dwyer & Schwartz 2010).

As countries in the region have struggled through the prolonged process of seeking membership in the EU, the price of accession has included the banning of the most egregious forms of discrimination, including that based on sexual orientation. The EU—and associated European-wide institutions such as the Council of Europe—have promoted antidiscrimination norms in postcommunist states applying for membership. Given a growing literature arguing that the EU has deepened democracy in the postcommunist applicant states, from the rights of ethnic minorities in the Baltics (Kelley 2004) to the reduction of political corruption (Vachudova 2006), it is only natural to look for a similar effect with regard to gay rights. Yet there are important questions about European institutions' capacity to bring about real policy change, especially given the very real possibility of provoking political backlash and, thereby, rights retrenchment.

This chapter attempts to sort out the EU's impact on gay rights in the region. It asks two central questions. First, has accession fostered gay rights despite the hurdle of still widespread societal homophobia? To put the question slightly differently, can differences in gay rights across the region largely be explained with respect to deeper differences in the level of societal homophobia? If so, then the EU's impact is insignificant. To the extent that the EU *does* have a demonstrable effect in promoting legal rights for gays, the second key question is: Does such rights promotion spark a homophobic backlash in the broader political sphere, particularly that of political-party competition? In answering these questions, I employ two different approaches. For the first, I look broadly at the postcommunist region, especially in comparison to Western Europe; for the second, I take a more intensive approach, focusing on the experience of Poland.

Most empirical analyses of the politics of gay rights in postcommunist Europe to date have relied on country case studies. The case study is, in fact, probably the best research strategy at this point, given the still underdeveloped nature of theorizing about even the basic contours of the region's gay-rights politics and the limitations of the extant comparative research. By and large, individual country studies have offered empirical support for arguments that both the communist legacy and EU conditionality have strongly imprinted themselves on the politics of gay rights. Yet the extant case-study research has also often raised questions about the limits of EU influence, struggling in particular to sort out what the backlash against gay rights—for example in Latvia, Lithuania, Romania, and Poland—reveals about conditionality's ultimate effectiveness (O'Dwyer 2010; O'Dwyer and Schwartz 2010; Ohlsen 2009). It has been difficult within the confines of studies of individual countries to separate the effect of the EU from possible confounding factors, such as different levels of societal tolerance and differing political cultural legacies based on the predominant national religion.

The first part of this chapter aims to expand beyond the individual country study, making use of a recent index of gay rights constructed by ILGA-

Europe. I compare the level of rights of postcommunist countries at different stages of EU accession, from those who became members in 2004 and 2007 to those at various stages of application for membership. To preview my findings, I uncover strong evidence of the benefits of EU accession. By looking at countries at different stages of EU accession, I find that the most recent members and those currently applying for membership have higher levels of rights than those further from accession. Unfortunately, ILGA-Europe's rights index does not allow for comparisons of the same countries before and after accession; therefore, this broader regional analysis does not rule out the possibility that EU accession might provoke a backlash and post-membership retrenchment at a second stage of the rights struggle.

In order to address the question of backlash, the second part of the chapter presents a brief study of one of the more difficult cases for gay rights in postcommunist Europe: Poland. If the extension of gay rights as the price for EU membership were to provoke a homophobic backlash—and later rights retrenchment—anywhere, it would be in Poland. Here, gay rights have been an especially volatile political issue, even by the region's standards. As elsewhere, Poland's legacy of Communist Party rule has hindered the development of a gay-rights movement. In addition to the communist legacy, Poland is home to an influential and politically active Catholic Church bent on preserving a traditional conception of the family. Yet as a recent entrant into the European Union (EU), Poland has had to adjust to the legal requirements and expectations of the wider concert of European countries, which are generally more liberal regarding gay rights. Thus Poland is an ideal site for studying the interplay between domestic and EU factors in shaping the rapidly changing politics of gay rights in postcommunist Europe. To preview my argument, I conclude that, in Poland, the expansion of gay rights occasioned by EU accession, limited though it was, *did* provoke a backlash of political homophobia. That said, from the vantage point of 2011, this backlash appears to have been brief, and the country's fledgling gay-rights movement has arguably become stronger as a result of it.

The State of Gay Rights in Postcommunist Europe: An Overview

How should we characterize the politics of homosexuality in postcommunist Europe? How can we compare the situation with that in other regions, especially Western Europe? My starting point in addressing these questions is to distinguish between three concepts: legal rights, societal homophobia, and political homophobia. Legal rights cover the narrow sphere of official practice: e.g., does the state recognize same-sex partnerships; does it limit freedom of assembly, for example, by banning Pride Parades? My baseline for comparing legal rights is ILGA-Europe's index, described below. By societal homophobia, I mean the broad cultural context within which a society forms its attitudes about LGBT people. Naturally, there is room for diverse attitudes at this level, since even the most tightly knit societies are never monolithic. Nevertheless, it is also clearly possible to speak about the prevailing attitudes toward homosexuality in a given society, especially in comparison to other societies. These prevailing attitudes are conditioned by factors such as religious practice and historical legacies, like that of communism, and these can be described with some accuracy by opinion data. Last, political homophobia captures the use of gay rights (or "homosexual propaganda," etc.) as an issue to mobilize people for political action, whether it be to vote for a certain party, support a particular social movement, or in some way influence state policy. While these concepts are interrelated, they certainly need not move in lockstep toward ever-greater progress. Legal rights may be relatively advanced in an otherwise homophobic society if, for example, those rights reflect outside pressures. Thus, to the extent that we find an empirical relationship between EU accession and gay rights, we must be very cautious about making the further claims that either the level of societal or political homophobia is on the wane.

Doubtless, one reason that most extant research on gay rights in postcommunist Europe has been case-study-based is that comparing legal systems for twenty-odd countries is extremely labor-intensive. Fortunately, the situation has now changed markedly for the better. In 2010, the Brussels-based LGBT advocacy group ILGA-Europe created an index of the legal situation of gays, lesbians, and bisexual (LGB) people across Europe.[3] Constructed by a team of legal and regional experts, this composite index rates fifty European states in terms of their legislation regarding the rights of and, to a more limited extent, their practice toward LGB people.[4] Each state receives a score between -4 and 10 depending on its legislation and practice. Points are given to countries recognizing same-sex partnership, parenting rights of same-sex partners, and recognizing homophobia in hate speech/crime legislation. Points are subtracted if countries have laws banning same-sex sexual acts, specifying unequal age of consent, or if they have violated the rights of LGB people to peaceful assembly and freedom of association.

While clearly a great advance for researchers, the ILGA-Europe index is not without its weaknesses. First, the rankings for 2010 do not incorporate rights for transgender people. Recognizing that this omission suggests invidious distinctions, ILGA-Europe reworked its ranking criteria in 2011 to include transgender rights. Yet even this step is not uncontroversial if we take Mark Blasius's argument that cross-national measures can be misleading when they include rights that have not been demanded in the countries that are being ranked. For this reason, and because the 2010 rankings put us that much closer to the date of EU membership in the countries in my analysis, I use the 2010 figures. As a second weakness, the ILGA-Europe index does not yet allow for direct comparisons over time.[5] This kind of over-time analysis of the politics of gay rights is necessary but, unfortunately, still absent for this region. Finally, measures such as ILGA-Europe's, which attempt to tap such multifaceted concepts as rights across different political and cultural contexts, risk flattening complexity and missing important nuances. To take one analogue, the Freedom House's rankings of democracy are invariably subjected to this critique. Yet scholars of democratization continually come back to the Freedom House scores for want of a better substitute and because failing to learn from differences among countries is a loss of its own. I will plead the same excuse here. By offering a broad comparison between post-communist countries at various degrees of proximity to EU conditionality, even the purely cross-sectional comparisons in the ILGA-Europe index offer the opportunity to disentangle domestic and international effects.

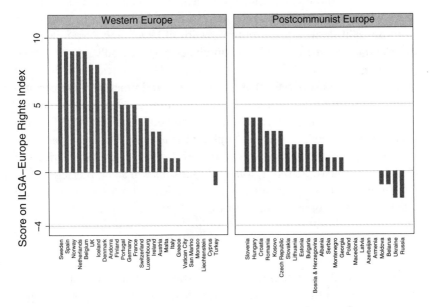

Figure 1. LGB Rights in Western and Postcommunist Europe Compared

To depict the wide range of divergence in gay rights across Europe, Figure 1 charts each country's overall score on the ILGA-Europe index in 2010.[6] Even a cursory inspection of the scores indicates an East–West divide. As will not surprise observers of European politics, it also reveals more fine-grained regional divides, notably between the gay-friendly Scandinavian countries and the generally less-so Southern European countries. (Spain is, of course, the notable exception. More recently, Portugal has seen rights gains, with the adoption of same-sex marriage.) Broadly speaking, however, postcommunist countries as a whole score lower in terms of legal rights. The average ILGA-Europe index reading for postcommunist states was 1.3 compared with 4.3 for the rest of Europe.[7]

Why do postcommunist countries, despite showing some internal variation, fare so poorly as a group on gay rights? Communist rule left two corrosive legacies in this sphere. First, the regimes' monopolization of and continual efforts to force participation in the public sphere poisoned the typical citizen's appetite for participation in social movements, volunteer associations, and political parties while at the same time engendering a deep distrust for things political (Howard 2003; Jowitt 1992). According to rights activists in the region today, this tendency is still quite noticeable: LGBT people often prefer to develop their own "underground" networks, clubs, and so on rather than publicly fight for acceptance.[8]

The second communist legacy is that of *de jure* and *de facto* homophobia. In legal terms, there was some variation among the communist countries. Homosexuality was criminalized in the Soviet Union and Romania, while in Poland it remained legal. In the unofficial sphere of daily practice, however, there was relatively little variation. Even where homosexuality was not criminalized, a host of official and unofficial discriminatory practices prevailed, from a higher age of consent for homosexual compared to heterosexual intercourse, to persecution by the secret police, to deep social stigma (Gruszczynska 2006, 2). Gays throughout the Eastern Bloc faced pervasive *de facto* discrimination and repression both from the state authorities and the broader society. As the regional comparisons will show, this legacy can be seen in the consistently less tolerant attitudes and more restrictive legal freedoms of postcommunist countries.

Theorizing the "EU Effect"

As powerful as it is, the communist legacy should not be assumed to be destiny. It is certainly not the only contextual factor at play in the politics of gay rights in postcommunist Europe. The other is the EU, which through both the leverage it exercises on states seeking membership and its "socialization" of both members and applicants in EU norms of minority rights and anti-discrimination has the potential to shape the political landscape regarding sexual orientation. In this section, I ask, first, how have scholars theorized the influence of the EU and, second, how might it practically affect gay rights in new and aspiring member states?

Extant scholarship on the EU's influence on postcommunist applicant and member states has focused on conditionality ("external incentives") and social learning as mechanisms driving so-called "Europeanization."[9] Conditionality is perhaps the EU's most powerful form of leverage, linking membership to compliance with EU legal norms. Scholars have argued that the leverage of conditionality depends on the clarity of EU norms, their credibility, the magnitude of the reward for compliance, and the number of domestic groups or institutional players that act to block compliance, the so-called "veto players" (Grabbe 2003; Kelley 2004; Schimmelfennig and Sedelmeier 2005, 12–17; Vachudova 2005). With regard to LGB people, the most directly relevant of the EU's norms, at least at the time of the first wave of enlargement to post-communist countries in 2004, was Directive 2000/78, which included sexual orientation among other banned discriminatory labor practices. All applicant countries were required to adopt Directive 2000/78 provisions in their labor code, often in the face of considerable domestic opposition (Bell 2001, 82).

The second Europeanization mechanism, social learning, describes a process whereby both applicant and member states are persuaded of the appropriateness of EU norms. This occurs, first, through the participation of national-level policy makers and other political elites in EU networks and, second, through the activity of transnational networks of domestic and European actors, who exert pressure on national governments and endorse European norms in the domestic political discourse. By fostering deliberation and by developing transnational networks that include domestic actors, European institutions can increase the perception of "norm ownership." Not only can this network serve as a channel for financial support, it helps legitimate these groups among otherwise indifferent domestic groups (Schimmelfennig and Sedelmeier 2005, 18). Unlike conditionality, the effectiveness of social learning does not drop off after an EU applicant becomes an EU member; in theory at least, social learning, which is a sociological process of norm persuasion, becomes more robust after accession because such norm-based change happens more slowly. The important point for the comparative analysis below is that both processes of Europeanization exert influence in the same direction, toward greater tolerance of and institutional protections for LGBT people. In theory, both mechanisms—which have been found to promote EU norms in areas ranging from ethnic minority policy to environmental regulation—have the potential to boost gay-rights advocates and their agendas in Eastern Europe, despite the obstacles of the communist legacy outlined above. The next section offers an overview of the empirical evidence, using the ILGA-Europe rights index as a yardstick.

The "EU Effect" in Practice: An Overview of the Region

As this section argues, there is compelling evidence that the EU has in fact improved legal frameworks regarding sexual orientation in postcommunist Europe. Countries that have recently acceded to the EU or that are currently in the process of application for membership have better legal frameworks for LGB people. In fact, some Polish activists I interviewed claimed that the whole of Poland's legal framework for LGB people, such as it is, is the result of EU pressure. This "EU effect" appears strong enough that it is evident even when we discount it by considering differences in the level of societal homophobia among postcommunist states. In this section, I also consider the impact of national religious differences, though this analysis is intended more as a suggestive caveat than a definitive statement. For both factors—the level of societal homophobia and national religious tradition—we would expect a strong relationship with the level of gay rights. For instance, highly homophobic societies will have weaker gay-rights frameworks. The following analysis shows, however, that both of these relationships are weak in postcommunist Europe—much weaker than in Western Europe. By implication, the pressures of accession largely account for why some postcommunist countries have better gay-rights frameworks than we would otherwise expect.

PROXIMITY TO EU ACCESSION

Taking a cue from the arguments about conditionality and social learning as means for diffusing EU norms, what does the ILGA-Europe index reveal about the effect of EU accession in a region whose communist legacy has proved so damaging to gay rights? To measure this impact, I have constructed my own index of "proximity to the EU." If the promise of membership is an effective lever for promoting EU norms of nondiscrimination, as external-incentives theorists argue, we should expect the greatest compliance among those countries closest to accession at the time the ILGA-Europe index was completed.[10] Following the social learning school's argument that, with increased exposure to and participation in EU policy networks, states are swayed by the EU's comparatively progressive stance toward LGB people, we should also expect better rights scores in postcommunist states that became members in 2004 or 2007.[11] To capture "proximity to the EU," I divide the postcommunist states in ILGA-Europe's index into four groups: EU members,[12] candidates and "potential candidates" for membership, participants in the so-called "European neighborhood policy" (ENP), and countries without formal arrangements for deeper integration of any kind. The candidates for membership—which include Croatia and the Former Yugoslav Republic of Macedonia—have all opened formal accession negotiations with the European Commission. Serbia, Montenegro, Bosnia and Herzegovina, and Albania constitute the "potential candidates" and, like Croatia and Macedonia, are working toward membership through the "Stabilization and Accession Process" (SAP). The European Neighborhood Policy (ENP) offers deeper integration without a commitment from the EU about future membership and encompasses Armenia, Azerbaijan, Georgia, Moldova, and Ukraine. With no such formal agreements with the EU, Russia and Belarus might be considered "permanent outsiders," states at the greatest remove from European integration of those in the ILGA-Europe rights index.[13]

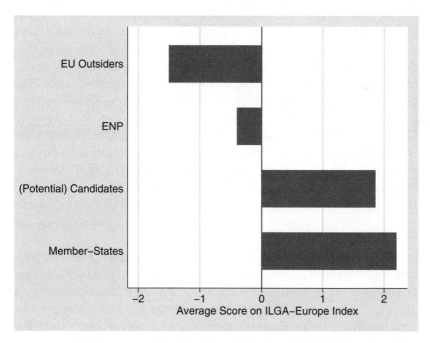

Figure 2. LGB Rights by Proximity to EU Accession in Postcommunist Europe

Figure 2 presents the results of this comparison, charting the average scores on ILGA-Europe's rights index according to the proximity of EU accession. Overall, these figures suggest that there is, in fact, a noticeable proximity effect. The largest differences are between countries that, on the one side, either recently became members or have reasonable prospects for becoming members in the future and, on the other side, those countries with unclear or no prospects of membership.[14] Interestingly, the difference in rights scores between actual and potential members is only 0.3 points.[15] Interpreting the absence of a proximity effect between members and potential members is difficult with these data. On the one hand, it could be evidence that there has been little backsliding on gay rights after accession. Alternately, it could also be seen as evidence that social learning after accession has been minimal at best. Adjudicating among these possibilities will require more nuanced data, and the case study of Poland that follows provides some suggestions.

Though this simple comparison indicates that the "EU effect" is real, a skeptic may, of course, suggest that generally better gay-rights frameworks in new EU members and potential members reflect deeper structural differences in this region. The possible candidates here are myriad, ranging from historical differences in socioeconomic development (Janos 2002) to political culture (Jowitt 1992). It may even be that the EU's own accession politics was influenced by these deeper structural differences. Capturing and controlling for these effects would require a more sophisticated statistical analysis than that offered here. Rather than exhaustively considering all the possible factors at play on gay rights in the region, my strategy is to focus on two obvious possible confounds, factors that either the conventional wisdom or common sense would suggest may be the "real" or deeper determinants of gay rights in postcommunist Europe, as opposed to EU accession and membership. The conventional wisdom would suggest that we consider religion; common sense would suggest that we consider society's general attitudes toward homosexuality. The next two subsections explore both of these in turn, asking, what happens to the "EU effect" when we consider these factors' separate impacts?

THE EU AND SOCIETAL HOMOPHOBIA

Societal homophobia is a gauge of deeper structural differences among postcommunist countries on the issue of gay rights. As mentioned earlier, I have in mind here the prevailing character of attitudes toward homosexuality in a given society, especially in comparison with other societies. Comparing the legal framework for gay rights among postcommunist countries with different levels of societal homophobia and at different removes from EU acces-

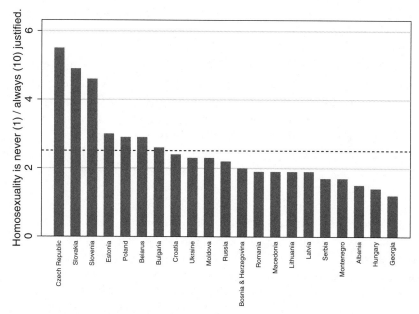

Figure 3. Postcommunist Country Scores on the World Values Survey Question "Homosexuality is never (1) / always (10) justified."
Note: The dashed line indicates the average score for the region.

sion allows a further test of the EU effect. As a starting assumption, I expect that more homophobic societies will have weaker legal frameworks for LGB people. If postcommunist countries with high levels of societal homophobia afford more rights to LGB people than one would expect, this anomaly is further evidence of an "EU effect." (On the other hand, of course, it is hard to draw firm conclusions about the role of the EU if postcommunist countries with low levels of societal homophobia also afford more gay rights.)

As a measure of societal homophobia, I use public opinion polling from the World Values Survey (WVS). The broadest available tool for comparing societal attitudes across countries, the WVS includes a question about tolerance that is a useful indicator of societal homophobia. It asks respondents to place themselves on the following 10-point scale: "Homosexuality is never (1) / always (10) justified."[16] As depicted in Figure 3, postcommunist countries show considerable, sometimes surprising, variation on this measure. Not surprisingly, the largely secular Czech Republic ranks the highest in the region. More surprisingly, the predominantly Catholic Slovak Republic also ranks as one of the most tolerant societies here. The largest surprises, however, come when comparing the data on societal tolerance with the ILGA-Europe LGB rights index, as we will see below.

Consider, for example, the case of Romania, which fares at the bottom of the region in terms of societal tolerance but matches the Czech Republic in terms of overall LGB rights. Moving for the moment beyond the scope of the ILGA-Europe index, it is instructive to consider the difference between the legal framework for antidiscrimination policy in the Czech Republic and Romania. Antidiscrimination policy is, notably, one of the chief pressure points that the European Commission has in the accession process. At a minimum, all applicant states are obliged to adopt into their national labor code EU directives preventing discrimination on the ground of sexual orientation. Romania—whose general EU-readiness was doubtful enough to delay its accession for two years and, moreover, whose reputation on gay rights was tainted by its criminalization of homosexuality up until 2000—went far beyond the minimum level of compliance in terms of antidiscrimination legislation. It adopted an antidiscrimination law banning discrimination on grounds of sexual orientation in all fields, not just the required field of employment. Moreover, it set up an independent state office to investigate and prosecute individual cases of discrimination, the National Council for Combating Discrimination, which commands considerable administrative resources. By contrast, the Czech Republic, a much stronger candidate for accession without a reputation for homophobic state policies, was much slower to enact antidiscrimination legislation, which in its final form hews more closely to the minimum for EU compliance.

Examples such as these are highly suggestive, but we can probe the relationship between homophobia and rights further by combining the above WVS polling data on societal attitudes with the ILGA-Europe index for 2010. To put the dynamics of the postcommunist region in broader perspective, Figure 4 plots the relationship between societal homophobia and LGB rights in both Western Europe and postcommunist Europe. The figure graphs the country scores on both measures and fits a line capturing the overall relationship suggested in each scatterplot.[17] The contrast is striking. Western Europe shows a clear pattern: the more homophobic the society, the weaker the legal framework for LGB rights.[18] By contrast, in postcommunist Europe this relationship is virtually nonexistent.[19] The absence of a relationship between societal homophobia and gay rights in postcommunist countries, despite considerable variation in rights across countries, suggests that something else—such as pressure from and the example of the EU—is driving some

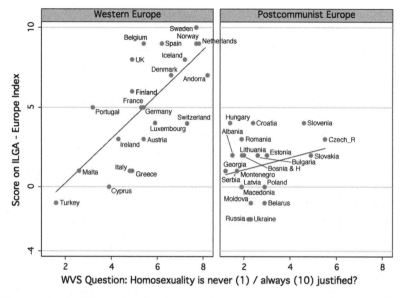

Figure 4. Societal Homophobia and LGB Rights in Postcommunist and West European Countries Compared

rather homophobic societies to adopt more rights than we would otherwise expect. The graph for the postcommunist countries illustrates this: Croatia, Romania, Hungary, and Bulgaria, all countries with high levels of societal homophobia, score as well on the rights index as much less homophobic societies, such as the Czech Republic and Slovenia. In sum, this broader regional analysis supports the intuition drawn from paired comparisons of antidiscrimination protections in countries of such different levels of societal tolerance as Romania and the Czech Republic. Without the prospect of EU membership, gay rights would be at an appreciably lower level in the region.

A CAVEAT ON RELIGION

One need only look at some of the more extreme instances of political homophobia in postcommunist Europe to find support for the proposition that national churches have often played a supporting role. In overwhelmingly Catholic Poland, top members of the Church hierarchy have condemned Pride marches as "demonstration[s] of sin" (Ramet 2006, p. 128), while less highly placed, but no less influential, priests such as Father Rydzyk have used religiously themed radio and television stations to agitate tirelessly against the "homosexual agenda." In Romania, a resurgent Orthodox church positioned itself as a staunch defender of that country's infamous Article 200 in the Penal Code, which criminalized homosexuality, and which was only abolished in 2000.[20]

Yet various examples suggest that the relationship between religion and homophobia is more complex than this. As others have argued, albeit in other contexts, the impact of the Catholic Church, a centralized and transnational organization, differs widely across countries, even where it constitutes the predominant religion and even on issues it deems fundamental (Connelly 2009). Consider Poland and Croatia, both strongly Catholic countries in which Catholicism and national identity overlap heavily. Croatia ranks at the top of the postcommunist world on ILGA-Europe's index (with a score of 4), while Poland scores a much lower 0. This comparison would actually seem to support the "EU effect" argument, as Croatia is not yet a member of the EU and, arguably, needs to do more to demonstrate its fitness for membership. As another striking anomaly, even a nominally Protestant and largely secular country like Latvia can rival the proudly Catholic Poland in the intensity of its antigay politics (O'Dwyer and Schwartz 2010). Finally, in the wider European context one finds apparent anomalies such as Spain,

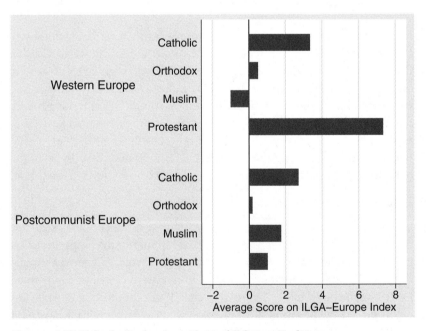

Figure 5. LGB Rights by Predominant National Religious Tradition

which, though predominantly Catholic, has not only registered partnerships but also same-sex marriage and adoption rights.

Thus examples abound suggesting that predominant national religion and gay rights are only weakly related, if at all. To get a sense of the broader relationship, Figure 5 classifies the countries in the ILGA-Europe index by their predominant religious tradition: Catholic, Protestant, Orthodox Christian, and Muslim.[21] Two important conclusions can be drawn from this figure. First, for Western Europe, there is a clear relationship between predominant religious tradition and gay rights. As one would expect, historically Protestant countries have markedly better rights frameworks than any other religious grouping. By contrast, in postcommunist Europe as a whole, the relationship between national religious tradition and LGB rights is quite weak: differences in gay rights are very small across religious traditions.[22] Second, in postcommunist Europe the character of the differences among religious traditions does not correspond with our expectations. Surprisingly, on average gay rights are more developed in Catholic countries than Protestant ones—and in Muslim countries than Orthodox ones. (In both cases, however, the number of the latter group is so small that it would be unwise to make too much of this difference.) No doubt, the weak effect of religious tradition on gay rights in the region in part reveals the legacy of communism—both its campaigns of secularization, which weakened the influence of national churches, and its persecution of homosexuality, which leads to uniformly lower rights for LGB people.

But at least part of religion's missing impact may again be due to the pressures of EU accession. If we look separately at the level of rights within postcommunist countries of the same predominant religion but at different removes from EU membership, here too we see evidence of an EU effect. Only the Orthodox category contains enough countries to make such a comparison meaningful, but among those countries, average scores on the ILGA-Index fall by at least one point for each degree of remove from EU membership. Thus there is some evidence that even the already small effect of predominant religious tradition can be weakened by the external leverage exercised in the process of EU accession.

A Case Study of Poland: Legal Stagnation, Political Mobilization

In the introduction to this chapter, I asked: "To the extent that the EU *does* have a demonstrable effect in promoting legal rights for gays, the second key question is: Does such rights promotion spark a homophobic backlash in the larger sphere of domestic politics?" I have shown that the incentive of EU membership does appear to have improved gay-rights frameworks in the difficult terrain of postcommunist Europe. Now I address the second question. Since, after a state enters the EU, the instrument of conditionality is greatly weakened, one might reasonably wonder about the durability of the "EU effect" over time. Absent the pressure to conform to EU norms in order to gain membership, a state could potentially backtrack on gay rights, especially if homosexuality remains an issue bound up in strong social taboos. Because the ILGA-Europe index does not capture the legal framework before accession, we cannot use it to assess such backsliding. A second blind spot of the index, and thus the comparative analysis above, is that by focusing only on the legal framework it may miss political change, especially homophobic political backlash. Of course, it may also miss improvements in the political situation of LGBT people that are not linked to *de jure* policy changes but to changes in the political discourse about homosexuality, mobilization by NGOs and social movements, and changes in public opinion.

In order to investigate the effect of EU accession on such shifts, this final section presents a brief study of gay-rights politics in Poland before and after EU accession, from the 1990s through 2011. In Poland, homosexuality has been and remains a controversial political issue, even by regional standards. In addition to the rights-dampening effects of its communist legacy, Poland of course has a politically active Catholic Church, which enjoys the mantle of defender of the nation under communism and before (Ramet 2006). As noted above, before gaining EU membership in 2004, Poland had to adjust to the legal requirements and expectations of the European Commission. Even with these adjustments, however, Poland as an EU member stands out for its comparatively poor LGB rights framework. In 2010, it scored a zero on ILGA-Europe's index, putting it at the same level as Latvia, Armenia, and Azerbaijan and just one point above Moldova and Belarus.

I would organize the Polish narrative into four parts. In the 1990s, the legal framework for LGBT people in Poland was very weak, and attempts to improve it proved futile. During this period, overt political homophobia was low, simply because homosexuality was not even on the radar politically. Around 2000, a shift occurred as the pressure of accession at last brought policy changes in the form of revisions to the labor code banning discrimination on the basis of sexual orientation—changes that brought new political attention to gay rights. The third act begins in 2004 with the finalization of Poland's EU membership and, immediately afterward, a sharp increase in political homophobia lasting through 2007. Since 2007, the legal framework appears to have stabilized, albeit at a low level, and militant political homophobia has ebbed. Surprisingly, in this last stage the political situation of LGBT people appears to have improved. There is an increasingly assertive, organized, and even influential gay-rights movement; moreover, in the domestic political discourse, the treatment of LGBT people has improved noticeably in the last few years. Thus the evidence is mixed; before attempting to draw any overall conclusions, I will first describe the different stages in the narrative in some more detail.

Gay rights were extremely undeveloped in Poland in the 1990s (Kliszczyński 2001, p. 166). Before the EU accession process began in earnest, the issue of antidiscrimination provisions covering sexual orientation arose just twice. The first episode occurred in 1992–94 in the discussions about the draft constitution (Kliszczyński 2001, p. 165). A handful of rights advocates argued for the inclusion of sexual orientation among the types of discrimination covered by the proposed Charter of Rights and Freedoms, whose draft form explicitly banned discrimination based on sex, race, nationality, ethnicity, and religion. The proposal appeared to have support, but then, in 1993, the government fell, and in the newly elected parliament that support disappeared. When the constitution was finally ratified in 1997, it made only a blanket, and largely toothless, protection against discrimination, stating that "nobody can be discriminated against in his or her political, social or economic life on whatever ground and for whatever reason."[23]

The issue became politically visible in the early 2000s, as Polish law underwent screening by the European Commission to ensure its fit with EU law. The Commission then determined that the constitution's protections were neither explicit nor strong enough, and it mandated changes to the labor code specifically. Despite strongly resisting the addition of provisions concerning discrimination on the basis of sexual orientation, the parliament eventually bowed to EU pressure and amended the labor code in 2002. While this legal change constituted undeniable progress, the highly public and controversial battle over the EU's intervention had two less positive repercussions: (1) it helped fuel a backlash of political homophobia from 2004 to 2007, and (2) it marked the end, in practical terms, of legal advances on gay rights until today.

Just a couple of months after joining the EU, Poland experienced a surge in political homophobia and rights retrenchment on a number of fronts. The most visible of these was the banning of Pride parades in Warsaw and several other major cities in 2004 and 2005, an infringement on the basic right of free speech. In 2005, parliamentary elections brought a euro-skeptic coalition of nationalists and populists to power, and homosexuality suddenly became a highly public and explosive issue. The new government consisted of the nationalist Law and Justice (PiS) party—one of whose leaders, Lech Kaczyński, had been responsible for the bans on Pride parades when he was mayor of Warsaw—and the even more nationalist and aggressively homophobic League of Polish Families (LPR).[24] Roman Giertych, leader of the LPR, was appointed education minister, from which position he declaimed repeatedly against the threat of "homosexual propaganda" in Polish schools. Giertych was also responsible for various violations of antidiscrimination policy in both form and spirit. In 2007, he fired the national director of teacher training for distributing a handbook on tolerance that included several paragraphs on homosexuality (Biedron and Abramowicz 2007). He also proposed legislation that threatened teachers who "promot[ed] homosexuality" with losing their jobs as well as with fines and even imprisonment (Biedron and Abramowicz 2007). Despite the outcry provoked by such actions, the PiS-led government ignored calls to remove Giertych as minister (Pankowski 2010, 182). This government also took an unprecedentedly conflictual tone with European institutions, most particularly on the issue of gay rights. When the European Parliament (EP) criticized Poland for homophobia, anti-Semitism, and xenophobia in June 2006, PiS sponsored a furious counter-resolution in the Polish *Sejm*, calling on the EP to safeguard "public morality." It stated further that even using terms like "homophobia" was "an imposition of the language of the homosexual political movement on Europe" and stood in conflict with "the whole of Europe's Judeo-Christian moral heritage" (quoted in Pankowski 2010, 189). The resolution passed with strong support.

The fourth, and ongoing, stage in Poland's gay-rights politics began with the collapse of the PiS-led government in 2007. Two trends are evident. First, Poland has not experienced more such flagrant violations of its legal commitments to LGBT people, though of course the absence of further legal backsliding should not be confused with progress. Second, overt political homophobia has fizzled. In the realm of social-movement mobilization and the political discourse, there are signs of improvement. As recently as the fall of 2011, the Polish gay-rights movement has even scored some stunning electoral successes. I will comment briefly on each of these developments.

The fall of the PiS-led government in 2007 ushered in another right-of-center government led by the Civic Platform (PO), a relatively new political party with a pro-EU stance and an emphasis on economic issues over cultural, identity-based ones. As respondents repeatedly emphasized to me in interviews conducted in Poland in 2009 and 2010, PO's strategy on gay rights is to avoid talking about them. In contrast to its predecessor, it has not sought to use this issue to mobilize socially conservative voters, but nor has it sought to be seen as sympathetic to gay rights, lest that alienate voters. The result is that, since taking office, the new government has not enacted any new legal rights for LGBT people. As can be seen from Poland's relatively poor showing on the ILGA-Europe rights index, the country still has a minimal framework in terms of antidiscrimination. There have been no serious attempts to expand antidiscrimination protections to other areas such as housing, education, health care, or goods and services. Such so-called "horizontal" nondiscrimination policy has been adopted by some other European countries, including, surprisingly perhaps, Romania. The PO government has also delayed redressing some of the manifest failings of its predecessor in implementing EU antidiscrimination policy. The implementation of extant labor-code provisions still was not fully compliant with EU legal standards as late as 2010, making Poland one of the last EU member states to be compliant in this area.[25]

At the risk of glossing over Poland's still-poor record regarding gay rights, I would argue, however, that the PO government marks a new stage in the overall arc of the Polish narrative. Actively antigay state policies are no more, and moving now to the second feature of the post-2007 chapter, there are clear signs that the *political* climate is shifting on this issue. The Polish gay-rights movement is increasingly better organized, and influential elements within the media and cultural sphere are becoming increasingly sympathetic. Space prevents a full discussion of these trends, but as an indication of the trend, I will give three examples since 2010.

First, during the summer of 2010 and under the leadership of the Polish NGO, the Equality Foundation, Polish gay-rights groups and NGOs from around the country organized the first Europride festival in Warsaw, the first such event in postcommunist Europe. While smaller than Europrides organized in Western European cities, this event was nonetheless a major logistical challenge bringing together activists, politicians, and participants from across Europe. Notably, the event went off without much political controversy, and more notably still, the largest Polish daily newspaper, *Gazeta Wyborcza*, gave the event extensive, even glowing, coverage for over a week. The second telling event from 2010 was the staging of an exhibition of homosexual-themed art entitled "Ars Homo Erotica" at the National Gallery in Warsaw, the country's central state-funded art gallery. The exhibit included overtly political art about the situation of LGBT people in Poland and the rest of the postcommunist region. Surprisingly, the event did not create a political controversy, despite its highly visible venue.[26]

Last, in Poland's most recent elections, in October 2011, three highly visible gay-rights advocates scored surprising electoral victories running as candidates of a newly established political party, the Palikot Movement (*Ruch Palikota*). Wanda Nowicka, a noted feminist and strong supporter of gay rights, was elected from Warsaw. Robert Biedroń, the longtime president of Poland's largest gay-rights NGO and political lobbying group, Campaign Against Homophobia, was elected from the Gdynia region. Most dramatically, the transgender candidate Anna Grodzka was elected from the notoriously conservative district of Cracow. Overall, the Palikot Movement won 10 percent of the vote, making it the third-biggest party in parliament. The success of this party, which loudly expressed its support for gay rights in the campaign, would seem to mark a sea change in Polish politics on this issue. Of course, social conservatives who oppose further rights are still very much present, but the discourse has changed, and rights activists are now *politically* represented in the debate.

Moreover, the elections underscored the organizational gains of the Polish gay-rights movement over the last decade. Since 2001, the year in which Biedroń's Campaign Against Homophobia was founded, a network of Polish gay-rights NGOs has been steadily increasing in density, organizing throughout—and seemingly even gaining focus from—the period of homophobic backlash of 2004–2007. These groups monitor discrimination, promote sex education, provide legal counsel, and lobby for civil partnership legislation. Some, like Campaign Against Homophobia, manage the seemingly impossible task—at least for NGOs in Eastern Europe—of maintaining full-time staff and a national network of branches. Poland still fares poorly in terms of legal rights, but the tide of political homophobia has turned, and all three developments indicate a new, far more tolerant, tone in Poland's public discourse about homosexuality.

Conclusion

In the end, this chapter offers hopeful answers to the two questions with which it began. First, despite having received its fair share of criticism, the EU's approach to fostering norms of minority rights and nondiscrimination appears to have improved gay-rights frameworks in postcommunist Europe. Second, the example of Poland suggests that fears of external pressure unleashing counterwaves of political homophobia and rights retrenchment may be overstated. While Poland *did* experience both a surge of political homophobia and some rights retrenchment after gaining EU membership, both phenomena proved temporary and, arguably, ultimately served to galvanize the Polish gay-rights movement, as its recent electoral victories attest. Of course, more comparative research is necessary before generalizing from Poland's experience, and, even there, time will tell whether the positive trend continues. Caveats aside, though, this analysis suggests that EU pressure can effectively counter homophobia. If we wanted to be critical, we might instead ask: Why has it not applied more pressure?

Notes

In addition to thanking Michael Bosia and Meredith Weiss for all their help and input, I gratefully acknowledge the feedback of David Cameron, Milada Vachudova, Ulrich Sedelmeier, and Michael Bernhard on an earlier version of this chapter.

1. The category "transgender" was essentially nonexistent under communism.

2. To avoid excessive use of acronyms throughout the paper, I will use "gay rights" to include rights for the umbrella grouping of lesbian, gay, bisexual, and transgender people. For much of the empirical analysis, my focus is limited to LGB people because my measure of rights, the 2010 ILGA-Europe index, does not include transgender people.

3. The 2010 ILGA-Europe rights index, which I use in the analysis here, did not include transgender people.

4. For a full description and the individual country scores, see http://www.ilga -europe.org/home/publications/reports_and_other_materials/rainbow_europe_map _and_country_index_may_2010.

5. The addition of transgender rights to the index in 2011 changed its scale, meaning that countries' 2010 and 2011 scores cannot be directly compared.

6. Again, the data are from http://www.ilga-europe.org/home/publications/reports _and_other_materials/rainbow_europe_map_and_country_index_may_2010.

7. A test of statistical significance reveals that we can be more than 99 percent sure that this difference is real, i.e., nonzero.

8. The difficulty of historically marginalized groups in mobilizing to demand rights after 1989 extends, for example, to the women's movement (Sperling 1999).

9. Europeanization is a broad concept, defined by one leading theorist to include "[p]rocesses of (a) construction, (b) diffusion, and (c) institutionalization of formal and informal rules, procedures, policy paradigms, styles, 'ways of doing things,' and shared beliefs and norms which are first defined and consolidated in the making of EU public policy and politics and then incorporated in the logic of domestic discourse, identities, political structures, and public policies" (Radaelli 2003, 30). Since measuring informal rules, styles, etc., is difficult to do across countries, much of the comparative literature focuses on legal and policy change; see, for example, Kelley (2004).

10. Whether one should expect a dropoff in compliance *after* accession is another question, especially in countries with strong societal-level homophobia. I consider this possibility in the case study of Poland.

11. Of course, the leverage of EU conditionality over these first postcommunist members would have been diluted by the time ILGA-Europe first constructed its index in 2010.

12. The postcommunist EU members include Estonia, Latvia, Lithuania, Poland, Czech Republic, Slovakia, Hungary, Slovenia—since 2004. Romania and Bulgaria became members in 2007.

13. I code Belarus as an outsider because, though potentially it is included in the "neighborhood," the ENP has not yet been "activated" since Belarus has not agreed to an Action Plan (http://ec.europa.eu/world/enp/policy_en.htm).

14. For the whole sample, we can reject with more than 99 percent confidence the null hypothesis that there is actually no difference among average rights scores of the different categories.

15. This difference is statistically insignificant even at the 90 percent confidence level.

16. In constructing Figures 3 and 4, I was able to use the WVS polls from 1999 to 2002 (Wave IV) for the majority of European countries. For five countries—Andorra, Cyprus, Georgia, Norway, and Switzerland—I had to use polls from 2005 to 2008 (Wave V). The WVS polling results are publicly available at http://www.worldvalues survey.org.

17. The fitted line is created using Ordinary Least Squares (OLS) regression.

18. The fitted line indicates that in Western Europe a 1 point increase in the WVS scale (i.e., increasing tolerance) translates into an approximately 1.5 point gain on the ILGA-Europe rights index (i.e., more rights). This sizable substantive effect is, moreover, highly statistically significant; as simple a model as it is, the bivariate regression explains about 55 percent of the variation in LGB rights.

19. Here, the fitted line indicates an only half-point increase in rights for each one-point rise in tolerance, and this effect is not statistically significant. Moreover, in postcommunist Europe, the bivariate model explains only 8 percent of the variation in rights.

20. See Buzogány (2008); Long (1999); Turcescu and Stan (2005).

21. My categorization of national religious tradition across Europe follows Norris and Inglehart's research (2004, 46–47). They divide the continent into Catholic, Protestant, Orthodox, and Islamic national religious cultures based on the plurality religion. For a discussion of their methodology and sources, see Norris and Inglehart, pp. 43–47.

22. The differences between the various religious traditions are statistically insignificant at the 95 percent confidence level.

23. Article 32.2 of the Polish Constitution (April 2, 1997).

24. The government contained a third party, the agrarian-populist Self-Defense (SO), but it was less concerned with homosexuality than its coalition partners.

25. The biggest problem of implementation under the PO government was the lack of legislation establishing an independent state office for antidiscrimination policy. While such noncompliance was less surprising under the PiS government, the PO government dragged its feet for several years, despite criticism by the European Commission. The Commission even initiated legal proceedings against Poland with the European Court of Justice, which could have led to financial sanctions.

26. Author's interview with the exhibition's curator, Paweł Leszkowicz, Warsaw, July 12, 2010.

Bibliography

Bell, M. 2001. "The European Union—a new source of rights for citizens in the accession countries?" In *Equality for Lesbians and Gay Men. A Relevant Issue in the EU Accession Process*, pp. 80–89. Brussels: ILGA-Europe.

Biedron, Robert, and Marta Abramowicz. 2007. "The Polish Educational System and the Promotion of Homophobia." In Marta Abramowicz, ed., *Situation of Bisexual and Homosexual Persons in Poland: 2005 and 2006 Report*, pp. 51–55. Warsaw: Campaign Against Homophobia and Lambda Warszawa.

Buzogány, Aron. 2008. "Joining Europe, Not Sodom: LGBT Rights and the Limits of Europeanization in Hungary and Romania." Paper presented at the National Convention of the American Association for the Advancement of Slavic Studies (AAASS), Philadelphia, PA, November 20–23.

Connelly, John. 2009. "Universal Church and National Body." Paper presented at the National Convention of the American Association for the Advancement of Slavic Studies (AAASS), Boston, MA, November 12–15.

Drabikowska, Agnieszka. 2010. "Marsz przeciwko homofobii. Radny PiS z kibolami" [March Against Homophobia: PiS City Councilor with Hooligans]. *Gazeta Wyborcza*, May 16.

Gruszczynska, Anna. 2006. "Living La Vida Internet: Some Notes on the Cyberization of the Polish LGBT Community." In Roman Kuhar and Judit Takács, eds., *Beyond the Pink Curtain: Everyday Life of LGBT People in Eastern Europe*, pp. 95–115. Ljubljana: Peace Institute.

Howard, Marc Morjé. 2003. *The Weakness of Civil Society in Post-Communist Europe.* New York: Cambridge University Press.

ILGA-Europe. 2010. "Rainbow Europe Map and Country Index." http://www.ilga -europe.org/europe/publications/reports_and_other_materials/ rainbow_europe _map_and_country_index_may_2010, accessed June 4, 2010.

Janos, Andrew. 2002. *East Central Europe in the Modern World: The Politics of the Borderlands from Pre- to Postcommunism.* Stanford, CA: Stanford University Press.

Jasiewicz, Krzysztof. 2008. "The New Populism in Poland: The Usual Suspects?" *Problems of Post-Communism* 55, no. 3: 7–25.

Jowitt, Ken. 1992. *New World Disorder: The Leninist Extinction.* Berkeley: University of California Press.

Kelley, Judith. 2004. *Ethnic Politics in Europe: The Power of Norms and Incentives.* Princeton, NJ: Princeton University Press.

Kliszczyński, Krzysztof. 2001. "A Child of a Young Democracy: The Polish Gay Movement, 1989–1999." In Helena Flam, ed., *Pink, Purple, Green: Women's, Religious, Environmental, and Gay/Lesbian Movements in Central Europe Today*, 161–68. Boulder, CO: East European Monographs.

Kochenov, Dimitry. 2007. "Democracy and Human Rights—Not for Gay People?: EU Eastern Enlargement and Its Impact on the Protections of the Rights of Sexual Minorities." *Texas Wesleyan Law Review* 13, no. 2: 459–95.

Leszkowicz, Paweł. 2010. *Ars Homo Erotica: Catalogue Accompanying the Exhibition "Ars Homo Erotica" at the National Museum in Warsaw.* Warsaw: CePed.

Long, Scott. 1999. "Gay and Lesbian Movements in Eastern Europe: Romania, Hungary, and the Czech Republic." In Barry Adam, Jan Willem Duyvendak, and André Krouwell, eds., *The Global Emergence of Gay and Lesbian Politics: National Imprints of a Worldwide Movement,* pp. 242–65. Philadelphia: Temple University Press.

Norris, Pippa, and Ronald Inglehart. 2004. *Sacred and Secular: Religion and Politics Worldwide.* New York: Cambridge University Press.

O'Dwyer, Conor. 2010. "From Conditionality to Persuasion? Europeanization and the Rights of Sexual Minorities in Postaccession Poland." *Journal of European Integration* 32, no. 3: 229–47.

——— and Katrina Z. S. Schwartz. 2010. "Minority Rights After EU Enlargement: A Comparison of Antigay Politics in Poland and Latvia." *Comparative European Politics* 8, no. 2: 220–43.

Ohlsen, I. 2009. "Non-Governmental Organizations in Poland Striving for Equality of Sexual Minorities: Differential Empowerment through the EU?" Master's thesis, Free University of Berlin/Humboldt.

Pacewicz, Piotr. 2010. "EuroPride, heterowstyd" [EuroPride, Hetero-shame]. *Gazeta Wyborcza,* July 19.

Pankowski, Rafal. 2010. *The Populist Radical Right in Poland: The Patriots.* London: Routledge.

Radaelli, Claudio. 2003. "The Europeanisation of Public Policy." In Kevin Featherstone and Claudio Radaelli, eds., *The Politics of Europeanization,* pp. 27–56. Oxford: Oxford University Press.

Ramet, Sabrina P. 2006. "Thy Will Be Done: The Catholic Church and Politics in Poland since 1989." In Timothy Byrnes and Peter Katzenstein, eds., *Religion in an Expanding Europe,* pp. 117–47. Cambridge: Cambridge University Press.

Schimmelfennig, Frank, and Ulrich Sedelmeier. 2005. "Introduction: Conceptualizing the Europeanization of Central and Eastern Europe." In Frank Schimmelfennig and Ulrich Sedelmeier, eds., *The Europeanization of Central and Eastern Europe,* pp. 1–28. Ithaca, NY: Cornell University Press.

Sperling, Valerie. 1999. *Organizing Women in Contemporary Russia: Engendering Transition.* Cambridge: Cambridge University Press.

Turcescu, Lucian, and Lavinia Stan. 2005. "Religion, Politics and Sexuality in Romania." *Europe–Asia Studies* 57, no. 2: 291–310.

6

Sexual Politics and Constitutional Reform in Ecuador

From Neoliberalism to the Buen Vivir

AMY LIND

In 2008, the Latin American and Caribbean Committee for the Defense of Women's Rights (CLADEM) released a report documenting violence against lesbian, bisexual, transsexual, transgender, and intersex women in Ecuador (Varea and Cordero 2008). Specifically, the report addresses the practice of reparative therapy in "rehabilitation centers" (*centros de rehabilitación*), where primarily women perceived as lesbian are forced to undergo various kinds of therapy, including electric shock therapy (Varea and Cordero 2008). The report demands the immediate closure of these centers, which aim to "dehomosexualize" lesbians. The authors state, "In these clinics physical and psychological punishment is practiced, including verbal humiliation, insults, permanent forced handcuffing, days without eating, whips, different forms of abuse and violence including sexual violence and the threat of rape" (CLADEM report, cited in Queiroz 2011: 1, my translation). According to the report, these centers have been operating for at least ten years and have forcibly interned hundreds of women perceived to be lesbian or to have gender dysphoria. Internees' treatment in the centers, the report states, is considered "torture" according to the Convention Against Torture, a convention that the Ecuadorian state has ratified and incorporated into its constitution. In 2007, there were approximately 205 such clinics in Ecuador, and only 55 of them appropriately reported to the two governmental bodies that oversee psychological treatment: the National Council for the Control of Narcotic and Psychotropic Substances (Consejo Nacional de Control de Sustancias Estupefacientes y Psicotrópicos, or CONSEP) and the Ministry of Health (Queiroz 2011). The report states that the Ecuadorian state is ultimately responsible for these actions, as it has been "inactive" in addressing the abuse and unresponsive to the very international agreements that it has ratified or supported.[1] It asks that the Ecuadorian state "investigate the complaints made regarding cases of torture and mistreatment of lesbian women in private clinics, and to apply the appropriate procedures and sanctions" (Varea and Cordero 2008: 7). It also asks for hate crimes based on sexual orientation and gender identity to be included in Ecuador's penal code. Interestingly, this practice has just recently, in the past decade, been made visible by activists and received regional and global attention. One recent study (Wilkinson 2012) suggests that the reparative therapy movement is more complex than initial human rights reports indicated, though it can be said that it is a "modern" phenomenon in that, with the historical shift in the mid- to late twentieth century toward emphasizing homosexuality as a disease versus as a crime, reparation-therapy proponents have further pushed for and institutionalized the practice, which disproportionately affects young women of middleclass or higher backgrounds in areas where psychological treatment is available.

Other forms of violence against lesbians occur as well that remain largely invisible in the literature on human-rights abuses against lesbian, gay, bisexual, transgender, transsexual, and intersexed (LGBTTI) people. Some stories are left untold, unpublished, and/or circulate primarily as rumor or as insider knowledge within specific communities. There is at least one account of two lesbian activists who were followed home after a public event and raped in their home by two men, likely for their activism and public personae as lesbians. The myriad ways in which trans people must negotiate transphobic institutions in order to access health care or sexual-reassignment surgery is another form of abuse that often remains invisible. Marcos and Cordero (2009) document the testimonies of several women who were forced to undergo psychiatric treatment, including at rehabilitation centers, because of their perceived identities. These forms of violence represent some of the ways in which violence is gendered and continues to be framed through a heteronormative lens, thus maintaining the centrality of the traditional, heterosexual family at the center of political, economic, and social life.

This chapter addresses the perpetuation of homophobia and transphobia as it is inherent in Ecuador's modernization project and as it has been politically contested in the context of neoliberal and post-neoliberal[2] governance during the 1990s and 2000s. Specifically, I analyze the 1998 and 2008 constitutional reforms as a discursive and institutional realm in which constitutional assembly members struggled to redefine the family and remake the nation. In 1998, Ecuador was the first country in the region to include an antidiscrimination clause on the basis of sexual orientation in its constitution. In

2008, an additional antidiscrimination clause on the basis of gender identity was added and the legal definition of "the family" was expanded to the new, socialist-inspired constitution. Given their progressive nature with regard to LGBTTI rights, these constitutions are often compared by political observers to post-apartheid South Africa's constitution and, more recently, to Bolivia's 2009 constitution. Given the general shift to the left in Latin America, which has occurred in two-thirds of the region, far outweighing any other region in the world in its resistance to global neoliberal capitalism, this case provides important insight into how both neoliberal and post-neoliberal forms of governance fare for LGBTTI people.

Throughout this chapter I argue that advances in LGBTTI rights legislation in Ecuador have occurred at the nexus of homophobic and homopositive discourses[3]: That is, they stem from sexual rights activism, yet also from discursive negotiations within the elected constitutional assemblies concerning homosexuality as a crime versus disease, as I outline below. Somewhat akin to homophobic mobilizations in Uganda (Kaoma, this volume), Namibia (Currier 2010), Southeast Asia (Weiss, this volume), and elsewhere, homosexuality and gender identity have become terrains of dispute for broader struggles concerning national sovereignty, westernization, and cultural modernity. While certain rights have been acquired for gays, lesbians, bisexuals, and transgendered people, new forms of homophobia and transphobia have emerged as well, often through and as a result of competing transnational discourses of sexual deviance and sexual modernization that have become articulated in complex and contradictory ways within national politics and social-movement responses to socialist-leaning President Rafael Correa's Citizen Revolution (2007–present). These contradictions emerge at the nexus of at least three interrelated phenomena: (1) The fact that homophobia and transphobia are not partisan issues; that is, both the neoliberal right and the post-neoliberal left have held antigay and anti-transgender views; (2) the increased presence of transnational religious networks in supporting antigay legislation in the country; and (3) the equally important increase in transnational networking among LGBTTI organizations, leading to new discursive and political imaginaries within Ecuador. Based on these phenomena, I argue that both homopositive and homophobic impulses are at work in the remaking of the post-neoliberal Ecuadorian state.

Before continuing, I wish to define the terms I use in this case study: First, by *homophobia*, I am referring primarily to its political deployment, "as an ideology and strategy individuals and groups use to police gender and sexuality." At the level of governance, homophobia is employed "for more than regulating gender and sexuality"; it is used as well to bolster masculinist control over the state apparatus (Currier 2010: 112). I view the political deployment of *transphobia* in a similar fashion, as an attempt not only to regulate gender-appropriate behavior and identities, but also as a way to invoke a heteronormative social order through explicit political rhetoric and, in this case, legal measures.

Homophobia and transphobia necessarily involve an understanding of heteronormativity, or the institutions, structures, and practices that help normalize dominant forms of heterosexuality as universal and morally righteous (Bedford 2011; Berlant and Warner 1998: 548). Regimes of heteronormativity, which help to regulate homosexuality and gender-appropriate behavior, have been central to, rather than secondary to, struggles concerning sovereignty, governance, and development in Ecuador. Homophobic and transphobic discourses operate alongside heteronormativity as well as racism and class inequality, an intersection emerging from Ecuador's colonial past. For example, the criminalization of homosexuality, and anti-prostitution and miscegenation laws all worked hand in hand to construct the ideal Ecuadorian citizen as of Spanish or *mestizo/a* origin, middle- to upper-class, urban, gender-appropriate, and heterosexual (Clark 2001; Prieto 2004).

As I argue in this chapter, the political deployment of homophobia and transphobia takes place in what I call the arena of sexual politics. By *sexual politics*, I am referring to the terrain in which contemporary actors struggle for the right to self-determination as sexual beings, freedom of sexual and gender expression, and the right to control one's own body. It includes but is not limited to the "rights, obligations, recognitions and respect around those most intimate spheres of life—who to live with, how to raise children, how to handle one's body, how to relate as a gendered being, how to be an erotic person" (Plummer 2001: 238; also see Cabral/Grinspan and Viturro 2006; Correa, Petchesky, and Parker 2008). This terrain thus extends far beyond the legal, formal, or public, and it includes political-cultural struggles over what constitutes citizenship and national belonging; how axes of personal/intimate life are structured, including along racial, class, gender, and geopolitical lines; and who "counts" as a citizen in the first place.[4] It also exemplifies how and why body politics (e.g., abortion, homosexuality) tend to take central place in national (and global) political discussions yet are simultaneously viewed as "private" issues.

Sexual politics often involve contestations over the developmentalist paradigm of (Western-style) gay and lesbian "liberation" as the primary model of sexual citizenship (Lind 2010). In this scenario, "sexual liberation" is linked primarily, if not exclusively, to sexual modernization, itself defined in terms of Western signifiers of visibility, rights, and empowerment. This narrative reinforces the idea that a nation's progress is defined by its level of citizen rights or sexual justice (Horn 2010). It also reinforces the notion that non-Western sexualities are "premodern" or "prepolitical" if they are not defined in Western terms (Cruz-Malavé and Manalansan 2002; Gosine 2005; Horn 2010). Yet as the introductory examples illustrate, and as lesbian and trans activists have pointed out, Western notions of progress and liberation—which are utilized by some local (i.e., "non-Western") activists as well—do not necessarily lead to sexual and gender justice for all. At the very least, the reality is much more complicated than these notions might indicate, as this study of Ecuador's constitutional reforms highlights.

Sexual politics, including both homophobic and homopositive discourses, are also contingent upon time and space—an idea noted as well in David A. B. Murray's 2009 anthology *Homophobias: Lust and Loathing across Time and Space*. Like elsewhere, the terrain upon which Ecuador's reforms have taken place involves spaces of social movements as well as those of state, religious, familial, community, and global governing institutions. It is also taking place in a historical moment when discourses of "homosexuality" and "gay rights" as well as of "global family values" are circulating across borders and within the realm of global governance (Buss and Herman 2003; Lind 2010). Social movements such as the feminist and LGBTTI movements have both worked to make the "private" public, and ultimately to challenge the many frameworks within which public/private boundaries are constructed and reinforced. Together, they constitute an important space of resistance that differs from the space of the assembly.[5] The spatialization of sexual politics, then, is important to note insofar as the outcome of rights-based claims depends upon where they are being proposed. In sum, then, the notion of "sexual politics" is informed by the transnational circulation of ideas and resources as they occur in a given time period (e.g., the globalization of a "family values" discourse beginning in the 1990s), and it encompasses a variety of spaces that help shape the specific forms that claims for legal and social recognition take in a formal arena such as a constitutional national assembly.

Finally, given Ecuador's colonial legacy as noted above, sexual politics are inherently racialized and classed from the start; one cannot discuss them without also accounting for how other categories of social recognition are understood in a given geopolitical, cultural, and legal context.[6] In the following sections I elaborate on the process of decriminalizing homosexuality in

Ecuador and remaking the nation through constitutional reforms, drawing out insights that are relevant to the points I outlined above.

Homophobia, Transphobia, and Sexual Politics before the 1998 Constitution

In 1997, Article 516, Ecuador's longstanding law criminalizing homosexuality, was repealed. This was an important victory in itself and set the stage for subsequent legal reforms. It also provided new opportunities for political organizing. Public debates that led to this repeal focused on a particular set of events that took place in Cuenca, Ecuador's third-largest city, which catalyzed a series of protests by the LGBTTI community and (for the first time at this scale) heterosexual supporters of LGBTTI rights. In June 1997, a Catholic group joined neighbors of Abanicos Bar, a gay and transgender bar, in complaining to police about what they viewed as "immoral conduct and weekend scandals." Police responded by raiding the bar and detaining up to fifty men who could not provide proper documentation.[7] These men were charged with intent to commit a crime against morality and released two days later; prior to their release, however, one of the men was raped by a jail guard, another was raped by an inmate as guards looked on, and a third was denied medical attention after experiencing a seizure. These events were publicized in the Ecuadorian media, and the Cuenca police force drew criticism from various social sectors. This prompted protests by local family members and friends, and later by individuals and groups in Guayaquil, Quito, and elsewhere in the country. The event marked a turning point in Ecuadorian history in the sense that heterosexuals began to publicly support the rights of gay men and cross-dressers who were arrested on false charges and violently attacked by state-sponsored jail employees. LGBTTI rights groups were then able to successfully push for the decriminalization of homosexuality during that same year (Saavedra 2001; Salgado 2004).

The decriminalization of homosexuality came about in a paradoxical way, however, as ultimately the argument used to mark Article 516's unconstitutionality was based on the argument that criminalizing homosexuality (with between four to eight years in prison) would simply lead (among other outcomes) to the "promotion of homosexual behavior in Ecuador's prisons" (Garbay 2003: 46–47, cited in Paez 2009: 77). In the ruling, language was used to discuss the "readjustment" ("*readaptación*") of homosexuals, and homosexuality was considered a type of "dysfunction" (Garbay 2003). Ironically, the Constitutional Tribunal that ruled unconstitutional Article 516 of Ecuador's constitution referred to the findings of the World Health Organization and the American Psychiatric Association regarding the depathologization of homosexuality as a mental-health disorder; this same tribunal used the above-mentioned homophobic logic and language to make its argument (Paez 2009; Salgado 2004, 2008).

Prior to this event, during the previous decade a small group of activists had worked hard to push for legal reforms and to educate the public on issues of LGBTTI rights. In the beginning, these individuals and their organizations developed coalitions with key social-movement actors from the feminist, Afro-Ecuadorian, and indigenous movements, in part by widening their representation in various public venues and decision-making processes. For example, in 1993, in the case of the feminist movement, speakers from all of these movements (indigenous leader Nina Pacari once spoke on one of these panels, alongside Orlando Montoya, a gay-rights and HIV/AIDS activist, and a representative of the Afro-Ecuadorian movement) participated on a panel on minority rights; the panel marked a clear shift from the primary focus on *mestiza*, middle-class interests represented by second-wave feminists. It was also one of the first times an "out" gay activist spoke openly at a public event. Efforts such as this one contributed in important ways to gradually changing public perceptions of gay men, lesbians, *travestis*, and transgendered people within the feminist movement, the local Quiteño culture, and nationally.

Following the Cuenca arrests, activists from a divergent set of organizations and loosely defined groups gathered signatures in support of repealing Article 516. The human-rights community, which traditionally had not addressed sexual rights, agreed with the call for an end to human-rights abuses of gay men and cross-dressers. The movement to repeal Article 516 had the historical momentum it needed, despite continuing homophobic impulses within legal and political sectors. These homophobic impulses as well as the new, more homopositive political environment shaped the context within which the constitution was redrafted in 1998.

Debates on Sexual Rights in the 1998 National Assembly[8]

Interestingly, the decriminalization of homosexuality was discursively framed both through homopositive and homophobic logics. How these logics acquire traction and meaning has depended in large part on the broader context of sexual, gender, ethnic, race, and class politics in the country, and on the broader political economy. Specifically, these changes occurred during so-

called second-wave neoliberalism; that is, during the region's second generation of neoliberal-inspired structural changes that have necessarily focused
more on the recognition of difference (e.g., affirmative-action policies and
laws) rather than on redistribution. This "second wave" stems from post-
Washington consensus ideologies that aimed to reintegrate social concerns
into market-led development, in contrast to the later attempt by the Correa-
led socialist state to move away from a neoliberal model altogether (Bergeron
2003; also see Ewig 2010).[9] The terrain of sexual politics has been made visible
largely through the struggles of the feminist movement and, more recently,
the LGBTTI movement.[10] Yet importantly, how sexuality has been legally
regulated and represented in public discourse also factors into how "sexual
orientation" became a visible and contested term in the assembly meetings. For
example, like elsewhere, LGBTTI activists have necessarily had to respond to
the historical and legal construction of sexuality as a "private issue" in order to
achieve recognition in the public realm of life. And they have necessarily had
to negotiate both homopositive and homophobic discourses of homosexuality as crime, disease, or form of liberation. The broader political-economic
context within which the constitutional reforms took place also figured into
how the language—and, ultimately, the constitution—unfolded. Throughout
the process, tensions existed between LGBTTI activists and feminist activists
(despite their shared interest in redefining the public/private split in law and
policy), and within these groups of activists as well, as they fought for inclusion in the assembly arena.

To begin, the National Assembly came into being following a particularly
turbulent year of politics. The severe political and economic crisis faced by
Ecuadorians in 1997–98 led to deep distrust in political and legal institutions
and for the state itself, as well as growing disdain for the neoliberal economic
policies that President Bucaram ultimately defended and upheld despite his
initial rhetoric to the contrary. Political groups had created monopolies of
representation, generating a crisis of representation in the congress itself
(Valladares 2003: 38). This situation caused numerous sectors of the state
and civil society to push for a national assembly, with the specific goal of
redrafting the constitution as a fundamental way to reconstruct failed political and legal institutions and develop a wider base of representation, a trend
already under way in other countries undergoing the second generation of
structural reforms that emphasized social rights in addition to market-led
development (e.g., Argentina, Bolivia, Brazil, Bolivia). During the period of
the interim government led by Alarcón, the National Assembly was ratified,
and in November 1997, seventy assembly members were designated who represented eleven political parties; among them, only seven were women, and

none of them had their roots in the women's movement (Valladares 2003: 39, 47). Within the National Assembly, two general ideological blocs, made up of party coalitions, developed quickly: a center-right bloc and a center-left bloc.[11] During the several-month-long process, assembly members heavily debated what should be included in the new constitution, with an eye toward stabilizing political, legal, and economic institutions and overcoming the crisis of representation. Throughout these discussions, rhetoric about "the family" as the foundation of the nation's citizenry stood out, and assembly members battled over how to define "the family" in relation to almost every realm of decision making: child and family welfare, protection of "vulnerable" groups (e.g., indigenous, Afro-Ecuadorian, female heads of household, children, women, gays, and lesbians), and the effects of broader economic and social policies and planning processes on Ecuadorian families and legally defined vulnerable communities or individuals.

Members of civil society and the state also participated in the assembly: in particular, representatives from the indigenous movement and the women's movement played key roles in the process; LGBTTI activists also actively participated, although in smaller numbers. They created working groups, designed proposals, and presented them to the assembly. Because of their ties to civil society, these representatives also received a lot of input from other individuals directly involved in struggles for the rights of LGBTTI people and other marginalized groups. Thus, importantly, civil society played a significant role in redrafting the new constitution, at least more so than in the "politics as usual" process in which only elected officials directly participate in decision making. Some of these participants played roles both in civil society and the state. For example, two feminist organizations, Coordinadora Política de las Mujeres Ecuatorianas and Foro Permanente de la Mujer Ecuatoriana, and the state women's agency, Consejo Nacional de la Mujer (CONAMU), jointly prepared a document with their proposals for constitutional change, *Nosotras en la Constitución: propuestas de las mujeres ecuatorianas a la Asamblea Constituyente* (*We Women in the Constitution: Ecuadorian Women's Proposals to the National Assembly*, CPME/FPME/CONAMU 1998). Several other women's organizations, including Movimiento de Mujeres de Guayaquil, Mujeres por la Democracia, Mujeres Luchando por la Vida, Coordinadora de Salud y Género, Frente Democrático de Mujeres, Movimiento de Mujeres de Pichincha, and women from political parties and other social movements, also participated in meetings with the three sponsoring groups to help draft the document. This document, which was sponsored by thirty-five assembly members, included several points about women's rights with no reference to sexual identity. Additional proposals from women's and feminist groups were also presented by members of the assembly. Some individuals and groups, such as the Colectivo Feministas por la Autonomía, explicitly chose not to be included in the proposal because in their view it did not go far enough in framing the issue of rights for all women (Cordero 2008; Rosero 2008). In the end, thirty-four out of the thirty-six proposals submitted by women were incorporated into the 1998 constitution.[12]

A significant discursive struggle took place within assembly meetings. For example, assembly observer Lola Valladares noted three sets of discourses that became visible in the meetings: discourses of motherhood, discourses of the family, and discourses of sexual and reproductive rights (Valladares 2003). Various commissions were established within the assembly to address topical issues. The commission named to analyze women's rights was called the Commission for Women, Children, and the Family (Comisión de la mujer, el niño y la familia, or Commission VII), automatically linking discussions of women's rights to those about child welfare and (presumably procreative) family health and well-being. Debates within the assembly regarding "the family" revolved in part around a proposal put forth by Commission I, which called for the following addition to the constitution: "The state shall recognize and protect distinct forms of nuclear families as household units with equal rights and opportunities of its members, with the aim of providing welfare, protection and mutual respect. It will support, in particular, minors and female heads of household." This proposal, stemming from the assembly's mission to redefine "vulnerable groups" in the constitution, led to a series of debates about how to define the family, much of which centered on whether the legal definition of the family should be expanded or whether the traditional model of a heterosexual two-parent household should be preserved. Some assembly members, for example, argued that including this language in the constitution would help "foment same-sex households," help "open the doors to same-sex marriage rights, and the freedom to adopt among homosexual couples," and therefore lead to the overall "degradation of the family."[13] In contrast, supporters argued that this proposal was not meant to "stimulate abnormal same-sex partnerships," but rather to support "households with integrity, above all those led by single women who have been expelled from the familial breast and are obligated to form a household without the complementary presence of a father." The language of this proposal was included in the final constitution, although as Valladares points out, it reinforces a heteronormative logic in that it legitimizes the nuclear heterosexual family while leaving unprotected other forms of kinship and domestic partnerships that are not constituted in state-sanctioned marriage or common-law marriage (*uniones de hecho*). It is only in the realm of marriage that "love, the exercise of sexuality, and reproduction are legitimate"; consequently, it is only through marriage that hereditary, conjugal, and other civil rights are legally defined (2003: 90).

Similar arguments were made by conservative assembly members during discussions concerning the inclusion of sexual orientation in the constitution's antidiscrimination clause. It was argued that, like expanding the definition of the family, protecting citizens on the basis of sexual orientation could lead to an increase in same-sex households, same-sex-parent adoptions, and the degradation of the heterosexual family. At least one assembly member linked HIV/AIDS to homosexuals, implying that gay men are the primary carriers and therefore culprits of the perceived epidemic in Ecuador (Valladares 2003: 142). Interestingly, however, some assembly members defended, and ultimately the majority supported, this clause. Indigenous leader, lawyer, and former minister of foreign relations Nina Pacari, for example, supported the proposal on the basis that all groups of people should be able to live free of discrimination. Others pointed out that historically, homosexuality has been treated as a crime according to Ecuadorian law and used as a justification for discrimination; still others cited the history of the pathologizing of homosexuality as a mental disorder as yet another way in which discrimination on this basis has been justified and condoned by a variety of societal institutions and actors.

It is important to note that the adoption of this language did not come about explicitly due to the presence of the women's movement in the assembly meetings. In fact, while the women's-movement representatives may have been sympathetic to including the language (and indeed, some of them are lesbians themselves), they did not centrally locate its importance in their documents, including in the most widely supported document, *Nosotras en la Constitución*. This caused some fallout between groups such as the Autonomous Feminists Collective, who fought for a broader definition of "women" in the language of the constitution, versus those who sought a more reformist (and, arguably, more likely to be approved) agenda that fell within the range of normative familial arrangements; that is, within the heteronormative social order.

The 2008 Constitution

Rafael Correa was elected into office in 2007 with the goal of once again revising Ecuador's constitution, this time with redistribution, and not just recognition, in mind. Specifically, he and his coalition government aimed to reprioritize the country's economic-development goals, from that of neoliberalism to that of state-led (and World Bank–free) development, and to implement the government's "citizen revolution," which focused on redistributive mechanisms that would reach historically marginalized sectors. His economic-development reforms were based on the idea of the *sumac kawsay* ("living well" in Quichua, also known as the *buen vivir* in Spanish), a notion of sustainable living that surpasses and puts into question traditional economic indicators of well-being found in Western, neoliberal development models. This notion of *sumac kawsay* or *buen vivir*, now common parlance in national political discourse, informed his constitutional strategy as well. One of the first measures initiated by his government was a referendum calling for a National Constitutional Assembly. Before the assembly began its work, civil society was invited to submit proposals. A committee of jurists representing the university community and the Ecuadorian government developed the contents submitted by nongovernmental organizations and interest groups (Marcos and Cordero 2009). Several LGBTTI groups submitted proposals that ranged broadly in theme and purpose; for example, some supported same-sex marriage, others, in contrast, were critical of that approach and supported redefining the family and marriage altogether (Vásquez 2008). The new constitution was passed in October 2008, replacing the 1998 constitution. The overall framework of the new Ecuadorean Political Constitution defines the state as "constitutional, rights and justice-based, social, democratic, sovereign, independent, unitary, intercultural, plurinational and secular." Following the principle of *sumac kawsay*, it is based on respect for sovereignty and self-determination in terms of "economy, political life, finances, food, culture, and environment" (Marcos and Cordero 2009: 3). Positive changes were made with respect to sexual and gender rights: Article 11.2 of the 2008 constitution now includes an antidiscrimination clause on the basis of gender identity as well as sexual orientation.[14] New hate-crime language is included in the constitution, and, although it does not make reference to specific groups based on social recognition, it has the potential to be used in cases of human-rights abuses and other forms of harassment against LGBTTI individuals (e.g., in the workplace).[15] In addition, the legal definition of "the family" was revised in sections of the constitution, specifically by changing the definition from one based on blood kinship to one based on other social factors such as household composition or living arrangement (Vásquez 2008). This opened multiple possibilities for the extension of state benefits and legal protections (including domestic partnerships) to non-normative families, including same-sex households but also migrant, transnational, communal, and other non-normative forms of kinship. In theory, individuals or couples could potentially draw from traditional common-law marriage laws to expand that form of legal recognition to same-sex couples; this, however, would need to be challenged in court and would occur in the midst of a political environment fraught with homophobic impulses as well.

Interestingly, although the definition of "the family" was expanded in the 2008 constitution, the Religious Right was able to coalesce within the assembly and successfully block same-sex marriage in the new constitution. A few key issues emerged during the referendum campaign as the most visible points of contention, including the right to decide on one's body, the right to abortion, and the right to same-sex unions (Marcos and Cordero 2009; Romo 2008; Rosero 2008; Vásquez 2008). A self-proclaimed observant Catholic, from the beginning of his term President Correa stated his position against the recognition of these rights. Alliances between lesbian-feminist and trans activists were key, however, for advancing their claims before the assembly. Their demands included: (1) a system for protection against discrimination; (2) a more detailed and progressive definition of sexual and reproductive rights, as compared to their description in the 1998 constitution; (3) recognition of alternative families and gender-neutral definition of de facto unions; (4) the inclusion of one article in the section on the right to life that will allow decriminalization of abortion in secondary legislation; (5) punishment for hate crimes based on gender and sexual diversity; (6) collective rights' entitlement and enforceable nature; (7) wide protections; (8) a nonpartisan Constitutional Court; and (9) secular ethics as interpretative principle for the law (Vásquez 2008; also see Marcos and Cordero 2009).

Of these demands, the recognition of alternative families did take place to some degree, as language addressing migrant/transnational families and families not based on kinship or blood was incorporated into some sections of the constitution. And likewise, gender identity was added to Article 11.2. Yet the decriminalization of abortion remained untouched, as did the (heteronormative) institution of marriage.

These demands were widely publicized during the campaign leading up to the referendum vote on the proposed constitution as well: In street pamphlets, on television and radio, and in public forums, both sides of the referendum (the vote for the "sí" and the vote for the "no") heavily campaigned throughout the country to gain support. At the time, only one known documented gay male–led gay-rights organization actually supported same-sex marriage (most lesbian and trans groups did not view this as their key strategic issue), an issue that they hardly publicized. Somewhat ironically, it was the "no" supporters, backed by a Religious Right supported in part ideologically and financially by non-Ecuadorian organizations (i.e., by transnational religious networks—see also chapters by Bosia, Kaoma, and Weiss, this volume), that publicly argued that voting "yes" for the proposed constitution would result in same-sex marriage and the "decay of Ecuadorian family values," as pamphlets distributed at that time claimed. Thus despite the fact that LGBTTI activists did not, for the most part, even mention the institution of marriage, it became a hotbed issue during the campaign—thanks in part to the transnational circulation of ideas about "family values," homosexuality, and same-sex marriage. What "sí" supporters did support was the "recognition of the rights of sexual minorities and other groups in situations of vulnerability." This phrase was found on pamphlets supporting the proposed constitution, alongside phrases such as "the right to live one's sexuality in a free, responsible and informed way, including being informed about one's reproductive health" (Unidad por el Sí 2008). In a country where homosexuality was publicly discussed at a national level beginning only in the late 1990s, these demands likely came across as "foreign," particularly in rural areas. Ironically, the push against same-sex marriage, based on homophobic impulses, was at least as "imported" as any other idea, be it positive or negative, about homosexuality.

Toward a Queer *Buen Vivir*? Assessing the Impacts of the 1998 and 2008 Constitutions

As human-rights activists in Ecuador have noted, and despite positive legal changes stemming from the 1998 and 2008 constitutions, the abuse of lesbians, gay men, and trans people continues to occur in Ecuador. And generally speaking, the Correa administration's agenda clearly promotes a heteronormative social and economic order. Following the passage of the 2008 constitution, President Correa dismantled the National Women's Council (CONAMU), which had been in existence since 1998, and which was built upon earlier institutional versions of a state women's agency dating back to 1980. Based on Articles 156 and 157 of the constitution, his aim was to "transition" the agency into a general council that addressed all forms of inequality. While a Transition Commission was set up in 2009 and continues to exist, to date a permanent council with a clear budget and purpose has not yet been established. Thus there is no state agency that oversees women's issues per se, leaving a wide institutional gap with regard to gender-equity policies, laws, and education, and an absence of mechanisms to address issues concerning sexual orientation and sexual identity as defined by law.

To some extent, the new constitution opened the possibility for new subjectivities to be imagined, including in a homopositive sense. It gave new legal protections and citizen rights to people on the basis of gender identity and included language concerning sexual orientation and sexual identity in the revised penal code. Furthermore, it expanded the definition of the family. These reforms built upon the earlier successes of the LGBTTI and feminist movements—most notably the decriminalization of homosexuality and the antidiscrimination clause included in the 1998 constitution. They also built upon the thirty-four proposals incorporated into the 1998 constitution from women's and feminist groups, which extended rights and benefits to women.

Yet interestingly, some of these achievements occurred through a strange mix of homopositive and homophobic logic. The gender-identity antidiscrimination clause, for example, extends protections to transsexual and transgender individuals, yet the overall constitution frames gender in a normative fashion, thereby reinforcing state paternalism vis-à-vis women, the patriarchal family, and dualistic gender roles. Valladares's examination of women's rights in the 1998 constitution concludes that women are viewed in an apologetic way: "In almost all of the discourses, including those of men as much as those of women assembly members, the recurring themes include the need to recognize women's rights in the context of the nuclear heterosexual family; the control of female sexuality; private space as the legitimate feminine space; . . . [and the representation of] women as victims, vulnerable, marginalized, wounded, hurt, such that they can only be subjects of rights under a conception of tutelage and protection" (Valladares 2003: 146).

Likewise, both the decriminalization of homosexuality in 1997 and the newly introduced antidiscrimination clauses were agreed upon by the majority in part due to an inherently homophobic argument. As noted above, these forms of legislation were passed because even homophobic jurists or assembly members viewed the brutal violence, torture, and rape of gay men or *travestis* as unwarranted, uncivilized, and therefore unacceptable. The argument for decriminalization rested in part upon the idea that homosexuality might dangerously be displayed in and spread through prisons if homosexuals were imprisoned; their identity was seen as a "dysfunction." Likewise, assembly members successfully argued that homosexuality was a mental-health issue, not a crime, thereby allowing for the antidiscrimination clause to pass in 1998. That is, a discursive and institutional shift took place with regard to framing homosexuality: Whereas historically it was viewed as a crime, now it was argued that public interventions should be left to mental-health professionals, not the criminal-justice system, thereby legitimizing support for the measures on behalf of antigay legislators who represented all sides of the political-ideological spectrum (Cordero 2008; Paez 2009; Salgado 2004 and 2008).

Fortunately, despite these paradoxes, the bottom line is that legal change brings about new political opportunities. What remains to be seen is how the 2008 constitution will actually be implemented, and how the Ecuadorian state will address the demands of LGBTTI activists. So far, the Correa administration has shown positive signs of addressing what has now become a major public-relations issue for the state, the reparative therapy centers: Indeed, as the news traveled across borders and was disseminated among global institutions and transnational networks, the Correa administration was pressured to address the issue at home. The CLADEM-sponsored report and additional reports filed by the Quito-based organization Taller de Comunicación Mujer were first presented to the Organization of American States (OAS) and also during the first round of Ecuador's Universal Periodic Review by the United Nations. Since the publication of these reports, additional social and political organizations have publicly demanded that the Ecuadorian state investigate the practices of rehabilitation centers. In response, in August 2011 the Correa administration closed down twenty-seven clinics that were offering to "cure" homosexuality. While over two hundred such centers still exist, this was the first acknowledgement by the state that this practice was potentially unjust or illegal. At the time, Ecuadorian activists were able to draw from the transnational, region-wide "Cures that Kill" campaign (Curas que Matan), which has focused precisely on ending illegal practices of reparative therapy. Activists utilized their social networks as well: In November 2011, a change .org petition in English and Spanish was circulated worldwide; by December 2011 it had received over 113,000 signatures (Fundación Causana 2011). In January 2012, Correa appointed a lesbian activist and outspoken opponent of reparative-therapy centers, Carina Vance, as the new health minister in Ecuador. The former executive director of Fundación Causana, one of the three organizations that has worked most visibly to demand that the state investigate the reparative-therapy centers, Vance has already declared in her new position that she will follow through on the promise to investigate these centers and end the unjust treatment of LGBTTI individuals. The context in which this occurred—in which Correa himself, who has publicly opposed homosexuality, appoints an "out" lesbian to a ministerial position—can be understood only through the messy logic of homophobia and homopositivity that characterizes sexual politics in Ecuador.

One issue that remains clear is that homophobia is not a partisan issue; LGBTTI people have been demonized by both the right and the left, historically speaking and in the current context. Natalia Marcos and Tatiana Cordero make use of post-neoliberal political discourse precisely to point out that not everyone "lives well" in the country: "[D]iscrimination, abuse and torture against lesbian and trans women continue, affecting their *buen vivir*" (2009: 5). In Ecuador, initial reforms related to sexual orientation occurred in a neoliberal context. The long history of feminism and the left is ridden with conflict and contradiction, and in the current New Left context women's rights continue to be framed largely in a paternalistic, heteronormative way, much like earlier generations of socialism (and capitalism, including the 1980+ neoliberal period). Like previous neoliberal governments, the Correa administration has yet to fully address or legally protect people on the basis of sexual orientation and gender identity; LGBTTI people's *buen vivir* is not yet clearly accounted for in the new redistributive agenda. President Correa may be "beholden to the agendas of national political forces and/or international institutions" (Friedman 2007: 16) or simply to his own "Christian socialist" beliefs, similar to other New Left governments such as that of former Sandinista Daniel Ortega in Nicaragua, who, religiously "reborn" since his era as a Sandinista leader, imposed some of the strictest anti-abortion legislation in the region upon his elected reentry into office in 2007, and Venezuelan Hugo Chávez, who did not allow for new legal protections for LGBTTI individuals during his time in office from 1999 to 2013. In this regard, I would argue that the set of reforms I analyze in this chapter, while framed through both homopositive and homophobic discourse, provided recognition to historically marginalized groups of people, a form of legal recognition greatly needed in order for them to potentially benefit from economic redistribution and sexual politics in the post-neoliberal order.

Notes

1. For example, the Beijing Declaration and Platform for Action recognizes that women have the right to control and decide freely their sexuality, without being submitted to coercion, discrimination, or violence. The CLADEM report argues that the Ecuadorian state is not acknowledging its own adherence to that declaration. In addition, the report asks the Ecuadorian state to consider their findings as part of the state's compliance with the Convention on the Elimination of All Forms of Discrimination Against Women, or CEDAW.

2. By "post-neoliberal," I am not implying that neoliberal policies no longer exist, but rather that they have lost their "quasi-hegemonic position," as new forms

of collective action and articulations of economic and social policy have gained salience (Fernandes 2007; Grimson and Kessler 2005).

3. Here I am drawing from Meredith Weiss's definition of *homopositivity* as "the acceptance of 'queer' people and practices, not necessarily per western binaries" (see Weiss, this volume).

4. For debates on sexual citizenship in Latin America, see for example Cabral/ Grinspin and Viturro 2006; Sardá 2007; Lind and Argüello 2009; de la Dehesa 2010; Viteri, Serrano Amaya, and Vidal Ortiz 2011.

5. Whereas social movements operate largely (although certainly not entirely) from the space of civil society, a space characterized by low levels of funding and grassroots (local and transnational) networks, the space of the National Assembly is comprised of assembly members and constitutes a formal political arena; an arena also influenced in myriad ways by institutions of global governance such as the United Nations, World Bank, and multinational corporations.

6. This certainly applies as much to the North as to the South.

7. There are conflicting reports on how many individuals were actually arrested. One report claims that fourteen individuals were arrested out of the fifty who were originally detained (Amnesty International 2002, 2005).

8. Portions of this section were published in Lind 2012.

9. By "post-Washington consensus," I am referring to the shift within the World Bank and other governing institutions from a pure neoliberal (i.e., free market) model of development to one "aimed at integrating economic and social dimensions of development, paying attention to broader goals such as sustainability, and challenging the old state versus market dichotomy" (Bergeron 2003: 397).

10. Here I am broadly defining *movement* to include an array of actors and organizations that do not necessarily work together cohesively. Rather, I view social movements as a contested terrain and field of action composed of various actors, institutions, strategies, and visions for social change that involve overlapping or shared ideas about what needs to be transformed or addressed (Alvarez et al. 1998).

11. The center-right bloc consisted of Democracia Popular, Partido Social Cristiano, Frente Radical Alfarista, and Partido Liberal Ecuatoriano; the center-left bloc consisted of Izquierda Democrática, Movimiento Popular Democrático, Partido Roldocista Ecuatoriano, and Movimiento Pachakutik-Ciudadanos Nuevo País.

12. These proposals included the rights to personal integrity and to a life free from violence; to equality before the law and to nondiscrimination; to equitable participation of women and men in the popular election process, in management and decision-making in public spaces, in the justice system, in controlling bodies, and in political parties; the right to make free and responsible decisions in one's sexual and reproductive life; to equality and mutual responsibility in the family and support for women heads of household; to nondiscriminatory education that promotes gender equity; to coeducation; and the state obligation to implement public policies and create a national machinery to advance women's equality (Marcos and Cordero 2009: 3).

13. Assembly members Ricardo Noboa (formerly of the right-wing Partido Social Cristiano) and Marcelo Santos (Partido Social Cristiano) made these arguments (Valladares 2003: 88).

14. Article 11.2 of the constitution states that "All persons are equal and will enjoy the same rights, duties and opportunities. Nobody can be discriminated against on the basis of her or his ethnicity, birthplace, age, sex, *gender identity*, cultural identity, marital status, language, religion, ideology, political affiliation, judicial records, socio-economic status, migratory status, *sexual orientation*, health status, HIV status, disability, physical difference, or any other personal or collective, temporary or permanent distinction, that aims at or results in a detriment or nullification of the recognition, enjoyment or exercise of rights. The law will punish all forms of discrimination. The State will adopt affirmative-action measures to promote substantive equality in favor of those right bearers that are placed in an unequal situation" (emphasis added).

15. The penal-code amendments include the revisions of Article 212.4 and 212.6. Article 212.4 reads as follows: "Whoever incites to hatred, disdain, or any form of psychological or physical violence against one or more persons on the basis of their skin color, race, sex, religion, national or ethnic origin, *sexual orientation or sexual identity*, age, marital status, or disability, in public or through any channel suitable for public circulation, will be punished with six months to three years of prison. If any person is harmed (as a result), the penalty will be increased to two to five years of prison, and to twelve to sixteen if the outcome of those violent acts would be the death of a person" (emphasis added; English translation found in Marcos and Cordero 2009: 4). Article 212.6 extends this same type of protection to the workplace.

Bibliography

Alvarez, Sonia E., Evelina Dagnino, and Arturo Escobar. 1998. "Introduction: The Cultural and the Political in Latin American Social Movements." In Sonia E. Alvarez, Evelina Dagnino, and Arturo Escobar, eds., *Cultures of Politics/Politics of Cultures: Re-visioning Latin American Social Movements*, pp. 1–32. Boulder, CO: Westview Press.

Amnesty International. 2002. "Ecuador: Pride and Prejudice." Amnesty International Report, March.

Amnesty International. 2005. "Ecuador: Continued Torture and Ill-Treatment of Lesbian, Gay, Bisexual and Transgender People." Available online at: http://web.amnesty.org/report2005/ecu-summary-eng.

Asamblea Constituyente. 2008. *Constitución de la República del Ecuador 2008*. Quito, Ecuador.

Bedford, Kate. 2011. *Developing Partnerships: Gender, Sexuality and the Reformed World Bank*. Minneapolis: University of Minnesota Press.

Bergeron, Suzanne. 2003. "The Post-Washington Consensus and Economic Representations of Women in Development at the World Bank." *International Feminist Journal of Politics* 5, no. 3: 397–419.

Berlant, Lauren, and Michael Warner. 1998. "Sex in Public." *Critical Inquiry* 24, no. 2: 547–66.

Buss, Doris, and Didi Herman. 2003. *Globalizing Family Values: The Christian Right in International Politics.* Minneapolis: University of Minnesota Press.

Cabral, Mauro (A. I. Grinspan), and Paula Viturro. 2006. "(Trans)Sexual Citizenship in Contemporary Argentina." In Paisley Currah, Richard M. Juang, and Shannon Price Minter, eds., *Transgender Rights*, pp. 262–73. Minneapolis: University of Minnesota Press.

Clark, Kim. 2001. "Género, raza y nación: La protección a la infancia en el Ecuador (1910–1945)." In Gioconda Herrera, ed., *Estudios de género*, pp. 183–210. Quito: FLACSO/ILDIS.

CPME (Coordinadora Política de las Mujeres Ecuatorianas) / FPME (Foro Permanente de la Mujer Ecuatoriana)/CONAMU (Consejo Nacional de las Mujeres). 1998. *Nosotras en la Constitución: propuestas de las mujeres ecuatorianas a la Asamblea Constituyente.* Quito: CPME/FPME/CONAMU.

Cordero, Tatiana. 2008. Lawyer and co-founder, Taller de Comunicación Mujer, personal interview, Quito, Ecuador, August 19.

Correa, Sonia, Rosalind Petchesky, and Richard Parker. 2008. *Sexuality, Health and Human Rights.* New York: Routledge.

Cruz-Malavé, Arnaldo, and Martin Manalansan, eds. 2002. *Queer Globalizations: Citizenship and the Afterlife of Colonialism.* New York: New York University Press.

Currier, Ashley. 2010. "Political Homophobia in Postcolonial Namibia," *Gender & Society* 24, no. 1: 110–29.

De la Dehesa, Rafael. 2010. *Queering the Public Sphere in Mexico and Brazil: Sexual Rights Movements in Emerging Democracies.* Durham, NC: Duke University Press.

Ewig, Christina. 2010. *Second Wave Neoliberalism: Gender, Race, and Health Sector Reform in Peru.* University Park: Penn State University Press.

Fernandes, Sujatha. 2007. "Everyday Wars of Position: Media, Social Movements, and the State in Chávez's Venezuela." Paper presented at the Annual Meetings of the Latin American Studies Association, Montréal, Canada.

Friedman, Elisabeth. 2007. Introduction to special issue "How Pink Is the Pink Tide? Feminist and LGBT Activists Challenge the Left." *NACLA Report on the Americas* 40, no. 2: 16.

Fundación Causana. 2011. "Ecuador Minister of Health: Close Remaining Ex-Gay Torture Clinics in Ecuador." Change.org petition, November 17. Available online at http://www.change.org/petitions/ecuador-minister-of-health-close-remaining-ex -gay-torture-clinics-in-ecuador?alert_id=CTiffEcuvq_PnJXCkMxfc. Accessed January 12, 2012.

Garbay Mancheno, Susy. 2003. "Algunas reflexiones sobre los derechos sexuales y la ciudadanía de las mujeres lesbianas." In Patricio Brabomalo, ed., *Experiencias del orgullo lésbico-gay, Ecuador 2002–2003*, pp. 43–50. Quito: Fundación Causana.

Gosine, Andil. 2005. "Sex for Pleasure, Rights to Participation, and Alternatives to AIDS: Placing Sexual Minorities and/or Dissidents in Development." IDS Working Paper 228, Institute for Development Studies, Brighton, England, February.

Grimson, Alejandro, and Gabriel Kessler. 2005. *On Argentina and the Southern Cone: Neoliberalism and National Imaginations*. New York: Routledge.

Horn, Maja. 2010. "Queer Dominican Moves: In the Interstices of Colonial Legacies and Global Impulses." In Amy Lind, ed., *Development, Sexual Rights and Global Governance*, pp. 169–81. New York: Routledge.

Lind, Amy. 2010. "Introduction: Development, Global Governance, and Sexual Subjectivities." In Amy Lind, ed., *Development, Sexual Rights and Global Governance*, pp. 1–20. London: Routledge.

———. 2012. "'Revolution with a Woman's Face?' Family Norms, Constitutional Reform, and the Politics of Redistribution in Post-Neoliberal Ecuador." *Rethinking Marxism* 24, no. 4: 536–55.

——— and Sofía Argüello, eds. 2009. "Ciudadanías y sexualidades en América Latina." Introduction to special issue on citizenship and sexualities in Latin America, *Íconos: Revista de ciencias sociales* 13, no. 3: 13–18. [Quito: FLACSO].

Marcos, Natalia, and Tatiana Cordero. 2009. "Situation of Lesbian and Trans Women in Ecuador." Shadow report, International Covenant on Civil and Political Rights. Quito: Taller de Comunicación Mujer/Global Rights/IGLHRC.

Murray, David A. B., ed. 2009. *Homophobias: Lust and Loathing Across Time and Space*. Durham, NC: Duke University Press.

Paez, Carolina. 2009. *Travestismo urbano: género, sexualidad y política*. Master's thesis, Quito: FLACSO.

Plummer, Ken. 2001. "The Square of Intimate Citizenship: Some Preliminary Proposals." *Citizenship Studies* 5, no. 3: 237–53.

Prieto, Mercedes. 2004. *Liberalismo y temor: imaginando los sujetos indígenas en el Ecuador postcolonial, 1895–1950*. Quito: Abya-Yala.

Queiroz, Camila. 2011. "Carta de acción de solidaridad contra las clínicas de rehabilitación: Comité denuncia actuación de clínicas anti-homosexualidad en el país." *Adital*, September 28. Available online at http://desafiandomitos.blogspot.com. Accessed October 13, 2011.

Romo, Maria Paula. 2008. 2008 Constitutional Assembly member, personal interview, Quito, Ecuador. August 22.

Rosero, Rocío. 2008. Former CONAMU director and assistant to 2008 Constitutional Assembly member, personal interview, Quito, Ecuador. August 20.

Saavedra, Luis Ángel. 2001. "Gays Harassed." *Latin American Press*, October 18.

Salgado, Judith. 2004. "Análisis de la intrepretación de inconstitucionalidad de la penalización de la homosexualidad en el Ecuador." *Aportes Andinos* 11. Quito: Universidad Andina Simon Bolivar, October. Available online at http://www.uasb.edu.ec/padh/revista11/articulos/judith%20salgado.htm. Accessed October 13, 2011.

———. 2008. *La reapropiación del cuerpo: derechos sexuales en Ecuador*. Quito: Universidad Andina Simon Bolivar/Abya Yala.

Sardá, Alejandra. 2007. "Resisting Kirchner's Recipe (Sometimes): 'LGBTTTI' Organizing in Argentina." *NACLA Report on the Americas* 40, no. 2: 30–32.

Unidad por el Sí. 2008. "Doce razones para votar por el Sí." Pamphlet, Quito, Ecuador.

Valladares, Lola. 2003. *Entre discursos e imaginarios: los derechos de las mujeres ecuatorianas en el debate de la asamblea nacional de 1998*. Master's thesis. Quito: FLACSO.

Varea, Soledad, and Tatiana Cordero. 2008. "Ecuador: Discrimination of Lesbian, Bisexual, Transsexual, Transgender and Intersex Women." Shadow report for consideration for review of Ecuador's compliance with the Convention on the Elimination of all Forms of Discrimination Against Women (CEDAW). Quito: Taller de Comunicación Mujer/IGLHRC.

Vásquez, Elizabeth. 2008. Co-founder, Casa Trans, and assistant to 2008 Constitutional Assembly member. Personal interview, Quito, Ecuador, August 23.

Viteri, Maria Amelia, Salvador Vidal-Ortiz, and José Fernando Serrano, eds. 2011. "¿Cómo se piensa lo *queer* en América Latina?" Special issue of *Íconos: Revista de ciencias sociales* 39. Quito: FLACSO.

Wilkinson, Annie. 2012. "Sin sanidad, no hay santidad: prácticas reparativas en Ecuador." Master's thesis. Quito: FLACSO.

7

Prejudice before Pride

Rise of an Anticipatory Countermovement

MEREDITH L. WEISS

The literature on social movements and contentious politics differentiates broadly, if somewhat imprecisely (see Lowery et al. 2005), between initial movement mobilization and reactive countermobilization. The sequence is implied, if not explicit: mobilization comes first.[1] And yet transnational discursive flows in particular may help to shift the sequence, yielding a form of anticipatory countermobilization. Present-day mobilization for and against lesbian, gay, bisexual, and transgender (LGBT) rights offers a stark example: rather than wait for an expected onslaught of LGBT rights claims, groups and individuals opposed to those claims have mobilized preemptively against them, deeming an eventual advocacy movement both teleologically unavoidable and an existential threat.

Homophobic activists do not tend to frame their mobilization as foundational, nor LGBT rights activists to frame theirs as an anti-homophobic countermovement; both tend to present LGBT rights claims as logically prior—even when these claims have not, in fact, been articulated locally, or articulated in the form or to the extent opponents describe as imminent. This particular identity politics, then, differs from most others, as the identity category at stake is not just refined, but may emerge in the first instance through the process of being undercut based on a borrowed optic. The resultant sequence is important not just for the evidence it seems to offer of transnational diffusion, but also for its effects on identity building and organizing among LGBT activists, likely allies, and cognate groups. In this chapter, I first examine the evidence for what I term a homophobic *anticipatory countermovement*, with reference primarily to Southeast Asian cases (especially Singapore, Malaysia, Indonesia, and the Philippines), then consider the roots and implications of such a sequence.

I choose these cases for their proximity (useful for evaluating the extent of global and regional discursive circuits), but also for their diversity: Indonesia and Malaysia are both Muslim-majority states, but Indonesia today is far more democratic than Malaysia; the Philippines is a Catholic-majority democracy; Singapore is a single-party-dominant state with important Muslim and evangelical Christian minorities. All four states technically adhere to secular governance, but Malaysia has a state religion (Islam), Indonesia's *Pancasila* (Five Principles) ideology requires monotheism, and the Catholic Church retains substantial political clout in the Philippines. While all but prosperous Singapore are developing states, all are highly exposed to global trade, media, and other circuits. Malaysia and Singapore criminalize homosex; Indonesia and the Philippines do not (although some Indonesian local governments have recently pursued anti-homosexual ordinances) and have far more open and elaborate networks of LGBT organizations. But as we shall see, all four states offer recent examples of high-profile homophobia, all with roots in Christian or Islamist discourse.

And a caveat: I use "movement" rather loosely here, including (coalitions of) social-movement organizations, coordinated state and religious authorities, and more discursive campaigns. I distinguish, though, between public, political claims or campaigns, and privately held beliefs and behaviors: I do not consider religious proscriptions against homosexuality, however fervently espoused, to constitute a homophobic movement for purpose of this analysis unless and until embodied in an outwardly directed, public, adversarial campaign. The same public–private distinction applies only imperfectly to LGBT relationships and praxis, given that the law may make no distinction, yet I am still concerned less here with "gay culture" and clandestine spaces than with public claims to recognition, protection, and equal rights. At the same time, what I label *homopositivity* (acceptance of queer[2] people and practices, not necessarily per received binaries) seems a necessary precursor to serious advocacy work, so the organizing and conscientization needed to develop that at least among LGBTs themselves is importantly pre-political, even if more internally than externally focused.

Political homophobia intercedes at the nexus of gender and sexuality, as state, religious, or other key actors proactively affirm gender roles. Homophobic countermobilization thus has an independent effect on both feminist and queer identities and mobilization, particularly given the close elision of state and societal anxieties about gender and sexuality (for example, Greenhouse 2010; Heng and Devan 1992), as well as the deployment of new collective-action frames and modalities for mobilization in an increasingly, fluidly, interconnected world. These anxieties go far in explaining the *why* of homophobic mobilization (see Bosia, this volume)—and the impacts of this mobilization may be profound.

Anticipatory Homophobia in Southeast Asia

We begin in Singapore, where a comparatively recent example of highly politicized homophobic mobilization aptly demonstrates these dynamics. That mobilization, while framed by participants as a countermovement, actually responded far more to developments in the United States and elsewhere than to the overt expression of non-heteronormative identities or rights claims in the local community, suggesting homophobia's transnational diffusion, but also presuming a normative (if derided) universal trope of "LGBT." The countermovement thus preempted in potentially critical ways the movement to which it claimed to respond, commandeering agendas and discourse, and affecting identity development through the elaboration of sides in an until-then relatively submerged debate.

In March 2009, a group of new members staged a takeover of Singapore's preeminent feminist organization, the Association of Women for Action and Research (AWARE).[3] Details emerged gradually: half the ringleaders (the "new guard") attended the evangelical Anglican Church of Our Saviour (COOS), home to the "ex-gay" Choices Ministry. A Choices staff member allegedly had pressed church members to join AWARE and support the new guard, while Senior Pastor Derek Hong, preaching against homosexuality amidst the fray, inveighed against Singapore's crossing of "a line that God has drawn for us"—drawing fire even from the National Council of Churches of Singapore (NCCS) for politicking (Ganesan 2010, 254–55). COOS and the new guard deemed AWARE too accommodating of lesbians and non-normative sexuality, citing especially the fact that AWARE's sex-education materials declared *homosexuality* a "neutral" term rather than inherently negative,[4] along with such ancillary issues as its screening of a lesbian-themed film at a 2007 fund-raising event and accommodation of (possibly gay) male affiliate members. Rallying women to the cause was seventy-one-year-old born-again Christian, former law school dean, and self-described "feminist mentor" Thio Su Mien (mother of outspokenly antigay politician Thio Li-Ann, and aunt-in-law of Josie Lau, AWARE's new-guard president), who cited concern that AWARE was promoting homosexuality (Au 2009d, 2009c; Lee and Choo 2009; Low, Yong, and Hussain 2009). Thio explained in an interview that AWARE appeared "to be only very interested in lesbianism and the advancement of homosexuality, which is a man's issue"; she preferred that it revert "to its original purpose" (quoted in Hussain 2009).

The coup caused a firestorm in Singapore. The new guard seemed bent on a specific moral agenda, raising the hackles of Singapore's non-Christian majority and secular state authorities, and aggressively shut out "old-guard" volunteers and staff. The old guard tabled a no-confidence motion, requiring an extraordinary general meeting in early May. An estimated three thousand women and men attended, many in red (new guard) or white (old guard) T-shirts. There, the old guard successfully ousted the new, amid an unprecedented show of overt feminism and queer-friendliness. The contest was front-page news in Singapore, finding its way even into the prime minister's annual National Day address.

AWARE regained its status quo ante in most regards. However, within a week of the May meeting, the government revisited AWARE's sex-education programs. Determining that some supplemental materials might "promote homosexuality" or premarital sex—adopting, as Au notes, the rhetoric of the American Christian right, including the assumption that homosexuality is purely learned behavior—the ministry suspended AWARE's school programs (Au 2009a). Moreover, the AWARE case raised key questions about the subtleties of queer mobilization in "conservative societies" (to use the Singapore government's usual phrase); the intermeshing of feminist and queer identities and agendas; and the nature and origins of homophobia in Singapore and elsewhere. (It also raised questions beyond the scope of this chapter, about the church–state divide in Singapore.)

Most important for present purposes: ironically, however ideologically open, AWARE had rarely advocated for lesbians or other sexual minorities. One prominent blogger dates AWARE's first public statement on a "gay issue" to 2007, when the organization joined a coalition supporting repeal of Section 377A, the law criminalizing sex between men. He details, too, a 2008 meeting at which then-president Constance Singam addressed a crowd of lesbians and bisexual women, who bombarded her with complaints that AWARE had thus far "paid virtually no attention to lesbian and bisexual women's issues" (Au 2009d).[5] Furthermore, the AWARE takeover was the most visible and controversial part of a larger campaign, spearheaded by increasingly weighty churches, responding to real or potential developments related to gender and sexuality in which LGBT activists had never been protagonists.

Christians are a clear minority in Singapore, albeit a fast-growing one. Just under 10 percent of Singaporeans were Christian in 1990; nearly 15 percent were a decade later. Evangelical variants are growing especially rapidly. Moreover, Christians tend to be disproportionately young, well educated,

English-speaking, and of high socioeconomic status; already in 1990, over 40 percent of Chinese university graduates (the ethnic majority) identified as Christian (Lee 2008, 542; Tham 2008, 18–19; Tong 2008, 38–40, 49–50). The AWARE saga launched a flurry of complaints that the government included a disproportionate number of charismatic Christians, lending that community undue policy influence.[6] Christians *are* overrepresented in Parliament, constituting a clear plurality of MPs, although those demographics say little about actual policy preferences or positions, and party discipline within Singapore's near-hegemonic People's Action Party is tight (Weiss 2010).

Indeed, almost six years before the AWARE debacle, the government had stirred things up by promising to allow gays and lesbians to serve openly in the civil service—a relatively low-cost but still politically perplexing move (given the small size of the relevant constituency in favor, and the backlash the gesture provoked) that I have argued elsewhere seems more calculated to appeal to international than domestic audiences (Weiss 2005; also Tan 2009). Then four years later, Parliament debated whether to decriminalize sex between men, thrusting homosexuality again into the public sphere—and again of its own volition, not at the behest of LGBT activists. At that point, the NCCS weighed in, urging that the law be maintained and augmented to include an equally "sinful, abhorrent, and deviant" crime of sex between women (Au 2010). And half a year after the AWARE debacle, Singapore's Anglican archbishop, John Chew, who served also as president of the NCCS, urged his flock of 30,000 to uphold "mainstream values" in the face of "alternative" and "fringe" cultures and family structures. Acknowledging the flow of religious ideas, he specifically urged local Anglicans to pay no heed to theological reforms, including the acceptance of female priests and gay bishops, in the church in North America and Europe (Feng 2009). Chew was subsequently elected to succeed vitriolically homophobic Nigerian archbishop Peter Akinola as head of the Anglican Global South, a breakaway confederation launched after the Episcopal Church (the U.S. branch of the Anglican Church) ordained openly gay Gene Robinson as bishop of the state of New Hampshire (Au 2010; Kaoma this volume).

This rising tide of homophobia seems not to have dampened the already tentative LGBT-rights movement in Singapore—especially since it dragged homosexuality squarely into public view—but it has obliged a particular reactive focus. For instance, echoing the "family values" rhetoric of their evangelical opponents, LGBT activists have increasingly stressed their own family-friendliness. The quintessential such efforts were well-attended (and well-reported) "Pink Dot" events, which appear to have responded directly to the Christian-led campaign but focused more on changing societal views through positive exposure than on any specific government policy. Hordes of pink-clad people—gay and straight alike, numbering 2,500 in 2009, over 4,000 in 2010, an estimated 10,000 in 2011, and over 15,000 in 2012—gathered in a downtown park to form a giant, human "pink dot." The themes for 2009 and 2011–12 stressed "Freedom to Love"; the theme in 2010 was "Focusing on Our Families" (with an unsubtle nod to the antigay Focus on the Family).[7]

In neighboring countries as well, we find organized homophobia, sometimes clearly in anticipation of LGBT rights claims, and other times responding to movement stirrings. In these cases, too, homophobia feeds into gender and sexuality-oriented identities and strategies, shaping the movements it claims to counter, sometimes from their inception. And here, too, even when some form of LGBT movement *is* already active, homophobic countermobilization invariably raises the specter of movements elsewhere rather than responding just to local realities.

For instance, in late 2008, amid a spate of cognate developments (see Williams 2009, 11–15, for a rather breathless account), Malaysia's National Fatwa Council issued a *fatwa* (an Islamic guideline, not yet legally binding) against *pengkid*, or (in the words of the *fatwa*): "women who have the appearance, mannerisms and sexual orientation similar to men" (loosely translated as "tomboys"), to be combated by appropriate guidance, especially for young girls, on "aspects of their clothing, behaviour and appearance."[8] Explained the director-general of Malaysia's Department of Islamic Development, while not all *pengkid* are lesbians, they are "heading that way"—"it starts with the clothes and the behaviour [but] . . . might go to the extreme level." He stressed that clothes are just a signifier for the real issue: lesbianism. Since Malaysian law forbids homosexuality (although the secular criminal code, applicable to non-Muslims, does not specifically criminalize sex between women apart from broad proscriptions of "unnatural" sexual activity), "anything that can drive or lead towards it should also be stopped" (quoted in Aniza 2008). Yet even while justifying the enactment as to safeguard "the family institution" per Islamic doctrine, the director-general raised the bugbear of the "west," noting efforts to "legalise these things" in Europe and the United States. To validate his fears, he insisted that homosexuality "spread to this country. That's proof that it's contagious. That's dangerous" (quoted in Aniza 2008). Echoing those sentiments, including the specific specter of family breakdown, former prime minister Mahathir Mohamad insisted in June 2012 that "men marrying men, women marrying women . . . It's not natural. . . . One generation and the whole human race is wiped out."

The rhetoric is not new; Mahathir, for instance, had warned his party five years earlier of neocolonial "European" efforts to force Malaysia to adopt "unlimited freedom for the individual," including "free sex," sodomy, same-sex marriage, and general "hedonism" and "satisfaction of base desires, par-ticularly sexual desires."[9] Indeed, the Malaysian state had been campaigning aggressively, combining diatribe with *fatwa*, laws, guidelines for media,[10] and general harassment, against homosexuality and any divergence from ascribed gender attributes and roles especially since the late 1990s, catalyzed by domestic power struggles (embodied in deposed deputy prime minister Anwar Ibrahim's two trials for sodomy[11]), but in line with rising religious con-servatism and heightened moral policing since the 1970s. Recent campaigns find their roots in the confluence of that Islamization process and Malaysia's export-oriented development push in the 1970s–80s; particularly as young, rural Malay women flocked to factories, "Islamic State bodies came to regu-late sexuality when families no longer could" (Lee 2011, 106). Nor were men immune, even beyond pressure to marry. In 2007, for instance, "confused" effeminate men were barred from teaching in Malaysian schools (Lee 2011, 107–8). In this sense, male (and lesbian) sexuality comes to share the stage with a heavy-handed focus on (presumed straight) women's modesty and chastity, largely, but not exclusively, focused on the Muslim majority (Zaitun 2006, 45–47).

Even when countermobilization was explicit, as with the formation in 1998 of the pro-government, antigay People's Anti-Homosexual Volunteer Move-ment, even the Malaysian AIDS Council and human-rights NGO Suaram—both of which at least condemned the group—said nothing further in support of sexual diversity. (Suaram did, however, issue a strong statement much later condemning state support for homophobia and transphobia.[12]) Nor did other advocacy efforts spark up for several years, beyond limited engagement on issues of women's sexuality (Zaitun 2006, 51, 54–55). Finally, in 2003, a group of LGBT rights advocates brought a petition to Malaysia's Human Rights Commission, in response to recent media reports condemning "effeminate men and masculine women" (Lee 2011, 108; Zaitun 2006, 44). Nothing seems to have come of those efforts. It is worth quoting the late Zaitun, herself a prominent advocate, at length on what it means to have public homopho-bia precede LGBT activism: "so potent is the stigma of LBGTIQ issues that even those who have begun to discuss the issue cannot fathom it in terms of advocacy. Women's groups wonder if taking on the issue will somehow undo and/or 'de-legitimise' the gains that have been made on women's is-sues. And groups that have organised to provide services to the LGBTIQ community seem reluctant to take the issue to a different level, that is, from service provision to advocacy, fearing the repercussions that it may have on the community" (Zaitun 2006, 55).

Some years later, a kerfuffle over the annual (usually somewhat under-the-radar) Seksualiti Merdeka (Sexuality Independence) festival proved how relevant Zaitun's concerns still were. Lawyer Ambiga Sreenevasan, the leader of Bersih (Clean), a popular movement for electoral reform, was slated to officiate at the opening of Seksualiti Merdeka 2011, to reinforce its antidiscrimination message.[13] Not only was Ambiga personally castigated for embracing LGBT rights and hauled up for investigation when the festival was banned, but state supporters broadly derided the Bersih movement—which *was* highly critical of the state, but not at all focused on gender or sexuality—as "infiltrated" by LGBTs and thus all the less legitimate. The incident kicked off an especially venomous round of anti-LGBT pronouncements and mobilization[14] that served to distract attention from the real concerns of Bersih in the run-up to general elections. Prime Minister Najib, in fact, made that connection clear when he proclaimed in July 2012, "LGBTs, pluralism, liberalism—all these 'isms' are against Islam and it is compulsory for us to fight these."[15]

Over around the same period in nearby Indonesia, two separate developments revealed state and religious authorities' quite similar anxieties over sexuality and gender, in the form of what likewise amounted substantially to a preemptive countermovement. Boellstorff describes the earlier stirrings of a specifically political homophobia in Indonesia starting in 1999—a time of democratic transition and general sociopolitical disarray. Boellstorff deems the real issue then less homophobia per se than pervasive heterosexism, and specifically challenges to normative masculinity posed by still-tentative local efforts to claim public space for lesbians and gays (brought to the fore by a network linked with the small Parti Rakyat Demokratik in 1998), the increasing visibility of gay men in popular culture, and global discourses (Boellstorff 2004). The countermovement in this case was ostensibly Islamist: several different groups of armed thugs who attacked gatherings of AIDS activists (many of them also sexual minorities), gay men, lesbians, and *waria* (loosely, "transwomen"), but who also menaced police and media, rendering punishment difficult (Boellstorff 2004; Oetomo 2001).[16] While less preemptive than responsive, these attacks preceded a long lull in public activity on both sides and laid the groundwork for a new phase.

In 2008, Indonesia's Parliament passed a sweeping new Pornography Law, upheld by the Constitutional Court two years later, to the especial dismay of regional authorities, who felt their local cultures under assault, and women's organizations, which bridled at new restrictions on dress and behavior (Khalik 2008; Maulia 2010). Within days of that court decision—implying that the court had thrust sexuality back into the public sphere—protesters from several Islamic organizations (including the official Indonesian Council of

Ulama, MUI) assailed the fourth regional conference of the International Lesbian, Gay, Bisexual, Transgender and Intersex Association (ILGA), sponsored by leading Indonesian LGBT organization GAYa Nusantara, in Surabaya. Having already convinced the initial conference hotel to withdraw and the police not to issue a previously agreed-upon permit, the vigilantes returned once the meeting had begun (less formally than planned, and at a different hotel). They threatened violence, "sweeping" the hotel for prey and forcing ILGA organizers to cancel the meeting, hire security forces, and evacuate participants. Vandals from MUI and the Islam Defenders Front (FPI) also attacked GAYa Nusantara's offices, spray-painting, "Gays and lesbians are moral terrorists" (Liang 2010; Tan 2010a).[17] Again just over a month later, FPI vigilantes stormed a training session on transgender rights (co-sponsored by the official National Commission for Human Rights and the Indonesian Transgender Communication Forum) in Depok; police seemed loath to investigate seriously (Jakarta Post, May 4, 2010; Liang 2010).

In both these cases, FPI and its allies declared LGBT genders and sexualities to be un-Indonesian and un-Islamic (Liang 2010). In the case of the ILGA meeting, at least, clearly there *was* an LGBT movement to which to respond—and yet the response was disproportionate, particularly for these relatively small-scale, community-focused activities. In Indonesia, as in Singapore or Malaysia, homophobes seemed to be mobilizing against something more than what was actually occurring locally. And in Indonesia, too, such aggression has rallied incensed liberal allies (and left many LGBT activists craving revenge), but has also encouraged advocates to adopt the same frame—in this case, focusing on such issues as Indonesian Muslims' obligation to respect diversity.[18]

The Philippines, too, offers examples of homophobic countermobilization, both "provoked" and otherwise. The most significant recent example involves the attempt to register an LGBT political party (the world's first), Ang Ladlad. The Elections Commission, citing both the Bible and the Qu'ran—despite the country's secular constitution and the legality of homosex—ruled in November 2009 that the party "tolerates immorality which offends religious beliefs" and thus could not register. The Supreme Court overturned that ruling, allowing the party to contest for the first time in the May 2010 Philippines elections.[19] Ang Ladlad's five-plank platform called for enactment of a long-tabled Anti-Discrimination Bill, to include sexual orientation and gender identity; support for LGBT-friendly businesses; LGBT-supporting microfinance projects as well as legal aid and counseling centers; and repealing the Anti-Vagrancy Law, which has been used to extort LGBTs. Neither same-sex marriage nor a controversial bill to recognize transgender Filipinos was included. Catholic leaders continued to voice their disapproval of the party, as, in the words of one Catholic Bishops' Conference of the Philippines (CBCP) official, "a group that's of abnormal human persons" (*Straits Times*, November 19, 2009; Yuan 2010). As in Singapore, homophobia in this case was clearly grounded in Christianity—in this case, in explicit concordance with Vatican policy. Moreover, opponents again trotted out same-sex marriage and family values as grounds for resistance, even though Ang Ladlad, anticipating that response, had purposefully avoided those issues (ABS-CBN News.com, December 9, 2009).

While the Elections Commission's and CBCP's homophobic resistance clearly followed LGBT rights claims, other local countermobilization has been more anticipatory. The most clear example—germane well beyond the Philippines—lies in feminist organizing. While the Philippines has long had an extremely diverse and active cohort of feminist organizations, many of them involving lesbians and bisexual women (both "out" and otherwise), nearly all have hesitated to speak to sexuality.[20] In a nutshell, homophobia tends to have an independent effect on women's groups: it deters feminists from addressing sexuality for fear of compromising their primary campaigns by being branded "lesbian" and delegitimated—which may happen if they engage stridently on any rights issue, but is especially likely if they defend lesbians.[21] As one Filipina feminist puts it, "Whether women activists like it or not, they are already being labeled 'lesbians' as they defy standards of femininity with their activism. They are compelled to defend themselves. So, eventually, they will have to confront that sexuality-baiting is not about LGBT issues, but . . . women's sexuality is being used to attack women's organizing" (Mary Jane Real, in Dinglasan 2006, 38–39).

Such "sexuality-baiting" (and "lesbian-baiting" specifically) does invite new dialogue across movements, but by highlighting shared vulnerabilities; meanwhile, it reinforces many activists' discomfort with homosexuality (Dinglasan 2006, 37–38).[22] Sexuality-baiting occurs even at the level of the UN, undermining advocacy work especially on campaigns that counter heteronormativity (Rothschild 2005, 4). That said, many lesbian organizations have roots in women's movements. Lesbian organizing developed in the early 1990s in the Philippines, for example, from women's groups and international meetings, including mobilization specifically against homophobia in the latter (Marin 1996a).

The same tension applies to groups organized around HIV/AIDS, which may hesitate to address gay or transgender populations despite a public-health imperative not being met by the state, not least due to homophobia (Weiss 2006, 672–73).[23] And in the Philippines, even broadly left-progressive groups have rebuffed not just LGBT rights claims, but openly LGBT members themselves (for instance, Editor 2001; Marin 1996b; and Estrada-Claudio 1991, who notes at least on-paper advances). These effects amount to a possibly subsurface countermovement at play: the expectation of a negative response, given homophobes known to be already ready to deploy, preempts LGBT-oriented mobilization or ties what engagement there is to a constrained and largely defensive frame.

The Roots of Anticipatory Homophobia

It is globalization that most clearly drives and enables anticipatory homophobia. However much its opponents decry homosexuality as foreign and imported, contemporary modes of homophobic engagement—the tropes of "gay" invoked, the inclusion of lesbians within the same frame, the melding of gender and sexual identity "deviance," the idealization of "family values" and "tradition," the specific verses and other language deployed—are far more clearly and widely contagious than either homosexual practice *or* apolitical disapproval of same. As we see, for instance, also in recent campaigns in several African states, where American evangelical Christian leaders in particular have lent resources and vitriol to further their own "culture wars" on fertile new ground, homophobic discourses and models are readily borrowed from elsewhere (even when layered over long-standing prejudices and cultural norms) and have distinct effects not just for gay rights, but also for HIV/AIDS outreach, reproductive and sexual-health campaigns, and more (*Economist* 2010; Gettleman 2010; Kaoma this volume; McVeigh, Harris, and Among 2009). The cases here are of a distinctly "modern," modular, activist homophobia, on the assumption that "homosexual" will diffuse in much the same manner (via media, tourism, military bases, markets, etc.), thus to be appropriately met with about the same response across venues: both gays and antigays access the same "reference model," however germane or not in practice (Broqua 2013). Drawing on Foucault, Massad (202, 374) hence describes a process of "incitement to discourse": the efforts of international LGBT organizations to extend their reach has forced state and other actors to take sides and either support or oppose LGBT rights (cf. Zeidan, this volume).

As a result, viewed from the ground, the response sometimes comes before the call. We know already that globalization has some bearing on sexual- and gender-identity categories, but that that link is easily over/mis-stated on the one hand (e.g., Altman 1996; Corboz 2009; Grewal and Kaplan 2001; Jackson 2009; Johnson et al. 2000), and used to undercut LGBT mobilization as invidiously "foreign" and/or driven by outsiders (e.g., Bosia 2007, 158–59).

Altman offers a cogent summation: "Economic changes mean that sexuality is increasingly commodified, whether through advertising or prostitution, which . . . is closely linked to economic dislocation and change. Cultural changes mean that certain ideas about behavior and identity are widely dispersed, so that new ways of understanding oneself become available that often conflict bitterly with traditional mores. . . . And the political realm will determine what forms are available for sexual expression, so that there is a far more overt 'gay' world in Manila than in Singapore, despite the considerable gap in wealth, in part because of different political regimes" (Altman 1999, 563). But since globalization independently tempers opposition to any challenge to heteronormativity (as understood, in these cases, per a dominant Christian or Muslim doctrine specifically), the dynamics are yet more complex than that.

State and societal discourse—especially religious strands—tends implicitly or explicitly to elide gender and sexuality. Norms of "reproductive citizenship," for instance, effectively stigmatize other modes of gender identity and sexual behavior (e.g., Blackwood 2005, 227). Hence in Indonesia, for example, as international images of lesbians and gays permeated nationally in the 1990s, both government officials and state-sanctioned clerics invoked a sex/gender binary to "explicitly disconnect lesbianism from normal womanhood": women were to become wives and mothers, with the household as their primary ambit, notwithstanding juridical equality (Blackwood 2005, 228). By the 1990s, Islamic discourses had regrouped to counter emerging international pressure to support sexual rights, including same-sex marriage.[24] It was in this vein that Islamic leader (and later president) Abdurrahman Wahid wrote in 1994 not just of women's duty to be wives and mothers, but that lesbianism is therefore deviant (Blackwood 2007, 298). After 1998's democratic transition, a conservative Islamic minority came to push for tighter laws restricting sexuality and the dominant discourse on marriage shifted focus, from gender normativity to legislating heterosexuality in the context of criminalizing sex outside marriage (Blackwood 2007). While there *were* at least limited examples by then of domestic LGBT-rights-advocacy initiatives in Indonesia, those efforts seem to have been less salient than international discourses and pressures in shaping state and clerical responses. This process illustrates a larger dynamic, most clearly apparent with regard to non-heteronormative women, but not limited to them.

Both "feminism" and *homopositivity* are most commonly framed outside the United States and Western Europe as at least partly (and incongruously) imported (e.g., Lyons 2000a; Marin 1997; Rohana 1999). (The direct counterpart to heteronormativity would be homonormativity, which likewise implies its own rules and rubrics for "proper" relationships and behaviors. I mean something broader: open acceptance, bracketing the question of whether, for instance, monogamous marriage is deemed superior to promiscuity.[25] That said, homonormativity is impossible to evade in practice, especially in an advocacy- or policy-oriented context. In some cases, feminism informs homopositiv- ity; in others, feminists only reluctantly encounter or embrace challenges to heteronormativity.) Even tentative expressions of queer identity (in gender or sexuality terms) raise boundary challenges for feminists and their organizations in particular, not least where understanding and performance of non-hetero- normativity has typically tended to privilege gender over sex dimensions. The recent surge detailed above in usually religiously justified homophobia throws those boundaries into relief, requiring immediate and precise specification of gendered identities amid a widening range of indigenous and extralocal alter- natives. Yet in the meantime, we find the emergence and anxious expression of homophobia even as homopositivity remains marginal and largely suppressed. Before we can examine the effects of that trigger-happy homophobia on gen- der- or sexuality-based mobilizing (feminist, LGBT, or otherwise), we need to understand why and how such anticipatory countermobilization happens.

These Southeast Asian cases are useful to study in part for what they allow us to rule out. Contemporary homophobia here stems not from tradition or ignorance, especially when the sins being cited are demands like same-sex marriage—not (yet?) voiced locally in any serious way, let alone historically contested. While religion is a motivating factor, it is the specific discourses that are of note: the reiteration of notions of "family values," for instance, thus pressing LGBT activists to defend themselves in those same terms. Singapore's Thio Su Mien, for example, acknowledged that what motivated her and the new guard were trends overseas toward redefining notions of marriage and family; they did not want marriage extended to "between two men or between two women or indeed between three women and three brothers or between a brother and a sister." More broadly, she believed there to be a "political homosexual movement which seeks to infiltrate into Singapore . . . It is a kind of neo-colonialism which we do not want" (quoted in Low, Yong, and Hussain 2009). (Note the parallel with Bosia's discussion here of nations in crisis.) For that matter, a local Christian news- paper, in detailing the AWARE saga, concluded with a lengthy explanation of the "homosexual agenda," detailing a five-step sequence (bolstered by evidence from the United Kingdom, United States, and Canada) by which "the lobby" moves unwaveringly from seeking decriminalization of sod- omy, to equity in age of consent, to antidiscrimination laws, to same-sex marriage and parenthood and adoption rights. The segment concluded ominously, "Christian leaders have reason to believe that [this program of action] is being aggressively initiated in Singapore" (Chua 2009). Interestingly, nowhere does this framing seem to account for differences in regime: Singapore does not have lobbies of the sort found in the United States, and its decidedly illiberal government is well insulated from societal pressure. Regardless, as Miranda Joseph notes, D'Emilio's (1997) juxtaposition of family versus gay identity is superannuated: cornered by Christian rhetoric, "gays have entirely given up the fight against family as an oppressive form and have instead joined it" (Joseph 2002, 89).

Yet this is not an issue of diffusion of a "western" model of LGBT activism, but rather of the disembodied response to that activism, primarily through reasonably sturdy and deeply transnational channels of organized religion. The evidence suggests that discourses of homophobia are frequently directly borrowed and significantly rattle LGBT communities, perhaps nudging their self-identities and reference groups so as to account for some proportion of the similitude of LGBT frames, terms, strategies, and objectives across contexts. The participation of Muslim-majority countries in homophobic blocs in international fora such as the UN offers additional evidence of sharing of discourses and frames; Malaysia, for instance, took a leading role in rallying Muslim countries to reject a UN resolution on homosexual rights in 2003–4 (Williams 2009, 10).

In all these states, religion is both highly prominent in the public sphere and heavily fraught. Singapore's Maintenance of Religious Harmony Act in particular leaves very little public space for discussion of religion. Malaysia prohibits proselytization of any religion besides Islam but has an active, state-supported program of propagating that. Indonesia has been struggling to sustain social peace since the late 1990s, its efforts peppered by both militant Islamists and a spurt of anti-Chinese/Christian violence in the transitional *Reformasi* period. The Philippines has a highly dominant Catholic hierarchy and long-running, geographically concentrated Muslim insurgency. Aversion to homosexuality, as so many of these religious leaders are quick to note, offers a point of convergence across religions, and hence can at least discursively neutralize the specifically sectarian focus of assertions of "morality" in public life even while raising the public profile of the sponsoring church.[26] Moreover, adherence to secularism, when required, is patrolled not just by the state itself, but also by religious figures chary of any one leader's co-opting too much space. Gay blogger Alex Au proposes that taking over AWARE offered the Christian right a comparatively stealthy way to attract public support, given that straitened space (*Economist* 2009). Hence, even as the NCCS took Pastor Hong and COOS to task for their involvement in the AWARE saga, it still asserted a right for Christians to involve themselves in public debates (Low, Yong, and Hussain 2009).

But it is the intersection or elision of gender and sexuality that offers the most analytical leverage.[27] LGBT population percentages are low everywhere, and nowhere in Southeast Asia (with the possible exception of the Philippines) do queers form a voting bloc or other organized constituency—especially when rebuked by homophobes before they even begin to articulate a program. But license to *be* LGBT implicitly challenges norms of gender; homopositivity argues for fungibility of gender roles and identities as natural, contra state and religious policies that resist such a conception either out of pronatalist angst (Singapore) or because accepting such flexibility would challenge the relevance of religious precepts and edicts. It matters that these developments coincide with an Islamist[28] resurgence in Indonesia and Malaysia that has, among other effects, brought to the fore questions of appropriate male and female behaviors and roles—from Malaysia's "tomboy *fatwa*" to whether the popular but female Megawati Sukarnoputri could become president of Indonesia; among the *fatwa* from Indonesia's MUI in 2005 alone, for example, were ones both denouncing feminism (as a form of liberalism) and endorsing polygyny (Wieringa 2005, 3). This trend has also brought forth a rash of intrusive or even violent vigilante groups in both countries claiming to act as moral guardians of Islam. Meanwhile, these dynamics render lesbians and lesbian sexuality near-invisible, including to scholars, except as bêtes noires to attack: heterosexism and general diminution of sexuality studies, inflected by homophobia (internalized or anticipated), molds feminist praxis and research, and much research on gay men (or "homosexuals" generally) pays scant heed to women (see, for instance, Blackwood and Wieringa 1999).

Lastly, to some extent, gays provide a scapegoat when known sociopolitical and moral orders seem to be crumbling. Hence Dédé Oetomo (2001) traces the rise of homophobic violence in Indonesia at the moment of increasing democratic space not to LGBT activism per se, but to greater public understanding of human sexuality, not least given media sensationalism of homosexuality and the global AIDS crisis. (Yet all transpired alongside a general breakdown in public order; brothels, bars, and other venues were likewise attacked.[29] Religion may have genuinely motivated some assailants, but alcohol, Oetomo notes, seems to have fueled others.) In this reading, religious/moral claims have inherent legitimacy, and prototypical gays fit readily into an (im)moral frame, regardless of what they themselves may have said or done. Beyond enforcing public morality, gay bashing asserts a pecking order among societal groups; offers a chance to vent (and perhaps extort); shows up the weakness of the state as a foil to "prove" the power of the mobilized group (to wit, the clearly outgunned Indonesian police); and both engages and bolsters transnational circuits, which may offer moral succor, replicable political repertoires, and tangible resources.

Implications

All of which brings us back to the question of homophobia's effects on collective identity and mobilization. At least two very different lines of analysis conjoin. One, drawing on critical race theory in particular, focuses on how collective identity categories come to be defined and understood, and when and how they come to be inscribed as legally or normatively inferior (for instance, Marx 1996 and 1998). The other, which cleaves more closely to a contentious politics approach, seeks to understand the effects of sequencing of movement and countermovement, when the latter can take on a modular, transferable form (thanks in this case to roots in transnational religious traditions) and be launched prior to the full articulation of the former. While couched in different literatures, these approaches work well together to disentangle homophobia as a widely prevalent response to a still-emerging collective-identity category and identity-based movement.

Both "feminism" and "LGBT" (variously named) are widely presumed to be inappropriately foreign. Even more ambiguous, than, for instance, "racial" categories commonly defined in terms of dubious biological measures, but embedded in very real socioeconomic histories and migration patterns, queer identities are always in flux. Emergent challengers perturb known categories as queer discourses disruptive of gender boundaries contest longer-established (indigenous or imported) feminist and/or gendered discourses and identities. In the meantime, new possibilities for solidarity arise—not just of religious activists espying grounds for legitimacy in borrowed antigay master frames, but also of LGBT activists, who increasingly develop their movements against a backdrop of weirdly uniform homophobic discourses. Here, too, we find tension: use of the term *LGBT* facilitates international solidarity (and hence is rapidly taking root), but at a potentially steep cost in terms of local self-identification (for instance, Dinglasan 2006, 33). Most trenchantly, Massad bluntly condemns the goals and discourse of ILGA, IGLHRC, and the rest of the "Gay International" as "missionary," "orientalist," and ultimately repressive in trying to force conformity with a specific sexual ontology and epistemology (Massad 2002, 361–65). (The *T* in particular may be an empty or dubiously appropriate signifier where gender categories are understood differently.) In the meantime, among those segments now organizing and asserting rights claims in Southeast Asia are those whose claims lie most clearly at the intersection of gender and sexuality—in particular, variously identified "transgender" women: for instance, Singapore's Sisters in Solidarity, launched by three transwomen in May 2010 (Tan 2010b), and the Society of Transsexual Women of the Philippines (STRAP). While it would be tempting to presume that a given array of LGBT organizations relates most directly either to the extent and success of prior LGBT rights claims or to the efficacy of state and societal homophobes, as the contrasts among these cases suggest, such variation may have more to do with organizational culture and freedom than actual acceptance or rejection of LGBTs. Hence the Philippines has a host of LGBT organizations, extending to a path-breaking political party . . . yet survey data suggests wide, strong aversion to homosexuality and homosexual people (Manalastas and Del Pilar 2005), and the powerful Catholic hierarchy rejects LGBT rights unequivocally. Now-democratic Indonesia, too, has an array of LGBT organizations, and at least as many that reject them; less liberal Malaysia and Singapore, on the other hand, lack any legally registered LGBT advocacy groups.

And yet how these groups identify collectively, frame issues, and mobilize is a larger issue, and is shaped in part by the fact of opposition that *precedes* or *predicts* their articulation. A rise in "fundamentalisms" in the global North, explains IGLHRC, "has ensured that defenders of sexual and reproductive rights are put in increasingly defensive positions, a condition that results in organizations finding themselves in the absurd position of spending the bulk of their time defending the most basic of their agendas and unable to pay attention to articulating and expanding liberatory agendas of their own" (Rothschild 2005, 15).

Experience of such baiting, or even just the reasonable expectation of it, encourages self-censorship, deterring public education and advocacy on issues of sexual rights, sexual orientation, and gender: any focus on sexuality comes to be deeply internalized as being both divisive (with lively reminders at any transgression) and too marginal to be worth the risk. At best, sexual-rights campaigns may be addressed obliquely or framed as "anti-violence" (Rothschild 2005, 17–20); rarely do activists stress a claim, for instance, to pleasure and eroticism (Dinglasan 2006, 39). Victims' and investigators' not wanting to lend credence to charges of being (for women's groups) "lesbian" complicates even documenting abuses—which further limits discursive space and reinforces the power of the accusation (Rothschild 2005, 22–23). And when, as is common in anti-feminist attacks, "any discussion of 'gender,' feminism, or 'sexual rights' is taken to refer to 'deviant' sexualities, or assumed to be 'promoting homosexuality' . . . [t]he effects are double: such attacks reduce the definition of 'gender,' and the scope of sexualities, to a single issue within the spectrum; and they exploit, and give added strength to, the stigma attached to homosexuality" (Rothschild 2005, 41). Hence, for instance, Malaysia's Seksualiti Merdeka was branded in 2011 as all about "free sex" (*seks bebas*), for addressing sexuality at all, while lesbian-baiting leaves feminists specifically in a double bind of needing to shed the label, but also to dismiss the negativity with which it is imbued (Rothschild 2005, 42).

And religion-justified homophobic campaigns in particular easily traverse state borders. In what IGLHRC bluntly terms "colonial ambitions," antigay, conservative Christian organizations in the North "have learned to disguise moral imperialism as a helping hand," insisting that they aim to preserve developing countries' sovereignty "against the twin dangers of 'sodomy' and human rights" (Rothschild 2005, 52–53). Not only does the resultant baiting impede women's ability to organize freely, or some LGBT groups' capacity to organize openly at all (Rothschild 2005, 53), but it may pit women's organizations against each other or gay men's groups against lesbian ones (Rothschild 2005, 55–56), and enduringly shapes the content and timbre of collective mobilization. Hence, for instance, a sex-positive frame remains scarce in Southeast Asia, even among LGBT organizations: the origins of so much activism in HIV/AIDS work on the one hand (Weiss 2006), and homophobic discursive assault on the other, makes proactive positivity difficult.

Indeed, while homophobic baiting is not a new phenomenon, nor is the defensiveness it engenders, its effects go well beyond curbing women's mobilization, especially where gender- and sexuality-based *mobilizing* is still nascent. Preemptive homophobia molds or impedes collective identity formation among LGBT communities—and the bogeys deployed to enforce quiescence can be deployed all the better against still quasi-imaginary as against real, live local communities. Nor are these dynamics necessarily unique to Southeast Asia, although there probably is a "late development" dimension (not to imply teleological evolution of identities, but in terms of collective political mobilization). In much of sub-Saharan Africa, too, for instance, hostility from state and other authorities (again, seemingly out of sync or proportion with actual advocacy work on the ground) seems to have spurred not just fear and flight, but more open and urgent LGBT collective action (Broqua 2013), while a sensationalizing (and likely politically motivated) fury over a purported "lesbian syndicate" preying on secondary schoolgirls in Kenya in 1997, per a local activist, "shut down all space for lesbian organizing" (quoted in Rothschild 2005, 26–27). And there, too, we can expect LGBT activist agendas, if not preempted entirely, to form not in their own mold, but in reaction to that temporally prior countermobilization.

Overall, then, the implications of not just homophobic countermobilization, but of *anticipatory* homophobia, may be wide-ranging: legitimacy on the religious right for what may amount to impressive-looking shadowboxing, a felt need to shape or restrict rights claims to reflect what terrain the countermovement has already claimed or declared to be critical, and pressure on gender-based organizations to confront internalized fears of appearing queer if they speak to sexuality. And in many cases, as IGLHRC notes, the result is invisibility: the "hatred and shame" attached to being branded a lesbian "ensures that lesbian women remain voiceless and unseen in many societies—and thereby only confirms the assertions of political leaders who claim that homosexuality is alien or unheard of in their countries" (Rothschild 2005, 63–64). The same applies logically to gay male, bisexual, and trans would-be activists. The result may be either a failure to develop mobilizable collective identities, or mobilization within parameters or around an agenda defined by the countermovement. Either way, the effects of such anticipatory countermobilization may permeate deeply, and far beyond its obvious targets.

Notes

1. An important (and germane) exception: Fetner (2008) traces the symbiotic maturation of LGBT activism and the religious right in the United States.

2. While used sparingly in the region beyond academic circles, *queer* offers a "shorthand to refer to non-normative sexualities connected with a range of erotic desires, relationships, identities or politics that involve overlapping sets of sex/gender domains associated with non-heterosexual, same-sex or transgendered subjects" (Wilson 2006; also Sinnott 2010, 19–22).

3. The takeover was simple and constitutional: around 80 percent of members who showed up for that year's (typically poorly attended) annual general meeting had joined within the prior three months, including nine of twelve executive committee members elected (Au 2009b).

4. Discussion of homosexuality took less than two minutes of the course, compared with thirty on the topic of abstinence (Teo and Soh 2009). Moreover, while AWARE had reached around five hundred students in twelve institutions by late 2008, the Ministry of Education had received no negative feedback (Au 2009a).

5. My own interviews with AWARE members dating back to the mid-1990s suggest, too, that the organization was deeply wary of being branded a group of "bra-burning feminists," let alone overrun by lesbians. Conventional wisdom has been that feminists are "loud-mouthed man-haters with unshaved legs" and "lesbians and just not nice" (Singam 1993, 2).

6. For instance, see "Religious Demographics of Our Politicians (Minus the Cabinet Ministers)," on *Singaporean Skeptic*, posted by Skeptic, February 10, 2010, http://singaporeanskeptic.blogspot.com/2010/02/religious-demographics-of-our

.html (accessed August 13, 2010); and "Religious affiliation of MPs," on *Yawning Bread*, posted by Yawning Bread, August 2007, http://www.yawningbread.org/ arch_2007/yax-784.htm (accessed August 13, 2010).

7. See http://pinkdot.sg for details, photos, and video clips.

8. Already by the mid-1990s, vigilante morality enforcers had begun attacking not just men and women thought to be involved in same-sex relations, but also men perceived as effeminate and women, as masculine (Peletz 2009, 221).

9. "Mahathir's verdict: you're greedy, sexual deviants," *Sydney Morning Herald*, June 19, 2003, http://www.smh.com.au/articles/2003/06/19/1055828425389.html.

10. Most obviously, 2010 Malaysian Film Censorship Board guidelines were relaxed to allow depiction of gay characters, but only so long as they repent, go straight, or suffer by the end of the film. (Locally produced films on other themes, particularly sexual or political, face strict guidelines as well.) Liz Gooch, "Film Pushes Malaysian Censorship Boundaries, but Not Too Far," *New York Times*, October 28, 2010.

11. Anwar himself has resisted being cast as a "gay" cause célèbre, however, most recently clarifying that while "archaic" laws should be amended "so innocent people will not be punished," still, Malaysians "do not promote homosexuality" and "uphold the sanctity of marriage." Lisa J. Ariffin, "Anwar Agrees to Discrimination against Gays to Uphold the Sanctity of Marriage," *Malaysian Insider*, July 18, 2012.

12. Natalie Khoo, "Suaram: Political Leaders Must Take a Stand on LGBT Rights," *The Edge Malaysia*, July 25, 2012.

13. See http://www.seksualitimerdeka.org for full press coverage and discussion.

14. For instance, Malay rights group Jaringan Melayu Malaysia (Malaysian Malay Network) organized an anti-LGBT rally one week before a planned Bersih rally, its president noting specifically that unlike Bersih, *this* rally was a "protest for the future of our nation." Shazwan Mustafa Kamal, "Anti-LGBT Groups to Rally against 'Unacceptable Lifestyles,'" *Malaysian Insider*, April 8, 2012.

15. Hafidz Baharom, "Najib: LGBTs, Liberalism, Pluralism Are Enemies of Islam," *Malaysian Insider*, July 19, 2012.

16. Ungar (2000) offers a plausible but, in this case, empirically unconvincing, counter-explanation: that transition to democracy (and attendant civil liberties) allows the proliferation and politicization of LGBT organizations; the latter's new visibility and activism provokes backlash amidst the travails of regime change, not least from the tense and troubled state itself.

17. See also the special May 2010 issue of *Bhinneka* (vol. 6) on the ILGA saga.

18. Interviews, June 2010.

19. Citing the constitution's equal-protection clause, the court asserted, "The denial of *Ang Ladlad*'s registration on purely moral grounds amounts more to a statement of dislike and disapproval of homosexuals, rather than a tool to further any substantial public interest" (pp. 15–16). Yet the decision cautions, "none of this suggests the impending arrival of a golden age for gay rights litigants" (p. 20). Ang Ladlad LGBT Party v Commission on Elections, G.R. No. 190582, April 8, 2010, available online at http://sc.judiciary.gov.ph/jurisprudence/2010/april2010/190582.htm.

20. Interviews, June/July 2010; Pineda (2001) also notes this deep-rooted heterosexism.

21. It is not only on sexuality that feminist groups reprioritize thus—consider the substantial literature on their circumscribing gender-specific or "strategic" claims in the name of unity toward a wider nationalist cause (among many others, Wieringa 1992).

22. Writing on Singapore, Lyons (2000b) offers perhaps a less cynical take: she suggests AWARE prioritizes an ethic of respect for all members' religious and other sensibilities, so eschews stances that might offend. Such avoidance is sufficiently widespread, however, and even AWARE, by now sufficiently willing to approach sexuality, that her explanation seems incomplete.

23. Conversely, explains Altman (1998, 17–18), some states intent on combating homophobia by decoupling HIV and homosexuality have gone too far, devoting disproportionate resources to lesser-risk hetero populations—so homophobia still drives the agenda, but through a different trajectory.

24. Blackwood mentions specifically the UN's 1994 Cairo Conference on Population and Development, at which Indonesia opposed a statement in support of same-sex marriage (2007, 298).

25. See Cantor (2006) for a trenchant, Philippines-focused critique.

26. IGLHRC offers specific examples of international alliances between "conservative Catholicism," "conservative Islamic states," and "wealthy right-wing NGOs" (Rothschild 2005, 51–52). One of their examples, Focus on the Family, is not only strong in the region, but is (as AWARE used to be) a state-approved provider of sex education in Singapore schools. COOS's Choices ministry is an affiliate of their other example, "ex-gay" ministry Exodus International.

27. I am less interested here in (clearly variable) taxonomies of gender/sexuality per se than in the ways those collective identities are deployed, particularly in terms of rights claims, which increasingly do adopt an "LGBT" frame for purposes of public articulation.

28. "Islamist" here refers to a specifically political agenda, not solely private devotion (see Emmerson 2009).

29. Some supposed manifestations of rising turpitude are more farfetched, like a cabinet minister's assertion (backed by MUI) that a 2009 earthquake was caused by declining morals, manifested in the sale of pornographic DVDs at street markets (Palatino 2009).

Bibliography

Altman, Dennis. 1996. "Rupture or Continuity? The Internationalization of Gay Identities." *Social Text* 48, no. 14: 77–94.

———. 1998. "HIV, Homophobia, and Human Rights." *Health and Human Rights* 2, no. 4: 15–22.

———. 1999. "Globalization, Political Economy, and HIV/AIDS." *Theory and Society* 28: 559–84.

Aniza, Damis. 2008. "Sunday Interview: Fatwa on 'Pengkid' to Prevent Lesbianism." *New Straits Times*, November 23.

Au, Alex. 2009a. "Education Ministry Suspends AWARE's Sexuality Education Program." *YawningBread.org*, May 7.

———. 2009b. "From Now On, Be Wary of AWARE." *YawningBread.org*, April 12.

———. 2009c. "Pirate Mother Ship Appears on Horizon, Guns Blazing." *Yawning-Bread.org*, April 24.

———. 2009d. "Pirates Ahoy! Gay Netizens and the AWARE Hijacking." *Yawning-Bread.org*, April 21.

———. 2010. "Singapore Homophobia Takes World Stage." *Fridae.com*, April 26.

Blackwood, Evelyn. 2005. "Transnational Sexualities in One Place: Indonesian Readings." *Gender and Society* 19, no. 2: 221–42.

———. 2007. "Regulation of Sexuality in Indonesian Discourse: Normative Gender, Criminal Law and Shifting Strategies of Control." *Culture, Health & Sexuality* 9, no. 3: 293–307.

Blackwood, Evelyn, and Saskia E. Wieringa. 1999. "Sapphic Shadows: Challenging the Silence in the Study of Sexuality." In E. Blackwood and S. E. Wieringa, eds., *Female Desires: Same-sex Relations and Transgender Practices across Cultures*, pp. 39–63. New York: Columbia University Press.

Boellstorff, Tom. 2004. "The Emergence of Political Homophobia in Indonesia: Masculinity and National Belonging." *Ethnos* 69, no. 4: 465–86.

Bosia, Michael J. 2007. "Guilty as Charged: Accountability and the Politics of AIDS in France." In P. G. Harris and P. D. Siplon, eds., *The Global Politics of AIDS*, pp. 155–70. Boulder, CO: Lynne Rienner.

Broqua, Christophe. 2013. "Male Homosexuality in Bamako: A Cross Cultural and Cross Historical Comparative Perspective." In S. M. Nyeck and M. Epprecht, eds., *Sexual Diversity in Africa: Politics, Theory, and Citizenship*. Translated by Michael Bosia. Montreal: McGill-Queen's University Press.

Cantor, Libay Linsangan. 2006. "Forcible Homonormativity and the (Truly Free) Lesbian Existence." *Women in Action (ISIS)* 6, no. 1: 107–12.

Chua, Edmond. 2009. "New Aware Exco: Real Coup by Homosexual Activists." *Christian Post*, April 24.

Corboz, Julienne. 2009. Globalisation and Transnational Sexualities. http://sexualitystudies.net/files/Globalisation%20and%20Transnational%20Sexualities.pdf.

D'Emilio, John. 1997. "Capitalism and Gay Identity." In R. N. Lancaster and M. di Leonardo, eds., *The Gender/Sexuality Reader: Culture, History, Political Economy*, pp. 169–78. New York: Routledge. Original edition, 1983.

Dinglasan, Anna Kristina M. 2006. "Bringing LGBT Concerns to the Forefront: Issues, Challenges, and Gains." *Women in Action (ISIS)* 6, no. 1: 32–43.

Economist. 2009. "Taken Unawares." May 9, 46.

———. 2010. "A Well-Locked Closet." May 27.

Editor. 2001. "Oscar Atadero." *Fridae.com*, February 23.

Emmerson, Donald K. 2009. "Inclusive Islamism: The Utility of Diversity." In R. C. Martin, ed., *Islamism: Contested Perspectives on Political Islam*, pp. 17–32. Stanford, CA: Stanford University Press.

Estrada-Claudio, Sylvia, writing as Sunny Langsang. 1991. "Gender Issues in Revolutionary Praxis." *Debate: Philippine Left Review* 1: 41–52.

Feng, Yen. 2009. "Fight Alternative Values." *Straits Times*, November 30.

Fetner, Tina. 2008. *How the Religious Right Shaped Lesbian and Gay Activism*. Minneapolis: University of Minnesota Press.

Ganesan, Narayan. 2010. "Singapore in 2009: Structuring Politics, Priming the Economy, and Working the Neighborhood." *Asian Survey* 50, no. 1: 253–59.

Gettleman, Jeffrey. 2010. "Americans' Role Seen in Uganda Anti-Gay Push." *New York Times*, January 4.

Greenhouse, Linda. 2010. "Hiding in Plain Sight." *New York Times*, August 12.

Grewal, Inderpal, and Caren Kaplan. 2001. "Global Identities: Theorizing Transnational Studies of Sexuality." *GLQ* 7, no. 4: 663–79.

Heng, Geraldine, and Janadas Devan. 1992. "State Fatherhood: The Politics of Nationalism, Sexuality, and Race in Singapore." In A. Parker, M. Russo, D. Sommer, and P. Yeager, eds., *Nationalisms and Sexualities*, pp. 343–64. New York: Routledge.

Hussain, Zakir. 2009. "Lawyer's Key Role in Coup." *Straits Times*, April 24.

Jackson, Peter A. 2009. "Capitalism and Global Queering: National Markets, Parallels among Sexual Cultures, and Multiple Queer Modernities." *GLQ* 15, no. 3: 357–95.

Johnson, Mark, Peter Jackson, and Gilbert Herdt. 2000. "Critical Regionalities and the Study of Gender and Sexual Diversity in South East and East Asia." *Culture, Health & Sexuality* 2, no. 4: 361–75.

Joseph, Miranda. 2002. "The Discourse of Global/Localization." In A. Cruz-Malavé and M. F. Manalansan IV, eds., *Queer Globalizations: Citizenship and the Afterlife of Colonialism*, pp. 71–99. New York: NYU Press.

Khalik, Abdul. 2008. "SBY signs porn law, protesters despair." *Jakarta Post*, December 9.

Lee, Edwin. 2008. *Singapore: The Unexpected Nation*. Singapore: Institute of Southeast Asian Studies.

Lee, Julian C. H. 2011. *Policing Sexuality: Sex, Society, and the State*. New York: Zed.

Lee, Terence, and Deborah Choo. 2009. "BREAKING NEWS: Staff Sent Out Email Asking Members to Vote at Aware EOGM." *TheOnlineCitizen.com*, April 27.

Liang, Jamison. 2010. "Homophobia on the Rise." *Inside Indonesia* 100 (April–June).

Low, Aaron, Jeremy Au Yong, and Zakir Hussain. 2009. "Should Faith-Driven Groups Take Over Secular Organisations?" *Straits Times*, May 2.

Lowery, David, Virginia Gray, Jennifer Wolak, Erik Godwin, and Whitt Kilburn. 2005. "Reconsidering the Counter-Mobilization Hypothesis: Health Policy Lobbying in the American States." *Political Behavior* 27, no. 2: 99–132.

Lyons, Lenore. 2000a. "A State of Ambivalence: Feminism in a Singapore Women's Organisation." *Asian Studies Review* 24, no. 1: 1–23.

———. 2000b. "The Limits of Feminist Political Intervention in Singapore." *Journal of Contemporary Asia* 30, no. 1: 67–83.

Manalastas, Eric Julian, and Gregorio E. H. Del Pilar. 2005. "Filipino Attitudes toward Lesbians and Gay Men: Secondary Analysis of 1996 and 2001 National Survey Data." *Philippine Journal of Psychology* 38: 53–75.

Marin, Malu. 1996a. "Going Beyond the Personal (Part One)." *Kasama* 10, no. 4.

———. 1996b. "Stolen Strands: The In and Out Lives of Lesbians in the Philippines." In M. Reinfelder, ed., *Amazon to Zami: Towards a Global Lesbian Feminism*, pp. 30–55. New York: Cassell.

———. 1997. "Going Beyond the Personal (Part Two)." *Kasama* 11, no. 1.

Marx, Anthony W. 1996. "Race-Making and the Nation-State." *World Politics* 48, no. 2: 180–208.

———. 1998. *Making Race and Nation: A Comparison of South Africa, the United States, and Brazil, World Politics*. New York: Cambridge University Press.

Massad, Joseph. 2002. "Re-Orienting Desire: The Gay International and the Arab World." *Public Culture* 14, no. 2: 361–85.

Maulia, Erwida. 2010. "Commission Slams Court for Supporting Porn Law." *Jakarta Post*, March 27.

McVeigh, Tracy, Paul Harris, and Barbara Among. 2009. "Anti-Gay Bigots Plunge Africa into New Era of Hate Crimes." *The Observer*, December 13.

Oetomo, Dédé. 2001. "Gay Men in the Reformasi Era." *Inside Indonesia* 66 (April–June).

Palatino, Moag. 2009. "Politics and Immorality in Southeast Asia." *UPIAsia.com*.

Peletz, Michael G. 2009. *Gender Pluralism: Southeast Asia Since Early Modern Times*. New York: Routledge.

Pineda, Roselle V. 2001. "Bridging Gaps, Making a Struggle: The History of the Filipina Lesbian Struggle in the Philippines." *Kasarinlan: Philippine Journal of Third World Studies* 16, no. 1: 131–62.

Rohana Ariffin. 1999. "Feminism in Malaysia: A Historical and Present Perspective of Women's Struggles in Malaysia." *Women's Studies International Forum* 22, no. 4: 417–23.

Rothschild, Cynthia (with Scott Long and Susana T. Fried). 2005. *Written Out: How Sexuality Is Used to Attack Women's Organizing*. New York and New Brunswick, NJ: IGLHRC and Center for Women's Global Leadership. Original edition, 2000.

Singam, Constance. 1993. "Faces of feminism." *Sunday Times*, March 7, p. 2.

Sinnott, Megan. 2010. "Borders, Diaspora, and Regional Connections: Trends in Asian 'Queer' Studies." *Journal of Asian Studies* 69, no. 1: 17–31.

Tan, Chris K. K. 2009. "'But They Are Like You and Me': Gay Civil Servants and Citizenship in a Cosmopolitanizing Singapore." *City & Society* 21, no. 1: 133–54.

Tan, Sylvia. 2010a. "Islamic Protestors Force Evacuation of ILGA Conference Participants in Surabaya." *Fridae.com*, March 26.

———. 2010b. "Transgender Women in Singapore Launch Campaign to End Discrimination." *Fridae.com*, May 5.

Teo Wan Gek, and Elizabeth Soh. 2009. "Face-off: The White Shirts v the Red Shirts." *Sunday Times*, May 3.

Tham Seong Chee. 2008. "Religious Influences and Impulses Impacting Singapore." In Lai Ah Eng, ed., *Religious Diversity in Singapore*, pp. 3–27. Singapore: Institute of Southeast Asian Studies.

Tong Chee Kiong. 2008. "Religious Trends and Issues in Singapore." In Lai Ah Eng, ed., *Religious Diversity in Singapore*, pp. 28–54. Singapore: Institute of Southeast Asian Studies.

Ungar, Mark. 2000. "State Violence and Lesbian, Gay, Bisexual and Transgender (LGBT) Rights." *New Political Science* 22, no. 1: 61–75.

Weiss, Meredith L. 2005. "Who Sets Social Policy in Metropolis? Economic Positioning and Social Reform in Singapore." *New Political Science* 27, no. 3: 267–89.

———. 2006. "Rejection as Freedom? HIV/AIDS Organizations and Identity." *Perspectives on Politics* 4, no. 4: 671–78.

———. 2010. "Democracy and Pluralism: Lessons from Southeast Asia." Paper read at Association for Asian Studies Annual Meeting, March 26, at Philadelphia.

Wieringa, Saskia. 1992. "IBU or the Beast: Gender Interests in Two Indonesian Women's Organizations." *Feminist Review* 41 (Summer): 98–113.

Wieringa, Saskia Eleonora. 2005. "Islamization in Indonesia: Women Activists' Discourses." *Signs* 32, no. 1: 1–8.

Williams, Walter L. 2009. "Strategies for Challenging Homophobia in Islamic Malaysia and Secular China." *Nebula* 6, no. 1: 1–20.

Wilson, Ara. 2006. "Queering Asia." *Intersections: Gender, History and Culture in the Asian Context* 14 (November).

Yuan, Elizabeth. 2010. "Philippine Gay Party on Ballot for the First Time." *CNN.com*, May 8.

Zaitun Mohamed Kasim. 2006. "Sexuality under Attack: The Political Discourse on Sexuality in Malaysia." *Women in Action (ISIS)* 6, no. 1: 44–55.

8

Homophobia as a Tool of Statecraft

Iran and Its Queers

KATARZYNA KORYCKI

AND ABOUZAR NASIRZADEH

Observers tend to see homophobia, as it relates to the politics of the Middle East, as a legitimate response, indeed the only one available to region's governments faced with the concerted "incitement to discourse" of Western human-rights groups (Massad 2002 and 2007); or as a result of the dissemination of homophobic norms from antigay networks in the West (Kaoma, this volume); or as a function of religion, Islam in particular.[1] As probable as the first two explanatory factors may be, they overestimate the power of human-rights and homophobic networks, and underestimate the reach and agency of Middle Eastern states. We, therefore, want to "bring the state back in" (Skocpol 1979). To do this, we treat antigay rhetoric as an analytical category and examine the content, the productive force, and the work it does for the deploying power. As such, we see religious anti-homosexual prejudice as a convenient frame to be used by states when it suits their purposes, not as a causally independent factor.

Tracing the story of the last two hundred years in Iran, we demonstrate that, far from being the pawn of Western machinations, the Iranian state has varied its stance toward homosexuality in pursuit of its objectives—namely modernization, consolidation, and most recently, deliberalization. In doing so, it has refashioned family and gender relations, positioned itself vis-à-vis the imperial appetites of the West, and centralized and expanded its power. To achieve these objectives, it first borrowed an anti-homosexual stance from the West, only to later claim homosexuality itself was a Western import. To trace how this remarkable twist happened, we anchor our story around three moments in which anti-homosexual rhetoric and practice have been deployed. First is the modernization moment lasting from the early nineteenth century to the onset of the Iranian Revolution in 1979. Second is the Islamic nation-state consolidation moment following the revolution. Third is the conservative backlash following the attempted liberalization of 1997 and persisting until today.

Throughout this chapter we do not use the term *gay* until Iranian homosexuals use it themselves at the turn of this century. In doing so we are guided by sensitivity to the historical meanings attached to the term *gay*: we wish to avoid sneaking in meanings and understandings that did not hold when our story takes place (see Blasius; Zeidan, both this volume). This is not to say that we uncritically agree with the Foucauldian act/identity distinction. In Foucault's account, when self-identified gays appear in modern Europe, they are produced by medical and criminal systems of classification and control (1990, 43). We want to offer a more historically attentive account—one that recognizes the different and more fluid categories of division and identification operating in premodern Iran, and why and how they were transformed by deliberate elite manipulation.

We do not use the term *homophobia*, either, until we reach more recent times. The concept is ideationally and semantically attached to the modern term *gay*. In the bulk of the paper we therefore use more descriptive terms, like *anti-same-sex*, or *anti-male-love*, when referring to concepts, policies, or law that appear homophobic to modern readers.

In exploring homosexual desire and practices in Iran, we deal with male desire only. Female homosexuality deserves its own exploration, beyond the scope of this work, especially given its complexity in Iranian history. Furthermore, although we are cognizant that both "Western" and "Iranian" or "Oriental" categories are mutually constitutive (Said 1979), and that the Iranian state instantiates itself in the context of the international structures and discourses, we bracket these categories in order to analytically map the space of autonomous state action. Finally, we are cognizant of the intersections between gender and sexuality, and signal them throughout the text. However, given our focus, we privilege state and sexuality in our analysis.

Religion as Explanation

The most pervasive view locates homophobic sentiment in Islam itself. We claim instead that all three Abrahamic religions display an ambivalent stance toward homosexuality. On one hand, their holy texts and laws contain strong formal prohibitions against same-sex desire or practice; on the other hand, enforcement of said prohibition has been historically uneven. Indeed, there are more similarities among the religions, in both their formal stance and weak enforcement, than differences in the severity of the practical sanctions within each religion over time.

Judaism and Islam approve of sex but confine it to the reproductive sphere of marriage between a man and a woman. Both religions contain strong formal injunctions against same-sex sexuality and weak and uneven practical sanctions (Afary and Anderson 2005, 155; Duran 1993; Eron 1993). The holy texts of both rely on the story of Lot to condemn homosexuality, with an additional Old Testament reference in Leviticus (18:22) to homosexuality as deviant and abhorrent. The Quran includes references to the demise of Sodom, which Islamic scholarship interprets as an allusion to a punishment for the sin of homosexuality (15:73–74 and 26:165–66).[2] More direct injunctions may be found in the *tafsir* and *hadith* (respectively, explanation of the holy text and reports of the Prophet's deeds), which equate homosexual and extramarital sex and punish them with death (Najmabadi 2005, 18). Judaism prescribes banishment (Leviticus 18:29) or death (20:13, 20: 33). Harsh direct or indirect penalties notwithstanding, neither tradition enforces them consistently or easily. The Talmud requires two witnesses and Sharia law four to establish that a transgression took place (Afary and Anderson 2005, 156; Duran 1993, 183; Eron 1993, 117). Each allows for repentance and cleansing rituals to reestablish offenders' good standing vis-à-vis the Divine and the community (Afary and Anderson 2005; Eron 1993, 184).

Christianity is less overtly hostile to homosexuality, but when it is, it imposes sanctions more consistently. It borrows the strict injunctions from the Old Testament and adds its own not entirely univalent condemnations, voiced by St. Paul (never Jesus himself) in Romans 1:26–27; 1 Corinthians 6:9; and 1 Timothy 1:10. The statements are ambiguous enough to warrant ongoing contestation of their meaning.[3] That being said, until the twelfth century, Christianity, influenced by Hellenic philosophy[4] and Muslim tolerance, was quite permissive of homosexual practice. This lenient stance changed with Thomas Aquinas, whose conceptions of nature, actions befitting human beings, and injunctions against those acting "against nature" prevail to the present day in Catholicism (Carmody and Carmody 1993, 142).

These disjunctures between scripture and practice and changes in attitudes over time are evident in all Abrahamic religions. We therefore claim, and use two hundred years of Iranian history to demonstrate, that reasons for variance in how homosexual desire is regulated need to be located in politics. To put it in provocative terms, if Khomeini were Catholic or Jewish, presiding over a revolution in a Catholic or Jewish state, he would find ample justification in the holy texts of either religion to implement his anti-homosexual policies.

Context: Premodern Iran

Premodern Iran did not organize sexuality along lifelong patterns of sexual orientation, nor along the lines of hetero- or homosexual desire (Najmabadi 2005, 20). This is not to say that individuals did not experience lasting preferences toward the same categories of people; nor does it mean that they did not self- and other-identify based on those desires. Rather, we suggest that the available categories were different than those toward which modern Iranians orient themselves.

At the risk of fixing that which was fluid, we propose that sexuality was organized according to three intersecting principles. These principles operated in a society in which love, friendship, desire, and pleasure were not naturally connected to marriage. Heteronormativity,[5] underpinning a connection between heterosexual love and marriage, had not taken hold. Indeed, later sections of this chapter show how this heteronormativity is constitutive of modernity itself and how it is inscribed by the erasure of the homosociability[6] and eroticism of the premodern era. Two examples of eleventh- and fifteenth-century ethics manuals make clear that the most valued relationships—friendship and love—as well as sexual desire were experienced among men ('ayn Unsur al-Ma'ali 1999 and Shuja'ayn 1971).[7] Relations between men and women were based on obligation, upkeep, and procreation. It is in this context that the three principles organizing the field of sexuality in premodern Iran have to be read.

The first principle was age. Young beardless males—*amrad* or *ghulam*—constituted a separate sexual category. They were desired, depicted, and described as "the beloved" (Shamisa 2002, 10, author's translation). The earliest expressions of this veneration may be found in Sufi writing. It reflected the belief that the greatness of God manifested itself in the beauty of a young man, here referred to as *shahed*, literally translated as "a witness to God's beauty." Later, the classical Persian poetry of Attar (d. 1220), Rumi (d.1273), Sa'di (d. 1291), Hafez (d.1389), Jami (d.1492), and Iraj Mirza (d. 1926) all evoke homoerotic ideals, as well as make explicit references to the beauty of young men (Afary and Anderson 2005, 156; Duran 1993, 185; Schimmel 1975, 289). One of the most prominent scholars of Persian poetry, Cyrus Shamisa, claims that "it was essentially a homoerotic oeuvre" (2002, 10, author's translation).

The second principle distinguishes between those who gave pleasure and those who submitted to pleasure (Afary and Anderson 2005, 156). It intersects with age in that once a young man became an adult and grew a beard, he moved from being an object to subject of desire. But not all adult males made the transition. Some, called *mukhannas* in early Persian texts, *amradnuma* in nineteenth-century Iran, and *'aynubnah* in medical literature, shaved their beards, appearing *amrad*-like, and by doing so declared their intention to be the objects of desire (Najmabadi 2005, 17). They may have been subjected to derision, but more often than not, they were accommodated through cross-dressing and incorporation into artistic professions, such as music, dancing, and recitation (Najmabadi 2005, 17). This distinction pits bearded adult males—the givers of pleasure—versus three categories of receivers of pleasure: the beloved *amrads*; women, with whom one had reproductive sex in the context of conjugal relations; and *amradnuma* of different class and social positions (including slaves and servants). The most prevalent homoerotic and sexual practices, as given by classic poets, included relationships between kings and slaves. Outside the courts, homosexual practices were accommodated in public spaces in male houses of prostitution (*amradkhane*), bathhouses, and military and clerical schools (Afary and Anderson 2005, 157).

The third principle concerns the private and public nature of morality. Although Islam contains a strong anti-homoerotic prohibition, its implementation in premodern Iran concerned the public sphere[8] only. Adult males were expected to marry. Once they did, the realm of desire and private pleasure was discreetly shrouded. As long as a man fulfilled his procreative obligation and did not appear to indulge excessively, he was free to love and seek pleasure as he pleased (Najmabadi 2005, 23).

The three principles organizing sexual space concern men. Women were assigned a procreative, private role (Najmabadi 2005).[9] The sexual preferences of men varied according to their age and social status, but it would be a mistake not to recognize that the general preferences of individuals did not go unnoticed, or that heterosexual desire was taken for granted. On the contrary, the general expectation to marry was accompanied by general acceptance of other sexual encounters, some of which may have involved exclusively male partners. The many examples of this praxis undermine the Foucauldian contention that homosexual does not emerge as a category of identity until modernity. The absence of the fixity generated by modern classificatory systems does not preclude a possibility of self- or other-identification based on the object of one's desire. Thus Shah Tahmasb II (r. 1736–47) "preferred one Joseph-faced to thousands of Zulaykhas and Laylis and Shirins" (Rustam al-Hukama 1974, 147), or famous court painter Bihzad "could not live a moment without ruby-red wine and ruby-red lips of a wine-bearer" (Soudavar 1999, 51), as opposed to Shah Sultan Husayn Safavi (r. 1722–32), who was "fully inclined to women" (Qazvini 1988, 79).[10]

Yet same-sex desires and practices outside of the prescribed boundaries were heavily stigmatized and in some cases criminalized. Relationships with pre-adolescent youth were one such instance and carried sentences that included the use of *bastinado*. Relationships in which force was used and which resulted in injury or murder were heavily criminalized, up to and including death (Najmabadi 2005, 22). Moreover, relationships between older men who had white beards and youth were stigmatized for the great age differential and the perceived undignified nature of an older man seeking sexual pleasure. In addition, as alluded to above, those who showed excessive displays of love, exclusive lust for *amrads*, or those who never married were also looked down upon socially (Najmabadi 2005, 23).

The memory of this fluid and complicated past in which same-sex desire and practice were common and accommodated was to be all but wiped out in the next 150 years. Homoerotic poetry would be reinterpreted as devotional; conceptions of beauty would become entirely feminized; and homoerotic desire, once entrenched in Persian culture, would become reinscribed in the social imagination as a Western and modern import.

Modernization from Below: Grafting a Western Anti-Homosocial Stance

By the beginning of the nineteenth century, Iran came into full contact with European colonialism. As a result, by 1828 it had lost close to half of its territory to Tsarist Russia.[11] In addition, the British Empire bribed and coerced its way to influence the Iranian royal court. To give just one example, Baron Julius de Reuter was granted a monopoly on railway construction, as well as access to Iran's mineral and forestry resources and to its banking. These concessions were seen as a "complete and extraordinary surrender of the entire industrial resources of a kingdom into foreign hands" (Lord Curzon, quoted in Gelvin 2005, 85).

The loss of the territory and the growing influence of foreign powers created a sense of crisis and loss of confidence. Many European-educated Iranian intellectuals, such as Mirza Jahangir Khan, argued that the traditions of Iranian society no longer provided a suitable guide for navigating the world. Other thinkers, like Fath-Ali Akhoundzadeh and Abd al-Rahim Talebof, identified a nation-state as the cornerstone of any attempt to modernize Iran. They began to reconceptualize the public sphere by imagining new categories of its inhabitants, shortly to be made into citizens. The profound sense of shame over the loss of prestige and territory precipitated a certain degree of mimicry and imitation of European models, although the process is better understood as "grafting," in which attractive ideas were adopted, but localized (Najmabadi 2005, 100).

This grafting was facilitated by frequent two-way contacts between the modernizing West and soul-searching Iran (see Blasius, this volume). By the turn of the nineteenth century, the reciprocal gaze of the elites produced a consensus that women's segregation was the main marker of Iran's backwardness; that religion, sustained by the veil and polygamy, was its origin; that the veil, in turn, led men to engage in homosexual practices, by then refashioned to be unnatural (Najmabadi 2005, 162). This remarkable transformation of gender and sexuality, and creation of a heteronormative public sphere, involved three interconnected intellectual paths, described below.

From the earliest encounters between Iranian and European travelers it became clear that male love was the most visible marker of difference between these societies and that Westerners considered it a vice. Iranian intellectuals responded, first by denying the pervasiveness of male love (and pointing out its presence in the West); later by equating the love of an *amrad* with frustrated desire for a female; and ultimately, by predicating Iranian modernity on the repudiation of male love (Najmabadi 2005, 39).

Furthermore, as Iranian men traveled in Europe, they encountered women who conversed with, engaged with, and even courted them. This public encounter was profoundly new and transformative. It permitted Iranian intellectuals to imagine a social space not exclusively populated by men. In time, the absence of women in public came to be seen as a cause of men's turning to one another for love and friendship. As Najmabadi suggests, this indicates a different path to heteronormalization than the one proposed by Foucault in Europe. Iranian intellectuals believed that once women entered the public sphere, the ensuing heterosociability, heretofore unknown in Iran, would remove the need for homosexual practice (Najmabadi 2005, 57). If men were backward owing to the public absence of women, and if heterosociability were to become normal, then new categories of actors were needed. Women had to remove their veils and renounce their own backward segregation. This new space had little room for those "still" stubbornly engaged in male love—they were first marginalized through "temporal boxing"—who were painted as backward and not yet enlightened. As the modernizing project progressed, other marginalizing moves were needed. These included now-familiar "othering" through medical and psychiatric discourses and, in most recent times, through "Westoxification" (Najmabadi 2005, 34). On this subject, nineteenth-century intellectual Mirza Agha Khan Kermani writes:

Men are *naturally* inclined toward socializing with and enjoying the compan-
ionship of women . . . If a people is forbidden from this great blessing and is
deprived of this great deliverance, then inevitably the problem of sexual acts
with boys and young male slaves is created, because boys without facial hair
resemble women . . . and it is for this reason that in the Iranian people/nation
this grave condition has reached saturation. And the ground for this situation
is the veiling of women that has become established in Iran . . . Sa'adi of Shiraz
and the obscene and shameful Qa'ani and other Iranian poets have big col-
lections of poetry that prove my word and relieve me of further explication.[12]

The creation of heteronormative social space did not proceed without
friction, voiced not by increasingly marginalized homosocial men, but by
women. The newly formed Iranian feminist movement supported the modernizing zeal of the male intellectuals. The feminists agreed with the unveiling
of women, ending of segregation, and increase in women's education. Despite
the general agreement, however, Astarabadi and other feminists claimed that
men did not go far enough, as they were protecting patriarchal institutions.[13]
Feminists thus pushed for the redefinition of the institution of marriage. They
wanted to change it from a contract for procreation to a contract based on
love. It was to be monogamous and to contain tough divorce rules protecting women. To achieve this new marriage contract, women demanded that
men forgo their homoerotic friendships (Najmabadi 2005, 156).

Allied with the broader modernizing movement, feminists began arguing
that traditional manifestations of same-sex love and sexuality were signs of
backwardness and causing Iran to succumb to the pressures of the colonial
powers. As such, the Iranian modernizers came to associate heterosexuality
with normalcy. This push for modernization among the Western-oriented
upper-middle classes in Iran during the late nineteenth century effectively
relegated manifestations of same-sex sexuality to the lower class and "backward" individuals who supposedly "lacked the capacity" to become modern.

Modernization from Above I:
Ataturk's Model of State Consolidation

The overall rate of change and modernization in Iran remained fairly gradual.
The efforts of the nineteenth-century modernizers led to the 1906 transformation of Iran into a constitutional monarchy. The parliament proved weak,
however, and the Shah bypassed it on many issues. Mohammad Ali Shah
even went so far as to bombard the parliament in 1908. Also, the Imperial
British and the Russians expanded their influence over Iran. Inspired by

Ataturk's policies in neighboring Turkey, discontented intellectuals, such as Hasan Taqizadeh, argued that unless every single traditional social norm were done away with completely, Iran was doomed to struggle in the modern world (Keddie 2003, 181). The only way to achieve that was to pursue Ataturk-style government policies of aggressive and authoritarian westernization and to break free from what was deemed traditional dogma and superstitions (Keddie 2003, 181). Advocates of radical modernization saw a political opportunity when Reza Shah overthrew the Qajar and established the Pahlavi dynasty in 1925. Many of the intellectuals articulating visions of social and political modernization found themselves in government.[14]

Reza Shah undertook radical, wide-ranging social and economic reforms that aimed at consolidating his power and accelerated modernization. What had been mused upon in intellectual salons, Reza Shah now turned into state polices. He began by eliminating autonomous networks of feudal power through concerted and successful military pacification (Migdal 1988). His second, much more challenging target was Ulama—Shiite clerics—whom he attempted to emasculate through a series of gradual reforms (Sedghi 2007, 67). He sought to eradicate their authority, which, although diffuse and decentralized,[15] had much local legitimacy. The Ulama had an independent source of income, as they collected religious taxes. More importantly, they were responsible for spiritual guidance, service provision, regulation of marriage, administration of justice, and education. Reza Shah implemented policies that challenged all these sources of legitimacy. To this end, he made marriage a civil institution as opposed to a religious one (Sedghi 2007, 73). Women were allowed to seek divorce when their husbands proved unfit (Mahdi 2004, 430). The minimum age of marriage was set at fifteen for girls and eighteen for boys (Mahdi 2004, 430). Reza Shah also aggressively expanded girls' education: in 1929, there were over 11,000 girls in schools, compared with 167 in 1910. This number grew to 50,000 by 1933 (Sedghi 2007, 71). The peak of such measures came in 1936 with *kashfe hejab*—a policy that banned women's veil and mandated Western dress (Mahdi 2004, 430).[16]

The Ataturk-inspired authoritarian policies of Reza Shah advanced the heterosexualization of the public space as gender and sexuality came under the purview of government, rather than religious, regulation. Reza Shah's reforms diffused norms of anti-same-sex love and sexuality, previously entrenched only in the upper echelons of society, among the lower classes in the late nineteenth century. The memories of eighteenth-century gender roles and homoeroticism that had been prevalent in public spaces now became a distant memory.[17]

Upon succeeding his father, Mohammad Reza Shah[18] undertook his own reforms aimed at further westernization of Iranian society. As part of his White Revolution of 1961, women were given the right to vote, and literacy corps, modeled on those in the United States, pushed universal education nationwide (Sedghi 2007, 133). Family planning, free contraceptives, and abortion became legal and available (Sedghi 2007, 133). More prominently, in 1975, Mohammad Reza Shah introduced the Family Protection Act. This law gave women the right to divorce, made polygamy contingent on the first wife's permission, transferred parental custody decisions from religious authorities to family courts, and raised the legal marriage age to eighteen for women and twenty for men (with exceptions for rural areas; Sedghi 2007, 136).

These concrete moves transformed gender relations throughout society (Sedghi 2007). Even though the reforms had no homophobic bent in themselves, they were part of a newly reconceptualized public and private sociability. This new heteronormative space was predicated on the total erasure of the homoerotic past, but not eradication of homoerotic love and practice. Indeed, an American residing in Tehran in the late 1970s describes his time there as a "sexual paradise" (Zarit 1992, 55). He tells of his multiple sexual encounters with Iranian males. Furthermore, despite all the Shah's policies, and in line with the growing visibility of homosexuals in the West, there were increasingly open displays of homosexuality in places such as cinemas, bars, and discos in Tehran (Afary 2009, 160).

Modernization from Above II: Khomeini's National Islamic Model

The 1979 overthrow of the Shah was the result of the confluence of multiple factors. Contrary to prevailing scholarship at the time, however, the revolution "was made" and sustained from below (Skocpol 1979 and 1994). The Iranian population, mobilized by multiple grievances against the Shah, found a powerful vanguard in the Ulama, who had access to valuable political resources (Skocpol 1979 and 1994). The clerics controlled cohesive and well-organized networks of the urban poor, delivering a resonant ideological frame that mobilized Iranians for a prolonged and bloody fight against the regime.

The grievances that united disparate parts of the revolutionary movement were threefold. First, the Shah's oil-wealthy *rentier* regime mediated its relationship with society through state expenditures. It facilitated consumption but failed to diversify the economy and develop many of its people. Flowing state expenditures, coincident with chronic inflation and unemployment, led to a gap "between aspirations and expectations" (Huntington 1968, 54) and constant, percolating dissatisfaction (Ansari 2003, 174).[19] Second, the Shah was almost universally despised for his servile relationship with the West, especially the United States. He was seen as more responsive to the interests of foreign business than of Iranians. The issue that powerfully catalyzed public imagination was the total immunity from Iranian law offered to the American personnel stationed in Iran.[20] Third, the Shah, through his much-feared secret police, SAVAK, engaged in extensive repression of dissidents, often involving torture and extrajudicial murders (Ansari 2003, 203). In Skocpol's words, "suspended above its own people, the Iranian state bought them off, rearranged their lives, and repressed them" (1994, 244).

Capitalizing on the political and ideological resources of the Islamic Republican Party (IRP), the Ulama, under the leadership of Ayatollah Khomeini, turned itself into the vanguard of the anti-Shah revolutionary force and mobilized sustained mass support (Skocpol 1994, 252). Their political resources took two forms. The institution of the bazaar, infiltrated by clerics, proved a powerful substitute for well-organized peasant communities of the previous successful revolutions (Skocpol 1994, 245–47), as it was a site of sociability and community-building for the ever-growing ranks of urban workers and merchants. During the Revolution, the bazaar supplied support and fostered mobilization able to resist well-organized army and SAVAK forces. The second political resource derived from the assertive interpretation of Islam: clerics adopted the role of true interpreters of Quran, which resonated with the disaffected and left-behind masses (Skocpol 1994, 252).

Post-Revolution, the victorious IRP moved aggressively on four closely related fronts, each equipped with its own discursive frame. First and foremost, the Mullahs wanted to consolidate power over opponents. Toward that end, attacking homosexuals as well as many undesirable others proved useful in demonstrating revolutionary resolve. Second, the IRP worked to create a national postcolonial narrative by simultaneously othering the West, the homosexual, and the Pahlavi regime. Third, the Mullahs wished to undo selected policies implemented by the Pahlavi dynasty, especially as they related to women, in the name of creatively reinterpreting national tradition. Fourth, they wanted to extend the reach of the state in an aggressive move to control private morality—this they accomplished by criminalizing homosexuality and regulating women. We explore all four processes in turn.

While consolidating power after the revolution, the IRP, buoyed by success, continued to command impressive political and cultural resources now deployed against weak and divided opponents. Backed by an assertive ideology and mass support, Khomeini proved willing and able to establish a centralized and coercive state.[21] He demonstrated his resolve to marginalize the liberals and social democrats, his anti-Shah allies (Skocpol 1994, 250), and feminist and ethnic minorities (Afary and Anderson 2005, 163) by staging mass public executions—over four thousand people were killed (Bakhash 1984, 221–22).[22] Public violence served a dual purpose: directly, it sped up the elimination of opponents, justified by readily available tropes of "corruption," "evil," "foreignness," and "unnaturalness" (Skocpol 1994, 252); indirectly, and more importantly, it signaled a resolve that silenced opposing factions and established Khomeini in a position of ultimate authority over his allies, the opposition, and society.[23] We thus see the post-revolutionary killings of homosexuals—two hundred were executed in the 1981–82 purges (Kafi 1992, 67)[24]—as primarily strategic. The deaths are only secondarily anti-homosexual in essence.

The view that the killing of homosexual men was strategic rather than essentialist is supported by Khomeini's own writing, in which he does not paint same-sex acts as more repulsive than other sexual acts. In his 1947 ethics manual, article 347 states, "if a person has sex and [his organ] enters [the other person's body] to the point where it is circumcised or more, whether he enters a woman or a man, from behind or the front, an adult, or pre-adult youngster, and even if no semen is secreted, both persons will become ritually polluted." This pronouncement is followed by instructions as to how such impurity may be cleansed (quoted in Afary and Anderson 2005, 159).

Lest we create an impression that Khomeini was in any way sympathetic to same-sex desire, we introduce his second move—the creation of a postcolonial national narrative. Like other postcolonial movements that rose to prominence during the 1960s and 1970s, Khomeini applied "us-versus-them" logic to draw the boundaries of his community. A "creator"[25] of the Islamic nation, he connected same-sex love to Western decadence and to the Pahlavi regime, constituting all three as foreign and deviant. This narrative resonated, as Iranians of all classes no longer held any memory of the long history of same-sex love and sociability; furthermore, they despised the Shah and saw the presence of same-sex practice as a result of his Western-induced permissiveness. This creative forgetting was maintained by casting the homoeroticism in Persian poetry as godly love between humankind and Allah, rather than worldly and physical sex (Moallem 2005, 116).

The third move of the new regime involved selective redrawing of gender relations. Thus, in the name of tradition, previously undermined by the "West-mimicking Shah," women were assigned a separate-but-equal status (Afary 2009, 265). This translated into strictly segregating public spaces such as public transportation, schools, mosques, and beaches; banning women's presence altogether in such spaces as sports arenas; tightening laws relating to divorce and custody of children (Sedghi 2007, 201); and limiting women's access to work.[26] The final and most dramatic change imposed a mandatory veil. The "separate but equal" doctrine harkened rhetorically to premodern Iran but had little in common with its reality. What had previously been a rural society, in which the majority of women, with uncovered heads, worked in the fields side by side with men, has been reinscribed on the urban and educated population of the centralized modern state (Sedghi 2007). These changes to women's status are significant for the argument in this work, in that they demonstrate the extent to which the regime was willing to use law to regulate previously customary conventions, and the degree to which it used an imaginary past to justify doing so.

The fourth move of Khomeini's regime blurred the boundary between public acts, which alone were heretofore subject to Sharia law, and private morality, which had been left unpatrolled so long as it did not manifest itself in public. Thus criminalization of homosexuality and the advent of police units—the *Nirooye mobareze ba mafasede ejtemayi*, popularly known as *Komiteh*, or morality police—that target "immoral" behavior are both manifestations of the state's increasing attempt to penetrate the previously unregulated domestic sphere. Thus, in the new Islamic laws, *lavat*, a penetrative or nonpenetrative sexual activity between two males, is considered a capital crime, for which both partners may be executed. Other homosexual acts including *tafkhiz*, which is the rubbing of the penis against another man's thigh, draw the punishment of 100 lashes for each partner (Islamic Penal Code Article 121).[27] Activities such as lascivious kissing and being found naked under the same cover with no reason draw 60 lashes and 99 lashes, respectively (Islamic Penal Code Article 123–24). Legalizing and criminalizing what had previously been private demonstrates the truly modern approach of this ostensibly traditional regime.

The four strategies and their tropes intersect. Using law to mandate the veil and criminalize some aspects of sex, othering the West and the homosexual, relegating women to the private sphere and then policing that sphere with special surveillance techniques—all in the name of tradition—reveal that the reinvention of the past and strategic deployment of anti-same-sex rhetoric are useful tools of statecraft. They also reveal the ingenious selective borrowing of modernizers' propositions, all in the name of the tradition that modernizers wanted to erase. Overall, the post-revolutionary Islamist government, in its attempts to "revive" religious "traditions," has effectively invented a whole new system of governance, utterly modern in nature (Moallem 2005, 13).

Modern Gays and Modern State Homophobia

Between 1997 and 2005, Iran experienced a brief moment of liberalization. Popular dissatisfaction with corruption (Abdi 2001) and regime repression (Poulson 2005, 254), as well as dramatically changing demographics, brought a crisis of legitimacy and led to the presidential election of Muhammad Khatami in 1997. The newly elected president reached out to the burgeoning ranks of young and not-Western-unfriendly citizens with ideals of rights, lawfulness, and civil society.[28] By the 2000s, the constituency had become mostly urban, highly educated, and under age thirty,[29] with little memory of the revolutionary struggle against Western domination and the Shah's rule. On the contrary, since it relies on satellite TV and the Internet, it follows Western consumerist values (Afary 2009, 327). For instance, young people arrange dates and matchmake on the Internet (Afary 2009, 333). Those of the middle classes increasingly hold favorable views toward sex, even premarital sex (Afary, 2009, 336). Moreover, the rapid expansion of the Iranian economy has led more people to marrying later in life, prioritizing their careers (Afary 2009, 340).

Despite the population's legitimate grievances and Khatami's popular appeal, regime "hardliners" moved to block most of his reforms, such that his legacy is felt mostly at the level of society rather than in the state itself. His presidency, which ended in 2005, opened a political space for discourse of rights and rights-based activism to flourish. The rise of this new discourse has manifested itself in the emergence of various nongovernmental rights groups, including feminist groups,[30] ethnic groups, and literary groups. At the same time, newspaper circulation, including publications with divergent political leanings, increased from 1.2 million to 3.2 million, and the number of journals jumped from 778 to 1,375 by the early 2000s (Abrahamian 2008, 191). Most prominently, rights-based discourse was evident during the post-election protests of 2009, with the main slogan of the demonstrators being, "Where is my vote?"[31]

It is in this context that we observe the emergence of gay Iranians. Although both the modernizing and revolutionary movements of the nineteenth and twentieth centuries succeeded in casting same-sex love and sexuality as unnatural, foreign, and criminal, by the end of the 1990s, Iran had a growing homosexual community, mostly in larger metropolitan centers such as Tehran and Isfahan. Members of these communities identified themselves by the English word *gay* (Afary 2009) and used the Internet to communicate with each other, to access material on gay rights, and to arrange sexual encounters. Some of these individuals eventually fled to the West as refugees and established diaspora-based politicized gay-rights movements. Indeed, a group called the Iranian Queer Organization (IRQO), based in Toronto, Canada, and with branches in Iran and around the world, was established by Iranian gay refugees in 2004. The group, through its publication of an Internet e-zine by the name of *Maha*, has attempted to change the Persian language surrounding sexuality to include the concept of sexual orientation, to record the experiences of gay Iranians and the problems they face, and to provide advice on coming out and health issues, including safe-sex practices (Afary 2009, 352).[32]

While in the first decade and a half after the Revolution state homophobia was a tool deployed to signal revolutionary resolve, create national narratives, and extend the state's reach into private morality, the nature of antigay policies is changing (Afary 2009). The new approach is designed to suppress the diffusion of this newly emerging gay identity among Iranian youth—or, to put it in more general terms, it is part of a wider campaign to close the space opened by the liberalizing tendencies of Muhammad Khatami. This liberalized space is demonized using familiar "Western invasion" tropes[33] and is actively constricted by periodic crackdowns on improper *hejabs* of women, tight clothing, and hairstyles deemed to be offensive. It also includes a ban on satellite dishes and raids to confiscate them, as well as the closing of newspapers that are seen to have offended Islamic sensibilities. Moreover, women's groups have come under severe scrutiny, with multiple feminist activists, such as Parvin Ardalan, Noushin Ahmadi Khorasani, and Delaram Ali, being sentenced to imprisonment in recent years.[34] Other human-rights activists, such as the Iranian Nobel Laureate Shirin Ebadi, are regularly harassed. And human-rights lawyers such as Mohammad Ali Dadkhah, Abdolfattah Soltani, and Mohammad Mostafaei have been detained or forced into exile for raising the profile of their clients.[35]

To arrest the spread of homosexuals specifically, the regime denies homosexuals' existence and continues to cast them as the Western other; to suppress human-rights discourse generally (used by many in Iran), the regime has increased the reach of its surveillance and control technologies. Homophobia as a tool of conservative backlash is proving useful yet again as a means of reasserting the coercive power of the state, in the wake of liberalization.

Thus Iranian officials have become more vocal in rejecting the existence of gay individuals in Iran, calling the phenomenon something that only exists in the Western world. For example, on April 29, 2000, a prominent Iranian Ayatollah, Ali Meshkini, "criticized the German Green Party for being pro-homosexual." Another prominent Ayatollah, Ebrahim Amini, on July 13,

2002, charged that "gay and lesbian marriages reflect a weakness of Western culture."[36] Echoing such anti-Western sentiments, the Iranian Supreme Leader, Ayatollah Khamenei, stated during a speech on November 18, 2007, "Currently, homosexuality has become a huge issue in the West. They try to pretend it is not a big issue. In reality, however, homosexuality now poses a painful and unsolvable problem for Western intellectuals" (author's translation).[37] Most prominently, the Iranian president, Mahmoud Ahmadinejad, proclaimed that gays do not exist in Iran during a speech at Columbia University in 2007: "In Iran, we don't have homosexuals, like in your country. We don't have that in our country. In Iran, we do not have this phenomenon. I don't know who's told you that we have it" (*Pink News* 2007).

In apparent contradiction to the above denials, the state is moving to increase its surveillance of gay activities. This proceeds in two ways. With growing use of the Internet, especially for arranging sexual encounters amongst people with same-sex desires, the security apparatus—including *Basiji* militia and the morality police—has moved to control the Internet (HRW 2010, 58). As such, the Iranian government has developed one of the most expansive Internet censorship regimes in the world, comparable only to China's (OpenNet Initiative 2009). Websites containing information on homosexuality are often blocked and filtered. Moreover, the morality police use the Internet for entrapment (Human Rights Watch 2010, 54). Furthermore, enforcement of morality proceeds through raids on suspected gay parties, with participants often rounded up and forced to become informants (HRW 2010, 52). Modern medical science has also made the Iranian state able to police sexual conduct in the most intimate ways possible.[38] Forensic rectal examinations or threats of such examinations are generally used to establish if the person has engaged in penetrative sexual activity or coerce the defendant into confessing to having had sexual contact with members of the same sex (HRW 2010, 53).[39]

Disavowal, othering, and increased surveillance achieve two objectives at once. First, they reaffirm the regime as a protector of "sexual sovereignty" of the nation against the neo-imperialism of the West. Second, as an element of a broader strategy to suppress the discourse of human rights, they serve to strengthen the regime's grip on power in the face of a changing society. The new approach is less decisive than the Pahlavi Shahs' and less resolute or violent than Ayatollah Khomeini's. It may also prove less effective—it is unclear why referring to sexual sovereignty would appeal to a young population seeking sexual liberation. On the other hand, the repressive and aggressive appropriation of the Internet may protect the regime for some time to come.

Conclusion

As this chapter has shown, in theorizing homophobia, scholars and activists should not take the West to be the sole agent creating and disseminating anti-same-sex norms to passive non-Westerners. "Incitement to discourse" by the "gay international" should not be seen as leaving no room for governments in the non-Western world to act in any but a homophobic manner. Rather, as in the case of Iran, the West should be seen as a referent in a "conversation," in which both parties create images of each other and produce anti- and pro-homosexual stances that vary across time (see Keating, this volume).

By suggesting a mutually constitutive conversation between the West and Iran, we do not mean to suggest the absence of power. On the contrary, we take exploitative military, economic, and cultural incursions of the West as a leitmotif of our account and wish, by way of conclusion, to raise a question of what follows from the inequality of positions for the questions of justice here and now. We propose that the normative thrust of much postcolonial resistance literature blunts its critical edge if it looks only to the West and does not address itself to ideational changes that have taken place within Iranian society (Massad 2002, 2007). Such a unidirectional stance essentializes and idealizes the past, and effectively erases two hundred years of interaction. Most importantly, it forces its proponents into a normative corner, from which they argue away antigay violence and repression as excusable because it is anti-Western or—better yet—as caused by the West (Massad 2002, 384). Our account means to redirect the spotlight onto creative processes of borrowing and grafting in Iranian society and to highlight new modes of self-understanding and identification. This perspective, we believe, is the only footing from which one can begin to articulate claims for just treatment of gay people in the Middle East and elsewhere. No matter how glorified by Foucault, the status-defined homoerotic love prevalent and tolerated in premodern Iran (and ancient Greece) seems hardly a model to look to in a society demanding broad citizenship, equality, and voice. The framework of human rights seems to provide the answers for now, but there is no reason to think that it is the only available framework, or even a sufficient one.

Notes

1. The assumption that Islam is anti-homosexual can be seen in the emergence of politicians such as Greet Wilders in the Netherlands, who view the Islamic Sharia law as a threat to gay rights and the Western way of life more broadly. Moreover, this assumption is also evident in immigrant orientation videos introduced in Germany

and the Netherlands featuring gay couples. A plethora of websites such as Islam-Watch.com and Answering-Islam.org that feature articles on the threat of Sharia to gay people have also arisen.

2. Scholars of Judaism and Christianity challenge this interpretation and locate Sodom's sin in denial of hospitality or rape. Islamist thinkers disagree (Duran 1993, Eron 1993, Carmody and Carmody 1993).

3. For a full exploration see Carmody and Carmody 1993, 137.

4. In ancient Greece, male love between citizens and young men was condoned and practiced; in Platonic and Socratic dialogues it came to designate the ultimate love (Afary and Anderson 2005; Carmody and Carmody 1993, 141).

5. We use this term to refer to a variety of social rules and norms that make the existence of two categories of sexual beings—male and female—appear normal and universal.

6. We use this term to refer to the way in which social spaces are organized and experienced. Men interacting with other men in most aspects of their social and intimate life will be seen as existing in homosocial space.

7. Quoted in Najmabadi 2005, 158.

8. The distinction between the private (*andarooni*, referring to "inside the home") and public sphere exists in premodern Iran and refers to a similar division of the social as the Western liberal concept.

9. Within which they found much scope for homoerotic sociability. We mention this here to signal, but we cannot explore it fully in this work.

10. Examples and quotes found in Najmabadi 2005, 20.

11. The Russian armies annexed what is the modern-day Daghestan and Georgia under the Treaty of Gulistan in 1813, and in 1928, under the Treaty of Turkmenchay, Iran ceded control of what are now Armenia and Azerbaijan.

12. Quoted in Najmabadi 2005, 56. Emphasis added.

13. For extensive quotes, see Najmabadi 2005, 174.

14. For example, an intellectual such as Hasan Taqizadeh became a parliamentarian and, later, minister of finance, during Reza Shah's rule, while Mohammad Ali Foroghi became the prime minister.

15. The Shiite branch of Islam is more hierarchical than the Sunni one, with four subordinate ranks of clergy under the Grand Ayatollah, the highest religious authority. Unlike in the papal system, however, multiple Grand Ayatollahs coexist, each with his own interpretation of religion and his own set of followers. In this way, the Shiites' system is both hierarchical and decentralized.

16. As noted by Millett (1979), Iranian feminists did not see these reforms as beneficial. The ban of the veil was just as patriarchal an act as its reimposition after the Revolution. What Iranian women sought was equality and freedom over their bodies—and neither Reza Shah nor Mohammad Reza Shah was interested in taking these demands seriously.

17. The only overtly anti-homosexual policy of this period was the removal of references to same-sex love in school textbooks (Afary 2009, 175).

18. The consolidation of power under Mohammad Reza Shah took time. His power, immediately upon his father's abdication in 1941, was undermined by popularly elected Prime Minister Mohammad Mosaddegh. Mosaddegh attempted to nationalize Iranian oil, but this was deemed to be a threat by the United States and the United Kingdom. The two powers undertook Operation Ajax, removed the prime minister from office in 1953, and backed the Western-friendly Shah.

19. Oil revenues averaged around $15 billion per year, which allowed Mohammad Reza Shah to expand state-development projects. This spending resulted in great social dislocations and a widening gap between haves and have-nots (Abrahamian 2008, 140). Expectations of living standards had risen due to increases in education, but so had the gap in consumption between the upper and lower classes. This pattern fostered widespread resentment, especially among the urban poor (Abrahamian 2008, 140). Moreover, toward the end of Mohammad Reza Shah's regime, escalating military expenditure left little money for social programs—in 1977, half of oil revenues were spent on military equipment from the West alone (Abrahamian 2008, 132).

20. Examples of aggravating double standards abound. For instance, foreign skilled workers generally received substantially higher salaries than Iranian skilled workers with the same level of education. Moreover, foreign workers' presence and spending habits led to growing inflation and a scarcity of housing (Keddie 2003, 160).

21. Despite the initial turmoil, the new Islamic Republic government rapidly moved to broaden and deepen central agencies of administration and coercion. To that end, they expanded the government bureaucracy rapidly; it grew from 304,000 civil servants in 1979 to 850,000 civil servants in 1982 (Abrahamian, 2008, 169). The coercive apparatus of the new state included the Revolutionary Guards, an armed force that existed in parallel to the regular army, and was charged with ensuring the regime's survival in the face of coups, domestic uprisings, and external threats. The new Ministry of Culture and Islamic Guidance was charged with ideological and propaganda dissemination amongst the populace.

22. The actual number of executions is uncertain since many killings took place after a hasty trial, without much documentation. Bakhash (1984) bases his numbers on evidence gathered by Amnesty International.

23. This interpretation may also apply to the taking over of the American embassy and its staff in 1979 (Harmon 2005, 62).

24. Feminist author Kate Millet, who was in Iran at the time, writes, "as for the homosexuals, they were shot right in the road, judgment took seconds" (1979, 109).

25. Ayatollah Khomeini is referred to as *Bonyangozare Jomhoriye Islami* in Farsi, which translates into "the creator of Islamic Republic."

26. While prior to 1979, women constituted about 12.9 percent of the Iranian labor force, in the first months of post-revolutionary regime, this percentage dropped to 8.2 percent, only to climb slowly toward full participation now (Sedghi 2007, 233).

27. The Islamic Penal Code of Iran is available at http://mehr.org/Islamic_Penal_Code_of_Iran.pdf.

28. Khatami used slogans of *Ghanoonmandi* (lawfulness), *Jameye Madani* (civil society), and *Goftegooye Tamadonha* (dialogue among civilizations) to propose reforms to the Islamic Republic's system. He implemented laws designed to ensure greater freedom of the press, expand ethnic rights, and increase gender equality. He sought to improve relations with the West. In each of these he was ultimately thwarted. For further exploration, see Abrahamian 2008, 182.

29. According to the CIA's *World Factbook*, close to two-thirds of the Iranian population is under the age of thirty, 71 percent of the population lives in urban centers, and 77 percent of the population is literate.

30. Feminist groups have held many demonstrations, and they initiated a campaign of gathering one million signatures for the repeal of discriminatory laws against women. For more, see *The Independent*'s coverage of the campaign: http://www.independent .co.uk/news/world/middle-east/lipstick-revolution-irans-women-are-taking-on-the -mullahs-1632257.html.

31. Based on author's personal experience in Tehran in 2009–10.

32. The publication has been discontinued. It was replaced by a new e-zine by the name of *Cheraq*; *Cheraq* was replaced by *Neda* in November 2008.

33. The Iranian Supreme Leader, Ayatollah Khamenei, often decries *Tahajome Farhangi* (the cultural invasion of Iran by the West) and warns of the dangers this poses to the Iranian youth.

34. For more, see the coverage of this issue by Human Rights First: http://www .humanrightsfirst.org/our-work/human-rights-defenders/iran/one-million-signature -campaign-timeline.

35. For more, see the Iranian Human Rights Documentation Center: http://www. iranhrdc.org/english/news/press-statements/3142-iran-human-rights-documenta- tion-center-calls-for-release-of-nasrin-sotoudeh-and-houtan-kian.html.

36. Quoted in Aman and Samii 2005.

37. The speech in its entirety is available in Farsi on Ayatollah Khamenei's website: http://www.khamenei.ir/FA/Speech/detail.jsp?id=860413A.

38. See also Lind (this volume) on a somewhat similar development in Ecuador, where there has been a shift in how homosexuality is treated, from a criminal offence to a medical disease.

39. In one telling exchange, an Iranian judge demanded a confession of penetrative sex. When the defendant conceded only that he had lustfully kissed and hugged other men, the judge threatened to send him for a forensic rectal examination (HRW 2010, 57).

Bibliography

Abdi, Abbas. 2001. "Iran at the Crossroads, " *Global Dialogue* 3, no. 2. Available at http://www.worlddialogue.org/content.php?id=144 (accessed June 25, 2011).

Abrahamian, Ervand. 2008. *A History of Modern Iran.* Cambridge: Cambridge University Press.

Afary, Janet. 2009. *Sexual Politics of Modern Iran*. Cambridge: Cambridge University Press.

Afary, Janet, and Kevin Anderson. 2005. *Foucault and the Iranian Revolution: Gender and the Seductions of Islamism*. Chicago: University of Chicago Press.

Aman, Fatemeh, and Bill Samii. 2005. *Iran: Is There an Anti-Homosexual Campaign?* Available at http://www.rferl.org/featuresarticle/2005/09/febbe245-8b6f-4d30-a77f -d0b40c23da05.html (accessed June 19, 2011).

Ansari, Ali. 2003. *Modern Iran Since 1921: The Pahlavis and After*. London: Longman.

Carmody, Denise and John Carmody. 1993. "Homosexuality and Roman Catholicism." In Arlene Swindler, ed., *Homosexuality and World Religions*. Valley Forge, PA: Trinity.

Bakhash, Shaul. 1984. *Reign of the Ayatollahs: Iran and the Islamic Revolution*. New York: Basic Books.

CIA. 2011. *The World Factbook*. Available at https://www.cia.gov/library/publications/ the-world-factbook/geos/ir.html (accessed June 21, 2011).

Duran, Khalid. 1993. "Homosexuality and Islam." In Arlene Swindler, ed., *Homosexuality and World Religions*. Valley Forge, PA: Trinity.

Eron, Lewis. 1993. "Homosexuality and Judaism." In Arlene Swindler, ed., *Homosexuality and World Religions*. Valley Forge, PA: Trinity.

Foucault, Michel. 1990. *The History of Sexuality, Vol. 1: An Introduction*. New York: Vintage Books.

Gelvin, James. 2005. *Modern Middle East: A History*. Oxford: Oxford University Press.

Harmon, Daniel. 2005. *Ayatollah Ruhollah Khomeini*. Philadelphia: Chelsea House, 2005.

The Holy Bible. 1962. Revised Standard Version. New York: New American Library.

Holy Qur'an. 1982. Trans. M. H. Shakir. Elmhurst, NY: Tahrike Tarsile Qur'an.

Human Rights Watch (HRW). 2010. *We Are a Buried Generation: Discrimination and Violence Against Sexual Minorities in Iran*. New York: HRW.

Huntington, Samuel. 1968. *Political Order in Changing Societies*. New Haven, CT: Yale University Press.

Kafi, Helene. 1992. "Islam." In Arno Shmitt and Jehoda Sofer, eds., *Sexuality and Eroticism among Males in Moslem Societies*. New York: Haworth Press.

Keddie, Nikki. 2003. *Modern Iran: Roots and Results of Revolution*. New Haven, CT: Yale University Press.

Khamenei, Ayatollah Ali. 2007. *Bayanate Rahbare Moazame Enghelab Islami dar Didare Grouhe Kasiri az Zanane Nokhbe dar Astanaye Salrooze Milade Hazrate Zahraye Athar*. Available at http://www.khamenei.ir/FA/Speech/detail.jsp?id=860413A (accessed June 20, 2011).

Mahdi, Ali Akbar. 2004. "The Iranian Women's Movement: A Century Long Struggle." *The Muslim World* 94, no. 4: 427–48.

Massad, Joseph. 2002. "Re-Orienting Desire: The Gay International and the Arab World." *Public Culture* 14, no. 2: 361–85.

Massad, Joseph. 2007. *Desiring Arabs*. Chicago: University of Chicago Press.

Migdal, Joel. 1998. *Strong Societies and Weak States: State-Society Relations and State Capabilities in the Third World*. Princeton, NJ: Princeton University Press.

Millett, Kate. 1979. *Going to Iran*. New York: Coward, McCann and Geoghegan.

Moallem, Minoo. 2005. *Between Warrior Brother and Veiled Sister: Islamic Fundamentalism and the Politics of Patriarchy in Iran*. Berkeley: University of California Press.

Najmabadi, Afsaneh. 2005. *Women with Mustaches and Men without Beards: Gender and Sexual Anxieties of Iranian Modernity*. Berkeley: University of California Press.

OpenNet Initiative. 2009. *Internet Filtering in Iran*. Available at http://opennet.net/ sites/opennet.net/files/ONI_Iran_2009.pdf (accessed June 20, 2011).

Pink News. 2007. *Ahmadinejad's Gay Comments Lost in Translation*. Available at http:// www.pinknews.co.uk/news/articles/2005-5566.html/ (accessed June 20, 2011).

Poulson, Stephen C. 2005. *Social Movements in Twentieth-Century Iran: Culture, Ideology, Mobilizing Frameworks*. Lanham, MD: Lexington Books.

Said, Edward. 1979. *Orientalism*. New York: Vintage Books.

Schimmel, Annemarie. 1975. *Mystical Dimensions of Islam*. Chapel Hill: University of North Carolina Press.

Sedghi, Hamideh. 2007. *Women and Politics in Iran: Veiling, Unveiling, and Reveiling*. Cambridge: Cambridge University Press.

Shamisa, Cyrus. 2002. *Shahedbazi dar Adabiat Farsi*. Tehran: Ferdows Publications.

Skocpol, Theda. 1979. *States and Social Revolutions: A Comparative Analysis of France, Russia and China*. Cambridge: Cambridge University Press.

Skocpol, Theda. 1994. *Social Revolutions in the Modern World*. Cambridge: Cambridge University Press.

Wehrey, Frederic, et al. 2009. *The Rise of the Pasdaran: Assessing the Domestic Roles of Iran's Islamic Revolutionary Guards Corps*. Santa Monica, CA: RAND National Defense Research Institute.

Zarit, Jerry. 1992. "Intimate Look of the Iranian Male." In Arno Shmitt and Jehoda Sofer, eds., *Sexuality and Eroticism among Males in Moslem Societies*. New York: Haworth Press.

9

Navigating International Rights and Local Politics

Sexuality Governance in Postcolonial Settings

SAMI ZEIDAN

As the world focuses its attention on the Arab/Muslim world against a backdrop of seemingly endless counterterrorism efforts, attempts to "accommodate" "cultural" issues with "Islam," and a wave of democratic Arab Spring revolts (and ensuing repression), one wonders whether trends in international human rights have been responsive to local political and historical contexts. More importantly, why have human-rights efforts in the Arab/Muslim world produced outcomes that often seem surprising? In December 2011, Hillary Clinton made the much-publicized announcement that: "Gay people are born into and belong to every society in the world." As if to remove any doubt she curiously added that: "Being gay is not a Western invention. It is a human reality." Government agencies in the United States are now directed to consider gay rights when making decisions about aid and asylum. Furthermore, the United States has announced that it will fight discrimination against gays and lesbians around the world by using foreign aid and diplomacy to encourage reforms. What do such developments tell us about the role of the state in discourses about sexuality? How are such moves received in the Arab/Muslim world?

In Egypt, state efforts to regulate sexuality have been "sporadic, short-lived and typically occasioned by political circumstances and the need to bolster regime legitimacy" (Dunne 1998, 10). In November 2001, Egypt raided the Queen Boat (a floating disco on the Nile known as a gay hangout) and charged Egyptian (but not foreign) "gay" men with obscenity and contempt for religion—despite the fact that Egypt has no specific law against homosexuality and that the arresting authorities had no proof that the individuals arrested were homosexual (Dahir 2001, 28). The Queen Boat men were actually tried by a special emergency state security court, which led Joseph Massad to caution that "the state considers this a national security issue" (Massad 2007, 182). The Lebanese equivalent of the Egyptian Queen Boat case was the governmental closing of a gay Lebanese website and the raid of gay-frequented Acid nightclub in 2005. In the raid, the police arbitrarily arrested a handful of people on allegations of "devil worshipping." However, both the intent and intensity of the raid have been disputed, as the incident may not necessarily have involved cracking down on non-normative sexualities and genders. Acid continued with business as usual, and the real problems might have been the "admittance of underage individuals and suspected drug use" (McCormick 2006, 251). There have been numerous other such incidents recently in the region.

This chapter goes beyond making the case that performing one's gender or sexuality is a right worth protecting and defending against sexist and homophobic intolerance. First, it calls attention to the potential confines of the labels brought to bear on non-heteronormative sexualities and genders by even the most liberal societies. Further, the chapter focuses on the tensions raised in balancing activism as it claims rights and struggles against the emergence of a borrowed homophobia implanted locally in a contested state (see also Bosia, this volume), and the more stable and durable forms of local sexual governance. While too easily dismissed as lifestyles that are performed in the confines of heteronormative imprisonment (that is to say, of something from which to be liberated), living one's life as a lesbian in the closet, or as a veiled transsexual, or as a gay parent in heterosexual wedlock can have tremendous ethical implications, particularly in the Arab/Muslim world. Slipping in and out of identities throughout one's lifetime sounds intellectually sexy but can be disturbing. Ultimately, the greatest social changes may be intentional or unintentional, rational or irrational, and quite possibly the result of living one's life as best one can while consciously being wary of token change as a superficial political (fashion) statement that earns one the title of being tolerant, sex positive, alternative, radical, respectful, or queer or of embracing diversity. Being open to change develops from varied life experiences that transcend intellectual musings or from perspectives derived from one's immediate vantage point. While coalitions are key to permeate the public sphere and to engage meaningfully with it, this does not necessarily mean that these coalitions must be based on coherent identities, especially, as others in this volume explore, when rights and identities raise a variety of global specters easily exploitable in local political contestation. Rather, we must ask "not whether we share a given position but whether we share a commitment to improve it, and whether we can commit to the pain of embarrassment and confrontation as we disagree" (Phelan 1994, 156).

In this process, unforeseen parallels invariably surface. Take, for example, that between Western LGBT persons and Muslim veiled immigrant women. The common ground is the fear of arrest or harassment for not conforming to appearance or dress codes: "After all, a dress code that can be used against a woman in *niqab* can target a drag queen next. Failing to recognize such potential understanding is not only a lapse in imagination; it is a collapse of politics—a failure to *be* political, to think beyond identity into possibility" (Long 2009, 132). At first view there is no obvious link between the political struggles of a veiled woman and a drag queen. There is space, then, for cooperation with embattled Muslim immigrants in the West against police misconduct and repressive policies, and this space *is* politics. Instead of working within a predefined box of LGBT identity-based activism, Western advocates could be sensitive to the fact that coming out in Lebanon and the Arab/Muslim world[1] is not on the radar of many non-heteronormative sexualities and genders. Some may go so far in valuing the institution of tradition and the family that their lack of sexual interest in the opposite sex does not stop them from entering a heterosexual marriage. Sexual-rights advocates could thus be sensitive to the historical pattern that Arab/Muslim society has been known to tolerate as long as an individual's sexual conduct does not challenge traditional institutions of marriage and religion. Arab/Muslim society has likewise at times indulged a wide range of gender and sexual behaviors. Nevertheless, there are people there for whom gay, lesbian, bisexual, transgender, or other categories do make sense, and Lebanese organizations like *Helem* ("Lebanese Protection for LGBTIQ")[2] are there to assist them, as I explain below. But the problem with some Western activists who fund and support these local groups is that they often, albeit unintentionally, filter the experiences of Lebanese men and women through reductive terminology. That is, to use Katyal's term, they presume an *exported identity* (Katyal 2002), and that projects the image that Lebanon somehow subscribes to a Western LGBT rights agenda, which in turn provokes significant backlash.

Despite recent criticisms aimed at orchestrated human-rights campaigns in the Arab/Muslim world, the issue is not whether concepts such as gay and sexual orientation are foreign imports, but whether they serve a useful purpose and include a right to self-determination asserted against and through disciplinary practices that constitute heterosexuality as normative.

Sexuality governance means that sexuality is constituted through social relations and then used as governance in a given society. In the Arab/Muslim world, governance has recently become an exercise in warding off dominant globalizing powers at the same time as it has turned inward to repress internal difference. *Heteronormativity*, a term developed by Michael Warner (1993) and inspired by Adrienne Rich's notion of "compulsory heterosexuality," captures the idea that a nonheterosexual individual (e.g., homosexual, bisexual, asexual, intersex, transgender) must struggle against the assumption that heterosexuality is the normal sexual orientation. As expected, heteronormativity is not a monolithic concept, because heterosexual family structures themselves have changed over time. The development of a sophisticated system of heteronormativity was possible as an operative form of sexuality governance alongside a parallel development of sexual rights that can be described as anti-heteronormative.[3]

Mark Blasius was among the first to elaborate the idea of sexuality as a "technique of government" (Blasius 1992, 649–50). In *Gay and Lesbian Politics*, he advances the case for lesbian and gay sexuality as an "insurrection on the part of subjectivity" (Blasius 1994, 83), affirmed by reference to sexuality as a technology of government of our selves: "It is, as such, a politics of our*selves* calling into question the power relations constitutive of us through our sexuality" (Blasius 1994, 83). In his work on governing societies, Mitchell Dean describes governing as "securing a particular form of life as something that is *normal* and, in doing so, deciding what is outside the limits to that life" (Dean 2007, 13, emphasis mine). Sexuality governance implicates discourses on gender and sexuality in national security, including the related U.S. "war on terror." As Mitchell Dean recently notes, it is a common but mistaken belief that globalization has undermined the state. He (rightly) dismisses the claim that globalization erases the binaries public/private, and state/society, both of which enable the project of governing society: "the first decade of the twenty-first century has seen an authoritarian reinscription of both of these divisions," as we have seen in "the events of 9/11, the rediscovery of the enemy in the form of Islamic fundamentalists, the war on terror"—as well as in the military occupations and the scandals of Abu-Ghraib and Guantanamo Bay (Dean 2007, 35).

Homosexuality and Homophobia in Lebanon

Sexuality governance was central to the colonizers' "civilizing" agenda, followed by a postcolonial nation-building exercise that saw sexual dissidence as a distraction at best. I suggest that Lebanon's historical uniqueness resonates with the experience of those with non-normative sexualities and genders, pitting Lebanon's own plurality and openness against more recent depictions of

Lebanon as political aberrance or a historical mistake. In political discourse it is at times listed among failed states, broadly defined. On the other hand, it boasts a relatively considerable civil society, with Beirut as the major Arab center (along with Cairo) of intellectual activity and publishing. One scholar went so far as to state that, although virtually "no political science research is being done in Arab countries," there is some such work "in countries like Egypt and Lebanon, which have scientific communities and a certain amount of freedom of expression, and a substantial amount of their work merits wider distribution" (Ben Néfissa 2000). Lebanon is constantly hailed as the only democracy in the Arab world; certainly it is still immature, but democracy would not even exist "if the people who live here had not demanded that much for themselves" (Totten 2006). In fact, the uniqueness of the Lebanese political fabric is that dictatorship is impossible. "Each sect's parliamentary bloc keeps the others in check. The result is a weak state and a de facto near-libertarianism" (Totten 2006). This is what, in my view, makes Lebanon an appropriate case study of (and for) nonconformist sexualities in postcolonial settings. There is resistance to change, first, because of the tradition of elite accommodation, which serves to cement existing identities; second, because the main allegiance of the individual is to her or his community or religious sect; and last but not least, because both government and society preserve and defend social foundations considered to be indigenous.

(Homo)sexuality is increasingly becoming a concern of the modern state, and "even in famously open and cosmopolitan Lebanon" there seems to be a "general moral panic" resulting in the policing of homosexuality (Azimi 2006). Hence Lebanese advocates have recently reoriented their efforts toward combating homophobia rather than selling the idea of a gay and lesbian identity worthy of protection. In these efforts, visible signs of Western support abound. Until recently, the Lebanese NGO *Helem*'s website indicated that it was supported in part by the Dutch Embassy in Beirut. The International Gay and Lesbian Human Rights Commission (IGLHRC) selected *Helem* as the 2009 recipient of the Felipa de Souza Award in recognition of its work to improve the human rights of those who face discrimination because of their sexuality or HIV-positive status. Yet Western support is carefully balanced with advocacy tailored to local needs, including publications in Arabic. As revealed in various campaigns, interviews, and its publication of the first book in Arabic on homophobia—*Rihab Al-Methliyya* (Ayyass 2006)—*Helem*'s avowed strategy focuses on publicly exposing homophobia and the hypocritical criminalization of homosexuality so that these subjects no longer remain taboo.

Many are surprised when they hear for the first time that a Lebanese NGO working on such issues has managed to operate legally for so long. How has this been possible? *Helem* opened its doors in Beirut in April 2004 and applied to the Ministry of Interior for official recognition in September of that year. Three months elapsed without any response, which is a legal assumption of tacit official recognition according to the Lebanese code of nonpolitical associations, unless the NGO in question expresses ideas that threaten national security or are conducive to organized crime. Reportedly, when Georges Azzi filed papers with the Ministry of Interior in 2004 to register *Helem*, an official shelved the file after writing the word "shameful" on it (*Rafei*); given the rules, the NGO could still claim recognition, despite the lack of explicit "authorization."

This ability is not to be taken lightly, as the Lebanese legal system was not always so progressive regarding the establishment of NGOs. The process of mere declaration (called *'aynIlm wa Khabar* in Arabic) replaced an earlier system of full-fledged authorization required for NGOs to exist. Today over five thousand NGOs are officially registered in Lebanon, and about two hundred new ones are established on a yearly basis (Howard 2006, 5). The reform enabled the state to exercise control following, not prior to, the creation of the NGO—hence alleviating the state's influence on civil society. However, according to *Helem's* website, the withholding of a registration number limits the organization's financial freedom and places it in legal limbo. In June 2006 the then–acting interior minister denied charges by conservative Muslim religious leaders that the Lebanese government had approved the establishment of *Helem*, but he stopped short of addressing the issue of the implicit approval three months after a noncontested declaration. The news line briefly stated: "A petition seeking prosecution of the gay rights group filed by a Beirut city attorney earlier this year was rejected by the attorney general's office, which ruled that the group's operation of an office and a Web site did not constitute an offense."[4] According to *Helem's* website, a lawsuit accusing it of "public indecency and corrupting the youth" was indeed filed against it in 2006 but was dropped following unsuccessful investigations to corroborate this claim.

That said, human-rights defenders working on sexuality constantly face dangers. For example, in 2000 the Lebanese government's vice-squad police arrested Kamal al-Batal, the director of a human-rights organization (MIRSAD), for advocating legal reform for Lebanese gays online. The charges arose from the organization's attempts to protect the privacy of information and to defend the organization's rights against police harassment. In 2001 the Military Court of Beirut charged both Batal and Ziad Mugraby, the managing director of the organization's Internet service provider (Destination), with defamation of the police in an email message:

> The message stated that it "deplored the blatant and unlawful attempts by the police to interfere in the freedom of the Internet as well as the freedom of expression of the gay community." They were charged under Article 157 of the Military Penal Code, which carries a penalty of three months to three years imprisonment. Police interrogated Mugraby in an attempt to extract the identities of persons running a gay Lebanese Web site. MIRSAD came to the defense of Destination and has suffered police harassment ever since. Condemning the arraignment before a military court the defendants stated that the charge "seemed to be an attempt to harass and intimidate a human rights defender to prevent him from carrying out his work." (Collins 2003, note 111)

The avowed governmental claim was to safeguard "public morals and national security" (imprisonment for defamation of the Lebanese army and the Lebanese flag), but the real aim was seemingly to punish a citizen for expressing a view that differed from the official position of the government (Collins 2003, 392).

Yet, interestingly, there has been increasing scholarship that depicts a seemingly greater acceptance of gender identity compared to sexual orientation (gays and lesbians) in the Arab/Muslim world. There has been more tolerance of transgender individuals in Iran and Saudi Arabia than elsewhere in the Arab/Muslim world and the West. But as Najmabadi and Habib note, the logic behind this acceptance is the reification of the binary gender paradigm that keeps men and women neatly apart in separate categories with strict presumption of heterosexuality. In other words, this seeming tolerance of transgender persons can have negative consequences on other non-heteronormative sexualities and genders. The enforcement of public homosociality is continuously threatened by the specter of homosexuality, and the anxiety generated by the delicate balance between upholding homosociality and forbidding homosexuality led to the acceptability of transsexuality and sex-change operations in Iran. The implication is that sex change could be legally imposed as a solution or alternative to execution of homosexuals.

Activists have therefore overlooked a general but important issue. The prevailing popular attitude toward non-heteronormative genders and sexualities (e.g., the argument that the decriminalization of sodomy will lead to men sleeping with men, women becoming promiscuous, and the crumbling of our nation/family/religion . . .) is a *real, sincere, genuinely held* belief, in response to which sexual-rights advocates simply must take the time to articulate their *own, substantive* rhetorical response. These moral panics target the sexually vulnerable and marginalized, because popular anxieties "of straight men, hegemonic and warring ethnic groups, the economically rapacious or insecure" find their way into the public sphere as the subtext of debates over morality, masculinity and femininity, and family relations (Parker et al. 2007, 10, 14).

I argue that the suggestion that non-normative sexualities and genders in Lebanon have a right to be treated equally may well be much harder to accept than public acknowledgment of their existence—hence the prioritization of working on combating homophobia over promoting LGBT rights per se. That is why *Helem* has made a slogan for itself in the word *Exist* and is developing the Homophobia Monitor, an online tool that collects information and resources related to the homosexual community in the Arab World. *Helem* lowered its visibility a few years ago and became relatively more of a service organization, explaining that it was important to take the time to convince society and not just do its work through a direct lobbying campaign against the government. *Helem* is also aware that a confrontation that is provoked too early could backfire, as it did on advocates of civil marriage in the 1990s.

Lebanese sexual-rights advocacy might, indeed, have to adjust to the fact that its empowered subjects—the beneficiaries of its rhetoric—are largely (in Western terms) in the closet and for the most part not struggling for free and equal interaction with heterosexuals (men). Like Manalansan, I question why practices that do not neatly align with Western scripts of how individual political subjects develop are written off as unliberated or at best homophobic. I argue that it is not so much access to the public sphere as much as it is the ability to move in and out of the public sphere with a minimal degree of safety that those with non-normative sexual orientations and gender identities crave in Lebanon. For newly "emancipated" LGBTs in the Arab/Muslim world, access to the public sphere could foster a particular form of identity conservatism, despite the initially liberal intent behind their movement. In this regard, my understanding and use of the term *public sphere* is to accommodate a notion of the public that is thought of as opposed to the private, *yet permeable to political redefinition.* The public sphere is generally where people deliberate "over matters of common concern, matters that are contested and about which it seems necessary to reach a consensus" (Dean, J. 2003, 95). But variations of this notion of the public sphere appear in distinctions between public and private, where *public* designates the state and *private* means the market and the family (Dean, J. 2003, 95). The point is to explore the necessity of a public sphere that allows those with non-heteronormative sexualities and genders to work out a local grassroots self-definition. In so doing, with what forces of globalization do they have to contend?

Which Side Is Globalization On?

Bearing in mind the way sexuality governance operates, I argue, like Boaventura de Sousa Santos (2007), that the task of emancipatory politics is not to work within a West/rest or global/local binary, but rather to transform both the practice and the very conceptualization of human rights into an appropriated and modified transgressive discourse. Avoiding entrapment in the binary begins by realizing that Western culture is not monolithic (any more than non-Western cultures are) and therefore neither is (nor can be) the locus of the conception of human rights. Oppressed groups need to develop the power to call themselves global, approximating a state's support of a transnational model of homophobia targeting local sexual minorities. For example, a non-Western rights-advocacy strategy for non-normative sexualities and genders could focus on local history to question the idea of an Arab cultural past that was premised solely on an authentic, opposite-sex sexuality. Strategies adopted could include, following El-Menyawi (2006), downplaying support from the West and publicly persuading the local population not on gay rights per se, but on issues that appear to have very little explicit connection with gay rights or gay identity—such as privacy rights; separation of state from religion; and open activism on issues such as economic revitalization, democracy, rule of law, and human rights.

Sexuality governance is commonly grasped at the level of the nation-state. However, as Mitchell Dean rightly notes, the "political project of governing societies" can also involve governing in the international domain by international law and international organizations (Dean 2007, 6). Since the end of the Cold War, energies at the international level have shifted away from strictly security issues and focused on increasing resources devoted to the monitoring of human rights. However, this move at the international level from exclusive focus on security issues to increased attention to human rights still faces national-security exceptions. For example, the UN special representative on human rights defenders said that states regarded sexuality data as part of their national security; they claimed that information whose publication was a threat to national security included "information on HIV/AIDS, reports of alleged human rights abuses by members of a governing political party," and "statements critical of the human rights impacts of government security policies" (Jilani qtd. in Corrêa, Petchesky, and Parker 2008, 230, note 7). This is perhaps why Mitchell Dean points to the role of globalization in remoralizing the individual (and states) under ever-more-intrusive sovereign surveillance; in the case of states, this is being done both multilaterally and unilaterally, such as by "coalitions of the willing" (Dean 2007, 5). This chapter looks at both of these aspects of international governance—that is, human rights as well as military intervention, with a focus on governance of sexuality. In this perspective, the goal of emancipatory political projects is not (only) to work within a binary of West/rest or global/local, but rather to transform human rights into a transgressive discourse that is appropriated and modified.

Sexual Identity as Both Problem and Solution

At the UN, human-rights law concerning non-heteronormative genders and sexualities emerged in relation to refugee claims. The 1951 Convention Relating to the Status of Refugees defines refugees as individuals who have a "well-founded fear of being persecuted for reasons of race, religion, nationality, membership of a particular social group, or political opinion." The term *social group* in this definition has been interpreted by several states to extend asylum to persons fleeing persecution because of their sexual orientation or gender identity. The legal concept behind granting refugee status is non-refoulement, which means that a person cannot be forcibly returned to a place where s/he faces persecution. There are numerous such asylum cases around the world, including in the United States. It is perhaps easy to forget that until the late 1980s, U.S. immigration laws regarded homosexuality, alongside communism and criminal conviction, as grounds for barring individuals from entering the country (Manalansan 1997, 498). Not surprisingly, the formulation of asylum claims tends to generate a discourse that upholds neocolonialism, nationalism, and an immaterial politics of identity that focuses on immutability: "Successful asylum claims generally require generating a racialist, colonialist discourse that impugns the nation-state from which the asylum seeker comes, while participating in an adjudication process that often depends on constructs of 'immutable' identity refracted through colonialist, reified models of culture shorn of all material relations" (Luibhéid 2008, 179).

Granting asylum also reveals the flipside of what some see as a haven for non-normative sexualities and genders resulting from the inability of a weak state to enforce the criminal laws that target them. Lebanon may be hailed as a gay-friendly destination in the Arab world, and it may indeed be tolerant while also being unable and unwilling to afford protection to non-normative sexualities and genders. This weakness of the state can in turn be leveraged as evidence for asylum, as a Lebanese man from Tripoli did to gain asylum in Belgium because of persecution based on his sexual orientation. A similar discourse was used in the case of Karouni in the United States, which I examine next.

In 2005 the U.S. Ninth Circuit Court of Appeals pronounced itself on an immigration case involving a gay Lebanese man suffering from AIDS named Nasser Mustapha Karouni.[5] Karouni came to the United States on a visitor's visa in 1987 after Hezbollah detained and threatened him as a result of his relationship with another man. He applied for asylum in 1998, stating that a former lover had been beaten and that a gay cousin was killed after having survived being shot in the rear two years earlier. Looking beyond the gruesome facts, the opinion is interesting insofar as it illustrates the way coming out as LGBT is a political (at times even existential) imperative for claiming and receiving rights on the transnational level. The issues examined in the opinion range from homophobia to antigay violence to outing in Lebanese society.

The person in question lived in the Hezbollah-controlled city of Tyre in southern Lebanon with his cousin, who was shot to death by Hezbollah because he, too, was gay. The opinion stated that Hezbollah (considered a terrorist organization by the United States) applies "strict Islamic law," as if to hint that the Lebanese state's government, police, military, or appointed leaders of the Shiite sect (to which Karouni belongs) have little to do with law enforcement. We are reminded that the reality on the ground is that the state has a fragmented role at best (that is to say that a set of religious local governments still exist, not unlike the Ottoman-style *zaim* system). "[T]he Lebanese government, or at least *local governments* within Lebanon, attempt to curb homosexual conduct through oppressive state action" (emphasis mine). The opinion correctly depicts Hezbollah as one of many local governments but curiously a privileged one that has access to oppressive state action. Indeed, in 2003, Hezbollah security forces had arrested a group of young men and delivered them to the Lebanese police to be charged under the penal code for engaging in same-sex acts (Saghieh in Scalenghe 2004, 235). As appellant, Karouni claimed "severe systemic intolerance," as exemplified not only when "Muslim militia-men repeatedly forced the barrel of a rifle" into his anus, but also when they had shot his cousin Khalil in the anus before killing him. "The perpetrators primitively and abhorrently believed that they were punishing Khalil for his perceived sins by mutilating, as Karouni characterized it, 'the locus of Khalil's homosexual sin'"[6]—i.e., the anus.

The other Shiite militia, Amal, which is Hezbollah's rival, "also played a role in this story. Amal forces interrogated and attempted to arrest Karouni at his apartment after they learned that he had been involved in a sexual relationship with a man."[7] They forced him to "confess to the crime of homosexuality" and "to name other homosexuals," thus forcing Karouni to come out and reveal a sexual identity deduced from having performed a specific sexual act. The undoubtedly related class dynamics were also made clear: "Karouni testified that his family name is so recognizable that it placed him at great risk because it identifies him as both a member of a prominent family and a Shi'ite. According to Karouni, many Islamic fundamentalists in Lebanon regard wealthy Shi'ite landowners as enemies and target them for no reason other than that they are Shi'ite and landowners" (Drexel 2005, 67). Karouni was thus portrayed as being of interest to Hezbollah because he belonged to a specific class.

The U.S. attorney general (Gonzales) had claimed that Karouni lacked a basis for asylum because of the fact that Lebanon only punishes homosexual *acts* but not homosexuals themselves. However, the opinion—probably inspired by the case *Lawrence v. Texas*[8]—replied in disagreement that this is an unfair demand because it involves giving Karouni a "Hobson's choice of returning to Lebanon and either (1) facing persecution for engaging in future homosexual acts or (2) living a life of celibacy"—both of which are unfair. The court qualified this persecution as being "on account of Karouni's membership in the particular social group of homosexuals." Coming out and having a sexual identity were imperatives for Karouni. First, he told the court he could not live anonymously in Lebanon since he was outed by a gay friend during a police interrogation. Second, Karouni said his identity in Lebanon would not be kept secret because of his AIDS treatment. Thus sexual identity became for Karouni both a compulsory problem in Lebanon as well as the inevitable later solution in the United States, around which his basic rights and very survival were at stake. Somehow, sexual identity became an issue of individual, national, and international security, and a discursive means of communicating with states at all those levels.

Whose "War on Terror"?

Corrêa, Petchesky, and Parker have recently drawn attention to the gendered and homophobic dimensions of U.S.-supported Islamist politics in Iraq, in particular the use of homophobia as a media tool to marshal support for the war on terror inside Iraq (Corrêa, Petchesky, and Parker 2008, 201). From the U.S. side, on the other hand, Scott Long has noted gay and lesbian activists' use of Islam as the resilient "other" against which to define sameness (a universal "gay") both violently *and* to deny difference (Long 2009, 130–31).

For our purposes, an interesting question is: To what extent is the U.S.-led "war on terror" after the September 11, 2001, terrorist attacks important in contemporary sexuality governance in both the West and the Arab/Muslim world? Corrêa, Petchesky, and Parker rightly note that "the continual breaching of the supposed 'wall' between public and private, secular and religious, is chiefly about regulating sexuality and gender" (Corrêa, Petchesky, and Parker 2008, 78). No doubt the geopolitical importance of the United States, combined with the context and timing of the attacks and their aftermath, has had significant effects on sexuality governance around the world. A neoconservative "moral" agenda included over $15 billion in U.S. foreign assistance to prevent and treat AIDS in the most afflicted countries, explicitly conditioned upon criteria upholding a "heteronormative, conjugal, and procreative model of sexuality so dear to the heart of the US Christian Right" (Corrêa, Petchesky, and Parker 2008, 36). After the September 11, 2001, attacks on the United States, a united front against terrorism was declared through a combination of police action and a general commitment to prevent future attacks. It was not long before the UN, among others, signaled dangers of violating international law and fundamental freedoms in the course of an unprecedented "war" on terrorism. In dealing with international terrorism post-9/11, the standard response by governments and the population at large has been to see law as irrelevant at worst and as a backup to the military response at best (Chibundu 2004, 898). The post-9/11 world has been described as an age marked by insecurities generated by the overriding fear of terrorism. As it turns out, the U.S. "war on terror" declared by the Bush administration became yet another incident in a larger historical pattern of colonial and postcolonial military conquests involving sexual appropriation and humiliation (Petchesky 2003).

The journalist Andrew Sullivan (Catholic, conservative, and openly gay), whose political blog is widely read, proposes a single link connecting the Taliban's persecution of homosexuals and the 9/11 events, and he describes it as a fundamentalist Islamic line (Wärn 2003, 107). Elsewhere, Sullivan is even more explicit about depicting monolithic distinctions between "brutal Islamic dictatorships" on the one hand, and the United States and Israel on the other, which have "the power to stop" them. His blogs addressing American gay readers illustrate how prominent Western (pro-)gay activists themselves feed the unhelpfully other-ing discourse that links sexual orientation to national security, especially since 9/11. Sullivan said, "I'm saddened that more gay organizations haven't rallied to the war against Muslim religious fanatics. This is our war too" (qtd. in Long 2009, 124). At the time, another link was being made in U.S. popular discourse between terrorism and homosexuality after 9/11: Three days after the attacks, Baptist minister Jerry Falwell blamed homosexual individuals for sinning and for bringing about God's anger articulated by the terrorists as punishment inflicted on the U.S. population (Shaban 2003, 13). All sides, it turns out, were governing non-heteronormative sexualities. Illustrating the "war on terror" as another postcolonial military conquest involving sexual appropriation is the following response by a U.S. gay soldier (to a blog by Sullivan on a controversial execution of two purportedly gay men in Iran): "Your post . . . confirmed for me that my recent decision to join the US military was correct. I have to stuff myself back in the closet [because of the U.S. ban on gays in the armed services at the time] . . . but our war on terror trumps my personal comfort at this point" (qtd. in Long 2009, 124). Similarly, members of the conservative gay group Log Cabin Republicans announced that "in the wake of news stories and photographs documenting the hanging of two gay Iranian teenagers," they "reaffirm(ed) their commitment to the global war on terror" (qtd. in Long 2009, 126). What this meant for the U.S. gay community was an existential self-definition via the articulated need to step in and speak for persons in the Arab/Muslim world imagined as the "same" but supposedly unable to speak for themselves. Curiously, then, the war on terror allowed (and encouraged?) U.S. gay activists to deny difference in the Arab/Muslim world and thus delineate the boundaries of a (Western) gay identity held to be universal (Long 2009, 130)—as echoed recently by Hillary Clinton. In this cultural exercise conditioning access to the public sphere, Islam became the convenient scapegoat. As Long eloquently puts it: "if pursuing recognition in the diffuse and sign-saturated public sphere of the modern West has led gay and lesbian movements into a mirror-realm of becoming similar, this quest for visibility requires at heart a more resilient opponent, against whom the self can be antagonistically defined. Islam serves that function for many activists in the USA and Europe" (2009, 131).

The question for American gay activists supporting the "war on terror" (supposedly for well-meaning human-rights causes) becomes whether it makes sense that Arab/Muslim gays and lesbians be "fought over and re-signified a continent away," through "promoting fear or engendering division" or even "selling the idea of a war" (Long 2009, 133). In sum, by insisting on stepping in and speaking for (instead of to) victims of homophobia in the Arab/Muslim world, American LGBT activists define themselves and identify with the hegemonic culture, and their human-rights activism (whether consciously or not) mirrors the treatment of Islam by the U.S.-led "war on terror."

Rise of the Individual

The link between homosexuality and self-reflection deserves our attention, if only because of its particular significance in the Arab/Muslim world. Most Arabs opposed to homosexuality repeatedly insist that such a lifestyle/identity goes against ancient social arrangements (such as heterosexual marriage and the traditional family as the societal unit). But it often turns out that, in fact, claims about "ancient" rules ("it has always been this way") do not date back more than two or three generations. Norms governing identities and relationships change over time and from culture to culture, and what is held to be indigenous can be the result of colonial intervention. The fact is that repressive authorities from various parts of the world summon culture as an argument for governing sexuality. This explains why, even as Arab Muslims charge that "perversions" come from elsewhere, officials in India had once not only denounced homosexuality as "against Indian culture," but also added that "Hindus don't have these practices—these are all perversions of the Muslims" (Human Rights Watch 2002 Report, qtd. in Long 2009, 129). Interestingly, this assertion has recently been superseded by the Delhi High Court ruling of July 2009 and its aftermath, delegitimizing Section 377 of the Indian Penal Code (entitled "Of Unnatural Offences") and recognizing that anti-sodomy laws are a relic from British colonial rule and that Indian "tradition" is much more pluralistic (see Ramasubban in Parker, Petchesky, and Sember 2007, 91–125).

In the contemporary Arab world, which is still emerging from arranged marriages and strong gender differentials, it is not just homosexuality, but individual lifestyle choices that present the shock of the new. The work of Abdellah Taia, who rose to fame as the first Moroccan gay and out autobiographical writer, illustrates the difficulties with the use of the first person in the Arab/Muslim world. In a recent essay he wrote: "'We' as opposed to 'I.' As most other Moroccans, I lived, for a very long time, as part of the 'we' of society, the 'we' of the group: the family was a single unit, the neighborhood was a single unit, the street was a single unit, school was a single unit, the nation was a single unit, Islam was a single unit. My own 'I' didn't exist, didn't have a chance to exist . . . The 'I' is operated by remote control" (Taia 2009). And Dunne's comparative study (of what can be thought of as as heteronormative practices of sexuality governance) explains that "*The greater success of the Middle Eastern patriarchal family* in maintaining intra-familial structures of male dependency otherwise undermined by economic change *may have inhibited that 'potential individuality' making possible egalitarian homosexual relationships*" (Dunne 1990, 75–76, emphasis mine).

Given the historical facts, surely it is not a sudden emergence of homosexuality that is prompting homophobic backlash. What enabled the emergence of a gay identity (a distinct lifestyle choice around which a sociopolitical movement was built) in the West was the onset of industrialization, urbanization, and the resulting decline of the family as an economic unit as well as the emergence in parallel of individuals actually able to make personal choices (about family and social arrangements) without the watchful eye of a tightly knit community (Heinze 2001, 303). Mitchell Dean writes that "there has been the emergence of a project for the reformation of character through the proper governance and cultivation of the individual" (Dean 2007, 5). The individual precedes the "homosexual," and it is therefore much more likely that the threat of the gay-rights agenda for Arab/Muslim states lies in the associated rise in individual autonomy.

Even heterosexual marriages and families have come to be based more on individual choice than on parental or community dictates. I want to emphasize here that heterosexuality is not some constant monolithic concept against which homosexuality emerged. Until scientific advances produced a discourse around sexuality, (heterosexual) marriage in the West was (and is still) much more than just about two biologically compatible individuals. Marriage had for a long time been as a union exclusively between aristocrats, or between Catholics, and so on. It is relatively recently that marriage has come to be understood as a biological union that represents both a given and the (heterosexual) standard against which all other relationships and identities are constructed (Heinze 2001, 304). All known societies have governed sexual conduct, whether through formal law or through social norms, and both heterosexual and homosexual individual lifestyles were the product of nineteenth-century radical changes in technology and market structures.

Colonized people were depicted as savages, in part because of their "unusual" sexualities, including same-sex or transgender practices. After World War II, the human-rights movement vowed to eradicate colonialism, but it was too late to change the colonial statutes on which political elites in non-Western states still rely today to defend discrimination against non-heteronormative sexualities and genders (Heinze 2001). Of course, it is not as if the colonies were havens of sexual freedom before the Europeans came along. Rather, the point is that today's homophobia as enshrined in laws such as the Lebanese Penal Code Article 534 (punishing same-sex acts as crimes against nature) is largely the vestige of colonial codification.[9] This provenance calls into question the characterization by postcolonial leaders of various non-heteronormative sexualities and genders as "un-Islamic" or "un-Arab."

Sexual-rights advocates must therefore be attuned to the subtle ways in which postcolonial leaders perpetuate the very thing that they accuse Europeans of having once done to them. Namely, they ignore the wide-ranging variety of histories of countless different African and Asian peoples with their different sets of varying social and sexual norms throughout large stretches of history. The result is, according to Heinze, a masquerade in which the East says to the West, "We'll pretend to have ancient traditions, you'll pretend to respect them" (Heinze 2001, 308). A similar concern must have prompted Garcia to call for "a critique of normative forms of nationalism that, in their obsession with the nativist past, colonize the nation's differences into a sameness" (Garcia 1996, 291). This auto-recolonization of difference echoes Long's critique of international human-rights-advocacy strategies, in which Western gay activists delineate gay identity by erasing internal difference and seeking (creating) a mirrored sameness in places like Iran that requires their help because the community there is unable to articulate its needs. Concepts such as human rights and homosexuality are historically and culturally contingent products of time and place. But they constitute a rhetorically and politically useful strategy that can be used by all sides of the definitional debate. The point is not to allow homophobic groups, including Arab governments, to appropriate them exclusively.

Whose Theoretical Languages?

A review of recent empirical work on Lebanese gay identities prompts the question of whether advocacy is inciting a Western-style identity revolving around sexuality and whether this is the main problem. I do not believe that inevitable westernization is as much a problem in Beirut as in other Arab/Muslim cities. There is a larger problem of representation in Lebanon. The society consistently says on the streets, in advertisements, and in magazines that Western is better. Although television programs produced in Lebanon for consumption in the Arab/Muslim world reproduce a Western idea of entertainment reality television, they contribute to the construction of an Arab identity while simultaneously provoking backlash because of perceived clashes with Islamic values. Youth demographics and urbanization have catalyzed the effect of information and communications technology as a mediator of Western-style global gay identities, but the Arab/Muslim world is incredibly diverse. A politicized sexual identity, then, need not be restricted to the reductive LGBT initials. An LGBT(/Q/I) identity in Lebanon may well be Western, but that is partly because Western models abound and are often the only visible cultural templates that seem available to non-normative sexualities and genders. The universalizing of gay terminology, which is often condemned as Western hegemony, can in fact have a locally liberatory function. The term *gay* may have become indigenized to mean many different things. *Globalization* is defined by Santos (2007) as the power of a given local position to *designate* itself as global while simultaneously designating rival positions as local. In other words, it is the power to categorize, draw boundaries, and control movement in and out of the categorical boundaries.

Massad uses the term *Gay International* to describe an orchestrated, missionary, human-rights campaign, guided by orientalism and inspired by "the white western women's movement, which had sought to universalize its issues through imposing its own colonial feminism on the women's movements in the non-western world" (Massad 2007, 361–32). Nevertheless, articulately blaming the West for "stabilizing" purportedly once colorful precolonial sexual practices is no substitute for substantive engagement in self-reflection, past and present. Why do more Arab and Muslim scholars not do the uneasy work of (re)presenting Arab and Muslim desire, instead of waiting for, as Warner (1993) puts it, "white US sexual politics" to carry out its "internationalization of the epistemologies producing" theoretical languages? Why care about the covert agendas of the Gay International if scholars in the Arab/Muslim world do not produce their own "theoretical languages"? In the past the Muslim world attracted Western colonial disapproval for "doing" sex, and today the Western Gay International occasions Eastern disapproval for "speaking" sex. Sexual transgressions abound everywhere, in ways that are sometimes similar and at other times different.

Is it then possible for sexual and gender dissidents to produce their own theoretical languages in today's globalizing world without dependence on Western genres or structures of hegemony? Building on the qualitative research of McCormick and others, the case can be made that language and identity categories are a field of contestation, hybridity, and fusion. As explained above, I argue that the threat of the gay-rights agenda for Arab/Muslim states lies in the associated rise of individual autonomy. I suggest that appropriated Western concepts and terms such as *LGBT* may, first, have different meanings in Arab/Muslim contexts and, second, be a bridge to developing more local, indigenous terms, which could include recovering older, precolonial histories and traditions.

A public sphere for non-heteronormative sexualities and genders in non-Western postcolonial settings exists and can allow access, legal reforms, and certain political gains. By describing instances of state regulation of non-normative sexualities and genders as well as oppositional discourses and actions of resistance, it is possible to argue, first, that we are all part of sexuality governance regimes (since, following Foucault, we are "inside" power); and, second, that living in the interstices, between categories, should also be recognized as a right—the right not only to claim and live, but also to avoid coherent identities and to move in and out of the public sphere.

Notes

1. I use the term *Arab/Muslim world* to define in a broad sense the geographical area in which Lebanon (my case study) is situated and to which it officially belongs. I recognize the risk of homogenizing the terms *West, Arab/Muslim world,* etc. These categories are reductive and ignore the huge class and other divisions within both regions (e.g., the wealthy Gulf versus North Africa). For the purposes of this chapter, I deploy these terms as tools for theoretical exploration of sexuality governance in postcolonial settings.

2. http://www.helem.net.

3. Scholars' use of the concept of sexuality governance is not new (see, e.g., Blasius 1992; 1994, 76; Cooper 1993; 2004, 98; Goodrich 1996, 650; Mischler 2000, 40; and Shalakany 2006; 2007, 43). Nevertheless, the underlying definition has been either assumed/ignored (Goodrich 1996; Shalakany 2007) or used with explicit reference to the state (Mischler 2000). An explicit link was made to Foucault's suggestion that what we call sexuality emerged through anatomo- and biopolitical governance (Blasius 1992; Blasius 1994). At best the term *sexuality governance* was summarily introduced, with reference to Foucault but strictly conceived in terms of regulation and deregulation, focused on legislative interventions by colonial and postcolonial authorities (Shalakany 2006). In other words, it has not been fleshed out, e.g., as having heteronormativity as an operative form.

4. http://www.dailystar.com.lb/article.asp?edition_id=1&categ_id=2&article_id =73289.

5. *Karouni v. Gonzales,* 2005 WL 517843 (9th Cir. March 7, 2005). http://bulk.re-source.org/courts.gov/c/F3/399/399.F3d.1163.02-72651.html.

6. *Karouni v. Gonzales,* 2005 WL 517843 (9th Cir. March 7, 2005). http://bulk.resource.org/courts.gov/c/F3/399/399.F3d.1163.02-72651.html.

7. *Karouni v. Gonzales,* 2005 WL 517843 (9th Cir. March 7, 2005). http://bulk.resource.org/courts.gov/c/F3/399/399.F3d.1163.02-72651.html.

8. *Lawrence v. Texas,* 2003 539 US. 558 (June 26, 2003). http://supreme.justia.com/us/539/558/case.html.

9. In 2009 a Lebanese district court remarkably found that same-sex acts could not be defined "against nature" and therefore could not be criminalised under that article. http://www.bekhsoos.com/web/2009/12/lebanese-judge-rules-against-the-use -of-article-534-to-prosecute-on-grounds-of-homosexuality/.

Bibliography

Ayyass, Abdel Rahman, ed. 2006. *Rouhab Al Methliyah [Homophobia: Views and Positions]*. Beirut: La CD-Thèque.

Azimi, Negar. 2006. "Prisoners of Sex." *New York Times Magazine*, December 3, p. 63.

Ben Néfissa, Sarah, et al. 2000. *NGOs, Governance and Development in the Arab World: Discussion Papers*. Management of Social Transformations (MOST-UNESCO) 46: 1–32. Available online at http://www.unesco.org/most/nefissae.htm (accessed April 7, 2008).

Blasius, Mark 1992. "An Ethos of Lesbian and Gay Existence." *Political Theory* 20 no. 4: 642–71.

———, ed. 1994. *Gay and Lesbian Politics: Sexuality and the Emergence of a New Ethic*. Philadelphia: Temple University Press.

Chibundu, Maxwell O. 2004. "For God, for Country, for Universalism: Sovereignty as Solidarity in our Age of Terror." *Florida Law Review* 59, no. 5: 883–920.

Collins, Antoine L. 2003. "Caging the Bird Does Not Cage the Song: How the International Covenant on Civil and Political Rights Fails to Protect Free Expression Over the Internet." *The John Marshall Journal of Computer & Information Law* 21, no. 3: 371–88.

Cooper, Davina. 1993. "An Engaged State: Sexuality, Governance, and the Potential for Change." *Activating Theory: Lesbian, Gay, and Bisexual Politics*. Ed. Joseph Bristow and Angelia R. Wilson. London: Lawrence and Wishart.

———. 2004. *Challenging Diversity: Rethinking Equality and the Value of Difference*. New York: Cambridge University Press.

Corrêa, Sonia, Rosalind Petchesky, and Richard Parker. 2008. *Sexuality, Health and Human Rights*. New York: Routledge.

Dahir, Mubarak. 2001. "More Fallout from the War." *Advocate* (November 20): 28–31.

Dean, Jodi. 2003. "Why the Net is not a Public Sphere." *Constellations* 10, no. 1: 95–112.

Dean, Mitchell. 2007. *Governing Societies: Political Perspectives on Domestic and International Rule*. New York: Open University Press.

———. 2008 "Governing Society: The Story of Two Monsters." *Journal of Cultural Economy* 1, no. 1: 25–38.

Drexel, Allen A. 2005. "Ninth Circuit Holds Gay, HIV+ Lebanese Man Eligible for Asylum." *Lesbian/Gay Law Notes* (April 2005): 65–88. Available online at http://www.qrd.org/qrd/www/legal/lgln/04.2005.pdf (accessed September 3, 2007).

Dunne, Bruce. 1990. "Homosexuality in the Middle East: An Agenda for Historical Research." *Arab Studies Quarterly* 12, no. 3: 55–82.

———. 1998. "Power and Sexuality in the Middle East." *Middle East Report* 206: 8–11.

El Menyawi, Hassan. 2006. "Activism from the Closet: Gay Rights Strategising in Egypt." *Melbourne Journal of International Law* 7, no. 1: 28–51.

Foucault, Michel. 1978. *The History of Sexuality Vol. I: An Introduction*. Trans. Robert Hurley. New York: Pantheon.

Garcia, Neil. 1996. *Philippine Gay Culture: The Last Thirty Years: Binabae to Bakla, Silahis to MSM*. Manila: University of the Philippines Press.

Goodrich, Peter. 1996. "Law in the Courts of Love: Andreas Capellanus and the Judgments of Love." *Stanford Law Review* 48: 633–75.

Habermas, Jürgen. 1991. *The Structural Transformation of the Public sphere: An Inquiry Into a Category of Bourgeois Society*. Trans. Thomas Burger. Boston: MIT Press.

———. 1996. *Between Facts and Norms: Contributions to a Discourse Theory of Law and Democracy*. Trans. William Rehg. Cambridge, UK: Polity Press.

———. 1996. "Three Normative Models of Democracy." In Seyla Benhabib, ed., *Democracy and Difference: Contesting the Boundaries of the Political*, pp. 21–30. Princeton, NJ: Princeton University Press.

Habib, Samar. 2007. *Female Homosexuality in the Middle East: Histories and Representations*. New York: Routledge.

Heinze, Eric. 2001. "Sexual Orientation and International Law: A Study in the Manufacture of Cross-Cultural Sensitivity." *Michigan Journal of International Law* 22: 283–309.

Howard, Stephen Burkett. 2006. "Civil Society and Democracy in Post-Ta'if Lebanon." MA Thesis, American University of Beirut.

Human Rights Watch. 2008. "This Alien Legacy: The Origins of 'Sodomy' Laws in British Colonialism." Human Rights Watch report. December 17. Available online at http://www.hrw.org/en/reports/2008/12/17/alien-legacy-0 (accessed April 13, 2009) .

Karouni v. Gonzales. 2005, Slip No. 02–72651. 9th Cir. of the U.S. March 7, 2005.

Katyal, Sonia. 2002. "Exporting Identity." *Yale Journal of Law and Feminism* 14, no. 1: 97–176.

Long, Scott. 2009. "Unbearable Witness: How Western Activists (Mis)recognize Sexuality in Iran." *Contemporary Politics* 15, no. 1: 119–36.

Luibhéid, Eithne. 2008. "An Unruly Body of Scholarship." *GLQ* 14, no. 2: 169–90.

Manalansan, Martin F., IV. 1997. "In the Shadows of Stonewall: Examining Gay Transnational Politics and the Diasporic Dilemma." In Lisa Lowe and David Lloyd, eds., *The Politics of Culture in the Shadow of Capital*, pp. 485–505. Durham, NC: Duke University Press.

Massad, Joseph Andoni. 2007. *Desiring Arabs*. Chicago: University of Chicago Press.

McCormick, Jared. 2006. "Transition Beirut: Gay Identities, Lived Realties." In Samir Khalaf and John Gagnon, eds., *Sexuality in the Arab World*. London: Saqi.

Mischler, Linda Fitts. 2000. "Personal Morals Masquerading as Professional Ethics: Regulations Banning Sex between Domestic Relations Attorneys and Their Clients." *Harvard Women's Law Journal* 23: 1–94.

Najmabadi, Asfaneh. 1991. "Hazards of Modernity and Morality: Women, State and Ideology in Contemporary Iran." In Deniz Kandiyoti, ed., *Women, Islam and State*. Philadelphia: Temple University Press.

———. 2005. "Mapping Transformations of Sex, Gender, and Sexuality in Modern Iran." *Social Analysis* 49, no. 2: 54–77.

———. 2005. *Women with Mustaches and Men without Beards: Gender and Sexual Anxieties of Iranian Modernity*. Berkeley: University of California Press.

———. 2006. "Beyond the Americas: Are Gender and Sexuality Useful Categories of Historical Analysis?" *Journal of Women's History* 18, no. 1: 11–21.

Parker, Richard, Rosalind Petchesky, and Robert Sember. 2007. *SexPolitics: Reports from the Front Lines*. November 8. Sexuality Policy Watch. Available online at http://www.sxpolitics.org/frontlines/book/pdf/sexpolitics.pdf (accessed April 11, 2009).

Petchesky, Rosalind Pollack. 2003. *Global Prescriptions: Gendering Health and Human Rights*. New York: Zed.

———. 2005. "Rights of the Body and Perversions of War: Sexual Rights and Wrongs Ten Years Past Beijing." *International Social Science Journal* 57, no. 2: 301–18.

———. 2009. "The Language of 'Sexual Minorities' and the Politics of Identity: A Position Paper." *Reproductive Health Matters* 17, no. 33: 105–10.

Phelan, Shane. 1994. *Getting Specific*. Minneapolis: University of Minnesota Press.

Santos, Boaventura de Sousa. 2007. "Human Rights as an Emancipatory Script? Cultural and Political Conditions." In Boaventura de Sousa Santos, ed., *Another Knowledge Is Possible*. London: Verso.

Scalenghe, Sarah. 2004. "We Invite People to Think the Unthinkable: An Interview with Nizar Saghieh." *Middle East Report* 230: 34–37.

Shaban, Fuad. 2003. "11 September and the Millennialist Discourse: An Order of Words?" *Arab Studies Quarterly* 15, no. 1: 13–32.

Shalakany, Amr. 2006. "Comparative Law as Archeology." *University of Texas at Austin Rapoport Center for Human Rights and Justice*. October 9. Available online at http://www.utexas.edu/law/academics/centers/humanrights/events/speaker-series-papers/Shalakany.pdf (accessed May 12, 2006).

———. 2007. "The Closeted Comparative Lawyer: On How to Pass for Human Rights Material." *The Harvard Human Rights Journal* 20: 41–46.

Sullivan, Andrew. 2003. "A Just Cause." *Advocate* (April 29): 72.

———. 2006. "World War on Gays." *Advocate* (April 11): 80.

Taia, Abdallah. 2009. "The Rule of I." *Reality Sandwich*. March 19, 2009. Available online at http://realitysandwich.com/print/12634 (accessed October 20, 2009).

Totten, Michael. 2006. "Lebanon the Model: Iraq Isn't the Arab World's First Democracy." *Opinion Journal: From the Wall Street Journal Editorial Page*. January 3. Available online at http://www.opinionjournal.com/extra/?id=110007758.

Wärn, Mats. 2003. "Stressing the Probable, Postponing the Improbable: Hizballah in the Shadows of the Al-Aqsa Intifada." *Civil Wars* 6, no. 3: 107–28.

Warner, Michael, ed. 1993. *Fear of a Queer Planet: Queer Politics and Social Theory*. Minneapolis: University of Minnesota Press.

10

Theorizing the Politics of (Homo)Sexualities across Cultures

MARK BLASIUS

This essay takes as its starting point an event in the history of sexuality, more specifically in the history of sexuality as a political issue.[1] In recent years, vastly diverse movements around the politics of sexuality have embraced the notion of "sexual rights." These "sexual rights" have been enunciated and have gained recognition around the world. This concept developed rapidly especially since the UN Conference on Women in Beijing (1995) and in the wake of the global AIDS pandemic (see Petchesky, 2001). More recently, rights specific to sexual orientation and gender identity have gained prominence, for instance with a 2011 Human Rights Council resolution on sexual orientation and gender identity and report to the UN General Assembly that analyzed in a preliminary way the universal human rights of LGBT persons under international law "that States have an obligation to address" (2011, 3).[2]

Issuance of this report and the resolution that commissioned it together signify a historical event in the politics of sexuality. While over a hundred years of advocacy, scholarship, and geographically disparate public awareness and legal reform around same-sex sexuality and gender diversity preceded it, this event took place on—indeed, created—a global platform, endorsed in advance by the UN secretary general and in its wake by the U.S. secretary of state and president, as well as by other international leaders. It marks an "arc" of official advocacy starting with the Beijing conference (where the sexual rights of women were addressed amidst controversy and only with caution) and demonstrates the percolation of issues specific to same-sex sexuality and gender diversity into global visibility, as a new dimension of perception and platform for action in the politics of sexuality across cultures. Similarly, the abbreviation *LGBT* represents the globalization of naming a particular politics of sexuality. Originating in western identity politics, adopted by transnational movements, and used open-endedly with indigenous terms by local human-rights defenders in non-western cultures, the moniker raises issues of cultural ontology and personhood as well as of governance and the enactment of social justice. The analysis of state homophobia, as in part a consequence and paradoxical signal of this historical arc that has created a platform for international recognition of same-sex sexualities and gender diversity across cultures, is therefore central to understanding politics today.

While remaining cognizant of and careful to avoid western triumphalism, we might ask, what are some terms of reference for intercultural debate and advocacy that this event at the UN suggests? What is happening now such that this moment—whether conceived as imperialist or liberatory or a combination of both—mandates taking stock of homosexuality, homophobia, and their relation to gender identity as political issues on the world stage? By "terms of reference" I mean something akin to "motifs," interweavings of thought and action that can be found in debate and advocacy, both "for" and "against." An example of the latter is the ideology that treats homosexuality as a foreign influence or as inconsistent with a culture's "traditional values" (e.g., Kaoma or Bosia, both this volume), and the homophobia and transphobia this ideology implies. As this volume collaboratively analyzes this dimension of the global politics of sexuality across cultures, I suggest not an outline of a theory, not a rubric or set of principles for thinking that can inform and in turn be informed by action, and not propositions that can be proven true or false. Instead, what is at stake in this debate and advocacy across cultures may be clarified by looking for *motifs*, with a motif understood as a historical confluence where both human personhood and social justice come to be recognized as differently constructed within governance through sexuality. Looking for motifs in the politics of sexuality helps avoid finding only what one has wanted or expected to find in advance of research. Looking for motifs in "working conceptions" of and ad hoc advocacy around sexuality can be more heuristic, leading toward reciprocity within intercultural dialogue through a search for reference—or "talking"—points, or recurring structures of debate across ideological spectra of thought and advocacy about sexuality as a political issue both within and across cultures.

This set of motifs seems to be at least fourfold. I frame these motifs as questions to provoke thought, ongoing interrogation, and reframing, not to suggest simply finding "solutions." First, to what extent and how has sexuality—that amalgam of sex, gender, and erotics—come to be coextensive with what it means to be "human" today? The language at least of sexual orientation and gender identity, while having a modern western etymology, changes meaning by *traveling*, in translation and in coexistence with other seemingly similar identities and practices, in the process reinventing referents for universal human rights. Second, how is sexuality related to governance conceived in the broadest sense, not only as power exercised formally or directly through the nation-state? This might mean, for example, that state homophobia even in its modular, anti-"western LGBT" form might be at times a composite, sometimes proxy, phenomenon, best addressed by deciphering and comparing "regimes of sexuality," wherein sexuality is constitutive of governing throughout the fabric of life. Third, how do people constitute *themselves* as sexed, gendered, and erotic agents in the ways they govern others and accept or resist being governed within regimes of sexuality? A nation-state-centered concept of citizenship is expanded when rights to sexual orientation and gender identity are asserted through identification, disidentification, and hybridization within relations of governance that shape subjectivity in accordance with moral, scientific, and other rationalities of "intimacy" or "feeling," thereby informing, even provoking a sense of selfhood or a personal ethos (Lind, this volume, following Plummer). How this dynamic becomes a political ethic motivating people in their engagement with various relations of governance, through "sexual" citizenship, involves a fourth motif. That motif interrogates how the widely used but culturally nuanced language of "social justice" mediates between international human-rights norms of sexual orientation/gender identity and the arena of "relational justice" where these norms are enacted. We might even be clearer by stating one perspective (*and corresponding hypothesis*) suggested within this interrogation: LGBT movements (*are successful when they*) shape debate and advocacy about same-sex loving and gender diversity across cultures through framing their specific cultural traditions within new ways of conceiving and enacting just governance.

The normative political significance of organizing this intercultural communication through some (not all) motifs lies in recognizing that the questions they raise do not demonstrate a shared given position, but rather a shared platform on which to express a commitment to creating a world together, and a commitment to the embarrassment of disagreement as well as the joys of learning how to create something new. The remainder of this chapter is thus organized by elaborating these four motifs to suggest how the questions they raise out of contentious debate and advocacy may help guide research into governance through sexuality across differing cultural formations of same-sex loving and gender diversity.

Traveling Sexualities

Note how I just replaced "homosexuality" with "same-sex loving" in the last paragraphs. This is not particularly original. I first heard the latter concept used in a conference of African sexuality scholars and activists I attended in Senegal in 2007, then again in South Africa in 2011, and have even been complimented for using it myself in transnational sexuality scholar-activist gatherings. This concept arose during the Senegal meeting because of the conferees' ambivalence about the usefulness of the concept of homosexuality and even "sexuality" in an African context. Many there believed that Europeans invented sexuality as understood today; stripped of cultural specificity, it became central to a colonial, postcolonial, and imperialistic discourse subjugating African peoples to this very day. I use *discourse* here in the narrow sense of how a regime of governance is constituted by means of knowledges—for example, medical, socio- and psychological, religious, or self-help—that authorize traditions or institutional practices of subjection through which power can be exercised. Discourses work through these practices (clinical, policing, pastoral, modeling, etc.) to shape how individuals or collectivities identify themselves as subjects who act by guiding them to act upon their own subjectivity and constitute themselves, while they simultaneously act upon the actions of others to shape their subjectivity—thus governing themselves and others. The historical concreteness of its regime makes a discourse contingent and an ongoing construction. Therefore, homosexuality can be said to be "un-African" even while same-sex-loving practices, including erotic practices that are considered practices of sexuality in a non-African context, are components of African traditions that still prevail today (Murray and Roscoe 2000).[3] What needs recognizing is that the discursive category of sexuality—for the human sciences and other forms of knowledge and corresponding practices governing what counts as human personhood (such as what is protected as a universal human right), and for the subjective experience of "having a sexuality"—emerged in Europe in the late eighteenth and nineteenth centuries and has a political history in Europe's interaction with the rest of the world. The genealogy of that discourse has to be placed into relief *as a motif* in the politics of sexuality across cultures. Of course, a similar discourse of sexuality developed in the United States, too, where the experience of a distinction among sex, gender, and the erotic was in large part a historical achievement of social movements on behalf of gender and sexual diversity (Meyrowitz 2002). This development corresponds historically to emerging analytical distinctions between sex and gender, and between sexual reproduction and erotic arousal; both developments resulted in a plethora of sexual and gender identities. Thus one motif for intercultural debate and advocacy is the historico-political status of sexuality. To be sure, this motif involves interrogating the concept of sexuality as, for example, what Durkheim (1898, trans. 1938) termed a "social fact" and Foucault (1978) later theorized as a "deployment," and as what UN and nongovernmental organizations now rely upon in their promotion of "sexual health" as central to human well-being across cultures. Almost an ironic application of western queer theory's questioning of the historical construction of a duality of homosexual and heterosexual persons, sexuality "travels." Not just individuals, but entire peoples, may come to "have" a sexuality, as in the emergence of an "African heterosexuality" (Lewis, 2011, 208–11) that could justify combat against homosexuality and non-heteronormative genders as "foreign." This motif also frames ambivalence about the extent to which sexuality is becoming one of the distinctive criteria of "human-ness," as historical capacities for pleasure when the corporeal embodiment of personhood encounters simultaneously limiting and transformative otherness; ambivalence about this discourse traveling includes whether it is functioning "as a control mechanism for maintaining unequal power relations in Africa [and] as an alternative and empowering force for challenging gender and power hierarchies" (Tamale 2011, 606; see also 23–27, 606–21 *passim*).

To specify, somewhat, the problem of political homophobia in this volume in a cautionary way: This motif involves sexuality's discursive relations linking truth, power, and subjectivity. Those relations not only fuel debate and advocacy within the international community meeting in Geneva and New York about whether to recognize and protect human rights of sexual orientation and gender identity. The relationships between truth, power, and subjectivity that inhere in the discourse of sexuality also travel to, for instance, Nepal, where they become codified as "third gender" citizenship, or travel elsewhere and result in (or are anticipated by) deliberately homophobic state policies, coupled ambiguously with transphobia and sexual secrecy (Kaoma, Weiss, Zeidan in this volume). Not surprisingly, the participants in the Senegal meeting proposed compiling a "thesaurus" of African same-sex-loving practices for use in the context of sexuality's traveling as a regime of governance.

Regimes of Sexuality

Understanding how concepts and discourses such as sexuality travel, as well as the practices of translating them within different cultural contexts, involves more than a simple "compare and contrast" form of intellectual work. Indeed, as literary critic Edward Said (1983) and political theorist Roxanne Euben

(2004) have argued, all theorizing is comparative because any standpoint from which to understand a human phenomenon emerges and is continuously transformed by encounters with multiple others. To explain sexuality as a central topic for political theorizing today, one refers, for example, to the emergence of AIDS through developing scientific technique and knowledge in relation to campaigns for sexual and reproductive public health (and who is thus empowered), and also compares this pattern with governing strategies in earlier sexual health, pro-natalist, and eugenicist campaigns.[4] One analyzes how selfhood with sexuality as a central reference, for example "LGBTI,"[5] can become intelligible in places where it had not existed before—diffused through, for example, online social media, mobile telecommunications networking, global human migration, and tourism. One historically traces the emergence of, domination by, accommodation with, and resistance to the economic organization of same-sex-loving relations through consumer capitalism or, for example, socialist programs for transformation of the so-called traditional economies of erotic relations (see, respectively, D'Emilio 1983; Herdt and Stoller 1990; Mieli 1980) into modern heteronormative regimes of sexuality (Berlant and Warner 1998; Lind, this volume) or neoliberal regimes of homonormativity (Duggan 2002) and homonationalism (Puar 2007). One also questions claims about ultimate values proffered by both fundamentalisms and liberalisms that invoke same-sex-loving practices (as, respectively, public or private) in order to justify governance through sexuality.

The framework for analysis termed "globalization," by specifying the global *within* the local and vice versa, as well as reactions against the effects of globalization coming not only from advocates of cultural authenticity with regard to gender and erotic relations, but also (as is seen in contemporary immigration debates within the global north) from some proponents of sexual diversity and gender nonconformity, suggests another motif in the politics of sexuality across cultures. This second motif, drawing upon these approaches for thinking politically about and advocating around sexuality across cultures, may involve how peoples (demographically and socially) and bodies (in accordance with populations that make them intelligible) are differentially sexualized through specific conditions of support and disallowance (Foucault 1978, 138–46). Strategies of "global governance" (including foreign aid and charitable-assistance programs) in which peoples and bodies are enmeshed stand in relation to political or other ideologies motivating, for example, "state homophobia" or a "virginity census" (see Ho 2008). These cultural articulations of truth-telling, of institutional interests and strategies of power, of practical ideologies relating individual and collective in "human nature"—let's call them a regime's "resources"—do not so much constitute sexuality as an object *to be governed* as specify *how sexuality is constituted (through knowledges, norms and institutions, and subjectivities) as itself a procedure or modus operandi of governance.*

This second motif involves, as suggested above, analyzing how discourses of sexuality "make up people" that are disposed to be governed in their relations with each other *through* sexuality (see Hacking 1986). To be sure, other governing regimes can be studied and may serve as resources for, or work together in a "complex" with, a sexual regime. It may be informative to draw upon regime theory in political science and gender studies (see Connell 1996; Keohane and Victor 2011; Walby 2004) to conceptualize and to explain regimes' traditional or institutional powers and forms of subjection, both to compare regimes of sexuality with each other and to show them in complex networks with other governance regimes, such as a criminal-justice regime, a social-welfare regime, an international legal regime, a racialization or race-formation regime, a public-health regime, an urban regime. For example, "homosexuality" within a regime of sexuality located in national and subnational cultures may engage (historically or contemporaneously) a criminal-justice regime (as "crime against nature"), a mental-health regime (as psychiatric perversion and gender dysphoria), a human-rights regime, a leisure regime (as "lifestyle"), a sports regime (deploying masculinist sex dimorphism), a racialized gender regime (with sociobiological epistemologies), and inscription within a regime of "governmentality" (combining external controls with self-management of sexuality ranging from cultural norms and socialization to biomedical science policies and pharmaceutical life enhancement [for example, see Nyanzi 2011]). The opportunities and dangers addressed by AIDS activism, when advocates use resources from different regimes to save their lives and protect those of others, have included remedicalization of (mostly male) homosexuality, coercive public health regulation with medical treatment and sequestering possible stigmatization of those with HIV leading to discrimination and criminalization, and consumerist subjection undermining a liberatory ethos with dependency on state agencies. In addressing these and other challenges through an interdependence of knowledge, regulation, and subjectivity in a discursive regime, AIDS activism influences how the HIV/AIDS pandemic has globalized and "glocalized" (to specific locales) governance through sexuality, and thereby contributes to this motif in the politics of sexuality.

The significance of analyzing state and modular homophobia through regimes of sexuality was evident in 2011 when several nation-states, most prominently the UK and later the United States, announced policies suggesting "aid conditionality" in their foreign policies to combat state homophobia. While Bosia and Weiss in their introduction to this volume suggest that conditionality might seek to restrict repression in an attempt to grant political space for sexual and gender minorities, such conditionality generally has involved bilateral deployment of foreign assistance within an international regime to create or shape a regime of sexuality. In the process, individuals in one nation-state are incited to adopt sexual identities of, for example, LGBT, to claim both recognition and protection from a foreign state when their own state misrecognizes them and limits or obliterates their civil status (not least given the cultural incoherence surrounding bodies, genders, and the erotic when sexuality travels). Aid conditionality is often presented as a form of support for human rights, or even as humanitarian intervention by the "donor," and as cultural or moral imperialism by the claimant, although ideologically it can revive a colonial "civilizing mission." There has been widespread debate among LGBTI advocates, transnationally and especially in claimant nations, about their governments' diverting attention from issues of good governance (Kaoma, this volume) and possibly scapegoating local LGBTIs for any aid withdrawal due to what the UK's David Cameron called "persecution of homosexuality" (that label itself reinforcing colonial legacies and stereotypes of homosexuality as "western"). This alarm extends to the effect sanctions will have on already vulnerable programs serving people living with HIV/AIDS, the cross-cutting effects aid conditionality will have on coalitions LGBTIs are trying to build with others in their communities on the basis of shared deprivations, and on the intersectional character of trying to live as an L or G or B or T or I person where a sexual- and gender-nonconforming identity is not privileged over one's other social identities.

What the debate highlights are the limitations of sanctions at the level of the state. My pointing to how sexuality itself is constituted as a governing regime is a cautionary tale about state power. Hence, for instance, a nuanced petition by social justice activists from West Africa following the UK announcement proposed rejecting the country-level approach and instead expanding assistance to community-based programs (LGBTI and otherwise) aimed at fostering dialogue and tolerance, supporting national and regional human-rights mechanisms to ensure inclusion of LGBTI issues in their mandates, and supporting the entrenchment of LGBTI issues into broader social-justice issues through the financing of community-based and nationally owned projects (AMSHeR 2011).

What a sexual-regime perspective can contribute toward understanding this political dynamic is to highlight the fact that despite the seeming prominence of state-centered actions—the ways in which donor nations' foreign policies shape recipient nations' foreign and domestic policies, for instance—there is an equally important level of "governance without government." This level includes the (self-)transformation of erotic acts into sexual identities; mobilization of a population as rights bearers even without institutionalized sexual citizenship, that is, protection of rights to sexual or gender identity and expression; and a potential separating out of a sexual identity from other identities, including a national one that may even be denigrated in the process of a homogenizing "global queering" (Ho 2008).

Ugandan scholar and activist Sylvia Tamale suggests one way of thinking about the interaction between local and global sexual regimes that could be a source for intercultural dialogue, and that avoids falling into the narrative either of a "sexual modernization theory" (Bosia and Weiss, this volume) or a colonizing "human-rights" mission. Tamale proposes that a "sexuality industry," building on 1970s-era campaigns against a population "explosion," then later the global HIV/AIDS pandemic, ties the commodification of sexual health to an "insatiable drive for profits and power . . . becom[ing] a multi-billion-dollar money spinner for national and international bureaucrats and pharmaceutical companies" (Tamale 2011, 22). To be sure, philanthropic organizations and research institutions have contributed to what Tamale sees as this "globalized, capitalist, and patriarchal" trend. This trend, too, has resulted in a backlash against western constructs of sexuality and studied ignorance toward non-western sources of sexual rights, particularly those arising from the African ethos of *ubuntu* (Tamale 2011, 7, 24, 26). Thus, just as the overreach of population campaigns spawned movements of empowerment amongst women, so the implications of AIDS for governance has opened the topic of erotic practices to popular discussion, reflection, and personal decision making. In this light, sexuality can be critically understood and acted upon as a regime that structures all social relations and the sense of personhood within them, but is distinct from a whole-cloth western imposition. It is in this context of a regime of sexuality entwined both with complex regimes of foreign aid, and with financial regimes that force structural intervention or "mere" adjustment, and even the "warehousing" of the unemployed from the global north to south through Christian evangelism (Dorothy Aken'Ova 2007), that the mobilization of state homophobia can be analyzed. Indeed, as Kaoma describes in this volume, there has been a demographic shift in the center of Christianity to the global south, with Africa becoming a colony for U.S. conservative churches to dominate by providing loans, social services, education, and support for research. At the same time we analyze state homophobia, studies like Kaoma's, as well as the chapters here by Weiss and O'Dwyer, suggest that the traveling modular homophobia of certain forms of Christian evangelism, Islamism, Catholicism, or other conservative movements may be effectively analyzed in the relations between embodiment, gender identities, and erotics within the regimes of sexuality they target. On the other side, transnational LGBTI activist movements and a culture of the erotic—of "how to relate" arising from same-sex sexualities and gender diversity in their relationship to other, nonidentity-based regimes of sexuality—may be flashpoints illuminating the way personal and collective agency exceed regulative constraints within these regimes, a third motif to which we now turn.

Sexual Ethics: Mediation and Agency

Another motif arising out of globalization and alter-globalization debates involves interrogating the status of narratives of progress or, framed bluntly, "sexual modernization theory" (Bosia and Weiss, this volume). That progressive narrative highlights the development of neoliberal or "post-neoliberal" global governance in conjunction with emerging cosmopolitan norms and human rights that include sexual orientation and gender identity, and the utility of identity politics in articulating these rights. Queer theory emerged as a critical master theory[6] (with the homo/hetero binary as a "master category of social analysis") to explain both historical development through, say, compulsory heterosexuality and heteronormativity, and insurrectionary sexual politics within neoliberal governance (Seidman 1997, 154; see also Lind, this volume). This third motif of envisioning sexual politics across cultures is invoked by sexuality theorists and activists resisting fundamentalisms and claims about "universals" through intersectional analyses that do not separate sexuality from other axes of social difference such as class, race, ethnicity, age, gender, religion, citizenship status, nationality, and disability but show how they inflect each other, and that often bear little resemblance to queer theory, particularly with regard to revaluing local traditions.

Take, for instance, Gloria Wekker's work on women's sexual culture in the Afro-Surinamese diaspora (Wekker 2006). Her research challenges the domination of women's erotic agency according to northern/western feminist and queer theory by tracing an erotic culture among women from migrant Dutch-Surinamese women, to Suriname and to West African traditions in which women's raising children and exercising agency within fulfilling erotic relations with both men and women were (and are) socially recognized and valorized. Wekker's approach does not suggest a golden age of precolonial indigenous sexualities, as do some approaches, critical of both fundamentalisms and queer cosmopolitanisms (e.g., Joseph Massad, 2007; c.f. Zeidan, this volume).[7] Indeed, Wekker recognizes the limits of a primary focus on what she terms "surfaces and commonalities" of globalization processes such

as circulations of people, capital, culture, and supposedly transnational categories of the lesbian/homosexual seeking recognition in the non-western
spaces of the unequally privileged nation-state system (and nation). Rather,
her template for thinking focuses on *subjective mediation* of these processes
by black diasporic women building on a West African cultural heritage in
the domain of "sexual subjecthood" (Wekker 2006, 74, 70). Wekker describes
how women exercise agency by means of specific practices of bodily and psychic pleasure with other women, "*mati work,*" as mediated by sociocultural
inequalities embedded in kinship, migration, and religious tradition. Her
relational methodology shows how women use same-sex sexuality as strategies, in governing themselves and others and in being governed, that resist
and reconfigure these regimes in their local specificities. Wekker's template
of subjective mediation and relational methodology revise transnational narratives about sexuality through comparative difference. Here, she contributes
to this motif in the politics of sexuality across cultures, a motif probing how
conceptions of "the human" or personhood emerge and are reworked at
sites of sexual ethics—where agency is mediated within (and also mediates)
regimes of governance through sexuality.

Judith Butler complements Wekker when she discusses the concept of
sexual rights. She writes:

> To assert sexual rights . . . means we are struggling for rights that attach, or
> should attach, to my personhood [but] if we are struggling not only to be con-
> ceived as persons, but to create a social transformation of the very meaning
> of personhood then the assertion of rights becomes a way of intervening in
> the social and political process by which the human is articulated . . . Sexu-
> ality is not simply an attribute one has . . . [i]t is a mode of being disposed
> towards others . . . sexuality is not this or that dimension of our existence,
> not the key or bedrock of our existence, but, rather . . . co-extensive with
> existence." (2004, 32–33)

Extending her analysis of sexual rights to frame those rights articulated, for
example, by the Yogyakarta Principles (2006) as ones of sexual orientation and
gender identity that already inhere in international law, I would use Butler's
words again: "International human rights is always in the process of subjecting
the human to redefinition and renegotiation. It mobilizes the human in the service of rights, but also rewrites the human, and rearticulates the human when it
comes up against the cultural limits of its *working conception of the human,* as
it does and must" (Butler 2004, 33; emphasis added). Referring back to the first
motif, a "working conception of the human" is central to intercultural political
work—in thought, debate, and advocacy—around the status of sexuality as a

governing discourse that translates versions of human-ness across cultures. The vernacularization of a transnational phenomenon—such as when having a *supi*, a close friend in a traditional relationship of female-to-female, often-erotic love in Ghana, becomes pathologized as "lesbian" by the community in which these women live (by churches, mass media, politicians)—and the possibilities for ethical hybridity this may open up (Dankwa 2009), is a site for ethical agency I find within the politics of sexuality (and inflections of gender through it) across cultures. To take another step beyond saying theorizing is always already comparative (and a step suggested by Euben): theorizing is a practice of translating concepts across cultures, or of translation from one context to other possible contexts; it is a kind of ongoing creation of a thesaurus that, in its encounter with and use by multiple others, becomes a toolkit for arts of living (compare with Ratele 2011, 410–11). Therefore, this third ethical motif of mediation and agency concerns how resources from diverse governing regimes, including regimes of sexuality, are used to translate *supi* into lesbian and how resources drawn from seemingly contradictory regimes that inflect practices and meanings of "traveling" sexuality (where tribal may coexist with national, continental, and transnational) can indigenize lesbian within Ghanaian sexual ethics as a hybrid erotic practice and subjectivity—"*doing it*," "*doing supi*"—to an extent that can be transformative within that Ghanaian regime (Dankwa 2009, 198–202). Comparing the politics of same-sex sexualities and gender identity as "self-determination" across cultures (while being mindful of one's own when using this language of rights) strives to make such practices of translation visible as ethical agency, where one's relation to oneself is mediated by one's relations to others through sexuality. As such, the "self" or one's personhood is not constructed once and for all but is ongoing; reflecting ethics as the relation one has to oneself, it is a "becoming." This motif of sexual ethics—theorizing, advocacy, intercultural disputation, listening, and learning—points not to a single moral code or traits of character but to *sites*: where a regime of living—a use of sexuality that makes the self intelligible to others—yielding personhood through an ethos of governing oneself and others and accepting how be governed; and where "flashpoints" of unintelligible, even outrageous, sexual agency make visible a regime's fault lines and opportunities for renegotiation of the "we" and "I" in addition to repetition of a tradition or a shared ethos (see Taia 2009 and discussion by Zeidan, this volume).[8]

My own fieldwork in Accra during 2007 indicates that there are women who identify as lesbians in Ghana—mostly younger ones who grew up aware, through increasing "outness" in the transnational cultural production that has filtered into Ghanaian popular culture, of the possibility of lifelong lesbian identity and partnerships. These young women are more likely than others to be involved in Ghanaian gay and lesbian or sexual-health organizations, or to have friends who are, and thus to find networks of same-sex-loving women. Within those networks, they socialize also with gay men, learning that they can be open about their sexuality and their girlfriends within specific circles of friends. While it is arguable whether most Ghanaians engaging in same-sex sexual relations also engage in different-sex ones (as well as the overall prevalence of such "bisexuality"), it is easier for men than women to remain unmarried. A woman's fecundity is considered part of the wealth creation of the community; she is thus expected to bear children (compare with Kaoma, this volume). As a result, women tend to be in erotic relationships with men and, except for the socioeconomically privileged (and for sex workers who are socially accorded greater sexual freedom), there has been no place for "lesbians" in Ghanaian society. Most women are at the mercy (especially for extortion) of whoever their partner may be, and "lesbians" may be ostracized from family and community life. One of my informants, an African-American expatriate, regularly held parties in her home, providing a rare space for women who had or wanted same-sex partners, but warned the twenty-something lesbian activist and her girlfriend who accompanied me to the interview that they would be pressured to marry and have children by the time they were in their thirties.

However, even she admitted that this expectation could change: with the increasing visibility of a Ghanaian lesbian and gay movement that promotes decriminalization, social services, and role modeling; as the growing cultural stature and financial stability of Ghanaian women make it easier for same-sex-loving ones to come out; with developments in the role of family in one's life—especially the ability to change one's family name (see Kaoma, this volume); and with a growing culture of receptivity due to the burgeoning student population, to the attitudes of Ghanaians who have lived abroad, to the culture of tourism, and to local elites lobbied by multinational corporations who want Ghana to be a sympathetic and safe home for their employees. Indeed, my expatriate informant believed Ghana to be, as South Africa is, uniquely positioned among African countries for (what she termed) an "LGBT movement" to encourage and support same-sex-loving and gender-diverse people so that they will stay there and not move away.

Serena Dankwa's research uses historical and ethnographic sources to describe the ethico-political flashpoint of *supi* relationships. Although historically, *supi* referred to a relationship between often older and younger adolescent girls ("having a *supi*") and involved a social identity ("being someone's *supi*") these relationships often continued on through life. Many of her informants described an erotic component, many did not, and many others insisted there was always such a component that would "wear off" or not. Nevertheless, due to family pressures and the stigma of the western concept of lesbianism, these relationships are highly problematic now. This "problem" contributes to lesbianism being talked about more openly and to traditional *supi* relationships, depending upon context, becoming suspicious and sometimes pejoratively identified. Although Dankwa does not argue this, the locutions "doing *supi*" and "doing it" appear as discrete ways of having a sexual identity distinct from lesbian and also distinct from the traditional and currently popular notion of *supi* that disavows a sexual component, yet locates it more in *a Ghanaian practice that any woman can engage in rather than in a fixed identity*. This may be a transforming practice for same-sex sexualities and gender identity in a Ghanaian regime of sexuality where one enacts (through legacies of tradition, cultural imperialism, and "private" rather than truly state homophobia) a hybrid erotic personhood through a relational ethos among women (Ratele 411). A relational ethos and its emotional (include here *erotic*) capital[9] as a resource in any regime of governance may be an ethical flashpoint indicating how these regimes persist and change and the significance of this motif in the politics of sexuality across cultures.

Human Rights and Social Justice Inclusive of Same-Sex Sexualities and Gender Diversity

A fourth motif that has achieved intercultural salience because of the enduring colonial legacy in much of the world and the intersectional politics of the postcolonial world involves *how* to frame sexuality as distinctively political. (By framing some aspect of life as "political," I refer to the activity of questioning any power relations and the truth claims and subjectivities that are constitutive of those power relations; politics objectifies and interrogates the ways we govern ourselves and others, with many possible outcomes.) One way of framing sexuality is to suggest that it is not a matter of politics but of "private" life, or, alternatively, of cultural traditions that are not appropriately questioned as political by individuals or social movements—especially with transnational support—and that the nation-state should "protect" these traditions rather than make them an object of deliberation and change through legislation. Just as has been the case for feminists seeking recognition of women's unequal status as *political*, across cultures and in transnational and international forums, sexuality-rights defenders strive to demonstrate the politicalness of sexuality, usually in the name of universal human rights (albeit often claiming that sexual rights inhere in existing international law and are not "new" rights). Challenging this claim, their opponents insist that such rights themselves involve the imposition of western values. Regardless, given the international and bilateral pressure (mentioned above) upon leaders and bureaucrats of both nation-states and civil society at least to debate cultural traditions in terms of "rights," it has been through this language that, as framed in Yogyakarta and at the UN, sexual orientation and gender identity, distinct but conjoined, have coalesced as a publically acknowledged political issue with a global platform. However, given the other motifs for politically theorizing sexuality across cultures— through a relational ethos of human personhood within regimes of sexuality in which "human sexuality" remains contested in cultural ontologies—this human-rights framework may be insufficient to relieve same-sex sexualities and gender diversity from repression, notwithstanding the political significance of the "right to be different" that recent democracy movements such as those of the Arab Spring have bequeathed to us.

Per the logic of an intercultural motif in the politics of sexuality for the short term, LGBTI human rights may be more intelligible to the extent they are joined to culturally nuanced formulations of social justice rather than framed primarily through the language of personal liberties or group rights (the genealogy of which is often ethnically derived). There are already re-visionings of cultural traditions, socioeconomic policies, and political in-stitutions, as well as local and transnational opportunities that enable sex-ual-rights defenders to work coalitionally toward recognition of same-sex sexualities and gender diversity as indispensable to local understandings of social justice. Recognizing sexual and gender identities as intersectional and engaging with languages and political processes of postcolonial and tran-sitional justice, say truth and reconciliation commissions or constitutional conventions, this "justice work" has reconfigured cultures that have been torn asunder, and LGBTI participation reconfigures social justice as inclu-sive of sexual and gender diversity (see Hackman 2009; Muholi 2009; Reddy, Wiebesiek, and Munthree 2011 for the example of South Africa). The long-term logic residing in this motif of the relation between rights and justice within sexuality involves explicit recognition of the place of capacities for erotic love among the shared values of any society, that is, recognizing not just what sustains human life, but what makes life worth living. Bodily, gender, and erotic self-determination evoke new consideration about what collec-tive goods—those required for a "good life" according to different cultural conceptions—are constitutive of global justice, to which human rights are supposed to contribute. Indeed, the logic of the motif of rights' and justice's dependence on a human-ness that is a "becoming" suggests why "new rights" arising from same-sex sexuality and gender diversity are a battleground. In the meantime, the distinctive politics of these "identity-based" rights as human rights emphasizes embedding a conception of same-sex loving and gender diversity, indeed, a regime of sexuality itself that constructs sex, gender, and erotics, as a necessary component of visions for and policies toward a common good that are perennial concerns of but take different forms within specific schemes and practices for governing today.

As mentioned at the outset of this chapter, the arc of international human-rights advocacy that established a global platform on which all these motifs, but especially the fourth, are publically visible, arose from at least sixteen years of sexuality-specific advocacy that in part grew out of gender advocacy across cultures, as well as from tensions within that advocacy work over accommodating rights of sexual orientation and gender identity.[10] Despite the increasing and important support at the levels of the UN, intergovernmental organizations, and transnational organizations monitoring and lobbying nation-states, it is not as though the most homophobic states have changed that much (even as this volume demonstrates the shift to an innovative, modular, and programmatic homophobia in domestic politics). The coalitions those states muster have become more fragile, and local LGBTI and HIV/AIDS organizations in networks with lateral and transnational others, as well as with regional and global funding sources, have helped create an advocacy infrastructure to complement the state-centric human-rights regime and critically monitor the "sexuality industry" to which Sylvia Tamale alludes. This infrastructure ranges from transnational organizations of scholars and policy makers such as Sexuality Policy Watch, to regional sexuality studies centers, to local LGBTI organizations throughout the world, building capacity through local and transnational philanthropy. On a regional level, local LGBTI organizations have questioned their governments and intergovernmental bodies such as the African Commission on Human and People's Rights, the European Commission, the Association of Southeast Asian Nations, the Commonwealth of Nations, and the Inter-American Human Rights Commission. Notably, the arguments for decriminalization and nondiscrimination have been made intersectionally, relating sexuality to such dimensions as violence, economic well-being, concepts of personhood, and childrearing and founding a family. For example, a comparatively UN-focused LGBTI-oriented NGO, ARC International, produced "An Activist's Guide to the Yogyakarta Principles," demonstrating how grassroots organizations in Belize, Sweden, Colombia, Guyana, Chile, India, and South Africa (to name a few) tailored human-rights claims around sexual orientation and gender identity to specific changes in local social-policy processes (Quinn 2010). While this achievement does not in itself suggest deliberative consensus on sexuality's place in just governance at a local level, these localizing projects engage a variety of other organizations that could potentially work in coalition toward greater recognition of it.

Among the most promising projects of local LGBTI organizations have been "livelihood projects" for the rural and urban poor among Philippine LGBT organizations, even when their explicit goal is "sexual rights." Due to relations of extended familial interdependence (and to gain cultural esteem), unmarried Filipinos are expected to be breadwinners. While what has transpired is not unique to the Philippines, the Philippine case is of special interest in my view because it involves a culture historically predisposed to the gender and erotic fluidity of "queerness" (this umbrella term has virtually no resonance; locals prefer choosing from among a cacophony of English and Filipino terms, depending on context), including social recognition of same-sex sexuality and gender nonconformity in spite of Roman Catholic and Islamic condemnation, a striking lack of legal protection of sexual orientation and gender identity, but also an ethos of care—a practice called *malasakit,* materially incorporating the difficulties of life of the other into one's own (as conceived by older *bakla,* gender-nonconforming MSM, see Abaya 2009). In the same vein elsewhere, David Kuria Mbote, a founder and former director of the Gay and Lesbian Coalition of Kenya (GALCK) and a prolific author (including of the locally popular *Homosexuality and Society*), campaigned as an openly gay senatorial candidate (from outside of Nairobi) with a platform quoting the Bible and emphasizing government transparency, non-tourism-based economic development, expanded state health care, social enterprise (livelihood projects), and what he calls second chances for "many people, particularly young men who have erred in judgment and given themselves to drinking, alcoholism, drugs and general lack of direction." David withdrew in late 2012 for financial reasons, and he wrote about the effects of his candidacy in a short book that offers an alternative LGBT "advocacy paradigm for Africa," including a rich discussion about "Broadening the Human Rights discourse" (*sic*) beyond a legalistic "niche area for the LGBT persons and their allies" that makes an easy target (for politicians) as special rights. Instead, "out" and LGBT activists should not fear to address "the people's experiences" by challenging authoritarianism, corruption and neo-patrimonialism, and socioeconomic inequalities that impede democratic social change in Africa (Kuria Mbote 2013, 33–34).

In cross-national analysis, what may appear to be the epitome of sexual social justice in some national contexts—marriage equality and even the normative "beyond normal sexuality" aspirations of some queer critiques of identity—may have slight relevance as a political strategy, or coherence for cultural translation, in others (see, e.g. Garcia 2008). On the other hand, an intercultural motif of "universal" (stating it generously) rights in conflict with universal claims of injustice inspires looking toward the global south not as a site of backwardness, victimization, and imitation in governance through sexuality, but as a site where, often in extreme circumstances, a relational ethos arising from same-sex sexuality and gender diversity mediates contested rights with ad hoc broader agreement to seek remedies for cross-cutting injustice.

To be sure, these cases and others like them do not make an argument for "LGBTI mutual aid," whether to compensate for the injustices of state homophobia or to assimilate and coexist with traveling modular homophobia by simply being an "out" Christian (both Filipino and Kenyan cultures involve deeply entrenched Christianity). Indeed, one fruitful area for activism around state bureaucracies has been documentation for the transgendered and intersexed. Nepal, for example, amended national citizenship categories in 2012 to allow Nepalese citizens to *elect* to be male, female, or other. (Very few other states allow this last category.) While the law here reflects the distinctive cultural ontology relating sex, gender, and erotics in Nepal and eases a burden carried by third-gendered Nepalese, through passports for international transit and by example this law potentially challenges one support for regimes of sexuality on the basis of which transphobic and homophobic state power is exercised. Although even this accomplishment suggests the limitations of a strategy that seeks justice primarily through national citizenship rights (most transsexual-identified Nepalese remain poor despite this victory), since *any* Nepalese citizen can elect this category, this is a political struggle over governance of the relationship of gender identity to the body and to erotic arousal that is ongoing. Moreover, even states of certain so-called "sexually progressive" societies continue to outlaw adoption by same-sex married couples and as of 2012, have required sterilization of transsexual persons. Historical analysis of sexual-liberation movements as components of revolutionary movements (as in Bolshevik Russia and contemporary Cuba) and postcolonial or anti-imperialist movements (as in South Africa and the Philippines) can yield insights into how LGBTI movements broaden themselves from rights-centered to social-justice- and even ecological- and disability-encompassing movements suggestive of intergenerational (Fernbach 1981) and a trans-human (McRuer 2010; Thomas 2006) justice, respectively.[11]

The limitations of human-rights-based movements, despite the appeal of the particular universalism of the state system, reside in historical skepticism about a globalizing political structure that helps elaborate capitalist economic development and the inability of those most disenfranchised due to poverty, stigma, and so-called "traditional values" pertaining to selfhood in relation to one's body and sharing bodily pleasures with others, to exercise those human rights (not to mention the costs of engaging cumbersome legal systems and their selective enforcement). This skepticism persists even when state leaders strive toward equal membership in the international community and agree to be monitored by its human-rights mechanisms. Hence, this fourth motif of intercultural dialogue and advocacy interrogates the extent to which sexuality is an issue of social justice including, but more encompassing than individual and group rights, and is also not merely postmaterial "icing on the cake" after other, supposedly more important injustices are addressed first, such as violence, economic inequality, sociocultural hegemonies, and deprivation of political participation—as though these were unrelated to sexuality (see Corrales and Pecheny 2010, 18). This is also why, in parts of the world in which injustice is widespread—that is, most of the world—treating advocacy for same-sex sexuality and gender diversity as social-justice work that demonstrates this work's indivisibility from "LGBTI rights" is an underrecognized, but potentially very effective, practical and theoretical strategy.

Recall that within this last motif of intercultural debate and advocacy, the significance of sexuality for politics is not taken for granted in any part of the world, where it may be conceived as something "private" or defined by its reproduction of cultural tradition, or as something natural. As advocates for same-sex-loving practices and politically correlated gender diversity gain an international platform, debate for or against their presence as human (equal) rights bearers focuses attention on how to conceive justice inclusive of sexuality and gender and how human relationships may accordingly be conceived of as just or unjust within and across national legal systems. This expands what aspects of life are political, as mentioned at the beginning of this section with reference to feminist revisionings of the political.

On the one hand, current understandings of cosmopolitan social justice could be informed by the inclusion of injustice within regimes of sexuality. For instance, Amartya Sen (2009) elaborates a "non-ideal" theory of "comparative justice" wherein justice would involve piecemeal recognition of expressed injustices of gender and sexuality in local, regional, and international forums and, with reference to all the four motifs mentioned here, the hashing out of agreement about how to eliminate them, transforming interculturally what justice is conceived to be across different forms of human association. On the other hand, the approach of sexual-citizenship theory, advocating sexual rights inscribed within international human rights and nationalized, has developed as most promising for a state-oriented legal approach. However, this approach presumes attentive, accurate reporting and monitoring through, say, the UN Human Rights Council's Universal Periodic Review—although this process lacks enforcement mechanisms that could effectively combat state homophobia (Cabral and Viturro 2011; Cossman 2007; Plummer 2003). A modified global-public-goods approach offers a third option; informed by World Health Organization guidance around sexuality and reproductive decision making as well as HIV/AIDS activism, this approach suggests that sexual health, literacy, and well-being be conceived as common goods available to all human beings and that, because cultural sanctioning varies, the means of access to these public goods of sexuality be internationally guaranteed within different regimes of sexuality governance. Each of these approaches points toward a combined effect with the others. Taken together they sexualize justice through an evolving conception of human capabilities that includes sexual ones needing material support; suggest rationales beyond cultural traditions (medical, educational, emotional, or psychic well-being from evidence-based social science); and invoke the force of law through accounts of sexual citizenship as also already gendered.

The historical arc that resulted in a platform of international visibility, debate, and political action around sexual orientation and gender diversity was successful due to global feminisms that interact with their challengers across cultures and continue, sometimes unevenly, to overcome them. Therefore, analyzing the motif that intertwines sexuality and social justice has to take account of recent feminist theories of justice (such as that of Koggle 1998) to conceptualize how advocacy around sexuality reframes both selfhood and political association in a relational way. Conceiving justice is dependent on the context of relationships in which it is invoked; these relationships are between historical, not abstract parties, and the differences between them include their historically-configured inequalities—of literacy, able-bodiedness, skin tone, etc. (see also Lyotard 1985). Here, the meaning of justice is *enacted* through relations of difference and inequality as these are inflected within governance regimes. Legitimizing truth claims inherent to those regimes suggest whether we "ought to" submit to being governed and govern others in certain ways, but we also "sense" whether we are empowered or disempowered through more or less institutionalized practices inciting us to shape our own and others' feelings of self- or personhood in relationships of professional occupation, sexuality, or citizenship, for example. The innovation that feminist and later queer theories bring to conceiving justice is a focus on "feeling" in "intimate" relationships, a focus on the situational thresholds, respectively, of self/not self and private/public—governing ourselves and others amid feelings of personhood that are ambiguous because they are mediated at once through relations of bodily intelligibility, gendered power, and erotic pleasure. The perspective of relational justice is sometimes described as "acting," "treating," "being treated," "living," justly, and helps decenter formal mechanisms of power exercised through the law and nation-state and introduces into reflective awareness a comparison of how interpersonal relationships are structured into regimes of sexuality and how personhood (ethical agency, Wekker's sexual subjecthood) exceeds their constraints even when it is produced within them.

The language of justice, particularly spoken in its broadest and most practical terms, may enable communication among adversaries who may each understand themselves as doing "social-justice work" and sometimes even cease being adversaries as a result, as Kaoma (this volume) notes of U.S. evangelist Rick Warren. Similarly, listening to claims of injustice suffered through non-normative sexed bodies, gender identities, and practices of erotic love and interpreting them with a language of relational justice, "how we relate," converts an interrogation of sexual rights into a lexicon that is translatable across ideological agendas and cultures. (A side benefit might even be recognition of how relatively central the "use" of sexuality is in living for different cultures.) A motif of sexuality and social justice also recalls early gay, lesbian, and "trans" liberation narratives from Europe, the Americas, and parts of Southern and Southeast Asia, that were already intersectional and cross-cultural in their approaches, even as it recognizes their historical limitations and configures them anew through transnational movements and the new comparative historiography of sexuality.

*   *   *

To sum up, observation of the historically developing platform that enables international recognition for same-sex sexualities and gender diversity suggests at least four motifs of intercultural communication and continuing contentiousness, but also of collaborative learning that opens up possibilities for political action. These motifs appear to weave together ideologies, debates, official proceedings, commissioned and independent research, and advocacy. First, relations of governance have historically come to link truth, power, and subjectivity into regimes through which same-sex sexualities and gender diversity have become widely intelligible but that load terms such as homosexuality, homophobia, and transphobia in different cultural formations. In the process, "sexuality" (inclusive of gender identity independent of birth-assigned biological sex) has become a key instance of translating conceptions of human-ness across cultures. Second, the ways in which sexuality involves a kind of governance without government is an important complement to frameworks for analysis within this volume, colored by both reactive and proactive state homophobia, that rely heavily on state power and legal rights. Hence, the need for comparative analysis of regimes of sexuality historically, culturally, and in relation to other governance regimes working to constitute sexuality, including what allows a modular homophobia to arise, travel, and take root in different parts of the world. Drawing on the historical perspective of the first motif, this imperative could suggest developing measures and types of heteronormativity to compare regimes of sexuality, using these to demonstrate what makes modular homophobia as well as LGBTI movements successful, and to discern whether or not state homophobia needs—a central concern of this volume—entrenched popular heteronormativity, and what kinds, in mobilizing homophobia. Third, "flashpoints" from alchemy among different working conceptions of self- or personhood and what, subjectively, makes that person's life worth living—clashing, hybridizing, glocalizing, and reiterating—within regimes of sexuality make visible when agency instantiates and when it exceeds regulatory constraints of a regime, providing an ethical framework for conceiving justice-as-relational through sexuality. As such (and fourth), justice, when it pertains to sexual governance, becomes intelligible to an important extent through interpersonal relationships and how they govern subjectivity; this historical situation requires attentiveness to how justice and injustice are conceived and may be explicated through those relationships in complex and locally specific interdependencies between sexuality and other governance regimes. The significance of sexuality in broader culturally nuanced debates about social justice is an under-recognized frontier for political thought, even though global political advocacy for LGBTI rights has outpaced it in conjunction with the strategies of sexual regulation explored in this volume. What seems to come clear in these architectonic reflections is that same-sex sexuality and gender diversity, inextricably intertwined politically today, form an axis around which just governance may be re-visioned contributing to how economic, intergenerational, transitional, retributive or reparative, cultural, and racial justice are conceived, too.

The historical event that gives same-sex sexualities and gender diversity an ongoing platform for international recognition is a battleground of competing views—even life forms, it sometimes seems—in relating sexuality to governance, ethics, and justice. Political thought at this frontier involves attending to disputations on the new global platform interrogating emerging human capacities occasioned by same-sex sexualities and gender diversity, as well as to practical reflections about human relatedness through sexuality by those "on the ground" that are informed by, say, *ubuntu* and *malasakit*—just to take two examples developed in these pages.

Notes

The author thanks Mike Bosia and Meredith Weiss for their editorial and, over the long term, substantive insights that improved this essay.

1. In titling this chapter, I have followed the theme of the book and discussions that gave rise to it, focusing on political or state homophobia. The analysis of homophobia cannot be separated from transphobia, and struggles for "homosexual" rights have historically been intertwined with struggles for (what are now termed) transgender rights, with same-sex sexuality often seen as manifesting a "third sex/gender" (Blasius and Phelan 1997). In my focus on the politics of sexuality and regimes of sexuality as objects of analysis, I have referred to gender identity in its relationship, theoretically and practically, to sexual orientation. Some transgender writers such as Audrey Mbugua insist "[t]he transgender community exists within the LGBT movement not because of their sexual practices or sexual orientation, but because of their gender identity" (Mbugua 2011, 243), and Mauro Cabral has rigorously theorized this argument, also including the intersexed (unfortunately untranslated, see here Cabral and Vitturo 2006). The contestations and interdependencies between a politics of gender and a politics of sexuality and what's at stake theoretically in the distinctions made by them are important, and I have not had the space to address this here. I am flagging this issue at the outset to recognize it, even as I highlight sexuality and its relation to governance in addressing, more narrowly, the focus on homophobia of this volume.

2. The report states: "The terms lesbian, gay and bisexual and transgender are used throughout the report, but often abbreviated to LGBT. These terms are used to refer to same-sex behavior, identities or relationships and non-binary gender identities. In several places in the text, discrimination against intersex persons is also addressed" (Human Rights Council 2011, 4n2). It concludes with, "A more comprehensive analysis of the human-rights challenges facing LGBT and intersex persons would require a more extensive study and, in future, regular reporting" (24). The report was commissioned in 2011 by Human Rights Council Resolution 17/19, the first UN resolution on human rights, sexual orientation, and gender identity.

3. Consider as an analogy U.S. president Bill Clinton's assertion that the fellatio in which he engaged with a young woman in the White House was not "sexual"; at that time (1998), most of my undergraduate students in an urban public U.S. university also did not consider engaging in the same act to be sex. "Having sex" for my students, then, involved penile–vaginal penetration.

4. For heuristic examples of the AIDS pandemic in relation to regimes of governance, see the essays collected in *AIDS and Governance* (Poku, Whiteside, and Sandkjaer 2007).

5. I use *LGBT, LGBTI* (*lesbian, gay, bisexual, transgender,* and *intersexed*), and other terms depending upon the relevant context. *LGBT* is used more in North America; *LGBTI* is used more often outside North America and in transnational

activist organizations. *MSM* and *WSW* (men/women who have sex with men/ women) arose through HIV epidemiology and are employed by international agencies and advocacy organizations; I use these where relevant, too. I am not making an argument here that this terminology should supplant local languages of same-sex sexualities and gender diversity; rather, what is important is the interaction among international, transnational, and local regimes of governance through sexuality, including the use of "homophobia," a concept and strategy to combat "homosexuality" that travels to non-western contexts, where it sometimes preemptively creates the phenomenon as a phantasmic imitation of its supposed western counterpart in order to mobilize political resources to "defeat" it (see Weiss, this volume).

6. What began as "queering"—a critique of heteronormative power relations exercised throughout culture—may have universalized a particular Anglo-American experience into a theory that homogenizes differences across and within cultures. More recent accounts of queer theory, by acknowledging limits in its translatability, are more promising (Hall and Jagose 2013, xiv–xx). One antidote to this, suggested by Wekker but left undeveloped by most queer theorists, could be analysis of the indefinite number of ways people materially reconfigure the relationship of sexed bodies to social categories and erotic practices around the world. In this vein, sociologist Steven Seidman would "imagine" social-organizing principles "beyond sexuality" as the pivot for queer politics (Seidman 1997, 229–30).

7. Bosia and Weiss, but especially Zeidan (all this volume), as well as Zeidan 2010, offer useful critiques of what Massad terms the "Gay International."

8. See Merry (2006) for examples of vernacularization, indigenization, hybridity, and repetition in cultural translation by human-rights defenders.

9. Compare here Wekker: "[T]here is a politics to passion . . . [that] speaks about the agency of women in the sexual domain . . . in which they protest the power inequities inherent in the dominant gender regime" (67–68). In addition to developing this theoretical point about power and erotics, Wekker conceptualizes female same-sex erotic relations emically as *mati work*, "a relational activity, where the sex of one's object of passion is less salient than sexual fulfillment per se," an ethical site where an "instance of the multiplicitous 'I' who loves to lie down with women is foregrounded" (193 and *passim*).

10. In a sense, Hillary Clinton's language emblematized the arc of at least official international advocacy in the politics of sexuality. At Beijing in 1995 as U.S. first lady: "women's rights are human rights and human rights are women's rights"; at Geneva in 2011 as U.S. secretary of state: "human rights are gay rights and gay rights are human rights" (Clinton 2011).

11. There is a treasure trove of historical studies on this topic across cultures and, to be sure, the record of modernity's "progressive" march is ambivalent and at best complex. For an example in one national context I have addressed, see Abinales's (2004) analysis and documentation of the inclusion of homosexuality within a program of sexual politics for the Philippine Communist Party's struggle against imperialism, and Estrada-Claudio's (1991) feminist analysis of the party's sexual politics generally.

Other, earlier primary sources specifically from LGBT movements are included in Likosky (1992) and Blasius and Phelan (1997).

Bibliography

Abaya, Eufracio C. 2009. "Ethic of Care: Growing Older as *Bakla* ('Gay') in a Philippine Locale." Paper presented at Eighth Conference of International Association for the Study of Sexuality, Culture and Society, April 16, 2009, Hanoi, Vietnam.

Abinales, Patricio N. 2004. *Love, Sex, and the Filipino Communist (or Hinggil sa Pagpipigil ng Panggigigil)*. Manila: Anvil Publishing.

Aken'Ova, Cesnabmiliho Dorothy. 2007. "Women and Girls' Sexual Health." Session on Sexual Health in Africa at International Resources Network-Africa Workshop, February 9, 2007, Saly, Senegal.

AMSHeR (African Men for Sexual Health and Rights). 2011. "Statement of African Social Justice Activists on the Threats of the British Government to 'Cut Aid' to African Countries that Violate the Rights of LGBTI People in Africa." October 27. http://amsher.net/news/ViewArticle.aspx?id=1200, accessed August 8, 2012.

Berlant, Lauren, and Michael Warner. 1998. "Sex in Public." *Critical Inquiry* 24: 547–566.

Blasius, Mark, and Shane Phelan, eds. 1997. *We Are Everywhere: A Historical Sourcebook of Gay and Lesbian Politics*. London and New York: Routledge.

Butler, Judith. 2004. *Undoing Gender*. London and New York: Routledge.

Cabral, Mauro (A. I. Grinspan), and Paula Viturro. 2006. "(Trans)Sexual Citizenship in Contemporary Argentina." In Paisley Currah, Richard M. Juang, and Shannon Price Minter, eds., *Transgender Rights*, pp. 262–73. Minneapolis: University of Minnesota Press.

Clinton, Hillary Rodham. 2011. "Remarks in Recognition of International Human Rights Day." December 6, 2011, http://www.state.gov/secretary/rm/2011/12/178368.htm, accessed August 9, 2012.

Connell, R. W. 1996. "New Directions in Gender Theory, Masculinity Research, and Gender Politics." *Ethnos* 61, nos. 3–4: 157–70.

Corrales, Javier, and Mario Pecheny. 2010. *The Politics of Sexuality in Latin America: A Reader on Lesbian, Gay, Bisexual, and Transgender Rights*. Pittsburgh, PA: University of Pittsburgh Press.

Cossman, Brenda. 2007. *Sexual Citizens: The Legal and Cultural Regulation of Sex and Belonging*. Stanford, CA: Stanford University Press.

Dankwa, Serena Owusua. 2009. "'It's a Silent Trade': Female Same-Sex Intimacies in Post-Colonial Ghana." *NORA-Nordic Journal of Feminist and Gender Research* 17, no. 3: 192–205.

D'Emilio, John. 1983. "Capitalism and Gay Identity." In Ann Snitow, Christine Stansell, and Sharon Thompson, eds., *Powers of Desire: The Politics of Sexuality*. New York: Monthly Review Press.

Duggan, Lisa. 2002. "The New Homonormativity: The Sexual Politics of Neoliberalism." In Russ Castronovo and Dana D. Nelson, eds., *Materializing Democracy: Toward a Revitalized Cultural Politics.* Durham, NC: Duke University Press.

Durkheim, Emile. 1938. *The Rules of Sociological Method.* Translated by Sarah A. Solovay and John H. Mueller. New York: Free Press of Glencoe.

Euben, Roxanne L. 2004. "Traveling Theorists and Translating Practices." In Stephen K. White and J. Donald Moon, eds., *What Is Political Theory?*, pp. 145–73. London: Sage.

Estrada-Claudio, Sylvia, writing as Sunny Lansang. 1991. "Gender Issues in Revolutionary Praxis. *Philippine Left Review* 1: 41–52.

Fernbach, David.1981. *The Spiral Path: A Gay Contribution to Human Survival.* London: Gay Men's Press and Alyson Publications.

Foucault, Michel. 1978. *The History of Sexuality, Vol. I: An Introduction.* Translated by Robert Hurley. New York: Pantheon.

Garcia, J. Neil C. 2008. *Philippine Gay Culture: Binabae to Bakla, Silahis to MSM.* Revised Edition. Quezon City: University of the Philippines Press.

Hacking, Ian. 1986. "Making Up People." In Thomas C. Heller, Morton Sosna, and David E. Wellbery, eds., *Reconstructing Individualism: Autonomy, Individuality, and the Self in Western Thought*, pp. 222–236. Stanford, CA: Stanford University Press.

Hackman, Melissa. 2009. "Emergent Sexual Identities: Ex-Gay South Africans." Paper presented at the International Resource Network-Africa Workshop, September 30–October 1, 2009, in Syracuse, New York.

Hall, Donald E., and Annamarie Jagose, eds. 2013. *The Routledge Queer Studies Reader.* London: Routledge.

Herdt, Gilbert, and Robert Stoller. 1990. *Intimate Communications: Erotics and the Study of Culture.* New York: Columbia University Press.

Ho, Josephine. 2008. "Is Global Governance Bad for East Asian Queers?" *GLQ: A Journal of Lesbian and Gay Studies* 14, no. 4: 457–79.

Human Rights Council. 2011. "Discriminatory laws and practices and acts of violence against individuals based on their sexual orientation and gender identity." Report of the United Nations High Commissioner for Human Rights, November 17. http://www.ohchr.org/Documents/Issues/Discrimination/A.HRC.19.41_English.pdf.

Keohane, Robert O., and David G. Victor. 2011. "The Regime Complex for Climate Change." *Perspectives on Politics* 9, no. 1: 7–23.

Koggle, Christine. 1998. *Perspectives on Equality: Constructing a Relational Theory.* Lanham, MD: Rowman and Littlefield.

Kuria Mbote, David. 2013. "Running as an 'Out' Political candidate in Kenya: Recording Lessons Learned." Kiambu Senatorial Campaign. http://kuriaforsenator.com/lessons_from_Campaign.pdf, accessed February 3, 2013.

Lewis, Desiree. 2011. "Representing African sexualities." In Sylvia Tamale, ed. *African Sexualities: A Reader*, pp. 199–216. Cape Town, South Africa: Pambazuka Press.

Likosky, Stephan, ed. 1992. *Coming Out: An Anthology of International Gay and Lesbian Writings*. New York: Pantheon Books.

Lyotard, Jean-Francois, and Jean-Loup Thebaud. 1985. *Just Gaming*. Translated by Wlad Godzich. Minneapolis: University of Minnesota Press. Sometimes cataloged under Lyotard or both Lyotard and Thebaud as authors.

Massad, Joseph A. 2007. *Desiring Arabs*. Chicago: University of Chicago Press.

McRuer, Robert. 2006 *Crip Theory: Cultural Signs of Disability and Queerness*. New York: New York University Press.

Mbugua, Audrey. 2011. "Gender Dynamics: A Transsexual Overview." In Sylvia Tamale, ed., *African Sexualities: A Reader*, pp. 238–48. Cape Town, South Africa: Pambazuka Press.

Merry, Sally Engle. 2006. "Transnational Human Rights and Local Activism: Mapping the Middle." *American Anthropologist* 108, no. 1: 38–51.

Meyrowitz, Joanne. 2002. *How Sex Changed: A History of Transsexuality in the United States*. Cambridge, MA: Harvard University Press.

Mieli, Mario. 1980. *Homosexuality and Liberation: Elements of a Gay Critique*. Translated by David Fernbach. London: Gay Men's Press.

Muholi, Zanele. 2009. "So They Have 'Eyes to See.'" Paper prepared for presentation at the International Resource Network–Africa Workshop, September 30–October 4, 2009, in Syracuse, New York.

Murray, Stephan O. and Will Roscoe. 1998. *Boy-Wives and Female Husbands: Studies of African Homosexualities*. New York: Palgrave.

Nyanzi, Stella. 2011. "Unpacking the [Govern]mentality of African Sexualities." In Sylvia Tamale, ed., *African Sexualities: A Reader*, pp. 477–501. Cape Town, South Africa: Pambazuka Press.

Petchesky, Rosalind Pollack. 2001. "Sexual Rights: Inventing a Concept, Mapping an International Practice." In Mark Blasius, ed., *Sexual Identities, Queer Politics*, pp. 118–39. Princeton, NJ: Princeton University Press.

Plummer, Ken. 2003. *Intimate Citizenship: Private Decisions and Public Dialogues*. Seattle, WA: University of Washington Press.

Poku, Nana K, Alan Whiteside, and Bjorg Sandkjaer. 2007. *AIDS and Governance*. Burlington, VT: Ashgate.

Puar, Jasbir K. 2007. *Terrorist Assemblages: Homonationalism in Queer Times*. Durham, NC: Duke University Press.

Quinn, Sheila. 2010. "An Activist's Guide to the Yogyakarta Principles." ARC International. http://www.ypinaction/content/activists_guide, accessed August 8, 2012.

Ratele, Kopano. 2011. "Male Sexualities and Masculinities." In Sylvia Tamale, ed., *African Sexualities: A Reader*, pp. 399–419. Cape Town, South Africa: Pambazuka Press.

Reddy, Vasu, Lisa Wiebesiek, and Crystal Munthree. 2011. "Military Mutilations: The Aversion Programme in the South African Defence Force in the Apartheid Era." Unpublished manuscript. Pretoria, South Africa: Human Sciences Research Council.

Said, Edward W. 1983. "Traveling Theory." In *The World, the Text, and the Critic* by Edward Said, pp. 226–48. Cambridge, MA: Harvard University Press.

Seidman, Steven. 1997. *Difference Troubles: Queering Social Theory and Sexual Politics.* Cambridge, MA: Cambridge University Press.

Taia, Abdellah. 2009. "The Rule of I." *Reality Sandwich.* March 19. http://realitysandwich .com/print/12634, accessed February 26, 2012.

Tamale, Sylvia. 2011. *African Sexualities: A Reader.* Cape Town, South Africa: Pamzabuka Press.

Thomas, Kendall. 2006. "Afterword: Are Transgender Rights *In*human Rights?" In Paisley Currah, Richard M. Juang, and Shannon Price Minter, eds., *Transgender Rights,* pp. 310–326. Minneapolis: University of Minnesota Press.

Walby, Sylvia. 2004. "The European Union and Gender Equality: Emergent Varieties of Gender Regime." *Social Politics* 11, no. 1: 4–29.

Wekker, Gloria. 2006. *The Politics of Passion: Women's Sexual Culture in the Afro-Surinamese Diaspora.* New York: Columbia University Press.

The Yogyakarta Principles. 2006. Principles on the Application of International Human Rights Law in Relation to Sexual Orientation and Gender Identity. http:// www.yogyakartaprinciples.org.

Zeidan, Sami. 2010. "Navigating International Rights and Local Politics: Sexuality Governance in a Post-Colonial Setting." PhD dissertation, City University of New York Graduate Center.

11

Conclusion

On the Interplay of State Homophobia and Homoprotectionism

CHRISTINE (CRICKET) KEATING

Referring to bias, discriminatory actions, attitudes, or beliefs directed toward people that either have or are perceived as having non-heterosexual identities such as lesbian, gay, bisexual, transgender, and queer people (LGBTQ), the term *homophobia* has been used by LGBTQ groups since the early 1970s to organize against discrimination and persecution. The essays in this volume center specifically on state homophobia, or what some authors call political homophobia, a neglected category of analysis, especially given its high-profile and often violent deployment in several contexts across the globe, and convincingly assert that states mobilize, consolidate, and foment homophobia to further particular ends, whether it be to consolidate national identity, to quash or to build opposition, and/or to legitimate the centralization of authority. By underscoring ways that political homophobia is tactical, purposive, and transnational, these essays highlight that there is nothing primordial, static, or traditional about homophobia, rather that it is a set of practices and discourses often generated and deployed by political elites for very particular political ends.

In this concluding essay, I will explore the interplay between state homophobia and discourses and policies geared toward the protection of sexual minorities, what I will call state "homoprotectionism." Like state homophobia, state homoprotectionism can also be instrumental and purposive, serving to legitimate political authority both on a national and on a transnational scale. Although seemingly opposed, I will suggest that these two approaches are closely linked and that political authorities rely on a complex interplay of both approaches in order to mobilize consent (or at least to minimize dissent).

Drawing on the essays in this volume, I will explore ways that activists might maneuver the interplay between state homophobia and state homoprotectionism in struggles for sexual justice. This maneuvering, as both colonial and postcolonial history exemplifies, necessitates a deeply coalitional approach to politics, one that challenges intra and intergroup hierarchies across a range of power relations and that fosters alternatives to state-centered configurations of sexual justice.

The essays in this volume underscore the centrality of state homophobia in contemporary national and transnational politics and point to ways that the state and other political actors consolidate heterosexist power and privilege through discriminatory, persecutory, and exclusionary legal frameworks and political discourse. All too often overlooked because homophobia, in the words of Michael Bosia and Meredith Weiss, "is reduced to nothing more than a variable [or a restraint] reflecting static religious values and traditional attitudes about sexuality," state homophobia is an approach to contemporary statecraft that is being developed, shared, and replicated in states throughout the world (Bosia and Weiss, this volume). Like the racial state, the bourgeois state, and the patriarchal state, the homophobic state gives legitimacy to heterosexist power and privilege, consolidating this power through laws and policies, and establishing mechanisms for the enforcement of these laws and policies.

In addition to state homophobia, contemporary politics is marked by what might be called state *homoprotectionism*, an approach in which political actors harness the power of the state to protect LGBTQ people from persecution and domination. In the protectionist framework, the state works to secure the allegiance of vulnerable groups by offering protection to these groups from other groups from within society. Indeed, whereas the homophobic state secures heterosexist power and privilege, the homoprotectionist state challenges it. Hillary Clinton's landmark 2011 International Human Rights Day speech is illustrative of homoprotectionist discourse and policy. In her speech, Clinton calls upon states around the world to protect the rights of their LGBT citizens and pledges the U.S. government's commitment to protecting gay, lesbian, bisexual, and transgender people on a global scale. In doing so, she positions the state as the vehicle for anti-homophobic social transformation, arguing that "progress comes from changes in laws . . . Laws change, then people will" (Clinton 2011).

Key to homoprotectionist narratives is a version of state–society relations in which the state functions as an arbiter between groups, working to ensure that one group does not dominate or persecute the other. In her speech,

Clinton outlines the many forms of homophobic discrimination, marginalization, and persecution that LGBT people face and notes that all too often, "authorities empowered to protect them [LGBT individuals] look the other way or . . . even join in the abuse." While acknowledging the participation of state actors in acts of homophobic abuse, Clinton downplays or occludes state homophobia as a mode of governance and gives little attention to how state actors structure or consolidate homophobia more broadly. In her framing, the primary obstacle to forging a "global consensus that recognizes the rights of LGBT citizens everywhere" is not the state in its homophobic guise, but rather the way that the people use "religious or cultural values as a reason to violate or not to protect the human rights of LGBT citizens" (Clinton 2011).

Although seemingly opposed, dominatory and protectionist approaches are closely linked and political authorities often rely on a complex interplay of both approaches in order to mobilize consent. Teasing out the interplay of homophobia and homoprotectionism helps make sense of the shifting justificatory logic and enabling collaborations upon which state power and authority rest. A first link between them is that state homophobic rhetoric and policy help shape the "traditionalist" politics that are the object of state homoprotectionist intervention. Second, although one approach or the other might be rhetorically dominant, both approaches are often concurrently pursued. Finally, both approaches help foster alliances that help to bolster state power. While homophobic rhetoric and policy are geared toward engendering the collaboration of dominant groups, homoprotectionism works to garner support from those who hope to put the state in the service of reform, obscuring the ways that the state helped to generate sexual hierarchies and its own stake (sometimes submerged) in their continuation.

Both homophobic and homoprotectionist approaches to governance are deeply imbricated in processes of colonialism, neocolonialism, and capitalist globalization. The essays in this volume speak to the close relation of homophobia with formulations of power within and between states that continue to privilege the global North over the global South. Indeed, despite rhetoric that holds that LGBT identities and mobilizations are themselves neocolonial impositions, this volume documents ways that homophobia, in the words of Frank Mugisha, is the "toxic import" (quoted in Bosia and Weiss, this volume).

Like homophobia, current homoprotectionist discourses and policies are also deeply linked to and embedded in inequitable global relations of power. For example, Jasbir Puar writes that contemporary projects of exceptionalism, "a process whereby a national population comes to believe its own superiority and its own singularity," in the United States are "furthered by attaching themselves to, or being attached by, non-heterosexual, 'homo-normative' subjects" (2008: 48). In this formulation of exceptionalism, "gay friendly" policies or discourses mark a nation as particularly forward-thinking, progressive, and/or democratic. Such a process "ties the recognition of homosexual subjects, both legally and representationally, to the national and transnational political agendas of US imperialism" in that it positions the United States as "the arbiter of appropriate ethics, human rights, and democratic behavior" (52).

In a similar vein, Sarah Schulman (2011) highlights ways that homoprotectionist rhetoric and policy are being used as cover for anti-immigrant and anti-Muslim politics in Europe and in Israel. For example, Schulman reports that "in 2005, with help from American marketing executives, the Israeli government began a marketing campaign, 'Brand Israel,' aimed at men ages 18 to 34 [which] sought to depict Israel as 'relevant and modern.' The government later expanded the marketing plan by harnessing the gay community to reposition its global image" (2011, A31). Such a marketing strategy, Schulman explains, enables a state to brand itself as modern and progressive, while at the same time pursuing a deeply racist and exclusionary agenda.

Hillary Clinton's 2011 International Human Rights Day speech is illustrative of the ways that homoprotectionism is linked to contemporary geopolitics. Although careful to note that the United States has a long way to go in terms of embracing gay rights as human rights, Clinton draws on a narrative of progress and positions the U.S. government as a leader in efforts to obtain equal rights for LGBT people worldwide. Addressing LGBT populations, she explains that "wherever you live and whatever the circumstances of your life, whether you are connected to a network of support or feel isolated and vulnerable, please know that you are not alone . . . you have an ally in the United States of America" (Clinton 2011). Such a framing is deeply seductive yet profoundly dangerous; if the U.S. state is an ally, the essays in this volume demonstrate that at best it is a fickle and unstable partner in the struggle for sexual justice. Further, as both Puar and Schulman note, while homoprotectionist formulations of transnational sexual citizenship may glean LGBTQ populations some policy benefits, these come at the high cost of acquiescing to unjust power relations within and between states.

Drawing on the articles in this volume, the remainder of this essay will explore ways to disrupt the interplay of state homophobia and homoprotectionism. I will suggest that the essays challenge the logic of both modes of sexual governance in three ways. First, they expose state homophobia as a form of statecraft in ways that serve to denaturalize intra- and intergroup power relations by underscoring the state's stake in such power relations. Second, the essays direct attention to the complex ways that both state homophobic and homoprotectionist agendas grow out of and interact with local and global political concerns and structures, and in doing so provide a valuable analytic model for interrogating the complex interplay between homophobia and homoprotectionism as modes of sexual governance. Third, they affirm the importance of challenging and dismantling neocolonial power relations but reject homophobia as a mode of doing so; similarly, they suggest strategies for challenging and dismantling heterosexism that refuse the neocolonial logic of homoprotectionism.

One of the primary contributions of this volume to both the analytic and political project of working toward sexual justice in a global frame is uncovering ways in which political homophobia is being exported by powerful transnational actors. For example, Michael Bosia points out that state homophobic practices have grown "increasingly modular," noting that these practices have a remarkable cohesion and consistency "despite differences in terms of region, religion, culture, historical experience, state capacity, and regime." In his essay, Kapya Kaoma gives examples of how such a modular form of state homophobia is being transmitted from the global North to the global South. Through a close analysis of the interaction between religious leaders from Africa and U.S. Christian religious conservatives, Kaoma argues that the U.S. religious right is exporting its culture wars to Africa and documents in impressive detail the exported weapons of this war: antigay talking points, workshops, and even laws. In an inversion of the cultural protection model, Kaoma claims that LGBT persons in Africa are suffering the "collateral damage" of U.S. culture wars. In this framing, it is homophobia that is unwanted foreign imposition, not identities and organizing based on same-sex desire. While Kaoma uses the metaphor of cultural war, David Johnson's essay focuses directly on the relationship between the U.S. military apparatus and state homophobia, highlighting the ways that the United States exported homophobic rhetoric and policy "both as explicit government policy and as a cultural model" during the Cold War.

Further turning the notion that LGBT identities and mobilizations are foreign imports on its head, these essays also highlight ways that instead of being a reaction to the mobilization of LGBT movements, state homophobic mobilizations often occur *before* LGBT political organizing. In her essay, for example, Meredith Weiss suggests that paying attention to this sequencing is crucially important in fleshing out the relationship between state homophobia and forms of queer organizing. Counter to the narrative that state homophobic policies are developed and deployed in reaction to local LGBTQ organizing, her examination of state homophobia in Singapore, Indonesia, Malaysia, and the Philippines reveals that state homophobia often, in Weiss's words, is "anticipatory." She explains that a close analysis of the timing of state homophobic mobilization reveals that "while framed by participants as a countermovement," such homophobic mobilization "actually responded far more to developments in the United States and elsewhere than to the overt expression of non-heteronormative identities or rights claims in the local community, suggesting homophobia's transnational diffusion, but also presuming a normative (if derided) universal trope of 'LGBT.'" This sequencing has many effects, not the least of which is forcing local LGBT groups to react to such efforts, which in Weiss's words has the ironic consequence of nudging LGBT communities' "self-identities and reference groups" toward their EuroAmerican counterparts. In this framing, it is the globalization of homophobia that prompts LGBTQ organizing in a particular form, not the other way around.

A second way that this collection of essays intervenes against both state homophobia and homoprotectionism is by paying close attention to the contingent and complicated ways in which sexual governance strategies play out in various political settings. Indeed, as analytically and politically important as the evidence of the ways in which political homophobia is exported from the West or the global North is, Katarzyna Korycki and Abouzar Nasirzadeh caution against overestimating the power of transnational homophobic networks and thus underestimating "the reach and agency" of non-Western state actors. Such an approach, they warn, perpetuates notions of the non-West as being perpetually acted upon. Further, it absolves non-Western states from their complicity in acts of state homophobia, as it locates the impetus of such action elsewhere. As such, this framing may have the effect of rendering "antigay violence and repression as excusable because it is anti-Western or—better yet—as caused by the West." Though not downplaying the disparity of power between the global South and the global North, Korycki and Nasirzadeh argue for close attention to the different ways that such homophobia plays out in relation to particular national political contexts. In Iran, for example, they explore the state's long history of sanctioning some and condemning other aspects of homosexual desire and note that "far from being the pawn of western machinations, the Iranian state has varied its stance toward homosexuality in pursuit of its objectives—namely, modernization, consolidation, and most recently deliberalization."

In her essay, Amy Lind also analyzes the complex ways that political homophobia and state support of sexual rights may operate side by side. Taking as her focus recent developments in Ecuador, a context marked by impressive victories in the struggle for LGBTQ justice, as well as by setbacks, Lind notes that newly articulated forms of heteronormativities (and homonormativities) remain central to political life, and in particular to new formulations of political economy. Lind's analysis underscores that not only is a careful analysis of what Sybille Nyeck (2010) calls the "contentious environment" of transnational and national political contexts crucial for grasping the complexity of state homophobia in any given situation, but also that an analysis of the state's approach to questions of gender and sexuality is critical for understanding contemporary political and economic life more generally.

Conor O'Dwyer focuses on the postcommunist regions of Europe (in particular Poland) and notes the back-and-forth nature of the sequencing of political homophobia in relation to pressure from EU actors to broaden and deepen sexual rights. In his analysis, O'Dwyer found an improvement of LGBT legal rights in response to EU requirements, which was then followed by a homophobic backlash. In his study, however, he pressed further and found that the initial uptick in homophobia was then followed by a LGB response that led to impressive gains in challenging heteronormative configurations of state and society in Poland. Given this success, Dwyer concludes by asking of the European Union, "Why has it not applied more pressure?"

If part of what makes homophobia so politically salient and efficacious is the way that state and state-seeking political actors have equated LGBT identities and mobilizations with challenges to national identity, then an important political project is to highlight the ways that homophobia itself has been deeply intertwined with neoliberal and neocolonial endeavors, as the essays in this volume do so well. A third step, then, is to work to build the equivalence between what Meredith Weiss calls a "homopositive" politics and a decolonial politics. Several essays in this volume point to ways to develop such a conceptual and political linkage. In his essay, Sami Zeidan suggests that a rejection of Western cultural hegemony should not mean a rejection of same-sex sexuality; rather, such a rejection makes imperative the creation of spaces at the local level, to deliberate over what it means to have same-sex intimacy. He emphasizes the strategic importance of fostering such a public sphere for conversations about non-heteronormative sexualities and genders in non-Western postcolonial settings. Such a public sphere, according to Zeidan, "allows those with non-heteronormative sexualities and genders to work out a local grassroots self-definition" and then enables the possibility of the translation of this discourse into progressive reform. In this framing, Zeidan mobilizes a decolonial impulse to press for the necessity of opening up spaces for dialogue about same-sex intimacies. Zeidan's vision for sexual citizenship is one of people turning to each other in dialogue without the mediation of the homoprotectionist state; for him such a dialogue might be state-enabled, but it is not state-centered.

In his essay, Mark Blasius turns to questions of strategy in the face of the accusation of the hegemony of Western forms of same-sex mobilization. He pays close attention to the power relations involved in making rights claims and notes that the dilemma is that through the language of human rights, sexuality has become a publically acknowledged political issue, but that these rights claims themselves are problematic, given that "their opponents insist that such rights themselves involve the imposition of Western values." Strategically, he suggests that LGBT movements broaden themselves from rights-centered to social-justice movements. He argues, "the distinctive politics of these 'identity-based' rights as human rights emphasizes embedding a conception of same-sex loving and gender diversity, indeed, a regime of sexuality itself that constructs sex, gender, and erotics, as a necessary component of visions for and policies toward a common good that are perennial concerns but take different forms within specific schemes and practices for governing today."

Taking up the pressing question of the globalization of homophobia, both with an understanding of its transnational, modular character and with an eye for the complexity of particular homophobic practices in particular political locales is powerful epistemically, in that it helps us to understand identity mobilization in various parts of the globe. It is also important to understand this phenomenon politically, in terms of building movements for sexual justice in both a transnational and a local frame. Given the imbrication of both state homophobic and state homoprotectionist discourse and policy with inequitable power relations within and between states, it is critical to pay close attention to their interplay, rejecting state homophobia while at the same time maneuvering state homoprotectionism in ways that preserves policy gains that enable LGBTQ people to live lives less marred by persecution, marginalization, and domination but refuses the racial and neocolonial alliances that Puar and Schulman argue so often are the price of such gains. This maneuvering is difficult, of course, and *Global Homophobia* gives us important tools—questions to ask, places to look, political projects to pursue—that enable us to do so more effectively.

Bibliography

Clinton, Hillary. 2011. "Remarks in Recognition of International Human Rights Day." December 6. http://www.state.gov/secretary/rm/2011/12/178368.htm.

Nyeck, Sybille Ngo. 2010. "Accounting for Paradoxical Emptiness in Contentious Intersections: 'Colonial Blackmail,' Token Causation and Sexuality in Africa." Paper read at American Political Science Annual Meeting, at Washington, D.C., September 4.

Puar, Jasbir. 2008. "Feminists and Queers in the Service of Empire" In Robin Riley et al., eds., *Feminism and War: Confronting U.S. Imperialism*, pp. 47–55, London & York: Zed Books.

Schulman, Sarah. 2011. "Israel and 'Pinkwashing.'" *New York Times*, November 11.

Contributors

MARK BLASIUS is professor emeritus of political science at the Graduate Center and La Guardia Community College of the City University of New York. His research and teaching are in contemporary political thought and the politics of sexuality and gender across cultures. His work includes: *Gay and Lesbian Politics: Sexuality and the Emergence of a New Ethic* (Temple, 1994); *We Are Everywhere: A Historical Sourcebook of Gay and Lesbian Politics* (co-editor, Routledge, 1997); *Sexual Identities, Queer Politics* (editor, Princeton, 2001); and articles in such journals as *Political Theory, APSR, Journal of the History of Sexuality,* and *GLQ: A Journal of Lesbian and Gay Studies.* He is completing *Sexuality and Social Justice* (a monograph to be published by Chicago) and a co-edited collection of studies on the politics of sexuality and gender nonconformity in the Philippines.

MICHAEL J. BOSIA is associate professor of political science at Saint Michael's College in Vermont. His work focuses on the intersection of the nation-state and transnational social movements, with a particular emphasis on French and U.S. politics, multiculturalism, the HIV/AIDS pandemic, and resistance to neoliberalism. His has been published in *Globalizations, French Politics, Culture & Society, French Politics, Perspectives on Politics, New Political Science,* and in edited volumes, and he is co-editor of a volume on globalization and food sovereignty.

DAVID K. JOHNSON is associate professor of history at the University of South Florida, where he focuses on the history of gender and sexuality, and gay and lesbian American history, including most recently the history of gay mass consumption before Stonewall and its impact on community and identity formation. He is author of the multiple-award-winning *The Lavender Scare: The Cold War Persecution of Gays and Lesbians in the Federal Government* (University of Chicago, 2004) and co-editor of *The U.S. since 1945: A Documentary Reader* (Wiley-Blackwell, 2009) and has published in journals including *The Journal of Social History*.

Rev. Canon Dr. **KAPYA J. KAOMA** is an ordained Anglican with a particular interest in human rights, ecological ethics, and mission. He is former dean of St. John's Cathedral and lecturer at Africa University in Mutare, Zimbabwe, and academic dean of St. John's Anglican Seminary in Kitwe, Zambia. Dr. Kaoma is a project director at Political Research Associates, where he produced a groundbreaking report titled "Globalizing the Culture Wars: U.S. Conservatives, African Churches, and Homophobia" that prompted invitations to testify before the United States Congress and the United Nations. He is currently the rector of Christ Church, Hyde Park, Massachusetts, and a visiting researcher at Boston University Center for Global Christianity and Mission. He received his doctorate in ethics from Boston University.

CHRISTINE (CRICKET) KEATING is associate professor in the department of Women's, Gender, and Sexuality Studies at the Ohio State University. She works in the fields of feminist political theory, decolonial feminisms, and democratic theory. She is the author of *Decolonizing Democracy: Transforming the Social Contract in India* (Penn State, 2011) as well as a number of articles in *Signs*, *Political Theory*, *Hypatia*, *New Political Science*, and elsewhere.

KATARZYNA KORYCKI is a doctoral student in political science at the University of Toronto and holds an MA degree in comparative politics from McGill University. She works on politics of memory and identity, using frameworks developed in race, gender, and sexuality studies to illuminate the political process of construction of nations.

AMY LIND is Mary Ellen Heintz Endowed Chair and professor of women's, gender, and sexuality studies at the University of Cincinnati. She has published on gender, development, globalization, and sexual politics in the Americas, with an emphasis on gendered forms of resistance to neoliberal governance and modernity; more recently, she has focused on LGBTQ and feminist political responses to the trans/national governance of intimacy and sexuality in Latin America. She is the author of *Gendered Paradoxes: Women's Movements, State Restructuring, and Global Development in Ecuador* (Penn

State University Press, 2005) and editor of three volumes, including *Development, Sexual Rights and Global Governance* (Routledge, 2010).

ABOUZAR NASIRZADEH is a doctoral student in political science at the University of Toronto and holds an MA degree in international relations from the London School of Economics and Political Science. He studies a variety of subjects, including politics of sexual diversity in the context of Middle Eastern countries, gay transnational activism, civil–military relations in developing societies, and the evolution of revolutionary armed forces.

CONOR O'DWYER is an associate professor of political science at the University of Florida. His research focuses on politics in postcommunist Europe's new democracies, including how the expansion of the European Union is changing the terrain of domestic politics and policy making in the postcommunist member-states. He is the author of *Runaway State-Building: Patronage Politics and Democratic Development* (Johns Hopkins, 2006) and has published in *World Politics, Studies in Comparative International Development, Comparative European Politics,* and *East European Politics and Societies.*

MEREDITH L. WEISS is associate professor of political science at the University at Albany, State University of New York. Her research addresses political mobilization and contention, the politics of development, civil society, nationalism and ethnicity, and electoral change in maritime Southeast Asia. She is the author of *Student Activism in Malaysia: Crucible, Mirror, Sideshow* (Cornell SEAP/Singapore, 2011) and *Protest and Possibilities: Civil Society and Coalitions for Political Change in Malaysia* (Stanford, 2006), as well as numerous articles and book chapters, and coeditor of three volumes, most recently *Student Activism in Asia: Between Protest and Powerlessness* (Minnesota, 2012).

SAMI ZEIDAN received his PhD in political science in 2010 from the Graduate Center of the City University of New York with a thesis titled "Navigating International Rights and Local Politics: Sexuality Governance in a Post-Colonial Setting." He also holds law degrees from Université St-Joseph (Beirut) and Harvard, as well as degrees from the American University of Beirut and California State University. He worked previously at United Nations headquarters and is currently a legal officer at the European Commission. He has published a number of articles in law journals and elsewhere.

Index

The University of Illinois Press
is a founding member of the
Association of American University Presses.

———————————————————————

Composed in 10.5/13 Adobe Minion Pro
by Lisa Connery
at the University of Illinois Press
Manufactured by Sheridan Books, Inc.

University of Illinois Press
1325 South Oak Street
Champaign, IL 61820-6903
www.press.uillinois.edu